AUSTIN LUNCH

Library of Congress Control Number 2004-110482

10 digit ISBN 1- 932455-08-6
13 digit ISBN 978-1- 932455-08-3

First published in 2005 by:
Cosmos Publishing Co., Inc
P.O. Box 2252
River Vale, NJ 07675
Phone: 201-664-3494
Fax: 201-664-3402
E-mail: info@greeceinprint.com
Website: www.greeceinprint.com
First reprint 2006

Printed in Greece

CONSTANCE M. CONSTANT

AUSTIN LUNCH

Greek-American Recollections

Constance M. Constant

COSMOS PUBLISHING

ACKNOWLEDGEMENTS

I would like to express my warmest thanks to all the good friends and family members who have demonstrated steadfast interest in the completion of this book.

And, my most heartfelt *EFHARISTO* (Thank You) is extended to these sympathetic and very helpful individuals for their valuable contributions to *Austin Lunch*, whether for family memories, stories, information, suggestions, and/or assistance.

Bob Constant
Nikos Constant
Helen Limberopulos
Nick Limberopulos

Helen Antonopoulos, Pitsa Captain, Mary Chryssopoulos, Jim and Argerey Constant, Frances Limberopulos Crocilla, Peter and Vivi Demopoulos, Dorothy Dixon, Akrevoe Emmanouilides, Maria Fotopoulos, Kathie Riedl Fuller, Catherine and Fotis Georgatsos, Carole and Ted Golin, Betty Hallock, Maita Houpis, Ann Kolevera Kardos, Connie Limber Kavalaris, Victoria Limberopulos Kourtis, Vasilike Kouveli, George and Rosemary Kuchuris, Chrisoula Kokinis Limber, Angie Limberopulos, Panagiotis G. Limberopulos, Stacy Menechios, Tessie Menechios, Sylvia Limberopulos Mitchell, Jim and Diana Pachares, George Pelecanos, Sophia Plessa, Marilyn Rouvelas, Christine and Perry Spanos, Athena Constant Stapakis, Isabel Wallace, Georgia Antonopoulos Zouvas.

Finally, I most sincerely thank

Judith Frost, my book editor at *Greece In Print*, for her most thoughtful and conscientious edit. Her kind words of approval lifted my spirits and inspired completion of this labor of love.

Rob Abeyta, Jr., a wonderfully gifted artist who created the cover for *Austin Lunch* by transforming family mementos into a work of art.

To Bob
with all my love

To Nikos, Vicky and Fran,
your Yiayia Vasiliki loved you
more than words can say

And
to Helen, Nick and Angie
with love and appreciation

INTRODUCTION

I n the Cro-Magnon days of my childhood, when radio listening was limited by parental control and television was still in its experimental stage, I was the little kid who discovered entertainment by listening in on family stories. These family chronicles revolved around two cataclysmic milestones in U.S. history of which I was not a part: the Great Depression and WWII. Those deadly serious events were recited with such vivacity that I came to believe that the times my parents and siblings lived through, before the beginning of my memory, were more fascinating than my own. The Great Depression was the background for stories about the "old country," coming to America, the old neighborhood, and our vast assortment of relatives. World War II coincided with the closing of my father's restaurant, the Austin Lunch, and the end of my siblings' childhood.

Unfortunately, many of my family's beloved anecdotes have already been forgotten because they depended on memory to survive; nobody wrote them down. Whereas nation-altering events are recorded, and the lives of powerful individuals like F.D.R. and Churchill are chronicled in numerous volumes, the stories of most of the plain people of that generation and their simple participation in life have been lost for eternity. *Austin Lunch* attempts to record and preserve the personal experiences of my family and the places where they lived and worked, most gone forever at this writing. I hope a flicker of time, of place, and of some of the good people who lived within them will not be completely extinguished.

My father, Paul, was forty-six years old when I was born; my mother, Vasiliki, had just celebrated her thirty-sixth birthday. My sister Helen, at fourteen and a half, was a high school student, and forty-five days after my birth, my brother Nick turned twelve. For well over a decade, all four of them had existed very well without me. Nine weeks following my arrival, Nazi armies invaded Poland, changing history forever. News of my impending birth into the established, hardworking, comfortable foursome known as the Limberopulos Family certainly must have given our own family history a comparable jolt. My entrance into the world at this late stage of my loved ones' lives has forever earned me an unending youth of sorts, along with the fondly bestowed titles, "baby of the family" and "kid sister." I, in turn, rejoiced in the time I could spend in their company, collectively and individually.

Our family's stories have been recorded here by me, Mama and Papa's 1939 intruder. Our family's experiences in the 1930s may differ greatly from those of neighbors who lived in the same section of town, from other Greeks in Chicago, and even from our relatives, but it was life in Chicago as our family lived it. My brother Nick provided many colorful details; we're thankful he remembers just about everything. My sister Helen, who remembers the "old days" clearly, provided stories about her and Nick's childhood in the 1930s and early 40s, and stories that she heard from our mother, whom she lived with and cared for until Mama's death. Without their input *Austin Lunch*, our collective memoir, could not have been written. I am eternally and enormously thankful to Helen and Nick for everything.

I am lovingly grateful to my husband Bob for his encouragement, ideas, and support for my efforts. Although Bob was not a part of the beginning of our family's history, he played a pivotal part in *Austin Lunch* because he discovered the bag of old letters, at Mama's birthplace in Greece, that re-kindled these remembrances. He also inspired, encouraged, and engineered our treasured tape recording of Mama's voice, retelling some of her story several years before her passing. My devoted appreciation is also heaped on our son Nikos for his attempt to inspire excellence in writing the story of his beloved grandmother, the only grandparent he ever knew.

The main characters of *Austin Lunch* are Mama, Papa, Helen and Nick, the first four blessings and loves of my life, for whom I am ever thankful.

Connie Limberopulos Constant

HELEN'S PROLOGUE

*G*arden variety green grass had become a forgotten species on the Chicago block where we grew up in the Thirties and early Forties. Inner-city weeds, persistent survivors that relish living on the edge under thankless city feet, never peeked out between sidewalk cracks. Green could only be spotted in the potted ferns that ominously lurked in the undertaker's window and in the rubbish of Wrigley gum wrappers and Lucky Strike packages before Lucky Strike green paled to white and went off to World War II. Powered by Windy City gusts, the green litter blew along curbs in tandem with the drab pages of yesterday's newspapers. Tiny Union Park, several blocks away, was the lone urban oasis of this cement world on the Near West Side of Chicago.

Even though we lived in the Prairie State, "prairie" was a geographical concept as foreign to us as "Great Divide" or "Painted Desert." For a century or so the great Illinois prairie, outsmarted and conquered by city slickers, hibernated under granite, asphalt, streetcar tracks, rat infested basements, and the formidable old Chicago Stadium in our neighborhood. Tons and tons of unbending cement and bricks, sans the luxury of greenery, covered the flat earth of our inner-city block as a stiff backdrop for its people. When I was a small girl, I thought all of us would go on forever.

Forty-five years later, the serendipitous discovery of old letters prompted me to return to my old neighborhood. It was like finding a skeleton: jarring, sad, and cold. A community once alive all day and night was dead, almost deserted of people. The Salvation Army's presence on Madison Street endured, but most of the buildings I knew, except for the very old New Ogden Hotel and its cumbersome black fire escape, were gone. Yet I found an ironic development: the prairie was back. Empty inner-city lots were littered with broken glass and shattered bricks, but thriving blades of grass triumphantly sprouted between them.

The streets were the same, though there was less traffic. Madison Street, Monroe Street, Ogden Avenue, and Washington Boulevard still memorialized great Americans. They were names that emerged from history books as white and Anglo-Saxon. I usually heard them mispronounced as "Madeeso Strree," (r's were usually trilled) "Ogthon Avenyou," "Monrrow Strree," and "Washytow Bouleevarr" by the awesome mix of immigrants in our neighborhood. Our Near West Side streets were home to a melange of eastern, southern and northern European and Asian immigrants, delicately blended with black and white Americans whose ancestors had come to America a generation or two or three before: the "melting pot." By 1910, seventy-five percent of Chicago's population was made up of first generation immigrants and their children; the percentage was still high in the Thirties. They were mostly emigres from country villages with clear blue skies where nature's green had been taken for granted, far different from their new urban landscape. Both my parents had emigrated from Greece and its province of Arcadia in the Peloponnesos. This was the very same Arcadia lauded for its pastoral beauty by the 18th and 19th century English poets I studied in school. Papa arrived in America in 1907. Mama squeezed in during July of 1921, minutes before drastic changes in U.S. immigration laws curtailed the "Give me your tired, your poor…" invitation carved on the Statue of Liberty.

They did not know that the prairie and its Native Americans, the Potawatomi, had preceded them in their Chicago neighborhood of Madison and Ogden. The great green prairie lay dormant under the buildings that sheltered them, waiting for a chance to sprout again when all of them were gone. It is the natural flow of life: virgin land, humanity, development, more humanity, decay, and prairie again. Newer city slickers are waiting.

The spirits of the Potawatomi, Madison, Monroe, Washington, and Ogden fused with the toils of Popper, Yakaitis, Sapinski, Christopoulos, Friedman, Vogel, Wong, Jones, Economou, Ahearn, Gallios, Garcia, Zapetti, and Limberopulos in my old Thirties neighborhood. We didn't have trees or grass, but we were as American as apple pie.

Long lost letters and a vacation note from my sister Connie prompted my nostalgic visit to the old neighborhood, and a deep look into the past:

July 25, 1984

Tripolis, Greece

Dear Mama and Helen,

Bob made an unbelievable discovery today at the house where you were born, Mama. We went there this morning. It was fun, but hotter than blazes. The kids whined about the oppressive heat and nagged about wanting to leave right away—after I had waited a lifetime to see your birthplace in Piali.

We walked around the ruins adjacent to Grandpa's house and were impressed by antiquities from the Golden Age where you played as a girl. The grapevine in the courtyard you always told us was so beautiful and productive isn't there anymore. While we looked around, Bob found a sack of envelopes with Chicago postmarks—from the Thirties—one mailed from 1458 West Madison Street. Papa's name was on the return address. Wasn't that the Austin Lunch??

Bob didn't know what to do with the sack—didn't think it was his to take. After all, it wasn't HIS grandfather's house. He didn't tell me about it until AFTER we left the village. Now I'm excited about the possibility of old letters in the envelopes but there's no way to go back. Brother Nick will retrieve the bag and bring it to you in Chicago. He's planning to go to Piali next week.

Bob, Nikos and I are having great fun with Nick, Angie, Vicky and

Fran over on this side of the world, including a visit to Mercovouni. Remember how Papa worried about their eternal lack of water? Now they've got enough to water grass! Mercovouni is turning into the Park Ridge of Tripolis. Have lots to talk about when we get back. See you at O'Hare on the appointed day. Love from all of us,

Connie

My brother Nick, my sister Connie and both their families had traveled to Greece in the summer of 1984. We delighted in accounts of their travels and visits to the villages where our parents were born, but none of us revealed to Mother the true condition of her birthplace in Piali. We never even showed her the snapshots. Grandpa's house, uninhabited since Grandma died in 1947, was a complete and sad wreck. It was so dilapidated that a villager was keeping his goats in what used to be Grandma's kitchen. When my brother-in-law Bob took his discovery of old letters down from behind an almost collapsed wall, two immense black rats jumped out at him from inside the burlap sack. We didn't tell Mama about that either. The destruction of Grandpa's cherished house, adjacent to the ancient site, was in progress: the bag was retrieved in the nick of time. On subsequent visits, chain link fences and Greek lettered warning signs, installed by the government to protect ancient artifacts beneath, fenced off Mama's birthplace. Grandpa's homestead is, forever, off-limits to family explorers.

Discovery of the dirty sack precipitated an unstoppable outpouring of recollections as my mother and I began our survey of its contents. In fractured English combined with her native Greek, Mama amusingly, poignantly, and painfully recalled stories of coming to America. In no time at all, she resurrected Chicago's Near West Side during the Depression and the dated restaurant where, with the mere opening of the front door, mundane toil could be elbowed in the ribs by risky excitement. That was my father's place, the Austin Lunch.

AUSTIN LUNCH

Greek-American Recollections

THE "LIVING DEATH"

Venerable father, we are both fine and happy to see our sisters again after so many years

Vasiliki to her father, July 10, 1921

*M*ama was gutsy and proud of it. She sought no one's pity. "Never. Ever. Period!" Yet, as she read through the crumbling letters rescued from her birthplace, she felt the need to share stories of her eighty-one year old life with me. The woman who began life in America as a seasick immigrant girl carried volumes of personal history; it took two of us to remember it all. Painful memories of leaving home sixty-three years before resurged, evoking in me an unexpected compassion, and tears, both hers and mine.

"Helen, you're the first born of my children. I never could send you away or Nicky or Connie either, for any reason. Period. But my father was getting rid of his children. Your grampa could have sold his horse and his donkey if he needed money. But he didn't do that because they was too important to him. Yet, he was giving his daughters away, one by one, and two by two. He didn't want to do it. But any way you look at it, he was getting rid of his own flesh and blood. Many fathers did the same thing in those years. But I know I never would do that to you, Helen, even if I had fifteen children. My heart breaks in little pieces to tell you all this, but back then the poor guy had no choice. And we had to go along with it." Mama paused to swallow back emotions, then continued in her distinctive broken English.

"My oldest brother Kosta come to America first from our big Krilis family, way back before 1905. Then in 1912 Athanasia, who we alloways call Thanaso, and Aphroditi, my two oldest sisters, came to Chicago. In 1916 Politimi, my next oldest sister, come here from the village. Thanaso, Aphroditi and Politimi was all married and had children by the time Tasia and me come in 1921. When we came here to Chicago, we lived with Aphroditi and Politimi and their families.

"We was so unhappy to leave the rest of our family behind in Greece. We all cry like we was at a funeral when we hug and kiss our mama and papa and brother Nicholas and little sisters Garifalia and Stamata for the last time. When we separated from them we know there was no chance to ever hear their voices or ever feel their hugs again, for the rest of our lives. They never came here to America.

"Was a terrible punishment for Tasia and me, like going to hell. And we didn't do nothing bad, nothing wrong. Me and my younger sister Tasia, we had to leave home. Had to! All because of the damn dowries my Papa couldn't pay. He got seven girls! How he supposed to have property to give dowries for seven daughters, then have enough left over to pass on to our brother Nicholas? I think about it and cry and throw up for two weeks, sick as a dog, while that damn boat rock back and forth and don't stop. There was no relief, Helen.

"Tasia and me we never been no place before, only around our little hometown, Piali, and other tiny villages in our Tegea. Farthest we ever go was Tripolis, maybe five miles away, to visit our aunt. Tasia was sixteen and I was eighteen. We never ride in a car or train or boat, not even a bus. Only way we get around was to walk or ride a donkey. When we go someplace special, we ride on top of our Papa's horse and wagon. Our house in Piali got no electricity, no running water. We go to the bathroom outside. There was no conveniences whatsoever. Tasia and me, we learn to read Greek but that don't matter because we don't know one word of English. And there we was, going to America."

Vasiliki Krili and her younger sister Anastasia (called Tasia by everyone in the family) began life at the start of the twentieth century. Piali was a tiny village with an illustrious ancient history, but in 1921 it lagged a century behind the American cities the sisters were sailing toward with such heavy hearts. They grew up within a family-protected, farming environment where children, especially female children, were to be seen and not heard. Their older sisters had not even attended school. Though no one in their patriarchal environment ever commended them for it, or had even taken notice, Vasiliki and Anastasia made history in their family. A revolutionary change in Greek law required parents to educate female school-age children for a minimum of four years. Mama and *Thea* (Aunt) Tasia were the first women in our family to learn to read. Modern legislation made a vital difference to their lives, but so did an unwritten old country tradition.

The dowry, a custom that had endured for centuries, was the particular dread of fathers of female offspring. It presented unachievable economic expectations; the excruciating solution was to send daughters away, forever, with no hope for reunion. These separations took place all over Greece and were referred to as the "living death." The mourned were still alive, but never expected to be seen, heard, or embraced again. In May of 1921, after heart and soul-wrenching goodbyes from their father, mother, brother Nicholas, and little sisters Garifalia and Stamata, eighteen-year-old Vasiliki and sixteen-year-old Tasia left the world as they knew it to begin their own bittersweet exile in America.

My grandfather Dimitrios Krilis accompanied his two daughters along with two other girls who were making the trip to the New World as far as Patras, port city of Peloponnesos. Stomachs churning, they waited in a state of confusion, anticipation, and fear mixed with regret for emigration paperwork to be completed under Grandpa's constant supervision. They were to board the ship *King Alexander*, which was already loaded with unmarried Greek girls who had boarded at Constantinople and Piraeus. In Patras, one of the other girls broke the heel of her shoe. Embarrased and heartbroken, she cried and cried because she had no other shoes to wear. Fifty years later I remember hearing her reminisce with Mama about how old "Uncle" Dimitri Krilis bought her new shoes so she could come to America with dignity, not limping on a broken heel. Her five decades of appreciation made me posthumously proud of Grandpa.

"Seems like we rush to leave the village. Everybody say, 'You're so lucky to go to America.' I never think about it too hard until we was on the boat in the middle of the ocean, dizzy and sick to our stomachs. By then I got lots of time to think. I was so sorry I leave my Mama and Papa, and I cry. Can't stop cryin'. I feel like I got a hole in my heart, in my stomach, and in my head, too.

"'Why?' I ask myself. 'Where I'm going? Why I'm going to America? I'm leaving a whole village full of people I know. Why I'm going to America where I only know half dozen people? Don't make no sense. Maybe I'm going to be sick like this forever. Better to die than not be able pick my head up from the bed for the rest of my life. What if the boat sinks? The fish is going to eat us and there won't be nothing left of us to even have a funeral. Poor Tasia, she's sick too and I can't do nothing to help her. If something happens to me, what's going to happen to Tasia? I can't leave my Tasia alone. I can't die.'"

Heavy hearted, my mother wept recalling old frustrations. Hoping to ease her pain, I attempted to steer her away from hurtful memories. While she reminisced, photographs from books about the great wave of European immigration at the beginning of the century came to my mind. "Mama, how did you feel when you saw the Statue of Liberty? It must have been a thrill."

"Helen, I guess I was feel so lousy that I never even lay eyes on her because I don't remember nothing about the Statue of Liberty. But I sure thank God to be off that damn boat when we finally get to New York. Took a long time to feel good because even standing on God's good earth we still feel dizzy and like we was moving up and down. Tasia and me we cross ourselfs and thank God, over and over again. Then we look up to see a big beautifool building. It look beautifool to me but what did I know? I was just a little girl from a tiny village who never seen nothing like it before."

Mama, Tasia, and the other girls from the *King Alexander* entered America after enduring confusing matriculations through Ellis, which immigrants had rightfully nicknamed "the isle of tears." Mama referred to Ellis Island as *Kastrigari*, the name Greeks used because it is said that early immigrants read and mispronounced either the "Castlegarden" or "Coast Guard" sign at Ellis Island as "Kast Guardi." Believing either to be the name of the place, the mistake eventually evolved into the word, "*Kastrigari.*"

The girls went through immigration like blind figures in a labyrinth. Mama told me, "We stand and wait and wait in big, long, long lines to get inside the building. And we feel like we was deaf and dumb because we couldn't understand nothing they was telling us. Finally some guy who speak Greek show up and give us directions. So, we wait our turns and go inside where they check our eyes, hair, bodies, our papers, and we finally pass. Took lots of time. Never see so many people in my life. Some poor souls don't pass tests and have to be put in special rooms to wait, maybe even be send back to their old country, after everything they been through already. All this happen in July of 1921. The fourth of July was the day Tasia and me enter into America.

"Anyway, a fat man come and take us from the beautifool building. And what do I see? My God! This guy's going to put us on another damn boat. Thank the good Lord, it was a short trip to take us off the island, the *Kastrigari*, into New York City and we don't get seasick again. That fat man was in charge of thirty of us girls. He walk us over to a truck, with no top on it, and push us into the back of the truck. We was standing up and when they start driving real fast, we fall down all over each other and get real scared. Some girls even get bruises and scratches.

"There we was, coming into America, like animals. Just like sheeps in back of an open truck. I was so scared. I say to myself, 'I'm never going to see America or my sisters in Chicago because I'm going to bounce out of this truck and if I don't get kill from the fall, the New York cars is gonna run over me. Our bodies was swaying sideways and our heads was bobbing up and down and we was holding on for dear life. The New York streets was packed with moving cars, and people, and trucks, horse-pull wagons, and streetcars. Everybody was going real fast, a different world from the one we know, and too too scary. I hold on tight to the truck and hold on tight to Tasia so she don't fall. I tell Tasia, 'Hold on tight, *kakomoira*!' I was think to myself everyone of us on that damn truck, we was all *kakomoires* (unfortunate ones). They drive us to a hotel in New York City and put us six to a room. Never been in a hotel neither. When we get inside, the fat man turn off all the lights on us, then close the door. And he left. Why he turn off lights? I don't know. So we go to sleep, I guess. Or maybe he think we was like chickens or pigs in a barn and don't need no light because there's nothing we was suppose to see. Only God knows.

"We was all dying of thirst. But, how we going to find water? We figure out how to make the light go on and we look around and see the sink. We twist the faucet but only hot water was coming out. We look at each other and say that maybe in America everything's so modern they only got hot water. Not like the village where we have to find branches and build a fire to heat water. We understand that we got no choice. So we drink American hot water, then get ready for bed, and turn off the light.

"After we was in the dark a little bit, we feel something crawling all over us. We turn on the light and see the room was full of bed bugs. TERRIBLE. Can't go outside to get away from the bugs because we don't even know where we was. We don't know nothing. Had to stay in the room because we was afraid. All we know is that we was in America. In New York. Where? We don't know. Not one of us *kakomoires* can even say one word of English. We know we not suppose to trust strangers and we got to stick together. Between being afraid and all the bed bugs, we couldn't sleep all night.

"Morning finally come and the fat man, he was kinda like our guide, he show up again. He take us to a restaurant for breakfast. Ha! What we know about American breakfast? We don't know nothing about nothing. We was like blind, new-born puppies. We was afraid to eat because the foods was strange to us, bacon and ham and waffles. But, we was too hungry because we don't hardly eat nothing on the boat coming over the ocean. Finally we see something that look so good, and even if we never had them in the village, we try them. Delicious DOUGHNUTS. We ate them up. They taste so good we decide to take some of those doughnuts with us to bring for a present to our sisters' little children in Chicago. You know, Helen, it's Greek custom to take sweets when you go to somebody's house.

"After breakfast they take us to a huge railroad station. You could put the whole Piali village inside and still have room left over. Never see nothing like it before. Tasia and me, we took the first train ride of our lives. Was real hot, humid, and sticky. Remember, it was July. But this was weather we never experience before. Even the weather was strange to us. Windows in the train was all open so people can cool off little bit, and when the train start moving fast, black smoke come in the windows and we get covered with soot. We was wearing our good dresses so we could meet our sisters looking nice. But we was getting black and sooty so we change into our everyday dresses for the train ride. Tasia and me come to America with only two dresses and one pair shoes apiece. We was lucky to have them because our Papa didn't have enough money to load us up with clothes for this trip. When the train get into the Chicago station we was so excited to see our sisters that we try to rush off. Then, just in time, we remember our good dresses was still hanging in the closet. So we run back inside the train to save the only other clothes we own in the world.

"We was so surprise to see such a big group of our relatives waiting at the station. Everybody was crying for being so happy. After we been by ourselfs for almost three weeks, sick and everything, was big relief to be with family. Thanaso, Aphroditi, and Politimi, all three of our sisters who come to Chicago years before us was there with their husbands and kids. Even our first cousins, Katerini Metropolis and Stamata Bellson, was there. I remember I was a little girl when they left the village for America. Stamata and Katerini was so good to us after we come here. They was like mothers to us. They was our Uncla Stathi's children and they come to America from Piali way before everybody else. They was good, good people. Everybody ask about families in Piali and about the village, too. We was all proud of our Piali and proud to be *Tegeatisses* (women of Tegea). Piali is just one village in our Tegea township. Tegea is in Arcadia. Arcadia is a province in the south part of Greece that they call *Peloponnesos*. Our Tegea's got a long and proud history. There was ancient ruins next to our house. They was our backyard.

"When we come to Chicago, Thanaso and her husband, Jim Koliveras, was living on the South Side of the city. My two other sisters, Aphroditi and Politimi, was living together with their families in one huge eight room apartment on Ogden Avenue, and we went to live with them. Aphroditi was married to Pete Kuchuris and Politimi's husband was Christ Ganas. When we get to their house on Ogden Avenue, we take out the doughnuts from New York which was going to be our present for the children. But the doughnuts soaked the paper bag with too much grease, and the doughnuts was hard as a rock. Tasia and me was so disappoint and embarass with our presents for the little kids.

"'What you got there?' your Uncla Pete ask. We open up the greasy bag and look inside and apologize. We tell him we bring sweets all the way from New York but they get too, too stale. Uncla Pete say something to make us feel better. 'Don't worry about those old doughnuts. We gonna to buy fresh ones tomorrow. Now you are in America. There's plenty to eat here. You finally going to get your fill and you not going to be hungry again.' Poor guy didn't know there was going to be a Depression.

"Well, after a little time go by, even after all we went through to come here, I feel real strong inside myself that I DON'T like America. Was hard being so far away from my Mama and Papa. It wasn't easy when we first come, Helen. I really want to go back home to my family in Piali. Politimi, she used to tease me and ask, 'You want to go back to Piali and get scared by the rooster every time you going to the bathroom? What bathroom? Got no bathroom in the village. Just a little private place under a tree, where the rooster comes to pinch you on the behind.' Politimi want to make me laugh. I miss them all, now. Politimi, Thanaso, Aphroditi and, of course, my Tasia. She was my sister but my best friend, too. They all gone. *Aionia tous i mnimi* (May their memories be eternal). All of them is resting in God's peace."

While we studied the letters, my mother continually spoke of our loved ones. Almost every one of them was gone. Mama's memories were wall-to-wall full of dead people and she lovingly invoked a fragment of a Greek Orthodox prayer for the deceased, repeating *Aionia tous i mnimi* like a mantra.

I found myself on the brink of breaking into a good cry or suddenly laughing out loud as papers from the Greek sack inspired Mama's memories, revealing details I had never heard before. My mother was a strong woman with presence. Hearing of her fear and readiness to go back to Greece, rather than sticking it out in America, showed me a side of her I did not know. I knew the adult Vasiliki who not only stuck it out when life surprised her, but strove to make the living better. Surveying the sturdy, undaunted woman of my youth, I saw her grayed, fragile, and vulnerable. Ah, but she was still spirited. Mama's lively eyes, now behind spectacles framed by octogenerian wrinkles, still transmitted the look I have known since childhood: her unspoken "I know." She never stared blankly; my mother always knew what was going on around her and far beyond, with never-waning interest.

The letters were spread out in front of her on a disposable plastic sheet to protect our dining table from the dirty burlap bag and its dusty contents. We never told her about the squalid conditions where the sack had been found, or about the village vermin that jumped out of it when it was discovered. Nonetheless, Mama wore yellow rubber gloves, procured from under the kitchen sink, to handle the crumbling papers after she announced, "Looks like rats was messing around in this stuff." You could never keep Mama in the dark about anything.

We sat at our dining table fitting fragments of crumbling letter parts together, like a tissue-paper jigsaw puzzle. Her legs were elevated onto the lower rung of the aluminum walker she used to help her move around. For ten years Mama had been taking medication for a heart condition, arhythmia, but osteoarthritis alone was the cause of all her pain. The fingers that balanced untold numbers of heavy restaurant trays and carried thousands of steins and schooners of beer were permanently bent at forty-five degree angles. The outer and inner contours of Mama's legs curved so much that when she stood up straight she appeared to have spent her life on horseback in Wyoming, not working for sixteen hours a day in a rickety Chicago restaurant.

When Mama was seated, her relaxed attitude and lively conversation might have fooled an outsider into not realizing she was limited in her movements and confined to eight hundred fifty square feet of living space. Our house was larger than those measurements, but Mama couldn't maneuver the rest of the space by herself; she couldn't walk upstairs to the second story or downstairs to the basement anymore. If a fire had broken out when she was home alone, she would have been trapped inside. It was impossible for me to believe that someone who had been so "in charge" was almost helpless. But whether she was eighty-one or twenty-one, Mama never gave up.

"Tasia and me, we don't write no letters back to our Papa to say we got sick as a dog on the boat when we was coming to America. And I don't tell them back in the village that I don't like it here. Why worry them back home? We just tell them how good it was to see our sisters after so many years. But even after two weeks of misery being on that lousy boat, I want to go back home and I tell them, 'Send me back. I don't like it here!' I miss my family in the village so much that it feel like I gotta a deep, deep hole inside me. I cry every day.

"One day my sisters send me to the grocery store, downstairs from where we was living, to buy onions. They tell me the word for what I got to buy and I go all by myself to the grocery store and I practice the word "onions" all the way down the stairs and into the store. 'Onions, onions, onions, onions.' As soon as I see the American lady and she ask me what I want, I get nervous. I was embarrass and I forget the word. I feel like such a dummy. My face get hot and I know I'm all red. The lady was nice and she take me all around the store and she ask me, 'You want this? You want that?' She show me milk and bread and other stuff and finally I see the onions and I point at them. I push the money at her and I run out of the store. I was so upset, so mad, so hot and so embarrass that I even forget the change. I go back upstairs and say to my sisters, 'Here's your onions!' and I throw them on the floor and cry again, 'Now send me back to my father!'

"We had to ride the streetcars to go visit Thanaso because she live far away on the South Side of the city, but I used to get dizzy and sick to my stomach on the long rides. One time, we was on the streetcar on a rainy day when my face turn yellow. It look like I'm going to get sick again. My sister Politimi give me her umbrella and she say, 'Here, throw up in here,' and I did because I was too embarrass to vomit all over the streetcar. Then for a joke she take the full umbrella to Thanaso. Politimi smile and say to Thanaso, 'Here, this is a present for you from Vasiliki.' You know what I tell them when they was laughing at me? I say 'I can't live here. Please send me back to my mother and father!'

"My sweet sister, Aphroditi, God rest her good soul, she tell me, 'I don't like it here either when I first come. I miss my family and I was so lonesome, I even miss my sheep in Piali. My sister-in-law who I was living with before I marry Pete, she treat me like a maid. But, I get used to it. And you will like it, too, Vasilo. Takes little more time.'

"And, your Thea Thanaso, *Aionia tis i mnimi* (May her memory be eternal), she was so good and so kind, too. She got lots of patience. She say, 'Wait a little while more, Vasilo. Everything's going to be all right.' But you know, Helen, nothing's ever all right all the time."

THREAT "TO ...OUR RACE"

*M*ama and Thea Tasia made their American debuts in 1921, along with Band-Aids, Lincoln automobiles, and Betty Crocker. It was a great year for Betty and the Lincoln, but not a particularly good time to be an immigrant from the sunny Mediterranean.

Most Americans lumped foreigners into two classifications that year: the celebrated who were called "great," "gifted," or "genius," and the multitudes who usually had demeaning epithets hurled at them. Charlie Chaplin, Rudolph Valentino, Amelia Galli-Curci of the Metropolitan Opera and Albert Einstein were among the heralded. Enrico Caruso, who died that year, was deeply mourned throughout the U.S. despite his native roots. The masses who belonged to the second category were poetically lauded on the base of the Statue of Liberty as "tired," "poor," "huddled," "wretched," "homeless," and "tempest tossed." Sacco and Vanzetti, sentenced to death in 1921, belonged to this group. Ku Klux Klan burnings were lavished on these newcomers, and KKK cross burnings multiplied in 1921.

Most immigrants didn't feel worthy enough to be welcomed into America as Albert Einstein had been. Quietly matriculating through Ellis Island, they put all their efforts into blending with the new culture, trying not to stand out, preferring even to be invisible to avoid disdain by ordinary Americans and harassment by vicious men wearing white sheets. Acceptance and success did not come easily to them as it did to Charlie Chaplin and Band-Aids.

Mama, Thea Tasia, and thousands of other naive immigrants sailing on ships headed for New York Harbor, during the first week of

July in 1921, were completely unaware that the United States government was hell-bent on keeping them out. Only a month and a half before, President Warren G. Harding had signed the Quota Act of 1921 into law, reacting to increasing fears among "restrictionists" in Congress that the United States was accepting too many immigrants. A special phobia permeated the U.S. about immigrants from southern and eastern Europe, like Mama and Thea Tasia. The Immigration Restriction League, founded by wealthy Bostonians in 1894, publicly referred to these newcomers as the "off-scourings" of Europe. One of the league's most prominent members was Massachusetts Senator Henry Cabot Lodge, who warned Congress that aliens from southeastern Europe were a threat "to the very fabric of our race."

Lodge ignored the fact that his Separatist ancestors, otherwise known as "Pilgrim Fathers," who began arriving with the more famous Mayflower crossing, were considered religious off-scourings of their homeland's teeming shore in the sixteenth and seventeenth centuries. When they left England to come to America, England's powerful were glad to be rid of them. The forgetful Mr. Lodge ignored the reality that these loathed Greeks and Italians were leaving lands that had contributed the foundations of western civilization and culture to his "race." The pompous old Brahmin's put-downs made me seeing-red angry, but inspired my ethnic pride.

The First Quota Act of 1921 ended the United States' open door policy by limiting and reducing the numbers of eastern and southern European immigrants entering the New World's "Golden Door." Those heading for New York's harbor in the early summer of 1921 had already suffered traumas of borrowing money for passage, heart-rending separations from loved ones and homelands to travel to the unknown, usually without the ability to communicate once they got there. Ships left European ports in May and June of 1921 with innocent immigrants aboard who did not know they would be turned back at the end of the voyage because of new legislation.

By law, even though a ship was already in New York it might not be allowed to disembark its travelers. Of the twenty ships rushing to

arrive in the harbor on July 1, 1921, only ten, carrying thirteen thousand passengers in all, arrived before midnight, when the new law was
scheduled to take effect. Vasiliki and Tasia's ship, the *King Alexander*,
was one of them. Ten others had been delayed by fog. Because the
Quota Act changed immigration law, Mama and Thea Tasia were the
last sisters in the Krilis family to migrate to America. Three older
sisters had preceded them: Athanasia, Aphroditi, and Politimi.

Mama always liked to say, "They close the door after we got in,"
but all she really knew was that she and her sister arrived on one of the
last immigrant ships allowed into the U. S. before a law was changed.
Mama never heard of Henry Cabot Lodge or The Immigration Restriction League, had no power over dowry traditions in Greece, U.S.
quotas, or attitudes about women, and never realized she was a pioneer. And in the end, none of them made a direct difference in her
life. My mother did what she "hadda do" with the only power she
had: power over herself. Mama used it smashingly.

"Helen, it's a good thing for you and me and all of us I got stuck
here. I love my Tegea, but I love my Chicago, too. After so many years
gone by—I'm in this country sixty-three years—and you know what
I say, don't you? I say, God Bless America. Even if, once upon a time,
I had to work almost like a slave at the Austin Lunch.

"Was the Depression that change everybody. It especially make
big big change in my life. I hope nobody got to go through anything
like it, ever again. For most of us who was poor, the Depression was
like this damn arthritis I got. Nobody get real excited about it because
it don't come all of a sudden, like a heart attack. It come slow and you
alloways hope it's going to go away. It hurt like hell and you suffer in
a quiet way because you're stuck in it and you can't get out. But you
don't die."

"GONNA BE LIVIN' IN THE STREETS"

Things are changing here in America. Times are tough. But don't worry about us.

—*Vasiliki to her father, November, 1930*

Mama skipped over the story of how she met and married Papa; that was to be remembered later. With the Austin Lunch on her mind, she asked if I recalled when she began working in Papa's restaurant and of course, the scene had been engraved on my memory very early in life, an event that affected our family like no other. It didn't take much encouragement for my mother to remember the autumn of 1931.

"Helen, your Papa was losing his restaurant. Busyness slow down and down and almost die after 1929 and '30. He come home at night to our nice apartment on the West Side and he was dead. I never see him so tired before. Not forty yet, but his hair was turn white. Papa feel terrible that he had to lay off restaurant workers because he couldn't pay them nothing—because he wasn't making nothing. Uncla Al stay, but Papa was paying him five dollars a day when the times was good in the Twenties. Of course, in the Thirties, most times Papa couldn't pay him at all and your father, he feel bad about it. Papa feel oblige to keep paying Al the five bucks. Al was living with us for free and get free food to eat at the Austin Lunch. He don't have to pay no rent, so he stay to help Papa. They was not only cousins but good friends. Al was like a brother to us. But your Papa feel bad because he couldn't pay him good wages for working so many hours. One day, Papa tell me he was three months behind in paying the store rent. He owe $375 to landlord Prevolos. That was a fortune for people like us. When I hear this I realize that the next step must be to close the Austin Lunch.

"'How about the rent for our beautifool apartment?' I ask myself. 'Must be we can't afford that either. We gonna be livin' in the streets just like lots of good families.' You know, there was families sleeping in the parks, in alleys, and in doorways of buildings because they was so poor? Every night Papa come home with more news about Greeks that lose their restaurants. Your Uncla Christ Ganas and your Uncla Pete Kuchuris they shut the doors of their places. They was looking for jobs as cooks or even dishwashers, but nobody need them. There was NO jobs whatsoever. Papa say he's hardly taking in ten dollars a day. Place was open 24 hours, he work more than sixteen of those hours and only take in ten bucks. And from those ten bucks he's got to pay the rent, Charlie the cook, Al the waiter, Harry the dishwasher, Mrs. Feldman, the lady who sell the meat for the restaurant, the electricity, the gas, the water, and more and more. The expenses don't stop. I was positive we was gonna be in the streets with ice and snow that winter. I was sick with worry, but try not to show it. Then Al, he tell me something else that make my blood pressure go up and my head hurt so bad I think it's gonna explode."

Mama then told me that one morning before he left for work, Uncle Al, my father's first cousin, confided his concerns about my father to her. Al said a bookie was in business next door to Papa's restaurant and Al admitted that when times had been better, both he and Papa bet a couple of dollars on the horses every now and then, hoping to get a big winner and take life easy. Al assured her that neither of them had gambled since hard times had come, but he warned Mama that bookies were coming into the restaurant for coffee everyday, and he feared that Papa, with debts mounting, was very vulnerable.

Mama learned of my father's "hobby" a few years into their marriage. Papa's weakness for playing the horses rattled her like the earthquake tremors she remembered as a girl in the village. Mama couldn't fathom laying out good money to wager on racing horses. It was impossible for her to believe that a man as intelligent and well read as Papa, a good businessman who enjoyed a deep interest in history and philosophy, could ever imagine that wealth might come from betting on a racing horse.

More masterful than Eliot Ness at getting facts, she excavated deeply and discovered that when Papa, Al, and other Greek boys were newly arrived bootblacks, they learned to pool their meager, hard-earned pennies to gamble on horses via a bookie whose shoes they shined. The illegal bookmaker (Chicago had thousands of them) advised that making money on the horses was a quick way to get rich in America, much faster than shining shoes. In spite of their incurred losses, a few wins proved the bookie right in the boy-immigrants' naive thinking. They became intoxicated by the rush of excitement that highlighted their otherwise monotonous lives when pennies sometimes multiplied into quarters. Perhaps thrills emboldened them more than actual monetary winnings.

Their hands almost permanently blackened with polish, the boys worked long hours staring at untold numbers of feet wrapped in socks in various states of cleanliness, and handling thousands of filthy shoes. Day after day, for hours on end, dressed in white shirts and dark ties, chests and slim waistlines covered by long, tan colored aprons reaching to their ankles, they shined shoes. But drab existences were occasionally enlivened with dreams of fresh air and sunshine at a rural but elegant racetrack. Colorfully attired thoroughbreds, their trappings sewn from nothing less than silk, raced to victory in their boyish daydreams. While perspiration dripped from the bootblacks' grimy, young faces, they worked hard and wished for something better in their lives. Hustling to bring out the shine on the toes of dirty shoes, they hoped that, with a little luck, their humble participation in the "sport of kings" might bring them and their dependant Greek village families relief from poverty. They lost their pennies, dimes and quarters, but hope and the rush of excitement over an occasional win kept them betting.

Mama remembered when Papa lost a serious amount of money to a bookmaker in 1925, a loss large enough for him to resolve never to deal with bookies again. She thought he had learned a hard lesson, but Al's sincere distress worried her.

"Was the first big argument your Papa and me ever had after we got marry. He holler and shout that I don't know what I'm talking about because I don't know nothing about gambling. I suggest to him that maybe gambling is only for rich people that can afford to lose money. Not for a little guy who needs to have two partners to own one little restaurant—and he hafta work sixteen hours a day to do it. When Papa argue, he holler so loud I think his head's gonna fall off from the noise he was making. Papa never hit nobody when he get mad, but he shout and get so red from his neck up, you get scared something bad's gonna happens to him. I tell him, 'Calm down, Paul.'

"But I never get scared by all the noise he was making to keep me from NOT tellin' him what's RIGHT and Papa know I'm no dummy. But he had that damn weakness. And we couldn't afford it. One of the reasons I had to go to work at the store in 1931—and there was lots of people who make fun of me and say mean lies and jokes about me behind my back that hurt me—was because I know I gotta keep Papa from gambling. So he don't lose the restaurant and we have to go on relief. Was big embarrassment to go on relief. It was a terrible thing to be on relief.

"Helen, I couldn't explain nothing about it to nobody. On top of it, I was innocent. Dumb. I didn't know much about the fire some guys got in them to gamble. I didn't know there's nothing I can do to stop him. When Papa's own self-control was working good during the worse part of the Depression, he didn't play. But if he want to play the horses, nobody can stop him. Not even me. I can't tell nobody about this problem because it was big shame for me, like saying husband is a drunk or drug addick. I only tell my sister Tasia because I know she's not going to go blah blah blah to everybody. Tasia was my best friend. Papa was in debt real bad, not only to Prevolos for the rent, but to that big company that supply restaurants with all the stuff they need, the Sexton Company. Your Papa, maybe he gamble, but he was honest man who didn't want to go bankrupt. He didn't want to spoil his good name. And I know I gotta help him keep it. Period. Even though Greek womans was only suppose to work at home, and lots of people blah blah blah against me when I make my decision."

In 1931, a Greek woman's purpose in life, whether she lived in the old country or in America, was to marry, stay home, keep a clean house, be a good cook, quietly raise her children, and be subservient to her husband as she had been to her father. In addition, new arrivals in America believed that anyone fortunate enough to be born in their *patrida*, (native land) the cradle of western civilization that had illuminated the dark, ignorant world with knowledge and democracy, couldn't allow that "light" to go out in their own homes now that they lived in America. They laid that very heavy responsibility on the good Greek wife and mother. How ironic that the survival and eternal continuation of the esteemed Greek Orthodox Church and its Christian belief brought to Greek shores by the Apostle Andrew, a venerable and rich language with roots in pre-history, and western civilization, itself, were left in the hands of thousands of earnest, hard working young women, most from primitive villages, who until then the Greek nation had not deemed worthy of education past the fourth grade.

My mother fit the description of the ideal Greek woman—until the Great Depression began. Mama never allowed herself to be intimidated. "You gotta stick to yourself," was her way of saying a person who knew she was right needed to stick up for herself. In spite of being an immigrant, speaking broken English, standing a mere five feet two inches, and having been born female in a time and place when it was considered a detriment to family and society, Mama had terrific self-esteem; she stuck to herself. She went to work a full ten years before anyone had heard of Rosie the Riveter and two years before Eleanor Roosevelt's aggressive independence astonished complacent Americans. Untold numbers of women were in the workplace before 1931. But not many immigrant, married Greek women with children, who only knew a few words of halting English, worked in public. My mother did.

"I was never scared of working. In fact, I liked it. I was used to it. In my family, back in the old country, when the girls get to be nine, we have to do farm work in the fields. We take care of our Papa's sheep, clean and cook at home. At nine years old we even make bread. My Papa say I couldn't go to school after fourth grade because I was girl. In the old days they say girls don't have to know anything more. And you know, Helen, I liked school. I was a good school girl." Working together with her at the Austin Lunch, Papa would come to discover what an amazingly fast learner Mama was.

"The hard part was to get Papa to say yes about me going to work in the restaurant. I was trying to change his mind by talking about it little by little when he come home after work. Then one day Papa tell me he got good news. Landlord Prevolos say he won't throw Papa out of his building. Prevolos say that Papa can owe him the rent money. Prevolos was going to collect it all when business get better. 'See?' Papa say, 'Everything is better.'

"Better?? By the end of one year Papa was going to owe Prevolos $1,500. That was like ten fortunes for people like us. I ask Papa, 'How many years is the Depression going to last? Are we going to be in debt to Prevolos until we die? Are you going to run the place by yourself? You can't even boil water. And you think things is getting better?' Then, Helen, I shut up and figure out my plan."

PAPA AND THE AUSTIN LUNCH

*A*postolos, eldest son of Nicholas and Eleni Demogeronta Limberopulos, and his small cardboard suitcase arrived at Ellis Island
from the port of Le Havre aboard the French Line's *S.S. La Bretagne*
on April 1, 1907. I don't know how a thirteen-year old child from the
village of Mercovouni in the middle of the Greek Peloponnesos got to
Le Havre, France in 1907. All Papa said during his lifetime was that
he traveled in the company of a family from Mercovouni also immi-
grating to America. By the time I came to wondering about the details, he wasn't there to answer the questions. Papa told us, however,
that our *Papou* (Grandpa) Limberopulos, borrowed money at thirteen percent interest in 1907 to purchase his thirteen-year old son's
steerage ticket. Steerage cost anywhere from twenty to sixty dollars
per person, an unfathomable amount of money for my grandfather.
Then in 1911, Grandpa borrowed additional money to pay for Papa's
fourteen-year old brother Vasilios's ship's passage.

Moved to tears when he remembered it decades later, Papa recalled searching for Vasilios amid a sea of newly arrived, bewildered
immigrants from all over Europe at the assigned New York entry point
in 1911. Papa said it was "like looking for a needle in a haystack the
size of two Union Stations." For hours he searched among the thousands of newcomers in the confused and frenzied throng of arrivals,
particularly zeroing in on boy faces. Gnawing uneasiness finally turned
to triumphant relief when he found his awed little brother, thanks to
the huge name tag with "LIMBEROPULOS, VASILIOS/CHI-
CAGO" safety-pinned to his jacket. Certainly, his younger brother
had grown in the four years since he had last seen him. Papa instantly

Americanized young Vasilios upon his arrival, and ever after called him "Bill."

Loyalty to family, permanently etched on their souls and forever engraved in their minds, obliged Papa and Bill to send money to the village to pay off their father's enormous debt. After tickets were paid for, the family had additional needs that the two boys were required to meet with American-earned money. The primary reason they were sent to America was to work to pay for dowries for their two sisters, Panagiota (who was older than Papa) and Georgia (youngest of their family), while their sisters were still young and of marriageable age. Neither Papa's sisters nor his youngest brother Kosta ever emigrated from Greece. When the uncles in America finally retired from the shoeshine business in 1917, Papa felt free to change jobs.

Until then, from the time he was thirteen, my father, Apostolos Limberopulos (in America, his first name became Paul), had been a shoeshine boy. He worked ten years for three of his father's brothers (Stephanos, Jim, and George Limberopulos), who owned several hat cleaning and shoeshine parlors in Chicago, in Boston, and in Albany and Rochester, New York. Papa told us he earned room and board plus minimum compensation for working as a bootblack in twelve-to-sixteen-hour shifts, seven days a week. Even his tips were turned over to his employers. Papa and five fellow shoeshine boys (his brother Bill, cousin Al, and several first cousins) shared one room near Chinatown, taking turns sleeping in the beds according to their work shifts. From what Papa and Uncle Bill told us, the sheets never cooled down between occupants, and neither they nor their cousins had time or inspiration for laundering them.

"Your Papa want to quit his shoeshine job, Helen, because he's not make enough money to send back to the village like he promise to do when he leave. Poor guy. They was all back there in Mercovouni waiting for the dollars to roll in. But Papa appreciate very much that his unclas in Chicago sponsor him to come to America, and he feel oblige to keep working for them. Even if they wasn't hardly paying him nothing."

Papa's history with the restaurant at Laflin and Madison Streets, that was to become known as the Austin Lunch, began during World War I when my father finally decided to change careers. The day he walked into the restaurant at 1458 West Madison, he left a life of shoe shining to become a waiter. Mr. Prevolos, proprietor of the restaurant and owner of the three-story building in which it was located, was Papa's *patrioti* (fellow Greek), an older gentleman who immigrated from the same hometown before the turn of the century. Papa volunteered to work for Mr. Prevolos, for free, until he learned to be a waiter.

Five years after our father's unpaid beginnings at Mr. Prevolos's restaurant, Papa, Uncle Bill, and their very close friend, Charles Kingos (my brother and I called him Uncle Charlie), formed a partnership, pooling hard-earned money to buy a restaurant on Chicago's North Clark Street. This was the original Austin Lunch, named for the corner street, Austin, which intersected with Clark. (Austin Avenue is no longer in that location.) At first, my father worked at the Clark Street location and in Mr. Prevolos's place at Laflin and Madison. In 1922, he and his partners managed to scrape together four thousand dollars, and they used that as a down-payment to buy Mr. Prevolos' place for eight thousand dollars. That restaurant became Austin Lunch #2. Prevolos allowed them to pay off the balance, at six per cent interest, in monthly payments of one hundred fifty dollars. As the owner of the building, Mr. Prevolos also collected one hundred twenty-five dollars a month for rent.

"A few years before the Depression, I think 1926, Papa, Bill and Charlie break up their partnership because Bill he get a chance to go in the laundry busyness in Lansing, Michigan. Was a terrific opportunity for him. So they pay Bill off in cash. Charlie take the restaurant on Clark for his own in the deal. And Papa keep the one on Madison Street because he was working there the longest. They break up very friendly. They was still the best of friends. Everything was hotsy totsy because the Depression don't start yet.

"But when the Depression start, Charlie lost the Clark Street restaurant. Then Papa hired him to be the cook at the Austin Lunch on Madison. It's funny that Papa get to be restaurant man, because he don't know nothing about cooking. Papa can't cook. Period. But he sure know how to work with the public. Charlie was a good, good man. He know how to cook better than excellent. But Charlie was a sourpuss with customers. Papa don't know nothing about the kitchen, but the customers love him."

Patrons came to eat great food but also to talk to "Mr. Paul." They sought and trusted his advice, respected his honesty and enjoyed his sense of humor and his stories, which were filled with fun and interesting facts of history. Returning home from work in the hours after midnight, Papa relaxed by reading books on Greek and American history, or works by the philosophers Plato and Aristotle, before he went to bed.

"Your Papa shoulda been a perfessor. He know the whole shebang about history."

Books written in Greek were scarce in the U.S. at that time, but Papa's English was so good he didn't need translations. He came to this country young enough to learn English very well and spoke it with just the mere hint of an accent. Papa lived in the United States long enough to be very American and that, combined with the influences of his Greek culture, made him a one-of-a-kind great guy. Mama, on the other hand, came to America when she was older, and even in Chicago she was sheltered by her Greek community. So she never had time to properly learn her adopted language. She listened closely, on the job, to learn English, and had a knack for picking up American slang and a gift for inventing her own jargon. Yet she never succeeded in shaking off her strong accent.

Papa's Austin Lunch (he spent so much time in the place that they were an integral part of each other) was located between a bakery and a combination poolroom/bowling alley at Laflin Street where it is intersected by Madison, about a half block east of slanty Ogden Avenue. The old restaurant and the bakery occupied both street level stores in Mr. Prevolos's brown brick, three-story building. Four huge seven-room apartments were available for rent on the second and third levels, but there were no amenities, not even hot running water. Chicago is renowned for the architecture of some of its magnificent buildings. This wasn't one of them.

"Papa and me, when we first get marry, we live in one of Prevolos's apartments, upstairs from the restaurant. I was expecting my first baby in that house. But one day the police come and I find out that somebody was murdered. Killed—in our building. I get real upset that some poor soul was murder, almost right under my nose. I was so upset, I lose our first baby—a little boy. I never forget it and I still feel sad when I remember. Of course, we move out of there. Papa find other apartment close to my first cousins, way out west, around 4600 Madison. Was wonderful neighborhood. My cousin Katerini Metropolis was living around there. She and her husband got seven children. We had a good time with them as neighbors. Katerini and her sister Stamata was like mothers to me and my sisters.

"At that time another cousin come from Piali to America. She live with Katerini and Stamata until they find bridegroom so she can marry. She was your Thea Athanasia Karabas. She was an excellent person— and so much fun. She tell lotsa jokes and make us laugh. Years later, I tell her she should be on the television. I remember, back in the Fifties or Sixties, her brother came from the old country. On his first morning in America, Athanasia gave him a shopping bag and she told him, 'When you go out walking today make sure you use this to collect all the gold you gonna find in the streets. You don't even have to share with me, Brother. Keep it all.' I laughed so hard when Athanasia tell me about it that my sides hurt. Her brother went back to Greece. Didn't stay here too long. Athanasia was a hard worker. She work outside her house too, years after me, at the Florsheim shoe factory. She was a wonderful lady and I miss her. That damn cancer take her away too, too soon. May God rest her good soul. They all gone. *Aionia tous i mnimi* (May their memories be eternal).

"We had a good time living over there in that beautifool neighborhood before the Depression come. Helen, you was born when we was living in that wonnerful part of the West Side, and Nicky, too. We could walk to Garfield Park. Was happy times for us. Papa take the Madison streetcar to go back and forth to the restaurant, but he work too many hours. We don't hardly see him like I did when we live upstairs from the restaurant in Prevolos's *saravalo* (rickety old building)."

Our Austin Lunch block had no fun loving cousins, no trees or grass, just lots of buildings and people; its sidewalks were well used. Private vehicles were unaffordable for most American citizens, so they walked and rode streetcars. White clad milkmen and muscular ice deliverymen walked from one address to the other while their horse-pulled wagons sluggishly traveled along the curb. Entrepreneurs selling pencils and shoelaces out of tan cardboard boxes, and skinny beggars, many of them veterans of World War I, walked by Papa's restaurant day and night. The uncountable unemployed, looking less and less spiffy as the jobless weeks turned to months and years, continuously searched for work in and out of the narrow storefronts that lined Madison Street.

The Salvation Army Building occupied space on the same block as the restaurant. Neatly uniformed, polite and ever-cheerful Christians brightened Madison when stirring music spilled out of their sparkling brass trumpets and tubas during improptu sidewalk concerts. Events at the Chicago Stadium, four blocks away, brought politicians and performers from the "Loop" right by the Austin Lunch. The good, the great, and the crooked continually went down Madison Street.

Laflin and Madison is a long walk from the Windy City's most famous intersection: State and Madison. Madison Street ends at elegant Michigan Avenue where the graceful oasis of Grant Park blocks urban Madison from reaching the western shore of Lake Michigan. Lake Shore Drive residents no doubt described our Near West Side neighborhood as "run down," but in the Depression everyone who had a roof was grateful, no matter where. Papa's restaurant was located in an area that had, indeed, been considered elegant, maybe fifty years before. It was one of the settings for Theodore Dreiser's novel, *Sister Carrie*. Refined brownstones and roomy coach houses lined some of the side streets off the intersection, but by the Thirties, aspirations and dreams of riches had faded, even though grace was not gone. The poor can have grace, too.

Aesthetics touched the dim interior of the Austin Lunch, but one had to look hard and long to uncover them. Entering from the Madison sidewalk, a customer's first impression was that of a long, dark, narrow hall; the left side of the restaurant was only twenty-five feet from the dark paneled wall on the right. Real walnut booths and tables were attached to that wall, whose panels were also made of walnut—the fake stuff we know today hadn't been invented yet.

The restaurant's most memorable feature was an endless white marble counter partnered with a row of stationary but pivoting tall-backed oak chairs. We referred to them as "stools," but they were impressive, elegant chairs, attached to the ancient floor by individual white porcelain pedestals. High above our heads, just below the ceiling, two faded murals faced each other from opposite walls, so out of reach they usually went unnoticed. Stately garden scenes depicted elegant colonnades and manicured topiary, Madison Street's only artistic glimpse into the life of the French aristocracy. Decades of nicotine, smoke and soot from the coal stove back in the kitchen had faded them to a dull, rotogravure brown.

Marble counter, stools, booths and tables covered in white cloths stretched toward infinity from Madison to the kitchen at the distant rear of the store. It was evident a waiter had never been consulted in the restaurant's layout. Tending to booths and counter meant a lot of walking back and forth, an especially back-breaking task when hands were weighed down with trays of food, heavy restaurant china and glassware. Three shiny commercial coffee urns stood behind the counter at the middle of the store. With their aching feet and backs, the servers never thought the trek from urns to tables was worth the five cents that a cup of coffee cost in those days. Tips were rarely given to servers at the Austin Lunch, and if a nickel was left with the remains of a finished dinner, the customer was thought to be a philanthropist.

In 1931, coffee was the best seller, and Papa was glad to take in every nickel.

When brother Nick was four and I was seven, Papa's restaurant became the center of our world. Our childhood years were very different from those of our parents, who were raised in the sunny, fresh air of rural Greek villages. Nick and I grew up in the Austin Lunch. We looked within its dark walls and tobacco-scented and smoke-filled air for parenting, comfort and sustenance. Yet even while we were restricted to its confines, it became our bridge to the world outside of Papa's eating establishment. The possibility of a new drama unfolding presented itself each time the front door opened and someone walked in. In 1931, Mama, herself, brought excitement through the door.

AUSTIN LUNCH "HOOD"

Write us some news from the village so we can forget the troubles and hardships of living in America.

—*Christ Ganas to his father-in-law, November 1931*

A strictly commercial and brassy look defined our Austin Lunch neighborhood in the Thirties. Yet, thousands lived off Madison on surrounding side streets that were truly residential. Seventy years before, the Abraham Lincoln family lived four blocks away on Washington Boulevard. The Christopoulos, Gallios, and Economou families, all Greek like us, lived one block south on Monroe Street at addresses which had been grand and prominent at the turn of the century. Those neighborhoods were still good, but the Depression forced many owners of once elegant homes and adjoining coach houses to take in boarders for additional income; strangers and transients became an integral part of the area. A childhood image of our Thirties neighborhood, like a yellowed black and white lithograph, is indelibly stamped on my brain.

I see Papa's restaurant standing on the north side of Madison at Laflin. The New Ogden Hotel, with its black fire escape looming above the street like an iron spider web, was located across the street and west of Papa's place. The New Ogden was a small, respectable, residence hotel, not grand like the Palmer House, but not a flophouse either; there were shabbier hotels in the city.

A narrow Chinese laundry, where shirts were hand-laundered and ironed for ten cents each, stood next to the New Ogden. The south side of Madison, across the street from Papa's restaurant, was also home to a used furniture store, a shoe repair shop, Green's Dance Hall, and the tiny Princess Hotel. Green's Dance Hall was the loudest and liveliest nightspot in the neighborhood. Dressed-up couples streamed in and out of its prominent double doors from Thursday through Sunday night when the music was loudest. Signs outside advertised promotions: "Hosiery FREE Thurs. and Fri." On hot summer nights, decades before air-conditioning, exhausted, perspiring dancers came out to cool off, chat, and smoke on the Madison Street sidewalk. Two saloons joined these Madison establishments when Prohibition was repealed. At the end of the block the rusty brown Flatiron Building soared eight stories into the sky.

Mama purposely plunked herself into this fading urban environment on an unseasonably cold day in the autumn of 1931 to transact business. She carried the assurance that her children were safe and sound. Mama had walked me to school that morning and had left my brother Nick in Thea Tasia's care. (Tasia was married and living on the West Side.) Coat collar pulled up to the rim of her hat to ward off an unseasonably sharp wind, Mama walked with a determined stride, the hem of her brown winter coat (haggled for on Halsted Street in better times) swaying just above her chunky ankles. A trademark coffee-colored, wool felt cloche covered her thick, shiny, almost black hair, parted in the middle and gently pulled into a bun with soft waves framing her round, attractive face. Every day, Mama used biting metal spring-clips to form waves in her naturally straight hair. Preoccupied with thoughts thrashing around in her mind, she marched briskly, trying to mask her apprehension with a smile. But it always revealed itself in her deep set, dark brown eyes.

The first item on her agenda was to evaluate a huge bear of a building that stood a mere half block west and on the same side of the street as the Austin Lunch. She was planning to move our family there, kitty corner from the towering Flatiron. She realized the V-shaped, four-story, brick structure looked too commercial and too dismal to be anyone's residence; it vied with the Flatiron for unapproachability, grizzly bear style. Both eyesores were located on a street that was not the finest for raising children.

Mama was well-acquainted with the neighborhood; my parents had lived there when they first got married. Nick and I were familiar with it, too, from the many trips the three of us took via the streetcar to visit my father when he was working. A corner drugstore, Wong's Chinese Restaurant, and Youngdahl's Jewelers were street-level tenants of the brown grizzly. Mr. Youngdahl, a pleasant, tall, blond gentleman, always wore a *pince nez* on the tip of his nose. When my brother and I peered into his storefront window, we wondered if his comic-book eyeglasses, which dug into his nose like a vise, made breathing a problem for him.

Apartments for rent started at the third level, but the grizzly's belly was virtually empty in the autumn of 1931; only four of the twenty-two units were occupied. Mama began negotiations by visiting a friend, Christina Fellas, who was one of the building's tenants. Under pressure from my mother, Christina helped her hunt down the janitor in the vast empty spaces of the bulky structure. The entire fourth floor was vacant, except for the janitor's apartment; an exhausting, four-story climb made the top floor difficult to rent. The janitor, Mr. Yakaitis, and his family lived up there because he received his apartment rent-free as partial payment for his duties. Christina told the janitor that her friend, "the Missus," was interested in one of the third floor units. He showed them the apartment immediately next door to Christina's. It had been vacated by a family with no rent money who had quietly moved out in the middle of the night.

Mama walked through the four rooms with secret service eyes accented by a scowl and raised eyebrow. The living room and bedroom windows overlooked noisy Madison Street, where the clanging of streetcars floated up and punctured the quiet of the third floor. Mama knew streetcars ran all day and all night on Madison, so she looked the janitor in the eye, shook her head and let out with, "*Poh, poh* too much noise! How you can sleep?"

There was no window in the bathroom. It was pitch dark unless the electric light bulb was turned on, an expense brought to the janitor's attention. "Light cost too much money. And how we get fresh air?" The kitchen had a window facing outside, but it was partially covered from above by the fourth-floor's open porch. A mere trickle of light eked into the kitchen. "Too, too dark—feels like I'm blind." The dining room's only window opened onto the inside of a dreary, dark hallway leading to the building's Ogden Avenue entrance; it was a dud of a window that only emitted darkness. "What's for?" she asked. "No light comin' in." The janitor let her know he had not designed the building.

As she explored the apartment, Mama wrinkled her nose. She was a master at communicating with her eyes and facial expressions, the universal language in which she was most fluent. Before Mama uttered a syllable, approval, disapproval, happiness, anger, the entire range of human emotions could be detected in her bright but sharp brown eyes. A "look" from Mama could pin you to the wall.

"Thirty dollar? No, NO. Too much. Fifteen is better."

With her limited English, Mama succeeded in bargaining the rent down to twenty dollars a month. After the janitor, representative of the landlord, settled on the amount, the little Greek lady, as he referred to her, (Mrs. Fellas was probably five feet five or six inches tall whereas Mama was barely five feet two) convinced him that she could not move in with her family until one more deal was struck.

"Can't bring children here. Pigs can't even live here. Too dirty. Need paint. You get twenty dollar, but first you clean up good and paint nice."

With no demand for eighteen unrented apartments and the country in an economic downslide, the janitor agreed to her terms but demanded deposit money before we could move in. Mama, finished with the first item of business on her agenda, thanked and hugged an astonished Christina, then aimed herself toward Papa's restaurant to negotiate her second order of business. She walked quickly in the feisty, cold wind, mentally arranging her convictions and arguments. Item two— convincing Papa of the merits of her plan and getting him to turn over ten dollars for the deposit—wasn't going to be easy. He didn't even know she was in the neighborhood.

SHATTERING TRADITION

Write to us at our new address. We moved closer to Apostoli's business.

—*Vasilki to her brother, December 1931*

*T*he familiar smell of simmering soup met Mama as soon as she was inside the door of the empty Austin Lunch. Papa's restaurant always smelled like good, "stick to your ribs" food; savory soups were especially appealing on a cool fall day. As she inhaled the appetizing aromas, Mama looked from the front to the back of the narrow store and found no customers to smell, order, or pay for food. She passed a freestanding glass cigar case with an ornate metal cash register resting on top of it, both dimly illuminated by light filtering in from the front window that faced Madison. The tobacco case was almost empty, and so was the tightly closed cash register.

Mama turned down her coat collar as the warmth of the restaurant comforted her, and she continued her business-like stride down the one hundred and forty feet of the middle aisle. She always walked like that. Mama never sauntered, even when she was dead tired. White glass light fixtures and metallic, oily ceiling fans designed to look like airplanes, hung down on black cables from the surface of the yellowed ceiling, twenty feet above her. The well-swept floor under Mama's feet revealed dark, hardwood planks below patches of old, mostly worn-out linoleum.

She spotted Papa sitting behind the counter at the back of the store, reading his usual morning *Tribune*. We didn't own a radio. The crude wooden newspaper stand outside his restaurant on Madison at Laflin Street was Papa's connection to the world. He read as many newspapers in a day as he could get his hands on, cover to cover.

Uncle Al was sipping a cup of coffee, perched on a counter chair at the front of the dimly lit store, nearest to the fancy but empty cash register. Mama approached him first and was going to comment on the cold wind blasting in from the lake when she saw that he was studying *The Daily Racing Form*. She couldn't read English, but the horse and jockey logo at the top of the page tipped her off, and a mere glimpse of the animal with his rider reddened her face. Scowling, she walked behind, then around him. Al didn't notice Mama until he heard her voice. She began berating him in Greek.

"*Sachlamares.* (Unacceptable nonsense) Garbage. That paper is a sign of the devil's wrath! Al, why do you waste your money and your time?"

Recognizing the familiar but uncharacteristically confrontational voice, he turned around, flustered and apologetic, lowering his eyes to answer guiltily, with a nervous and stiff laugh. "Vasiliki? What are you doing here? Ah—oh—don't worry. I can't afford to play the horses. And Paul can't either. Paul can't even afford to pay me anymore. A customer left this on a stool. I'm just passing time. There's no one to wait on."

She slowly and resolutely shook her head. Her entire upper body subtly emitted signals of disgust when she strongly disapproved of something and it showed most distinctly in her eyes. Mama's smile was gone. "Paul'd be cutting his own throat if he started up with the damn horses again."

Al quickly changed the subject. "Where are the children?"

She continued toward Papa, with her back to Al. "Helen's at school and Nicky's at Tasia's house." My brother and I may not have been present, but through the years we came to know the details of that day as if we had been eyewitnesses.

Papa came forward to greet Mama. Al, his shift over, removed his apron and moved toward the coat rack. With her uncanny knack for "not missing a thing", Mama spied Al slipping the folded racing form deep into his gray overcoat pocket. Then he donned the familiar black felt fedora atop his movie-star handsome face. He looked like an ordinary uncle to me, but I had overheard Greek women whisper that he was better looking than Rudolph Valentino and far more appealingly masculine.

"Need anything? I'm going home, Vasiliki."

"Thank you. Nothing."

"Then, see you both later."

Al had begun working at the Austin Lunch at five dollars a day. Now he was lucky to get one dollar for a day's work. There was no payroll checking system at the Austin Lunch; employees and purveyors received daily payment directly out of the cash register if Papa had enough money in the till.

With Al out the door, my father turned back to look at Mama. His square young face contrasted with prematurely graying hair that now matched the gray uniform jacket he always wore over the dark tie and clean white shirt that Mama faithfully ironed and starched for him. Papa's long white half-apron was tied around his waist.

"It's biting and miserable outside, Vasiliki. Nobody waits on windy corners for streetcars on a day like this unless it's absolutely necessary. Why are you here?"

Papa's hazel eyes peered over his eyeglass frames. He had a way of making you know he meant business by the way he looked at you over those glasses, especially if he raised his voice. But he was quiet and casual. "What brings you here without the children?"

Mama forced a laugh. "I came for a job!"

Papa looked over his eyeglasses again. "What? Not that again. You don't know what you're talking about!"

"I sure do. I want to work here."

"Nothing doing! You've got plenty of work at home with two kids." Papa impatiently picked up a damp towel and started wiping the counter even though it was clean.

"You're right, Paul." Mama sat at the counter and watched him interrupt his chores to look over his glasses again.

"You've brought this up before, Vasiliki. Nothing doing. You can't work here. You've got plenty to do at home and besides you're a woman."

"You've got that right, too."

Mama's warm smile re-appeared and her eyes smiled, too, for a moment. But her face was flushed, betraying her anxiety.

"Tell me, how come you're here without the children?" Papa thought he was changing the subject, but Mama kept him on track.

"Charlie lost the Clark Street restaurant. Right, Paul?"

"Yes."

"You still have this place because Prevolos isn't collecting rent right now. He knows if you move out, nobody else can afford to move in. There are no tenants for anybody's buildings anymore. If you move out, this place will…"

Papa nodded and continued her train of thought, "…fall apart. The pipes will freeze and burst this winter. The rats will take over, and Prevolos knows his building will be good for nothing. I know all that, Vasiliki. Tell me, where have you been?"

"One minute, Paul. Let me finish. Remember when Charlie Kingos lost the Clark Street store, and came to beg you for a job here? One of the best chefs in Chicago works back in this hot, dark and rickety kitchen, cooking twelve hours a day, for three dollars."

"I know, Vasiliki. I can barely scrape it together. Charlie's worth more than three lousy bucks, but I can't afford it! Remember? He told me, 'I have a wife and five kids. I can't take care of them for less. You guarantee me three bucks a day, and I'll cook for you.' I know all that, Vasiliki. Charlie's the first one I pay every night. What else can I do?"

Mama looked up at him. Listening to Papa, she unconsciously fingered a menu stuck in a shiny steel holder attached to the counter. Along the white marble, at six foot intervals, groupings of white ceramic sugar bowls were clustered with glass salt and pepper shakers and cardboard menus, within easy reach of hoped-for but very absent patrons.

"Glad you asked." Mama's response caused both of them to smile. "Look, you're not paying Al and you feel guilty about it. He's a bachelor, lives with us, eats here. Al has no responsibilities, except for money he has to send to his father in the old country. You're probably keeping him from finding a real paying job. Let him go. His situation is not like Charlie's. It'll be easier for Al."

"Banana oil! How can I let him go? I need more than a day cook, a night cook, a dishwasher, and me to run this place. It's open twenty-four hours a day. I'm over my head with money problems. I owe Prevolos and Sexton and I have to pay the good people who work for me."

"Wait a minute, Paul. My father always asks, '*Ti stelni o Theos pou then ta vastai i yeis?* (What does God send down that earth cannot handle?) The answer is 'nothing.' God only sends what he knows we can deal with. You can handle this, Paul, because I can help. I will replace Al and you will save the money you're paying him."

"Impossible. We have children! You can't work and take care of children." His voice was getting louder and he was crossly looking at her over his eyeglass frames again. "Women work at home. Who do you know that works in her husband's restaurant? Nobody! There isn't a married Greek woman we know who works outside her house."

"*Mnistheti mou Kyrie!* (Remember me, Lord.) There are lots of Greek women whose husbands lost their businesses. Their husbands aren't working anyplace. They don't have restaurants or jobs—they don't even have houses anymore. They gather their children and quietly move out of apartments in the middle of the night because they can't pay the rent!" Now Mama's voice was louder.

"And how can you be at home on the far West Side and here at the same time? Who will be with the children?"

Mama had been waiting for just that kind of opening to tell her news. "Well, that means we have to move here."

"Live here? What kind of nonsense is that? Have you lost your reasoning, Vasiliki? I suppose we'll put our beds in the dark, smoky kitchen and live in back of the store, like the Gypsies do on Maxwell

Street? Better yet, are you suggesting we make our home downstairs in the basement with the rats?"

"No, no, Paul, I've just come from the building right over here, on the corner, at Ogden and Madison. It's a half block away and on the same side of the street. They have too many vacant apartments. In fact, I made a deal."

"Hold your horses, Vasiliki. Leave our nice apartment with trees and grass to come and live here? With hoboes who chew tobacco and spit all over the sidewalks? Thieves, bootleggers, streetwalkers, bums, the Mob, you name it. They're all here walking these sidewalks. You think I want my children to live here? No siree! Nothing doing."

"Paul, you think we don't have to keep an eye on our children where we live now? How do I know who is out and about in that neighborhood, no matter how lovely it is? My mother and father kept an eye on a dozen of us children in our little village of Piali, and we knew everyone in town. It's more important in this country where there are so many different kinds of people. We must watch our children carefully, no matter who, what, or where. We brought them into this world and we're going to raise them to be good people no matter where we live. Our children have no choice about growing up to be good people. Period. I guarantee it. And we've got no choice about lowering our expenses, especially house rent.

"Paul, we pay sixty a month for rent now and can't afford it. Here, on the corner, we can have an apartment for twenty. I just saw a place with Christina Fellas. She and John live in that building with their little girls, and you yourself know they are very good people. Lots of good people live around here because they can't afford to live anywhere else, just like us. Christina took me to see the building manager."

"And what did Christina say to you about moving over here?"

"The truth?" Mama smiled again. "She told me I'm crazy to leave our nice, sunny apartment to live in that old crumbly building. But I'm not crazy. Sure I'd rather stay where we are now. But I know what we want and what we can afford are two different things. The janitor, he's acting as manager, wanted thirty dollars a month. But I got him down to twenty, and he's going to paint it, too."

"He volunteered to paint it?"

"No, I told him we couldn't take it unless it was cleaned and freshly painted."

"Wait a minute. How did you manage these high level negotiations, Vasiliki? You don't speak English, and I'm positive he doesn't speak Greek."

"Christina knows him. She helped."

"Christina? " Papa laughed. "Christina can't speak English either!"

"Never mind that, because between the two of us, we managed to communicate. I got him to agree on twenty dollars. But I have to give him a ten-dollar cash deposit. How about it?"

(Dead silence.)

"Didn't you hear me? How about it, Paul?"

"How about what? I don't like it. My family living on this lousy street in that dreary building? You working in here? I don't like that either. Our kids growing up in this environment? Never. You don't know how this business is run and you don't speak English." Papa's voice pierced the dead air of the silent restaurant. "WOMEN STAY AT HOME. Especially GREEK WOMEN. What will people say?"

"What do I care what 'people' will say? Is their hair turning white like yours? Do 'people' pay our bills? People always criticize. I will learn. Hard work doesn't scare me. We'll both be with the children, except when they're in school. I promise you, we won't let our children go to the dogs. Your long hours make it almost impossible for them to see you now. And, walking to work will save carfare. Seven cents each way. We'll save fourteen cents a day on carfare alone. Look, I'm the only one you know who's willing to work for no pay. Do you want to lose this store? I don't think so. I'm tough. I'm a *Tegeatissa* (woman of Tegea). I can do it. But I need ten dollars to give the janitor for a deposit."

(Dead silence.)

"Paul?"

"I haven't got ten dollars! Here, give him five. And tell him he's lucky to get it. But remember, I don't want you to get sick working in here. And don't be shocked when you hear that people are saying nasty things about you working in here. No other women from Tegea work in their husbands' restaurants."

"So, I'll be the first. You know, Paul, we have no choice."

Papa knew that.

Mama remembered the pivotal day fifty-three years later.

"Helen, your Papa was waiting for customers to come in the restaurant to eat and pay. There was hardly any customers in 1931. Period. Nobody was paying for nothing because there was no money. Pockets was empty. People was starving. What I know about busyness then? Nothing. Papa told me there's no money to pay Al anymore. Well, I catch on, real fast, that there's no money to pay apartment rent, either. Don't take a genius to figure that one out. Thank God, we had food to eat at the restaurant. I figure out I got to go work with Papa and we must live close to the store so I can take care of you and Nicky. There was no other way. Sure I like it better to live someplace nice. I like nice things, too. But was no better choices in 1931."

LIKE AN OLD MOVIE

I never dreamed I'd live in such a big city with huge red trolley cars going by my door

—*Vasiliki to her brother, April 1932*

*I*t was like watching an old movie, except the screen was somewhere behind my eyes and the actors were my mother and father. Images of loved ones long dead, of places already demolished, and recollections from my Depression childhood popped in and out of my head as Mama spoke. A streetcar hit me when I was a kid. I relived it while Mama and I reminisced.

The huge red trolley ran into me one day in the early Thirties, after Mama had gone to work. Neither she nor Papa even thought of suing Chicago's public transportation system to find relief from their economic problems; my parents were both unsophisticated and honest.

I was alone, returning from an aunt's house on a stormy afternoon when I stepped off the trolley and slipped on one of the wet bricks that paved Madison in front of Papa's Austin Lunch. In an instant I was down on the cold, wet rails, staring up at the red iron monster that, like everything else, was dripping with rain. Before I could stand, the streetcar slowly started up and hit me. The motorman stopped and came out to find an embarrassed, petrified, seven-year-old girl on the ground in front of his trolley frantically trying to save herself and her mother's umbrella. I quickly stood up, wishing fervently that the motorman and his monster would simply evaporate without attracting a crowd. My bones weren't crushed, but my ego smarted and I trembled with thoughts of Mama spanking me hard and Papa yelling at me for not heeding his constant warnings to be careful. Within minutes they knew of my mishap because Uncle Al witnessed the accident from the restaurant window. I was quite confused when my parents seemed to be more concerned with making sure I was okay rather than giving me a sound scolding.

That's not to say that Mama didn't use the incident for a decade or so to remind me that she and Papa were always right. Hadn't she warned me to use four, forty, even four hundred eyes when I crossed the street, rode the trolley, or merely breathed on terra firma? My accident earned her the privilege of asking, "Remember when the streetcar hit you, Helen?" for the remainder of my childhood.

As children, my brother and I were entangled in a safety net of rules. Mama's favorite answer to our requests to do something exciting was "No." And Papa's response when we asked him to bend rules was, "Go ask Mama." They had to know of our whereabouts at all times, and they expected us to work at home and at the restaurant before we were allowed to play, with no exceptions. Papa sharply and loudly raised his voice when he was displeased with our behavior; I wondered if he could be heard in Michigan. Mama spanked.

Neither parent specifically explained the evils we could encounter in our neighborhood. In their day and culture, children were not told about sex, pregnancy, disease, crimes of passion, drug addiction, mental illness, or even divorce. These were adult topics, which if mentioned at all, were discussed in whispers, away from children. Our parents dogmatically believed that children were to remain innocent of "worldly" subjects for as long as humanly possible. I must report, our parents' efforts were successful.

What my mother and father considered discussable topics to teach children were caution (keep in mind that we lived on a block where drunks, prostitutes, and hoodlums integrated with "normal" pedestrians) in crossing the street and not drinking from another person's glass. "*Tha sas piasi panoukla!*" (You'll get the plague!) We didn't even know what a plague was. But Mama said it was so bad it had to be avoided and we took her word for it. She'd say in her stilted English, "Don't let nobody kiss you on the mouth, neither. Give them your cheek or the top of your head if you know them real good. And strangers? NEVER. They not allow to even get close to you. Bad people steal little children and you must be very careful. You're never going to see Papa or me again if some bad guy steal you." Streetcars, too, were a safe topic with no illicit overtones. All day and all night streetcars, our only means of transportation besides walking, ran down the middle of Madison. How many times did I hear, "Be careful! Remember when you get hit with the streetcar?"

Mama and Papa learned parenting techniques by example as they were growing up in the old country. There it was said, "*To kalo tou paidiou sou na to xeri i kardia sou alla ohi i glossa sou.*" (The good traits of your child should be rejoiced in your heart, but not praised by your tongue.) A child was not to be commended lest "*to pari apano tou,*" lest he grow too big for his britches. Many of my generation grew well into adulthood before we realized we could do something right.

Nick and I religiously lived according to our parents' irrefutable, custom-made regulations, sometimes like obedient child robots. Our alternatives were too painful to consider. Those rules snapped us into submission like an invisible bullwhip, but they always wrapped us in comfort, like a thick comforter on an icy night. One could say that our childhood wealth could be measured in parental attention. As involved as they were in their Austin Lunch labors, our parents never neglected us, although materialism and mushy parental doting were completely absent from our lives. We were not hugged and kissed a lot, nor did we witness physical shows of affection between our parents. They did not heap praise on us or on each other, even when it was well earned. There was no doubt, however, that we all loved each other even though the word "love" was not spoken.

We were surrounded by the sins of the inner city, but Nick and I were unaware of most of them. In fact, we lived in a slum and didn't realize it; we were poor and didn't know it. And there was no television to cut short our innocence. We grew up safely under four very watchful eyes. No matter how busy Mama and Papa were, they guarded and shielded us from all the dangers they knew about, and then some. They knew it was paramount to our survival.

Multitudes of good people lived in our Madison Street neighborhood. What I know now and didn't know then was the proximity of crooks and shady characters. Mama and Papa shielded us well, dedicating their lives to keeping us away from our neighborhood's vices. Papa's Austin Lunch was located in Chicago's 27th ward, where good people co-existed with scoundrels and crooked politicians, and where police couldn't be trusted because they were "on the take." After Prohibition, when policemen came into our store during the holidays, Papa "knew" that when the cop said "Merry Christmas!" and stuck his hand out to shake my father's, Papa was expected to put a fifth of whiskey in it. Local police and cops from station houses all over Chicago came to wish him well, and lavished saloonkeepers throughout the city with honored Christmas visits.

Organized crime, better known as "the Syndicate" or "the Mob," existed as a subtle presence all around us, yet we successfully and amazingly avoided involvement. Of course there were those unfortunate incidents when innocent Chicagoans, the overwhelming majority, became shockingly aware of the Syndicate's potential. I was not conscious of this until I was a teenager, able to read about Frank "The Enforcer" Nitti, Paul "The Waiter" Ricca, and Jake "Greasy Thumb" Guzik in newspapers, and hear their names on grim radio news reports about the occasional and unfortunate dead body, throat slashed from ear to ear and back peppered with bullet holes, discovered in a neighborhood doorway, alley, or familiar street.

The Austin Lunch was a family-run business, a "Mom and Pop" operation, not lucrative enough for the Mob to exact payment of the "street tax" in exchange for "protection" from their thugs. Our parents were fiercely resolved to avoid anyone remotely related to organized crime. The Mob, which ran illegal liquor sales and distribution before repeal, had already turned to other ventures once liquor sales were legalized in 1933, the year Papa got into the liquor business. Papa's business style was very low key, and he avoided Syndicate attention.

Local hoodlums heightened our parents' dread that their own children could get "mixed up with the wrong people." It was unusual for girls to belong to gangs in those days, but my parents were afraid that my brother would become involved with local gang members, who often graduated to the Mob. Mama and Papa's way of keeping us out of trouble was to keep us so busy at the restaurant, at home, with school work, and with our relatives that there wasn't a spare minute for delinquent friends. One of Mama's favorite excuses for keeping us "out of play" was that the house needed cleaning. Nick and I invariably whined when she used that excuse to quash a Saturday afternoon at the movies. Mrs. Clean trained us in the art of house-keeping very early in our lives and I still recall one of her thousands of specific instructions: "Use your little finger to get in the corners. Looks lousy when the middle shines and the corners is filthy." Nick's Greek maleness did not exempt him from these house-cleaning chores.

My parents were a threat to no one, except their children. Their philosophy was, "Don't bother anybody. Be nice, be honest, be careful, be helpful"—and "mind your own business." The enormous respect and admiration "Mr. Paul" and "Mrs. Paul" garnered from the people in our neighborhood protected us from most harassment. When business finally got better, Mama could walk the half block home, all alone at two in the morning, and safely carry all the day's receipts on her person without fear, because she was "Mrs. Paul." Even two-bit punks didn't dream of harassing her.

Our lives revolved around Mama, Papa and the Austin Lunch. Our neighborhood was not like downtown only fourteen blocks away, not like the affluent North Side, and not like swanky Michigan Avenue. On our block, it was common to find men sleeping in doorways huddled under dirty overcoats of brown, black, or gray wool, with caps and fedoras pulled down as far as possible to keep their ears and noses from freezing in Chicago's harshly frigid winters. Sometimes they were covered with unfolded, colorless black and white newspapers, the shapes of their huddled bodies blending into shadows of brown brick walls and gray city sidewalks occasionally lit up by brightly-colored neon signs promoting post-repeal beer and booze. The brightest hues of my childhood emanated from those signs.

Even though we traveled alone as children to visit our West Side aunts who lived in "good" neighborhoods, our home-based childhood world did not extend beyond Ogden Avenue or Bishop Street. Except, of course, for the half block that got us to the Century movie theater when we finally were allowed to attend, after enormous pleading and promises to return directly home the minute the show was over. I was a teen before I knew that at Throop Street, several city blocks east of the Century, two night club clip joints, "The L and L" and "The Soho," featured live floor shows with strippers. Of course neither of our parents explained that in those joints women were entertaining customers by showing off their birthday suits. That kind of information we picked up through youthful curiosity and the osmosis of overhearing when we were supposed to be minding our own business.

Except for nighttime honky-tonk neon, there wasn't a whole lot of color in my life when I was a kid; I didn't know there was supposed to be. I rarely saw fresh flowers or cheerful bright yellows in my surroundings. It was a time when all telephones were black and all radios were brown; we had neither in our home. Automobiles were usually either black or another somber color; we didn't own a car either. Clothing, more often than not, also came in somber hues. No matter how poor they were, most men, women and even children wore hats, especially in winter. The hats were usually gray, black, or brown. And as hard as it is to believe today, most men wore long-sleeved, starched white shirts and neckties all the time, even at baseball games and picnics.

I remember life as serious, colorless, and formal. Formality brought an ersatz dignity to lives plunged in poverty. Movies of the time portrayed rich people dressed in tuxedos and evening dresses. The least an unemployed man could do to measure up was wear a hat and tie, even at the beach. I believe that Papa wore a tie 95 percent of the waking hours of his life, looking like a businessman even when he dozed off in his chair at home.

Of course there were joys for a kid. When a child has few material goods, the smallest treats become lavish gifts. The corner drugstore in our drab building featured a 5-cent ice cream cone that was a five-star gourmet dessert in the Depression. When our neighbors, the Joneses, treated us to a 20-cent sundae or malt, that very same drugstore became our version of Disneyland. Who could forget the deliciously cold sensation of sipping a lavish blend of rich ice cream, chocolate syrup and malt flavoring through a straw until rude slurping noises broke through the respectable quiet of the pharmacy? Ice cream was rarely enjoyed at home because our kitchen iceboxes had no freezers.

An annual childhood delight was peering into Christmas window displays, the only way for us to enjoy toys that we didn't expect to own. The finest in our neighborhood was on Ashland Avenue, at our nearby Wieboldt's Department Store. Nick admired Lionel electric train sets and Schwinn two-wheel bikes. I was entranced by beautifully dressed dolls.

Mama told me my interest in dolls dated to my toddlerhood when she was pregnant with my brother. I spotted one in a store window and refused to leave the front of the store until I could have it for my own. Mama tried to explain that she did not have enough money in her purse to buy a doll, but finding no success in reasoning with her unruly child, she yanked me away from the window and I cried and screamed all the way home. Months later, my parents surprised me with my very own baby doll with eyes that opened and closed, and curls I combed in a motherly way until, to my dismay, they became straggly and came unglued.

Nick annually begged for a bike and was annually reminded we couldn't afford one, and that even if we could it was unsafe to ride bicycles on our city streets. "Someday," Mama promised, "when you're old enough, Nicky, and if you're a good boy, Papa will buy you a car." How's that for putting off gratification?

When Papa had business in downtown Chicago, he often took Nick and me with him. We'd ride the Madison streetcar to the "Loop," then alight to walk passed palatial movie theaters, fashionable department stores and ritzy restaurants. We were surrounded by bustling masses of people dressed in "swell" outfits, like women with chic hats who wore gloves, even in summer.

Clinging tightly to Papa's solid, stubby hands, we'd enter a very tall building where Papa had business, then soar upward in a mahogany-paneled elevator attended by a uniformed operator wearing white gloves. At the end of our flight, we'd emerge to discover a window in the sky from which we could stare breathlessly at our marine-blue, life-sustaining Lake Michigan.

"The Lake" was a mere two miles away from the Austin Lunch, yet it was not a part of our world. Our parents were always working at the restaurant, and most of the time we were there too, under their watchful eyes with no time for diversions, like going to the beach. Papa's veteran establishment never closed. If there was a key to the front door, Papa himself would have had a hard time finding it.

"SHE'LL RUIN HIM"

Vasilo should make time to visit her sisters.

—Christ Ganas to his father-in-law, March 1932

A torrent of vile tongue-wagging was set in motion when word got out that my mother had started working at Papa's restaurant, by Greek men of course, but even by some Greek women. Laboring outside the home was certainly not the ladylike behavior expected of a Tegeatissa. A few "friends" and some of Papa's village acquaintances were devastatingly harsh and critical.

"A woman's not intelligent enough to do a man's job. She'll mess up his business for good. He'll never recover."

"Women and business don't mix."

"Who in the hell does Paulenna think she is? She's got her goddamn nerve."

"You mean Paul can't make it in business without a woman's interference?"

"She'll ruin him. Just watch. He'll be closed in two weeks."

"She's probably good for scrubbing floors and doing dishes. He'd better keep her out of sight, in the back of the kitchen someplace."

"What does a stupid woman know about a restaurant?"

"If women were smart enough, they'd be called 'men.' Last time I looked, the whole bunch of them are still called 'women.' They ain't smart enough yet."

"What kind of a mother takes her children to live on Madison Street?"

"They took their children to live in that neighborhood? He'll lose his wife and his children, too."

"Working on Madison Street? Is she going to take up streetwalking? There's lots of those women doing business on Madison, too."

"She brought down the whole family. She's lower than low."

"That damn woman won't last. She probably quit already."

Neighborhood criticism rudely aimed, in-person, at Mama came from a group of Greek immigrant bachelors who lived in rooming houses a block away from the restaurant. They worked Chicago's West Side as horse-and-wagon peddlers who sold fresh produce and lived in the back barns of old coach houses on Monroe Street, in very close proximity to their horses. When I entered Papa's place, I knew without looking that they were at the counter because a strong stable stench polluted the restaurant.

The peddlers resented Mama's presence, and they took every opportunity to put her down by making disparaging and hurtful remarks about women within her hearing. They told her right to her face that she didn't belong behind the counter; that her place was at home. They bluntly concluded that she had to be an inferior wife and a poor mother. (I sit here, fifty years later, surmising they either remained life-long bachelors or married women who became miserably unhappy.) Not admitting their own English skills were far worse than hers, they came into the store every day and made fun of the way she spoke. Still, Mama retained her dignity, rose above their demeaning gibes, and paid no attention to their taunting. She waited on them, ignoring their derogatory comments and nasty name-calling.

"They never know nothing better than me, anyhow. They don't even know enough to take a bath. Their horses was smelling better than they was. Why should I want to stand around and listen to those guys? I hadda do what I hadda do!"

Mama was twenty-eight when she began her new career, Papa was thirty-eight, Nick was four years old and I was seven. The Congress of the United States and the President had serious economic problems confronting them that year. They responded by enacting safe, noncontroversial legislation; they officially named "The Star-Spangled Banner" the country's national anthem. There wasn't much to sing about. Two popular songs of the year, "Minnie the Moocher" and "Life Is Just a Bowl of Cherries," reflected life in a depressed economy.

The price of a Hart Schaffner and Marx suit was $29. Bifocal glasses cost $4.95. Our family didn't know anyone who was buying any kind of a new suit, much less a "swanky" brand, and a good number of Americans needing eyeglasses doggedly squinted with eye strain because new "cheaters" were unaffordable. Twinkies were born in Chicago that year. So was Dick Tracy; he debuted in *The Chicago Tribune* as the creation of Chester Gould. Babe Ruth and Lou Gehrig tied as home run champions in 1931 after they each hit forty-six homers for the New York Yankees. Chicago was enthralled with its own memorable home run champion, Hack Wilson of the Chicago Cubs. The previous year he had broken all records by hitting fifty-six homers in a single season.

Herbert Hoover was employed at the White House, but 15.9 percent of Americans were unemployed. By 1932, unemployment would reach 23.6 percent. President Hoover's Wickersham Commission had determined that Prohibition was ineffective, and many were calling for repeal of the eighteenth amendment. A bank panic was gripping the country. Three hundred banks closed in September of 1931, and an additional five hundred twenty two banks shut down in October. Hungry, out-of-work Americans all over the country were standing in bread lines for free food.

Moving to the third floor apartment at 1524 West Madison forced many adjustments on our family, but Mama herself shouldered the most traumatic changes. She courageously initiated our family's move from a pretty flat in a desirable neighborhood to a run-down, noisy tenement. She disciplined herself into learning a difficult language on the job as quickly as possible, labored on her feet for more than half of a 24-hour day and, as a result, suffered excrutiating backaches. At the same time she silently endured baseless, vitriolic backbiting trickling back to her from "friends."

I don't remember moving out of the sunny surroundings of our "beautifool" apartment, but I do recall Mama's efforts to turn our next apartment into a home. Even though the walls were freshly painted before we moved in, much cleaning remained for Mama to do before she felt remotely comfortable in the place. The first chore she set for herself was attacking the old wooden floors to plug up holes that the rats used to enter and leave the apartment. She initiated hostilities against the scummy little beasts by bringing home empty tin cans from the restaurant, smashing them with a hammer, then nailing the flattened tin in place over the holes to seal out the enemy vermin. Waging her unrelenting war on cockroaches, she took great pains to close off even the most minute openings in the kitchen and its pantry with wads of paper and anything else she could get her hands on cheaply. The place had never been so immaculate as when Mama finished with it, and its cleanliness, subject to such impossible conditions, was perpetually under her watchful but frustrated inspection. It was at this juncture in her life that Mama, shouldering a new work load at the store while being weighed down with an onerous one at home, added two more English words to her vocabulary: "hell" and "damn."

Our third floor apartment had only one bedroom. I slept in the living room on a sofa that turned into my bed every night; Nick slept on a small daybed in our parents' room. When Green's Dance Hall, across the street, opened in the evening, we could hear the muffled strains of Chicago jazz, blues and honky tonk dance tunes. The music mixed with the grating noises of metal streetcar wheels scraping iron rails as they passed below us. On hot, steamy summer nights, with all the windows wide open, sounds were louder and cigarette smoke from Green's wafted up and over Madison Street directly into our apartment window.

We got used to the noises, including the constantly marauding sirens and clamorous comings and goings of fire engines that were housed in the station about a block away, at Laflin Street. In warm weather, firemen sat outside in front of the fire station, on sturdy captain's chairs, waiting for a call. Alarms came too often in winter, when carelessly placed makeshift heaters and unattended coal stoves set living quarters on fire in apartments and homes built before safer steam-heat radiators and central heating had been invented. More often than any other time of year, we heard fire trucks raucously rushing down Madison during the week between Christmas and New Year's when faulty wiring or sizzling colored lights and careless smokers caused tinder-dry Christmas trees to flare up without warning. Ultimately, we slept through most of the sounds of our very noisy neighborhood.

In no time at all, we felt comfortable with our new next door neighbors, John and Christina Fellas, and their two very young daughters. The Fellas family was like us: Greek with immigrant parents. Christina was an accomplished seamstress. Mr. Fellas owned a barbershop less than a half block from our father's restaurant. Papa, Nick and I went to John Fellas' shop for our haircuts. His bachelor brother, who lived with them, was the second barber. I remember when Mr. Fellas ordered new electric clippers and was displeased the first time he tried to use them. He asked me to write a letter in English to the president of the clipper company that he could send to the factory along with the faulty clippers. "Tell him his lousy clipper make more noise than strrreeeetcar. It scare my customers away." Mr. Fellas was furious as he told me what to write in the letter, and he fully believed that I was capable of communicating his ire in my English translation. I did my best. I was only in the third grade.

Learning English presented a Himalayan-sized hurdle for most immigrants, since the new language was filled with alien sounds and a strange alphabet. Still, Mama picked up English faster than anyone dreamed possible because of her daily contact with American customers and her own determination to learn. The Austin Lunch gave her one of her many crash-courses in Americanization. Still, it took months before she could carry on a conversation in English. More than once a customer, preoccupied with what he was reading in the news, pushed the paper in front of her. "What do you think of this, Mrs. Paul?"

"So sorry," Mama would respond, digging her hands in the pockets of her crisp, beige uniform. "Guess I forget my eye-glasses home today."

Mama also dreaded being put on the spot when customers who were illiterate or couldn't afford reading glasses asked her to read the menu.

"So I memorize the bill of fare every day because the foods on it was changing every single day, breakfast, lunch, and dinner. Every morning I go in the kitchen and ask Charlie 'What's on the menu today?' I listen careful and remember every single item on the long list he tell me. I alloways know everything on the menu by heart. Prices and all. So nobody ask and I get embarrass because I don't know good English."

Mama didn't even start wearing glasses until she was fifty. Although she gradually learned to read English, she was always most comfortable with words printed in capitals, and she couldn't read cursive writing at all. Too busy raising children and working, she learned all she knew by listening. Correctly or not, Mama pronounced words as she heard them. Her efforts to communicate sometimes resulted in "Mama-isms," her own word inventions like, "Blow zero" (colder than zero degrees Fahrenheit), "Hotsy totsy," (her version of Hunky Dory), "It's the really McCoy," "Happy Universary," "Goodgradulations," "Rosie bush" (shrubs bearing fragrant flowers), "Marshow Feel's" (Marshall Field's) and "Alleluia on the bum!"

"When we first come to America, your Uncla Pete (Aphroditi's husband), *Aionia tou i mnimi* (May his memory be eternal) he told me, 'Go to school. Learn English! You be sorry if you don't do it.' Pete was right. But when Tasia and me come to America there was no English classes for big people. You had to go to first grade class if you want to learn English. I tell him, 'I'm not going to school with babies. I'm too old to be in first grade.' I make big mistake back then, Helen. I should listen to your Uncla Pete. He was right. May God take care his good soul."

Mama fondly remembered Pete Kuchuris for the advice he·gave her whenever she struggled with her adopted tongue. It was Uncle

Pete who gave Mama her English name, "Bessie," but when she went to work at the restaurant, Mama was called "Mrs. Paul" by our neighbors and customers. Referring to her as "Bessie" seemed too familiar during the Thirties, and "Mrs. Limberopulos" was a mouthful. But Mama was accustomed to being called by various names. She was baptized with the beautiful Greek name *Vasiliki*, the feminine form of *Vasilios* (Basil), which means royal or kingly. Although she was very down-to-earth and unpretentious, "kingly" was an appropriate name for a take-charge lady like Mama. It fit. She was also accustomed to hearing herself called "Vasso" by friends and relatives from the village, but her sisters and brothers-in-law referred to her as "Vasilo," their pet name, which she also liked. Papa called her "Vasiliki" when he spoke in Greek and "Bessie" when he spoke in English. She reluctantly accepted "Bessie" when Uncle Pete told her it was the American equivalent of "Vasiliki." Years later she found out that wasn't true, but by that time "Bessie" had stuck.

"Paul" was my father's English name, but in Greek it was *Apostolos*. Papa used to say that most people had one patron saint, but he had twelve, the Apostles. I don't know how "Paul" was derived from Apostolos except that each contains a "P" and an "L." After they married, Mama was called "*Paulenna*" and "*Apostolenna*" by Greek acquaintances outside the family, especially people from Papa's village. The old country custom was to refer to a wife by her husband's first name with the feminine suffix. If the husband was "George," the wife was called "*Georgenna*," a carry-over from the not-so-distant years in Greece when women had no individual identity outside their family. A woman's identity was always derived from a man; her last name was always formed with a possessive ending, marking her as belonging to either a father or husband. When Greek women came to the United States, their last names became the same as that of their husbands or fathers – the possessive endings were dropped

Even though it seemed to Mama that many of their Greek friends and acquaintances turned against her when she went to work, and her feelings were assaulted by their lack of understanding, she knew she had several friends who understood the whys and wherefores. Christina Fellas understood first-hand why Mama found it necessary to begin a new job because Mrs. Fellas had one of her own. She was a seamstress who worked from home to assist her family. In addition, Mama found comfort and aid in another very special ally, Dimitra Limbers. Early in Mama and Papa's marriage, to help Mama learn English and assimilate into her new country, Papa introduced his bride to the wife of a fellow villager he called "Uncle George." Distantly related to my father, Uncle George was a Limberopulos, too, but he trimmed his name down to "Limbers" in an attempt to simplify life in America. George Limbers and his family lived a few blocks from the Austin Lunch in the Twenties.

Uncle George's wife was our Thea Dimitra, a warm, friendly woman with pure white hair who gladly helped Mama feel comfortable in her new American home. Dimitra knew all the Greek customs and all the American ones, and she spoke English perfectly. She taught Mama how to make pancakes, waffles, American-style potato salad with mayonnaise, and gave her lessons on turning out the perfect apple pie. Of course, Dimitra was an excellent Greek cook, too.

Known in English as Marie Limbers, Dimitra spoke Greek very well considering she had been born in Dubuque, Iowa of German parents and knew nothing about Greek culture or language until she married George Limbers. She had never been to Mercovouni, but knew about the villagers as if she had grown up there herself. She made good Greek Orthodox Christians of her four children who were much older than Nick and me. She insisted they learn to read and write the language of the old country at a church-run Greek school, and eventually influenced them all to marry Greek-Americans. Like our mother's sisters, she was an important part of Mama's life and our own childhood because as an American-born woman, she could help us understand American ways. I was fascinated with stories about her girlhood on an Iowa farm and membership in a Woman's Club. Even more exciting, she was an enthusiastic Cub fan who attended Ladies' Days baseball games at Wrigley Field.

I remember a visit Thea Dimitra paid to us in the Sixties. She and Mama recalled their youthful years and the adventures they enjoyed together before Mama began working. Their conversation was full of poignant reminders of life before the Depression.

As I listened, I remembered that even when I was young I was dimly aware of class structure; as I grew older I realized how important wealth was in determining many aspects of American life. Jim Raklios, the Donald Trump of Greek immigrant Chicago, who was said to have owned 45 restaurants, primarily cafeterias, was looked up to as a role model for the hard working immigrant population of the city. He gave money to charity, owned a limousine, and socialized in places where men dressed in swanky tuxedos, like movie stars. When he lost his fortune in the Depression, dreams of poor immigrants were vexed; they ached for the great man and for themselves.

Who could really make it in America if the great Greek millionaire, Raklios, couldn't? News about the renowned Mr. Raklios reached Papa's ears when a fellow businessman confided, "You won't believe what I'm going to tell you. Raklios came into my place yesterday. He asked ME for a job." Mama pondered Raklios's job-hunting differently. "At least he didn't jump out windows like lots of them millionaireys did when the Depression come. He go out and look for honest job. Raklios got really McCoy dignity."

Signs of wealth in Greek-American Chicago during the Twenties were also signs of Americanization. They included owning a lucrative business, being in a profession (like medicine, law, or engineering) with a steady income, owning a home and a car, sending offspring to private schools, vacationing in Benton Harbor, Michigan, having a credit account at Marshall Field and Company, and maintaining a checking account at the Continental Bank. Some American businessmen had Greek immigrant business partners. Less affluent Greek-Americans looked up to the wealthier ones and paid their respects in various ways.

"Thea Dimitra, you remember how your Thea Ourania expect us to wash the dishes and clean her house when we go to visit?"

"Sure do, Bessie. She had nerve, didn't she, treating us like maids? It wasn't as if we were girls who needed training. We were married women with places of our own to clean. I had four children. She was a snob."

"And got no reason to be acting so high class. Just because she was from a town in the old country that was little bit bigger than my Piali."

"And she looked down on me because I was from an Iowa farm."

"Banana oil, like my Paul used to say. She was farm girl in her village, too, and you was a really McCoy American. You speak perfect English and good Greek, too. What she know? Not much. Just how to stick her nose up in the air and act delicate. Like she was a cream puff."

"Worst part, Bessie, was that you and I went ahead and did what she expected. We showed up on her doorstep for a visit wearing our hats and gloves, with our homemade sweets arranged on our best china dishes for our elegant hostess. And then we wound up doing her housework. Whenever my George invited his Uncle Sam and Aunt Ourania to our house for dinner, they arrived empty-handed. And she thought her behavior was high class. We learned better manners than hers on our Iowa farm. My Mama was a real lady."

"Elegant hostess? She was a sellafish cheapskate. Her husband had few more dollars than the Mercovouniotes. He don't even come close to what Raklios got before he lose it all. They was both full of banana oil."

"Selfish she was, indeed, but she was shopping downtown at Marshall Field's, Bessie, and…"

"And acting like she was Mrs. Potta Palma (at one time Potter Palmer was the wealthiest man in Chicago). I alloways hear how they was going to fancy dances and big doings at the best hotels in Chicago with rich Greeks. I know there was lots of good people in the high class bunch, too, but I alloways remember what my relatives told me about how Ourania's husband act at my wedding."

"I'll never forget it, Bessie. Everybody talked about it afterwards, and I saw him with my own eyes. Land sakes, he was rude. And so greedy. That guy went into the kitchen and helped himself to the leftover lamb at your wedding. He carried out an entire roasted lamb over his shoulder—roasting pan and all. "

"It really shock my relatives. They was the poor folks, but the richest guy at the wedding take the leftovers home. There's a Greek saying my Mama used to tell us about people acting that way. '*Voetha me ftohe na me sou moiaso.*' It mean 'Help me, poor man, so I don't get to be like you.'

"But life change for them when the Depression come. Poor Sam, he lost both his big restaurants. Then they was in bad shape just like the rest of us. My Mama had another saying for that. '*Opoios gyrevei ta polla, hanei ke ta liga.*' Means 'Somebody goes to get too much and then loses the little bit he got already.'" Unknowingly, Mama was paraphrasing the punch line from a two-thousand-year old Aesop's fable.

"That didn't stop Ourania from viciously criticizing you for going to work, Bessie."

"She was just one of them who talk against me, Thea. But you never did. You was working hard with Uncla George in your grocery store, and you know the whole about everything. You alloways understand. You been so good to me, Thea Dimitra, and I can't ever say thank you enough for everything you done for me."

Reviewing her past in 1984, Mama credited her sisters and Thea Dimitra with holding out soul-soothing lifelines to her when she was over her head with frustrations.

"It all come at once on me, but I know I got to manage it all. I had to be patient and strong. Their friendship make it a little easier. There was plenty of times I cry. All by myself so nobody see me. Papa was right, I did miss our beautifool apartment with grass and trees. And I miss the sunnyshine coming through the windows there, too. Anyway there's no time to sit home and enjoy nothing. I had to work. Remember, Helen, how dark it was in that Madison and Ogden apartment? Was dark at home and dark in the store. Had to go out in the middle of

Madison, where streetcars could run over you, to see the sun. Remember the noise? That noise never stop. It was in our ears day and night. My head get dizzy and hurt like hell from all the damn noise."

The constant din and darkness that meant my eyes were shocked everytime they saw sunlight were unforgettable. Most of all, however, I remembered how my mother's young, pleasant face became hard and haggard, and how she smiled less and less.

Mama's eyes filled up again recalling old frustrations. Papa was up to his ears in debt and she, weary but determined, lived on her feet for half the day while an occasional complaint from her sister Politimi, of all people, came back to add guilt to her burdens.

"Lots of days, we only take in eight or nine dollars. In twenty-four hours. Busyness was dead, dead, dead. Even with no customers coming in we had to be on our feet to clean. There's never rest from cleaning up, and alloways slavery in a restaurant. My back and my feet was killin' me. It was like somebody was taking a hatchet and hitting me in my spine and in the backs of my legs. While I work I was think about my sisters because I miss seeing them. Lots of times I cry, in private, so nobody see me. When we lived on the farther West Side we could walk to their houses, except for Thanaso, because she lived so far south. Politimi complain because I don't go to visit them anymore. She never realize how much I miss her. How much I want to visit and be with her and the rest of my sisters. She don't understand how much I cry. How much my body hurt from working and being so damn tired.

"Then, every time one of them bookies from Drell's cigar store come in to talk to Papa, my blood pressure go up because I'm not sure he's gonna start up playing the horses again. We could wind up in the poorhouse no matter how much we sacrifice and sweat and our bodies hurt when we work. And on top of everything, people saying mean lies about me that break my heart, too. But I couldn't complain to nobody because I, myself, had the idea to go to work. Nobody force me. But that's all right. It didn't kill us, Helen."

MATCHMAKING 101

*I*ris and George Jones, immigrants from England, resided in the seven-room apartment next to us at Ogden and Madison. The Fellas family lived on one side, the Jones couple on the other. Iris's yellow hair was fashioned into a short bob, absolutely straight except for frizzy curls which stuck out from ear to ear right above the nape of her neck. George was a tiny bit on the portly side. To me, a kid surrounded by people struggling to speak English, Mr. and Mrs. Jones sounded like British royalty. They were the only people I knew in the United States of America who spoke truly flawless English; at least it sounded flawless to me. The two of them lived in the kitchen and one bedroom of the apartment next door to us, renting out all their remaining rooms for extra income. They were childless with a great love for kids, and immediately took a liking to Nick and me. We enthusiastically returned the affection. Mr. Jones was a sports enthusiast and once presented Nick with a brown leather punching bag and two sets of boxing gloves. To say that Nick was thrilled doesn't come close to describing his boyish awe. My brother still smiles when he remembers Mr. Jones's generous gift.

The Joneses first introduced my brother and me to the American practice of going to the movies and enjoying ice cream afterward. We had never been to the corner drugstore ice-cream fountain, even though we lived directly upstairs. Our environment had been so Greek, immigrant style, when we went to live at Madison and Ogden, at ages seven and four, that we never before had attended a motion picture theater or had eaten at an ice-cream fountain. The Joneses took us to both on the same day, and I still remember it with joy and appreciation. Iris and George did much to open the eyes of two children of immigrants to the childhood pleasures of the United States. They helped brighten our Austin Lunch existences. The Joneses became good friends of our parents mostly through contact at the restaurant because work didn't allow much socializing at home. The four of them engaged in wonderful conversations at Papa's white marble counter while Nick and I listened in. We learned much about our parents by tuning into their conversations with friends and customers at the restaurant. That's how I learned how my parents met each other.

"Mrs. Paul, St. Valentine's Day is almost here. Have you made a Valentine for Paul yet? He's your sweetheart, isn't he?"

"Sure, Paul's my sweetheart, Mrs. Jones." Mama looked puzzled by the question.

"Iris and I have often wondered, did you marry in Greece?"

"Oh no, Mr. Jones, I don't even know Paul in the old country. He's from different village. I was only four years old when Paul come to America."

"How did you meet?"

"A matchmaker lady. She know Paul and she's friends with my sisters here in Chicago. She know my sisters got two girls to marry off, my sister Tasia, and me. She know we come from good family. I was the oldest so I had to be marry off before Tasia. That's old Greek custom.

"Matchmaker is still good friend of Paul and me. Before Paul meet me, he told her that he want to get marry and he want a girl that's not too young and she got to be smart. No dummy.

"The matchmaker ask him, 'What you going to buy me, Paul, if I find a good girl for you?' And Paul tell her, 'I buy you a new dress.'

"So, matchmaker set up the meeting. Paul come to my sister Politimi's house, where I was living, and bring his Uncla Jim and a friend, too. I serve them all sweets and coffee and I look at Paul and he look at me. We hardly talk to each other. Just 'Howdyado' and 'Nice to meetchyou.' Paul, my brother-in-law, my sister, and his Uncla Jim they talk to each other. I was very embarrass. What can I say? Not much.

"Next day Paul find out I'm a relative of his Uncla Jim's mama-in-law who is living here in Chicago with Uncla Jim and his family on the North Side. She tell Paul, 'This girl's grandma is my sister. She's a very good girl from a very good family back in our Piali. You be lucky man if you marry her.' And she recommend me as a bride for Paul.

"Next day Paul come to see me again and he talk to me more and I guess he see that I was no dummy and I like him, too. He don't blah blah blah too much. I don't like those guys that talk all the time and don't say nothing. Matchmaker and Paul's relatives tell me and my sisters and brother-in-laws that Paul's a good person. On top of it he's got two restaurants." She laughed. "But they don't tell me he's got two partners, too. Anyway, he look like nice person. He didn't talk no nonsense. My sisters and brother-in-laws tell me he's a good man for you. And so did Uncla Jim's mama-in-law. So in one month after we meet, we get marry. On June 10, 1923. And the matchmaker friend she get a new dress from Paul. That's the whole story, Mr. and Mrs. Jones. Here we are. But let me ask you something. What holiday is coming? I don't understand you before when you say it."

"St. Valentine's Day, Mrs. Paul. The day to remember a sweetheart."

"American saint Mr. Jones? I don't know about him. Yesterday was Febyouary 10, Saint Haralambos Day. He's a Greek saint. They start trimming the grapevines in the old country on St. Haralambos's holiday. My Papa's got one in our courtyard. It's so beautifool. I remember it all the time. His grapevines will be beautifool in summertime. The one growing on our house has the sweetest grapes in the world. Sweet as sugar! So sweet you can't never forget them."

"Mrs. Paul, how can you even think of pruning grapevines when the snow outside is ten inches deep and not likely to melt until April?"

Papa answered Mr. Jones's question with a look of longing in his eyes.

"George, the old country is even further away from us during these below-zero winters. Someday, though, Bessie and I will take our children back to Greece to see our parents, our villages and the vineyards again. And when we do, I'll send you a postcard from the Acropolis."

Mama's Depression daydream was over for the moment.

"Don't hold your breath, Mr. Jones. We all going to be real old people by that time."

Another match-making expedition came to mind while Mama and I were poring over the old letters from Piali. She remembered one of the happiest weddings in our family, which took place at the start of the very desolate year of 1932.

"We work hard but wasn't making no profit. Not even close. Alloways in debt and stuck in the dark smoky restaurant. And you and Nicky was stuck in there with us. I know it was no fun for you or for me, but that way I don't have to worry about where you was or what was happening to you. Because I could see you with my own eyes."

With Mama and Papa in the restaurant for twelve to sixteen hours a day, the deeper we became entrenched in our drab Austin Lunch bunker, the more we looked forward to news, visits, and excitement coming to us at Papa's store. Mama stationed Nick and me in a booth toward the rear of the restaurant and kept a laser eye on us. I was to help my brother with homework because I was older and several grades ahead. Certainly, both of us had restaurant responsibilities. At seven, Nick worked at helping Harry, the dishwasher, and I was trusted to take cash from customers before I was ten. Socially, however, the four of us rarely went off together as a family, except to attend funerals when Nick and I were dragged along too. But then there was "the" wedding when Papa's brother, our dear Uncle Bill, married Chrisoula Kokinis.

"Your Uncla Bill come from Michigan because his friend want to introduce him to a bride he can marry. We all go to meet her. Bill say, 'This is the one' and we was all happy for him. Everyone look forward to a wedding. It was a happy time in the Depression misery."

When Mama told my brother and me we were to participate at Papa's brother's marriage ceremony and there would be a party afterwards, we soared with excitement. Parties weren't a part of Depression life; they were unaffordable. We celebrated Christmas and Easter religiously, with no financial extravagance, and I don't recall big birthday celebrations or dinner parties. On our name days, when the Orthodox Church celebrates our patron saints' heroic and faithful lives, Papa pulled on our earlobes for good luck. If Mama had a break from restaurant duties, she'd bake Greek sweets. That was it. We considered ourselves well-lauded when we received a mere two words, the traditional wish of *Hronia Polla* (Living many years). Papa's affectionate ear tug and Mama's Greek cookies that she baked with love in a precious moment of free time extracted from her heavy work schedule were stupendously special. Uncle Bill's wedding, coming as it did during the economic hardships of early 1932, stood out as glamorous and lavish.

Late in 1931, Papa's brother, Bill Limber, came to Chicago from Lansing, Michigan, to be introduced to a single, young Greek woman, Chrisoula Kokinis. He shortened his surname from Limberopulos to Limber when he went to live in Lansing. Many Greeks shortened and Anglicized their names to escape hateful discrimination; small town prejudice against foreigners was sometimes worse than big-city intolerance.

Uncle Bill had been introduced to other prospective brides but didn't like any of them enough to marry. When he went to Chrisoula's home to meet her for the first time, my uncle showed up at the front door on Canal Street with six members of his family; this was preferred etiquette. The gentleman was proud to show he had family in America who were interested in his welfare. Their opinion counted when it came to adding a new member to their group.

The candidate for bride had been born in Chicago, but when she was nine years old her parents moved back to Magoula, one of the eighteen villages in the township of Tegea. After five months, her father decided to return to the United States, but her mother, sensitive to the obligations of a daughter-in-law to care for his aging parents, refused to go. Chrisoula pleaded to return with her father. She despised village life but loved the big American city where she was born. For nine years, she pined away and wrote tear-stained letters, imploring her father to bring her to America. Finally, at eighteen, Chrisoula left her mother and siblings behind in Greece and jubilantly returned to the shining lights of Chicago. Her father, a fruit and vegetable peddler, had been living alone in one room. Because housing for himself and his daughter was unaffordable, Chrisoula made her home with her father's sister and brother-in-law who treated her like a daughter.

Uncle Bill was introduced to Chrisoula at her aunt and uncle's house on South Canal Street, an old two-story, wood frame building, which probably pre-dated the Great Chicago Fire of 1871. After Chicago's infamous holocaust, city laws required new buildings to be constructed of brick. The family's living quarters were on the second floor. The ground level housed her uncle's business, a cooperage. Many of his customers were immigrants from Mediterranean countries who produced their own wine in their basements every autumn and needed his barrels for storage. In the 1930s, wine-making was legal if it was produced for personal consumption. Most of his hand-made wooden barrels, however, were sold to "bootleggers" and were destined to hold "bootleg hooch," alcoholic liquor made and sold illegally during Prohibition. Repeal of the eighteenth amendment was still a year-and-a-half away.

At home receiving guests on the prospective bride's side that evening were Chrisoula, her father, her aunt, her uncle and the matchmaker, a gentleman who was a friend of both families. Present on the prospective groom's side were Uncle Bill (who Chrisoula and her family were reminded was part owner of the Capitol Laundry in Lansing, Michigan), my father, my mother, Uncle Al and, more importantly, Uncle Jim, the Limberopulos family patriarch in Chicago who had sponsored Papa and Uncle Bill's immigration to America. Jim Limberopulos was no longer in the shoeshine and hat cleaning business with Papa's other uncles. When they sold all their shoeshine parlors in 1917, Jim's brothers returned to Greece for the rest of their lives, and Jim went into business on his own. He was especially well known in the Greek-American community as a successful North Side real estate entrepreneur. His wife, Koula, and one of their three daughters, thirteen-year-old Evelyn, were also in attendance at the introduction of Bill to Chrisoula.

As was expected and proper at such meetings, Chrisoula served sweets and coffee to the guests, so that the prospective groom and his family could observe her manners and upbringing. Her aunt's best china and serving pieces were brought out for the occasion. First introductions could be stressful but thanks to Uncle Bill comfortable conversation filled the room. And it turned out that Uncle Bill liked the spirited, petite and pretty Chrisoula. Earlier, he had confided to Papa that he would absolutely not consider marrying a girl who was too young for him. And Chrisoula had told her aunt, uncle, and father that she was not interested in marrying a man over thirty. Chrisoula was twenty-one, and Uncle Bill was thirty-four. Even though Chrisoula was a bit young, Uncle Bill decided that he'd gladly make an exception in her case, if she'd have him. And Chrisoula, though she suspected that her prospective groom might have already turned thirty, was taken with his unassuming nature and sense of humor. She saw a bump on the back of his head. He had it all his life and it was usually not visible under his mane of straight, dark brown hair. When Chrisoula got up enough nerve, she asked about it and smiled at his reply.

"Too many brains! They exploded and I have a hard time gettin' them to stay still in there." Sixty-three years later, Chrisoula remembered that she had liked Uncle Bill right away because "He was jolly and the minute I met him it was like I know him for years." It was easy to love Uncle Bill.

When the visit ended, it was understood that on the following day the matchmaker would contact both families to see if there was interest in matrimony. Chrisoula's aunt asked what she thought of Uncle Bill, but Chrisoula didn't want to let on that she was seriously interested and casually said, "Let's see what the other side says tomorrow."

Her aunt reminded her that the gentleman lived far away in Michigan and that Chrisoula had no other family there for companionship and comfort. She hinted it might be best to reject this candidate, but Chrisoula suggested that Mr. Limber might want to move back to Chicago. Her aunt told her not to count on it because the gentleman's successful laundry business was in far away Michigan and that he was lucky to have a thriving business when there was so much poverty and unemployment in Chicago. "Well," Chrisoula countered, "I'd be marrying the man and not the city. And Michigan City is much closer than you think. I could take the train and visit you in Chicago once a week."

Both families approved of the match; Bill and Chrisoula were engaged. The wedding date was set for the end of January, 1932, and Bill returned to Lansing. Before he went back to Michigan, he entrusted Mama with one hundred dollars to buy the wedding dress, veil, shoes and anything else the bride-to-be might need for the big event. He also told Mama to buy appropriate new outfits for Nick and me since we were to be in the wedding party. Evidently, the laundry business in Lansing was far more lucrative than the restaurant business in Chicago in 1932.

"I remember that I tell Bill a hundred dollars was going to take care of everything he want me to buy for him. And I promise that I'm going to give him plenty of change back, too. Papa and me, we don't got no hundred dollars to spend on fancy stuff. We still owe money to too many people." Mama and Chrisoula shopped for all the wedding clothes in the stores on Halsted Street, just north and south of Twelfth and close to Maxwell Street, where bargaining for merchandise was encouraged. Mama's older sisters had taken her there for the first time when she came from Greece. Mama's own 1920s waistless, white-beaded wedding dress was purchased in the same neighborhood in 1923. Papa paid ten dollars for it.

Greek-American custom in those early years dictated the groom pay for most wedding expenses, including the bride's dress, veil and shoes. Because there were many more single Greek men than single Greek women in the United States at the time, most bachelors were so delighted when they found a bride that they dismissed "old country" dowry obligations. As a result of this economic advantage, unmarried girls were sent to America to marry. Most fathers-of-the-brides, thousands of miles away, were not expected to contribute as much as a nickel for the nuptials. They, no doubt, harbored the hope that from time to time a new son-in-law would send American cash to them instead.

Our excitement over Uncle Bill's wedding reached Alpha Centauri by the beginning of 1932. Nick and I even infected George and Iris Jones with it, and they would have come to the church to admire us as "wedding attendants" (Mrs. Jones's words) had it not been for the blinding blizzard that raged the night before, and its lingering aftermath.

WEDDING

We have happy news. Apostoli's brother is getting married.

—Vasiliki to her parents, December 1931

*T*ime went into slow motion (as it does when you're a kid) until January 31, 1932, the day of Uncle Bill's wedding. Mama was seriously ill with pneumonia, and Chicago was deeply stuck in snow. When Nick and I gazed out our third floor window that morning, awesome whiteness and a great host of icicles dazzled us. The inner city always looks its best when snow is drifting down on it, before it turns into brown slush and human discomfort is worsened by frigid misery and inconvenience.

All our neighborhood's dark and dirty blemishes were submerged in deep, clean snow. Glassy icicles hung from power lines, windowsills and fire escapes; streetcar service on Madison was interrupted by ice-laden electric trolley lines. We marveled at light poles and street signs coated with glistening, translucent layers of ice, and at the thick crust of snow that stuck to one side of the Flatiron Building. Windows in buildings across the street from our living room were covered with dense sheets of frost. In fact, we had to scrape crinkly patterns of opaque ice off our own windowpanes to see the world outside.

Dr. Charles E. Pugh, Sr., our family physician, visited our apartment several times to attend to Mama while she was sick with pneumonia that January. He came that icy Sunday morning, too. Papa quickly trudged home from the store through a half-block of deep snow to be present while the doctor was there. It was exciting to see the distinguished older gentleman with his white hair and mustache, so highly revered by all of our family, when he arrived at the front door. He was the family doctor for all of Mama's sisters, their husbands and children. In those days, doctors kept personal contact with their patients. He greeted Nick and me by our first names because he had brought both of us into the world and knew our short medical histories by heart. As soon as the doctor removed his snow-encrusted galoshes and placed them next to Papa's in the dim hallway, Papa instructed us to take his hat, coat and scarf and lay them neatly on the sofa in the living room.

Dr. Pugh greeted Mama and brought out the cold, shiny instruments he always carried in his familiar black leather bag. Mama's face was flushed and she was almost hidden under a stack of blankets in the double bed of my parents' bedroom. It was a tiny room with just enough space for Nick's daybed, a small dresser, and my parents' double bed. A grouping of religious treasures hung on the eastern wall against the feather-plume design of aging wallpaper. The most dramatic was an icon of the Crucifixion in a wooden frame, showing the Holy Mother and Apostle John standing on either side of Jesus, nailed to the cross. The dark muddy colors, Jesus's suffering face, and the grief of both mourners reflected the worst kind of sorrow. The larger icon was a needle-worked brown cross, embellished with red poppies—Mama's own handiwork. She had embroidered it herself when she was a girl and brought it to America from Greece with her other sparse belongings in 1921. The third was a tiny, framed print of a white-bearded, solemn St. Nicholas attired in Bishop's robes that didn't make him look at all like Santa Claus. A red-glass vigil light glowed on a dark corner shelf along with the tiny brass censer. Mama used it to burn incense on important religious holidays, like Good Friday. The vigil lamp was filled with olive oil and burned by way of a floating wick; Mama faithfully kept it lit near the icons year round. No matter how dark it got in that room, Mama's vigil always offered a glint of light.

The doctor ducked into the bathroom to rinse and disinfect a thermometer, and Mama motioned for us to be quiet by putting her finger over her lips seconds before he returned and placed the instrument under her tongue. Then he began his examination. Dr. Pugh listened intently through his stethoscope, then tapped Mama's back with his fingers. She modestly arranged her thick flannel nightgown to keep herself covered as he examined her. Papa mentioned to the doctor that the children were exceptionally excited that day because we were going to his brother's wedding.

"This lady's not going to any wedding today, Mr. Limberopulos," he said. Mama agreed with Dr. Pugh that a stormy day in January was no time for a pneumonia patient to leave the house, but she reminded him that she was needed at the restaurant. The doctor responded with a question. "You want to die, Mrs. Limberopulos, and never see these kids grow up?" He answered himself. "I don't think so. You're a smart woman. I know you'll stay in bed until I say you can get out of it. Mr. Limberopulos can get along in his restaurant without you—until I say you're one hundred per cent well. The way this country's going, he probably hasn't got any customers in his place anyway."

He wrote a prescription on a small piece of paper; his name and office address were printed at the top. I don't remember where his office was located when I was very little because we didn't go there when we were sick. Dr. Pugh usually came to us. Later he moved to an official-looking modern office building at the northwest corner of Crawford and Madison.

Papa assured the doctor he'd go down to the corner drugstore to buy Mama's medicine before he dressed for the wedding. As he helped the doctor into his heavy coat, Papa asked how much he owed him. Hat with extended earflaps and wool scarf in place, Dr. Pugh announced his fee. He had climbed multiple flights of stairs and caught his breath on multiple landings in a poorly lit hallway to get to our third floor apartment. He was about to descend those same wooden steps to attend to his next home visit through miserable ice and snow.

"Two dollars. If that's not easy to do today, just give me one dollar. And, if you haven't got it, that's all right. Pay me some other time."

One of Mama's sisters arrived on the streetcar to care for her while we went to the wedding, and she filled us in on the difficulties of traveling through the city in the aftermath of the blizzard. Mama and our aunt supervised our dressing up in our new wedding apparel, then made sure we were warmly swathed in our heaviest coats, leggings, wool hats, itchy scarves, mittens and galoshes. Barely able to walk from the bulkiness of our arctic apparel, we departed with Papa for our streetcar rides to Holy Trinity Greek Orthodox Church on Peoria Street, in the neighborhood of Blue Island and Twelfth.

Mama and Papa had been married there, nine years before. Uncle Bill's bride, Chrisoula, all our cousins, Nick, and I had been baptized at Holy Trinity. It was the first permanently established Greek Orthodox Church in Chicago, selected by Chrisoula's father for her wedding because she had begun life as a Christian there. The reception was to be held in the hall at St. Demitrios Greek Orthodox Church on the distant North Side because Uncle Jim Limberopulos had connections there; he was president of the church council that year. When plans were being made for the wedding, no one expected a snowstorm.

The ceremony was to begin at four in the afternoon, but most of the guests did not own cars in 1932. Getting to Peoria Street meant riding streetcars, and all public transportation had slowed down because of the blizzard. Papa, who always showed up at appointments on time and sometimes a half hour too early, had been informed that we needed to be at the photographer's studio for a formal, group wedding portrait prior to the ceremony. He was agitated because the storm delayed us. Papa, Nick and I found Uncle Bill there happy and resplendent in his rented tuxedo and Thea Chrisoula looking beautiful in her bridal dress and soft veil. The only one missing was the best man. Papa blamed his absence on the snow.

After a long wait, an official photograph was taken of the wedding party: the bride, the groom, five bridesmaids, Nick and me. As I look at that photo today, I can plainly see that it was not the custom for bridesmaids to wear matching dresses. Each young woman wore a different dress and carried a bouquet that didn't match the others.

Nick and I had been positioned in front of all the adults. Nick, in his light blue outfit with short pants and matching shirt with Peter Pan collar, sat on a tiny metal chair to the right of the bride, with her long veil spread out in front of her. I was placed to the left of Uncle Bill and in front of Uncle Jim Limberopulos's eldest daughter, Sylvia, one of the lovely brunette bridesmaids. I was wearing my pretty pink dress with flared short sleeves and new white shoes with straps, called "Mary Janes." The adults in the photo look young and terrific, like Thirties movie stars. I, however, am sitting, slouched over, on some sort of fancy piano bench. It's obvious Mama had not been there to pay attention to detail and, as always, remind me to sit up straight before the click of the shutter.

The familiar and comforting smell of incense surrounded us when we finally entered the vestibule of the church on Peoria Street. With Papa's help, we each took off our mittens to light a slender candle and venerate the somber-colored icons of the Holy Trinity and of the Holy Mother. Nick and I crossed ourselves and kissed each icon as Mama had taught us to do. The holy pictures were far above our heads so Papa gave each one of us a boost so our kisses could reach their sacred destinations. Mama came to mind and I asked God to make her well again because I had never seen her so sick before.

I finished my quick silent prayer as Papa opened the door and ushered us into the warmer interior of the church. Tall, narrow icons of Jesus, the Holy Mother and many saints lined the front and side walls of Holy Trinity. A triangular icon with a large eye painted in the middle of it looked down on us from above the altar. Mama told me on previous visits that it represented the All-Seeing Eye of God. Although it wasn't Westminster Abbey by any stretch of the imagination, the glowing candles, incense and saintly icons, somber as they were, always emanated a feeling of peace inside God's small house on Peoria Street. Holy Trinity is no longer in the "old neighborhood." The venerable old parish was relocated to the Northwest Side of the city during the Sixties when the revered brick building was knocked down to make room for the University of Illinois Chicago campus.

Moments after we were inside the church, confusion broke our tranquility as a loud, complaining group of wedding guests approached my father. Papa was angrily informed that the best man had never been told about studio picture taking before the wedding. His wife, the best lady, vehemently complained, appalled that wedding pictures would not include the most important member of the wedding party, the *koumbaros* (best man).

Indeed, in the Greek culture, the *koumbaros* of a wedding was as important as the bride and groom. In accepting the honor of becoming best man, he automatically took on traditional wedding expenses that, at the very least, included buying the *stephana* (wedding crowns), the candles used during the ceremony and the gratuities for the priest and chanter, an outlay especially difficult during the Depression.

The best man, his wife, children, parents and siblings were considered members of the bride and groom's family for life, and this esteem was reciprocated. The best man was the first to be asked to baptize the couple's first child, and when a male child grew up and married, he would traditionally ask his godfather to be the *koumbaros* at the wedding. The groom usually determines who the best man will be. The church itself honors the spiritual bond between godchildren and their godparents by forbidding marriage between them and their children; they are assumed to be members of the same family.

Chrisoula, the shy bride, apologized for not informing the *koumbaros* about where wedding pictures would be taken, but she had never been to a wedding in America before and didn't know what was expected. To lighten a strained situation, Uncle Bill expressed regret tempered with humor. "I'm new at this swanky stuff myself. First time I ever got married!"

As late guests arrived, we lined up in the vestibule of the church for the march down the aisle. It was six o'clock; the wedding was starting two hours late. When the first of five bridesmaids smiled and began her walk down the aisle, loud arguing erupted between two older gentlemen who were standing on either side of the bride, each tugging on the bride's arm closest to him.

While the bridal tug-of-war ensued, Nick and I were stationed at the far end of the bride's veil and instructed by one of her female relatives to pick it up and carry it down the aisle. She told us that when we finally got up to the front of the church we were to gracefully lay it down and keep our positions behind the couple until the priest instructed us to pick up the veil again during the ceremony. The woman reminded us to stand up straight, walk tall, and be proud because we were, indeed, fortunate to be part of such an aristocratic wedding. Nick and I knew we couldn't start following the bride down the aisle, however, until she had settled her problems with the two older men who were making a noisy fuss and still trying to pull her apart.

They were Thea Chrisoula's father and uncle, each loudly insisting to the other that it was his privilege and right to walk the bride down the aisle. As the fifth bridesmaid reached the altar, we overheard the bride's decree, "OK. Both of you come." She grabbed the older men, one to each side of her, and the arm-linked trio started walking toward Uncle Bill's smiling face at the front of the church; we followed. A father and uncle team gave Chrisoula Kokinis away to Bill Limber.

As Nick and I carried the end of the bride's veil down the aisle, I was aware, without looking, that women, girls, and very young male children were gathered to my left, separated from men and boys who, by tradition, participated in religious services from the right side of the church. The tradition of separating the sexes during worship, carried over into Christianity from Judaism, was finally abandoned by American Greek Orthodox Churches during World War II. Even so, for years afterward I felt an obligation to sit on the left side of the church because when Mama drilled rules into you, they stayed drilled.

Standing behind the bride and groom, Nick and I waited a very long time for a signal from the priest at the front of the church. He was attired in beautifully embroidered blue vestments that hung from his shoulders to his shoe tops. The bride and groom blocked our vision, but every now and then we caught a glimpse of the cleric's richly colored vestments as he performed his priestly duties. I diligently watched for his signal.

The first part of the ceremony, the betrothal, commenced, and I strained to look between the bride and groom to catch a glimpse of shiny gold rings being placed on their fingers by the priest. The best man took part, too, but I saw none of the action. I only recognized the names "Vasilios" and "Chrisoula" during the priest's singing and the melodic "Amen" of the chanter who responded in Byzantine chant to all the priest's invocations. Uncomfortable, I longed to be sitting in the pews behind me. Then when I glanced up, I swallowed hard and froze in place. The immense "Eye of God" was staring down at me. Nick, too, was tired of standing behind it all. His eyes sent signals of his having achieved martyrdom, and he shifted his weight from one leg to another, contorting his body at the waist; the kid was in more agony than I was. I tried to imitate Mama and give him the high voltage "look" she flashed when she wanted us to stand still, but Nick knew I wasn't Mama. Then I sensed the crowd closing in. "Why don't they go back and sit in the seats? I'd give anything to be sitting," I silently complained to myself. Nobody told us we'd have to stand throughout a ceremony that took an hour to complete.

Finally, after some more chanting, I saw the top of the priest's head approach Vasilios and Chrisoula; he touched their foreheads three times with the wedding crowns, a pair of small, white, floral wreaths, as he again integrated their Greek names into the prayer. "The servant of God, Vasilios, is crowned to the handmaiden of God, Chrisoula." "The handmaiden of God, Chrisoula, is crowned to the servant of God, Vasilios." Every symbol of the ceremony was repeated three times in honor of the Holy Trinity while the chanter sang melodic Greek responses, non-stop. But the only one I understood was "Amen."

Then, I watched the priest place each of the pretty wreaths, joined by a length of white satin ribbon, on the head of my uncle and new aunt. As the ceremony continued the best man came between Nick, me, and the bridal couple and stood behind the bride and groom. After more chanting and waiting in pinchy shoes, we watched him switch the pretty white *stephana* from the head of the bride to the head of the groom, exchanging them three times. At that point the wedding guests pushed in against us even more forcefully, and I was positive we'd be crushed by them.

It was then that I caught a glimpse of Papa, forcing his way through the crowd to rescue his offspring who were about to be trampled and unceremoniously tangled in the bride's long veil. It never occurred to my child's mind that the grown-ups may have been leaning in, as close as possible, to catch blessings and happiness for themselves during the celebration of the joyful sacrament. Perhaps they were putting off the hard times which would resurface at ceremony's end when, exiting onto snow-clogged Peoria Street, icy snows would slap them into reality again.

Papa squeezed closer to us as the priest approached the couple again. Holding the gold-covered book of Holy Gospels in front of them, the priest began walking with our uncle and his bride, daintily joined together by the pretty white crowns and satin ribbon. The best man followed. They began orbiting a small table close to the *ikonostasion* (a wall of icons separating the altar from the congregation) at the front of the church. The gigantic "All-Seeing Eye of God" surveyed us from above, verifying that a whole church full of His children, young and old, were behaving themselves, just like Mama did. With each step, the best man gingerly kicked away folds of diaphanous and silky white fabric splashing like surf around his shiny black shoes. Yet he succeeded in following the couple while hanging on to their wedding crowns.

Without any warning, a woman behind me jabbed me sharply in my ribcage, impatiently gesturing for Nick and me to pick up the veil and follow the bride in the short circular procession. "Go around three times," she instructed in a whisper that could be heard on Peoria Street. The symbolic mini-walk is called the "Dance of Isaiah." The priest chants a prayer as he leads the bride, groom and *koumbaros* in a circle around the table. This walk symbolizes the bride and groom's journey through life together following God's Word (signified by the Book of the Gospels), as king and queen of their own new family (symbolized by the white crowns). I have since learned that this is the most important and joyous moment of the Orthodox wedding.

Prodded by the woman's whispers, my brother and I reached for Thea Chrisoula's veil and carried it around the table, bringing up the rear of the small procession. I guessed we were doing the right thing because nobody yelled at us. In a minute we came to a stop, stood in our places again, then waited through more chanting. Finally, the priest removed the crowns from the couple's heads and separated their hands by gently sliding the thick, gold Book of Gospels between them. The bride and groom turned toward Nick and me, and I could tell by the look of relief and the smile on Uncle Bill's face that the ceremony was over.

Hanging on for dear life to the bride's veil, we quickly followed the newlyweds to the back of the church where guests kissed and congratulated them. Nick and I were overly kissed, too, our chins and cheeks painfully pinched by hundreds of admiring sandpapery fingers. We were relieved when well-wishing was over. At the back of the church, the bridesmaids handed out Jordan almonds wrapped in white tulle and tied together with white ribbon, symbolizing the sweetness and bitterness of married life, to the guests.

I don't recall how Papa transported us to St. Demitrios's Hall for the party through the mountains of snow and sheets of slick ice, but I remember seeing Uncle Charlie Kingos cooking in the church kitchen after we arrived. Wedding guests feasted sumptuously on his roasted lamb, golden brown potatoes, cheese, olives, salad, and sesame-covered bread. Wine toasts were offered throughout the celebration. After dinner, a Greek band began playing folk dance music that inspired the best man, bride and groom to lead their guests in a huge semicircle of traditional dances. Papa said our Greek dances had their beginnings in ancient times. It was the custom for the *koumbaros* to have the honor of leading the first dance; if he was married, his wife was the next one to lead; then the bride and groom had their turns. Familiar Greek melodies filled the souls of guests and pure elation synchronized movements on the dance floor. Men, women and children danced together. Men moved with deliberate and spirited steps while ladies danced in the same circle, just as lively, but more gracefully and demurely. Children studied the feet of adults on either side of them in the semi-circle, attempting to master the fast moving *syrtos* and *kalamatianos*.

Another traditional dance, the slow moving *tsamikos*, was easier to keep up with. A line of dancers lingered behind a man who proudly jumped and twisted in perfect rhythm to the music, while holding on to a white handkerchief held high by the second dancer in the line. All eyes on him, he prolonged his display by masterfully performing even fancier steps while the clarinetist showed off his own artistry with an intricate solo. The enticing melody of "*Enas Aetos*" (An Eagle), the most popular piece for dancing the *tsamikos*, filled the room and more dancers jubilantly joined the semi-circle. Discarding his suit jacket for ease of motion, the dancer leapt and whirled in perfect cadence to the music. Mesmerized, unmindful of the devastating Depression and treacherous ice awaiting him on Chicago's dark and frigid streets, he became engulfed in exuberant melody and rhythm. Dancing the *tsamikos*, he was no longer an unemployed dishwasher, counterman, or cook attending a wedding in a damp and drafty church hall. As the lyrics suggested, he was an eagle soaring in the sun, and for an instant he metaphysically returned to his warm, bright homeland.

Our parents expected us to learn the centuries-old Greek dances and pass them on to our progeny. No matter how young, children were encouraged to join the dancing and learn to lead at the front of the semi-circle. Traditional dances were a source of comfort, a vestige of the "old country," for our immigrant parents who had been plunged into the strangeness of a new country. Music and dancing were another link to those familiar customs and loved ones they had left behind, thousands of miles away. Uncle Bill's wedding and reception provided a flash of brightness in the serious dark Depression. The entire cost of bringing joy to so many was three hundred dollars.

After the reception, Bill and Chrisoula paid a visit to our apartment at Ogden and Madison so Mama could wish them happiness and see the bride and groom in their handsome and lovely, once–in–a–lifetime, wedding attire. After loving congratulations were bestowed, they departed into the icy night again, wearing new street clothes, for their honeymoon at the elegant Edgewater Beach Hotel. The Edgewater Beach is gone now, but until it was torn down in the late 1960's, it reigned on the shores of Lake Michigan as one of Chicago's finest hotels.

Later in the week, Bill and Chrisoula drove to Michigan to begin their new life as Mr. and Mrs. William Nicholas Limber. A short distance out of Chicago, when the road began rounding the southernmost curve of Lake Michigan, Chrisoula spotted a road sign.

"Looks like we're almost home, Bill. The sign over there says 'Michigan City.'"

"We've got a long way to go Chrisoula—we're not even halfway there yet."

"But, that sign says 'Michigan City.' That's where we're going isn't it?"

"Where'd you get that idea? Michigan City? Michigan City is in Indiana. We're on our way to Lansing, Michigan. Lansing is a city in the state of Michigan. We've got at least another four hours of driving to get there."

Uncle Bill's Capitol Laundry in Michigan's capital city is gone. It's heartbreaking for me to say that Uncle Bill is gone, too. But the good news is that Thea Chrisoula still lives in Lansing, Michigan. She had married the city, too.

CONVERSATIONS OVER THE WHITE MARBLE

*F*ollowing Uncle Bill's wedding in January of 1932, our lives moved as slowly and uneventfully as the sooty icebergs we climbed and jumped off in the shadowy alley behind Papa's restaurant. It took forever for them to melt away in spring after multiple snows and frigid temperatures had cemented them in place. New baby cousins brought happiness and the World's Fair did, too, but we'd have to wait until 1936 for major excitement in our household.

There was much to be troubled about in 1932. Mama's concerns about her offspring expanded to kidnapping after the baby son of Charles Lindbergh, America's flying hero of 1927, was taken from his home and murdered. The tragic but sensationalized incident brought fearful anxiety to every parent, famous or not.

Unemployment in the U.S. reached 23.6 percent. In the spring, out-of- work veterans of the First World War, who had been guaranteed a government bonus for laying their lives on the fighting line to make "the world safe for democracy," suffered personal and economic sacrifices to travel to Washington. Their intent was to peacefully remind our government that over a decade had passed since the bonus was promised, and it was most desperately needed. Bureaucrats, including President Hoover, were perturbed to find thousands of veterans camped around the White House, Capitol and along the Potomac in "Hoovervilles" (shabby tents and make-shift lean-tos of the homeless). Our leaders, however, couldn't conceive of a graceful way to convince the veterans to leave town without the bonus. So, they devised an ungraceful way to get rid of them.

At the end of July, Hoover commanded General Douglas MacArthur, his aide Major Dwight David Eisenhower, and his tank officer, Major George S. Patton, all of glorious and heroic future fame, to disperse the patriotic old soldiers. MacArthur, it was reported, rode majestically down Pennsylvania Avenue on a white horse and ordered U.S. military units to use bayonets, rifle butts, tear gas and tanks against fellow Americans who had worn the same uniforms fourteen years before. Shantytown "Hoovervilles" were set on fire by the U.S. Army, and the embittered, heart-broken "Bonus Marchers," many accompanied by their wives and children, left Washington without causing massive riots. President Hoover said, "Thank God, we still have a government that knows how to deal with a mob." This was just one of many imprudent statements credited to him, during the early years of the Depression, that demonstrated how out of touch he was with common Americans. Thanks to a Congressional bill, the bonuses were finally paid in 1936.

If 1932 had a theme song, it had to be *Brother Can you Spare a Dime?* One of its most moving verses refers to the plight of the "Bonus Marchers."

> *"Once in khaki suits.*
> *Gee, we looked swell,*
> *Full of that Yankee Doodle-de-dum.*
> *Half a million boots went sloggin' through Hell,*
> *I was the kid with the drum.*
> *Say, don't you remember, they called me Al—*
> *It was Al all the time.*
> *Say, don't you remember I'm your pal—*
> *Brother can you spare a dime?"*

Mama remembered, "Business was bad because there wasn't any."

It was early summer in 1932. Papa shuffled from the coffee urns toward a customer for the billionth time. Chatting with patrons was one way he freed his psyche from the confines of a restaurant owner.

"Where'd you go to school, Paul?" The gentleman ate peach pie and drank coffee with cream and sugar.

"Me? I went to the ninth grade. Left Greece when I was thirteen. That was it."

"You never went after that?"

"Well, I went to night school a couple of times." Papa smiled. "That unexpected pleasure came because of a pair of shoes I shined. You know, I was a shoeshine boy for ten years after I came from the old country. Until I was twenty-four. That's another story. Anyway, the customer whose shoes I was cleaning was a regular client, a high-class gentleman with a short beard. My uncles, our bosses, made sure we took good care of him, hovering around us when we shined his shoes. So I knew he was a big shot. I was shining away, real good when the guy asks me, '"Hey, kid. Where do you go to school?'

"My uncles never let me answer. I was whisked away and asked to run an errand. Next day, my uncles enrolled me in night school. But after the second class, they put me on a train to work in Albany, New York. They had another shoe shine parlor there. See, I was brought to America to shine shoes, not go to school. The big shot customer was Judge Kenesaw Mountain Landis."

"The baseball commissioner?"

"That's right. Landis was a very well-respected judge in Chicago. He was appointed commissioner of baseball in 1921 to bring integrity to the game after the White Sox baseball scandals."

"Uncles tried to cover up, huh?"

"Guess so. Looks like I was supposed to be in school for part of the day. But I had a thrilling experience in Albany, before they brought me back to shine shoes in Chicago again. I shook hands with President Woodrow Wilson. I heard he was going to make a speech in Albany, so I went to listen. Afterwards there was a big long reception line for him. And I just got in it. Simple as that. I got to shake Wilson's hand. I'm still thrilled by it. You know what it means to a shoe-shine boy when he can shake the hand of the President of the United States? The King of Greece never would have extended his hand to a guy like me. This is a great country. Always admired Woodrow Wilson. He never got cooperation from Congress. That narrow-minded Henry Cabot Lodge was a thorn in his side."

Mama came out of the kitchen and joined Papa behind the counter.

"Mrs. Paul, I'm surprised your husband only went to school up to the ninth grade. He knows so much about history, about so many things. I was sure he'd been to college."

"I tell Paul long time ago he should be a perfessor. He's good at that stuff. He's very intelligent man." She looked at Papa and teasingly added, "Most of the time." Smiling, Mama moved toward the front door and walked home for her afternoon break while Papa continued chatting about the news of the day.

"Looks like Roosevelt is THE man, Mr. Paul. Convention finally got him nominated last night."

"Yeah, I read it was a grueling session. Al Smith had his hopes, but Roosevelt finally got the votes. F.D.R. may even fly to Chicago to accept the nomination. That's never been done before. I wish I had a radio so I could hear some of that convention business myself. But I guess I'll have to take the *Tribune*'s word for it."

"Mr. Paul, you only missed a lot of malarky those chiseler politicians are full of. Did you read any of Will Rogers' columns this week? He had a good one about opening ceremonies at the Democrats' Convention at the Stadium. And you know, I found something in the paper I didn't know anything about. I read that the Chicago Stadium's the largest indoor arena in the world. How about that?"

My father had witnessed the Stadium's construction. "The Stadium? I watched them build it. Only four blocks away from where you're sitting. It was quite a project. You know, the Republicans were in town last month, meeting at the Stadium, too. I saw them going by on the street in big black cars—big black fancy cars. But a few Democrats came in this week. It's so hot and steamy in that Stadium they've got to get out and cool off.

"Big push is for repeal, Mr. Paul, at that Republican shindig last month and now at the Democratic. The smart guys finally figured out that Prohibition don't work. The 'drys' versus the 'wets'—that's all Chicago newspapers write about these days. And the rest of the news is about people flying all over the place—Lindbergh, Amelia Erhart, even Roosevelt. Do you think you' ll ever go up in one of those airplanes, Mr. Paul?"

Papa smiled. "Sure I will, but only if I can keep one foot on the ground." He continued speaking when the laughter from his counter patrons ebbed. "Say, I got a kick out of one of the campaign buttons those delegates wear on their lapels. A guy came in yesterday wearing one that spelled out, 'Anyone but Hoover.'" Papa laughed again and shook his head. "That's a good one. I've been looking for Will Rogers to come in now that he's in town for the Democrat's convention. Ha! Ha! Just joking fellas. I don't really expect Will to come into this joint, but I always try to read his columns. I like how that guy thinks."

"Then you'll like this, Mr. Paul." Joe took a folded newspaper out of his pocket and placed it on the white marble next to his coffee cup. Then he found his place on the newsprint.

"Will writes, 'There was a delegate with his little boy standing beside me on the floor of the convention, and during the opening prayer I heard the little fellow ask his daddy; "Is that man praying for the convention?"

"'And his daddy told him: "No! He took one look at the convention, and he's praying for the country.'"

Papa laughed hard. He'd always been an appreciative Will Rogers fan.

"The guy's good. Shows common sense when he writes about the dumb things that go on in this country. Remember what he said about Republicans? 'Republicans have a habit of having three bad years and one good one. But the good one always happens to be the election year.'" Papa laughed again and so did several customers at the counter who had been listening.

"Not this year, Mr. Paul. Even Republicans can't cover up this

Depression. There are seven hundred thousand unemployed workers in Chicago alone. I'm one of them. The city's broke—and so am I."

Joe spoke up again. "I was reading that the city owes twenty million bucks in back pay to the schoolteachers. Those very same unpaid teachers take money out of their own pockets to feed kids that go to school hungry everyday."

Papa joined back in. "To think that kids in this country go to bed hungry every night. It's unbelievable. See how the banks are failing? They're dropping like flies. It's not just scary. It's terrifying. Not only here, but all over the country. Since the Insull Utilities flop, forty banks in and out of this city alone have closed and more of them are on the verge of collapse."

"Hey, Paul, remember there was supposed to be a chicken in every pot? Ain't got no chicken in my pot. In fact, I don't even have a pot to…"

Papa and the Austin Lunch patrons were startled by what they saw and heard next. The kitchen door at the back of the restaurant abruptly opened with a bang, and Uncle Charlie's voice, loud, angry, and strong, came from inside.

CHILDREN UNDERFOOT

"*P*aul, get that kid outta here! It's hotter'n hell in here. And on top of it he's driving me crazy with that whistle."

My cute little brother seemed to come out of nowhere. Nick's head was downcast, his cheeks were flushed, and glistening sweat trickled over his forehead under his straight, thick brown hair. Dejection was evident in his cheerless eyes because he had just been ousted from the sweltering kitchen of the Austin Lunch by one of his all-time favorite people. Nick approached Papa from behind the counter that was still an inch higher than his sweaty head. Papa didn't know he was back there.

"Pa, how come Uncle Charlie's sore at me?"

"I don't know, Nicky, were you a bad boy? Did you spill something? You break something back there?"

Nick looked up at Papa with serious brown eyes and a disappointed, flushed face. "No, Pa, I was just watching Uncle Charlie. He was shoveling coal in the stove he cooks on. And all of a sudden he hollered, "'Stop that damn whistling and go find your father!' Uncle Charlie yelled it real loud."

Early in life, Nick had learned how to whistle. He constantly entertained himself by whistling away, his little lips pursed into a tiny pink funnel to blow out the tunes he knew; he was good at it, too. Sometimes, instead of whistling, he sang words of songs out loud. It was an especially hot and humid day. Evidently, Charlie Kingos had heard enough of my brother's cheery music by mid-afternoon in that dreary, torture rack of a kitchen.

"Nicky, Uncle Charlie works real hard and he's real tired right now. That old kitchen's real hot today. He wants quiet. Say, I don't want you to say 'damn' again." Papa stared at Nicky over his eyeglasses, his voice getting louder. "Charlie says it, but you can't. Have you heard me talk like that? Of course not! Where's Mama?"

Whenever Papa didn't know how to handle a situation with his children, he always asked where Mama was. I heard the familiar question as I walked through the front door carrying the white enamel coffee pot from home.

"At home, Papa. She's resting. Mrs. Fellas said she'd make coffee so Mama and her could visit for a little bit, but Mama told her not to bother because coffee's always ready at the store. Papa, Mama says to please pour three cups of coffee in here so I can take it home to them."

My father reached over the counter, took the pot out of my hands, removed the lid, and held the open mouth under the center coffee urn's spigot. Then he gave instructions.

"Tell Mama to rest up good because we might be busy for a change tonight. Democrats from the Stadium have been trickling in. The Stadium's so hot and steamy the delegates got to cool off and get refreshments. Nicky, you help Helen take this thing home. Be careful now, it's very hot. Don't spill it and don't burn yourselves."

My brother and I had carried the hot enamel pot home before, and Mama usually needed to re-heat it when storefront distractions slowed our delivery. Fifty years have passed and that series of buildings is more clearly stamped on my brain than the one where I live right now; a funeral parlor, a coop with live chickens, and a bowling alley were a mere sampling of the twenty businesses renting street level stores on Madison, between Bishop Street and Ogden, our childhood front yard.

Mama and I remembered our neighbors on Madison, one by one, as we reminisced in 1984. "Ida Popper and me was good friends. She work in her grocery with her Sam just like Papa and me was doing. They take care their family, just like us. Mrs. Popper come and have a cup of coffee with me every morning so we can relax and chew the rag together. Good people live on that block. Bad guys was coming from outside."

Mama remembered John Garcia, the used furniture and upholstery man, Baker's Dry Goods that always smelled like mothballs, and Popper's Grocery Store with Feldman's meat counter in the back; two entrepreneurs shared the rent in one store. The meat for Papa's restaurant was purchased there daily.

Every morning Mrs. Feldman came to the restaurant where Uncle Charlie gave her the day's meat order; then Mr. Feldman cut, prepared and delivered the order. Before she went home at night, Mrs. Feldman returned to stand soldier-like in front of the cash register until she received payment for the day's provisions. By that time of the evening, the Austin Lunch had sold enough meat for Papa to pay Mrs. Feldman. Without realizing it herself, Mrs. Feldman was a pioneer in the women's rights movement, emphatically declaring that she was the owner of the meat counter and that her husband worked for her.

Sam and Ida Popper lived in an apartment upstairs from their grocery store, and the Friedman Family lived in the same quarters. Mrs. Popper and Mrs. Friedman were sisters; their families doubled up in one unit during the Depression. Mr. Friedman did not have a store. Everyday he went out with a large tan cardboard box filled with caps and shoelaces to sell door-to-door. The Austin Lunch was one of his many stops.

Nick and I were friends with the Friedman children, Ethel and Jack, and walked to school with them everyday. The Poppers had two children, Anna and Lester, but they were older than the rest of us. Anna gave piano lessons up in their apartment and Mama paid for me to take a few lessons from her once, but it was a short-lived musical study. Mama and Ida Popper shared cups of coffee everyday over the white marble at the Austin Lunch. Work and motherhood prevented them from enjoying a real social life, so they sipped coffee and visited with each other about family, neighborhood, and weird characters who surfaced on the street. The mutual lack of paying customers was discussed daily. While nobody during the Thirties would have acknowledged them as such, they were two businesswomen who were also very good friends.

A few cages filled with live chickens for sale were always in front of Mrs. Popper's store, part of the Feldman meat concession. Eating a tasty chicken, when it could be afforded, started with buying a live bird and killing it. Mama and our aunts would have nothing to do with "cold storage chickens" that had already been "dressed" because of their distinctive and unpleasant gamey taste. The mere thought of eating distasteful cold storage poultry made Mama shudder. Chickens were the object of my very first lesson in disection, which came from Mama, of course, years before high school biology.

"I learn to kill chickens when I was little girl like you back in the old country. First you got to cut the throat, then you get a big *katsarola* (cooking pot) full with boiling water and stick the chicken in it so you can pull out the feathers. When all the feathers is off, you make a cut in the belly to take out all the guts." (Interruption: "With your hands, Mama?") "You think you going to do it with your feet? Of course with your hands, Helen. See this part that's attached to the guts? This little greenish thing is the gall bladder. But we throw guts and gall bladder away. Now, over here is the good stuff, the liver, the gizzard, and the heart. We going to cook them in the *tigani* (frying pan) with olive oil and *rigani* (oregano), salt and pepper. When they all cooked and brown and crispy, we gonna squeeze lemon on top. Going to be wonnerful, very delicious." After purchasing the live bird, Mama kept it penned in our apartment bathtub until she was ready to cook it. There were live chicken stores in neighborhoods all over Chicago, but she always bought our poultry from Mrs. Feldman's coop.

Between Popper's Grocery and the Austin Lunch was a large store that housed a billiard parlor and bowling alley. In contrast to the immense, automated bowling emporiums of today, this operation was miniscule; there were two or three alleys. The pins were re-set by young men who steered clear of the powerfully heavy balls, but who instantly popped out from mysterious reaches in the back to replace pins when necessary. The pinsetters came into the Austin Lunch to eat on their breaks. Papa played billiards there when business was slow. When Mama got too many customers to handle by herself and

Papa was "next door," Mama would send one of us to fetch him, usually Nick.

"Pa, Mama's busy."

"O.K. One more shot. I'll be right there."

When he delayed and Mama was deluged with work, the message was, "Mama says, 'Come now.'" Sometimes Papa needed three and four reminders.

Through the years, sympathetic customers convinced Mama that if Mr. Paul had a sport, then Mrs. Paul should have one, too. They taught her how to bowl so she could go "next door" for recreation, too. At first, our aunts took the news of Mama's bowling as a disgrace because "Ladies" from their village simply didn't do things like bowling. Mama thought her sisters were making too much of an innocent pastime. For her, bowling brought relaxation and good exercise. It never took long for Mama to learn to do something well, even bowling. She eventually improved her skills to earn a two hundred average. She also learned to ignore critics who didn't know what bowling was all about.

The heavy, wood-framed glass door in the middle of the block, next to the bowling alley/pool hall, belonged to the Austin Lunch. Early in July of 1932, Nick and I exited that familiar doorway bearing the weight of Mama's white coffee pot and three generous cups of steaming coffee.

Neither of us was aware that within the next ninety minutes, without needing to step outside of our tenement apartment at Madison and Ogden, we would look out our obscure living room window and thrill to an exciting and unforgettable glimpse of the next President of the United States.

OUR BLOCK, OUR WORLD

I am writing now and I have written before. You have not responded.

—Vasiliki to her brother Nicholas, April 1932

Sharing the handle of the steaming coffee pot, Nick and I began walking the half block of Madison toward home. A few steps out the restaurant door, I choked on a rank odor. It was a familiar smell that invariably made hot, steamy days and nights feel hotter and steamier in Chicago. The stench permeated the humid atmosphere around us.

"Pheeou! What stinks?" Nick pinched his nose and distorted his mouth.

"The Stockyards! They're stinking bad today."

The first open door in the brown brick building next to Papa's restaurant and Vogel's bakery brought the usual smell of tobacco. Louie Drell's Cigar Store exuded an aroma that partially masked the Stockyard stench wafting from the South Side. Nick dragged me over to peek into Mr. Drell's window.

"Come on, Nicky! Mama and Mrs. Fellas want coffee now."

"Wait a minute, Helen! I'm looking for horses."

"What horses?"

"I heard Uncle Charlie bawl out Pa about going in there to play with the horses."

"Where'd you get that dumb idea? Who ever heard of horses in a cigar store?"

Then I made the connection. "Oh. The horses aren't in the store. They're at the racetrack. Remember a long time ago when Papa took us way out in the country and we watched a bunch of horses run around a big circle?"

"Yeah, and Pa got all 'xcited?"

"Those horses got something to do with going into Louie Drell's cigar store. And its got something to do with little books, too, because I heard Uncle Al call them 'bookies.' There's newspapers and magazines in there, but I never saw little books for sale. It must be some kind of a secret because people always whisper when they talk about it."

"Uncle Charlie didn't whisper to Pa when he told him he couldn't 'ford to play with the horses. I heard Uncle Charlie real good."

"Mama doesn't want Papa to do it either. I heard her tell him she's not working sixteen hours a day to feed the horses. Mama was mad and she and Papa were hollering. I hate it when they holler like that. It's scary."

"And too loud. Hey, Helen, what do the horses in there eat? Uncle Charlie's leftovers?"

"I already told you. There's no horses in the cigar store, Nicky. And besides, Uncle Charlie's food's too good for old horses. He wouldn't let them eat it."

Nick persisted. "Only horses I seen are the ice man's and the milkman's—and the raksolion man (junk man who yelled "Rags, old iron" from his horse and wagon). Sometimes fruit peddlers got horses. But I never seen no horses going into Mr. Drell's. When I went in there with Pa and he buyed a paper, I looked all over. But I never seen no horses."

"I don't ask questions, Nicky, because Mama and Papa get mad when they talk about horses. Come on. Let's don't talk about it."

We retrieved the pot and quickened our pace passing the vacant store that was to become Tom Charlas's saloon, Papa's closest competitor after repeal. He was the "bad guy" on our block and, ironically, Charlas was a fellow Greek. The next door we passed belonged to the Great Atlantic and Pacific Tea Co., known to all as the A & P, a minuscule establishment compared to future supermarkets. The smell of freshly ground Eight O'Clock Coffee wafted from inside the A & P, reminding us Mama was waiting. Nick let me carry the pot by myself as we crossed the front of the next façade, which was decorated with thin columns that Papa had told us were Corinthian. The startling and deafening sound of grinding equipment at work came from beyond the seedy Grecian splendor. Grinding stones were made there.

"What are grin'ing stones?"

"Don't know. Ask Papa."

I routinely speeded up whenever we reached this point in our walk because the next storefront was the neighborhood funeral parlor. Green ferns in the eerie mortician's window were decoratively displayed in front of secretive gray drapes which were always drawn, and I liked them that way. The very word "undertaker" was gruesome. I refused to be present when a casket was being carried in or out, empty or full. It was my little-girl habit to deny the parlor's existence and to race by.

"Move it, Nicky. Walk faster!"

"Why?"

"Because there's dead people in there."

"What are they doing?"

"I don't know. Scary stuff. They keep them in boxes in the back room."

"Why?"

"Because that's where they get them ready—to bury them."

"How do you know?"

"Mama told me. And lots of weird-looking people come out that door, too. So MOVE IT. Wish we didn't have to live on the same block with a spooky undertaker. Don't ask me why. Just MOVE IT."

"Why?"

"Hey, Nick. Let's look in the Ben Franklin's window." Our neighborhood mortician did business next door to an enticing Ben Franklin "dime" store with a small toy department that featured unattainable dreams for Depression kids like us.

The neighborhood dry cleaner was next to the dime store. It always emitted the stench of throat-tickling chemicals and steam, another hot spot on the Madison Street sidewalk. "Everything stinks today. Let's look in this window." Nick peered into a street level office below a large blue sign that announced, "Western Union." He wanted to see if the man with the neat uniform was there. He wasn't. "How come there's lotsa people out here today, Helen? Who's these guys with the big tags on their suits?"

"Must be the Democrats."

"What are Demmacrass?"

"Don't know, except Papa said they're having a big meeting at the Stadium. Come on. Mama is waiting. Shake a leg, Nicky." Singlehandedly, I struggled with the pot as we rushed by the Salvation Army Building, the newest and best kept structure on our street. Their house of worship was located on the first floor, toward the back alley. Apartments for rent were available on the second floor, and Tom's Restaurant, similar to Papa's place, was the Army's street-level tenant. Restaurant competition was plentiful on our block, all friendly. A grocery store, owned by a fellow Greek, was next to Tom's; Mama sometimes sent us there on shopping errands.

Finally, we passed the most mysterious enterprise on the block, Mr. Wong's Chinese Restaurant, closest to home, but most exotic and remote. That ancient Asian culture with one of the world's finest cuisines, like our own Greek one, was so alien to our Mediterranean roots that Mama simply could not relate to it. She smiled and nodded at Mr. Wong when she passed him on the street, but Mama claimed to have inside information on the mysterious operation of his restaurant. "So bad it will make you want to vomit." After enough pestering by Nick and me, she explained the enigma of our neighbor's exotic offerings as a warning about eating in Chinese restaurants. Mama had been informed, quite confidentially by an eyewitness, that Wong's menu listed many dishes with celery that retained its crispness even after it was cooked. She reminded us that in Greek recipes, celery softened as it was ordained to do with heat. (Greeks usually overcook vegetables.) Wong's secret method of keeping celery crunchy (she shuddered) was to store it stalk ends down in the bathroom toilet bowl.

Mama was one of many new immigrants who naively believed just about anything they heard concerning other ethnic groups in America. Comfort meant staying among your own people, so with scant social integration and poor English skills, people of different nationalities, including Europeans, were often feared and avoided. There was little opportunity for discovering commonalities. I wonder what juicy, untrue tidbits Mr. Wong had heard about the Greek families on the block?

Mr. Wong and Papa both worked long hours in their restaurants, but by the time Papa realized their shared predicament, it was too late to strike up a friendship. Sometime in the late Thirties, a foul stench permeated our block. Irate neighbors called authorities and several days later, police and fire departments arrived to investigate. Mr. Wong's body was discovered in his locked up restaurant: he had been dead a week. "Too bad we never knew him. Poor guy, he kept to himself. He died a hostage of his chop suey parlor. Owning a restaurant doesn't give you a chance to get out much." Papa, disturbed by our Asian neighbor's demise, sadly pondered whether Mr. Wong's fate would one day be his own.

The doorway next to Wong's was marked 1524. Nick, the cooled coffeepot, and I had finally arrived home on that hot July day in 1932. We climbed the scuffed and worn wooden steps to our grizzly bear's third floor. Mama opened the front door of our apartment as soon as she heard our voices in the hallway.

ROOSEVELT

We worry about our parents, please write.

—Tasia to her brother Nicholas, July 15, 1932

"*M*ust be cold coffee by now, but thank you, *poulakia mou.*" Often, Mama called Nick, me and other kids her *poulakia*, (little birds), a Greek term of endearment. Conversations at home in our early years were entirely in Greek, one way for us to learn our noble ancestral language. Our responses were most often delivered in a mixture of Greek and English.

"Coffee needs heating, Christina. And did you say hello to Thea Christina?" Mama and our aunts made us call Greek ladies "Thea" (Aunt) to show both respect and affection.

"Hello Thea Christina. Mama, it's too hot to drink that stuff. We oughta have ice cold Coca-Cola today and we should drink it with ice cubes and a straw. And we should go to the lake to cool off like lots of people do. Jackie Friedman told me their whole family might go to the lake tonight." Nick complained to Mama as he climbed up on the shiny, white kitchen chair. Once seated, he laid his face on the blue and white porcelain tabletop to cool himself.

"How come you're so hot, Nikolaki?" Mama felt Nick's forehead for fever.

"He was bothering Uncle Charlie in the kitchen and Uncle Charlie yelled and threw him out."

"I told you to come home with me when I left the store, Nicky. You should listen to Mama. I told you not to play in that hot kitchen. Poor Charlie did you a favor. It's so hot today that if I didn't have to go back to the store, maybe we'd go to the lake, too."

Mrs. Fellas remembered the old country. Grownups were always doing that. Longing for Greece's kinder climate, she wiped perspiration from her face with a crocheted white hankie. "Even on the hottest days back home, nights are cool. During the heat of the day in my village, you can cool off in the shade of an immense plane tree. These apartments are like concrete ovens. Imagine having to sleep in public parks and on the beach to cool off. How can a place that is bitter cold and frozen stiff with ice and snow in winter be so hot and steamy in summer? It's even hard to breathe today."

"I remember summers back home, too, Christina. We didn't know how good we had it then. Haven't had a letter from the village for a long time. The old folks are dependent on my brother and younger sisters to write. I worry when we don't hear. Aahh, it's so good to be off my feet. My back's been killing me since yesterday and the humidity's choking me." Mama's eyes seemed to sink back into her head as she sat on one kitchen chair and lifted her legs and feet onto another. She wiped the trickles of perspiration streaming down the sides of her face with a folded pink handkerchief procured from her beige uniform pocket.

"You know, Christina, my sisters and I want to know details about our family in the village. My younger sister Garifalia is newly married. Is her husband a kind man? My mother's sister in Tripolis, who is also my godmother, has adopted our baby sister, Stamata. My father won't need to give her a dowry and Stamata will inherit from my aunt and uncle who are childless. How is Stamata adjusting? My godmother demanded so much of us older girls when we went to Tripolis to visit her. Every year we had to knead her holiday breads and help her bake sweets for Christmas and Easter. My older sisters say she's too bossy, and they're right. She commands like a general. Even as I sit here in my own kitchen, I can hear her. 'You must perspire to make good bread. You're not perspiring enough. Knead more. Perspire! Turn red, like a beet.' But I remember her with love. I was named for her.

"Before official papers came through for me to come to America she offered to adopt me because I'm her goddaughter. My father said, 'I don't care what the benefits are. I don't give my children away. They aren't servants.' What changed his mind? I think about little Stamata living with that difficult woman and wonder how she's coping. My brother Nicholas doesn't write those details. He hardly writes anything. We're cut off from news we really want to know."

"Vasiliki, we're closed off from the old country and still not a part of the new one. It's like we're stuck in a sidewalk crack."

When I heard "sidewalk," I remembered the Democrats crowding Madison Street and that I had forgotten to give Papa's message. "Mama, Papa says to rest up good because you might be busy tonight. There's Democrats at the Stadium. What are Democrats, Mama?"

"Men who want to put in another president in place of Hoover. That's what they're doing in their meetings at the Stadium. Papa says that if they select a good man he can help the country better than President Hoover."

"I thought 'Hoover' was somebody's dog," Nick interrupted.

"How'd you get that idea, Nikolaki?"

"When we go over to Thea Aphroditi's house and I hear Uncle Pete talk cuss words he says, 'That dog, Hoover.'"

"Well, that's because Uncle Pete lost his restaurant. He had his own place before he came to work for Papa, and he's angry that he had to go out of business. He says bad words about Hoover because he blames the Depression on President Hoover."

Nick's question brought a phrase to mind that I had been wondering about, and I interrupted. "Mama, what does '*Ptou Colombe*' mean? I hear lotsa Greek guys say it and they spit when they say the 'Ptou' part. I hear them say cuss words, too."

Mrs. Fellas laughed.

"That's kind of a joke. It's like they're wishing Columbus had never found America so they wouldn't be out of a job and poor now or working too hard and not making money. It's a way of saying they're sorry they came to America."

"They're spitting at Christopher Columbus?" I was appalled. "He was a great explorer. Our school closes on his holiday."

"Helen, lots of men who lost their businesses are out of work and very angry. They blame Hoover and even Columbus. They knew about being poor in Greece, but never expected it to happen to them in America."

A shadow quickly crossed our kitchen window, blocking the dim light coming through the screen door. We heard a cheerful, familiar voice speaking perfect English with an English accent. "Hi ho, everyone!"

We knew without looking that it was Mrs. Jones. Our gray wooden porch was shared by other apartment dwellers on the third floor of our building, making all our kitchens accessible to each other. Mama's Greek conversation instantly turned to English and she quickly took her feet off the chair.

"Come in Mrs. Jones. Come and have a cup of coffee with us or maybe you like it the tea better?" Mama motioned for her to sit on the chair between Nick and Mrs. Fellas.

"Hello, Christine, Helen and Nicky. Is it hot enough for everyone? Actually Mrs. Paul, I just finished some tea while listening to the radio. Do you know about the convention at the Stadium?"

"Yes, Democrates is picking new man for president. Paul told me. Democrates is even coming to the store to eat. Restaurant more busy than usual."

"It's very exciting. Franklin Roosevelt has just flown to Chicago by airplane to accept the nomination. It's never been done by any candidate, Democrat or Republican."

"Airplane? My goodoness. Must be he like new job very much."

"He won't be president until November and actually won't take office until March of next year. If he's elected, of course."

"Next year? Whooooo. That's a long time from now." When Mama said or rather sang "Whooooo" she made a gesture with her right hand, palm up, wrist in circular motion, slicing through the air to indicate something in excess, too big, too long, too much, too something. "What's big hurry to come on the airplane?"

"I heard they are expecting Governor Roosevelt to arrive at the Stadium in Mayor Cermak's car this afternoon. Radio said they'll probably use the route from downtown, right up Madison Street. The motorcade may go by this building."

Nick leaped up and took off for the living room. Almost immediately we heard his voice. "Mama. MAMA. Look at all the people on the sidewalk!"

We all followed to see what was going on. Nick had already pushed aside the beige organdy curtains and was hanging out the open front window of our apartment. I stuck out my head, too, and saw people lining our side of the street. Another crowd was gathering along the base of the Flatiron Building.

"DON'T do that!" Grabbing Nick and me by the waistbands, Mama jerked us back into the living room. "You gonna fall downstairs and kill yourself! Don't you dare to climb up on the windowsill, Nicky! You gonna fall out."

"Mother is right, children. It's very dangerous. Keep both feet on the floor when you look out. That's much better. I haven't seen anything like this since I lived in England. We British gather in crowds like the one below us when we know Their Majesties, King George and Queen Mary, will pass by."

Mama instantly had business on her mind. "My goodoness! I gotta help Paul. Maybe he be busy. Too many people down there. Helen and Nicky, let's go downstairs to help Papa!"

"Mrs. Paul, how would it be if I were to stay here with the children? Then we can all see Governor Roosevelt if he comes by. I'll go get my George and we'll watch together from your living room window. We can't see from the Ogden Avenue side."

"Sure, sure Mrs. Jones. Christina you stay, too." Mama was pressed for time.

"No, no, Vasiliki. I go tell my girls. We see it from our own window."

Already wearing her waitress uniform, Mama ducked into the bathroom, pulled the light string, and glanced in the mirror to make sure her hair was combed. She still needed rest, an uninterrupted year's worth, but she had re-charged herself with a cup of coffee and an hour of sitting.

"Helen and Nicky, you be good. Mrs. Jones, too much bother for you to bring children to the store after while? I worry after poor little Lindbergh baby he be take from his house. I don't want them to be by themselfs. There's all kinds bad people around. I'm leaving the key on the table, Mrs. Jones. And don't forget, Helen and Nicky, be good and be careful."

Papa was relieved to see Mama rush into the restaurant, but she was surprised to find only two people at the counter. "Where are the children, Bessie? Roosevelt's supposed to come down Madison any minute now. The children should see him. This is historic." Mama smiled when she saw the excitement in his face and heard it in his voice as he questioned her in English (my father never spoke Greek in front of customers). Mama knew to reply in English, too.

"Calm down, Paul. Mrs. Jones told me the whole about it. She and Mr. Jones take care the children and see Roosevelt from the front room window. When everything's over they going to bring the kids here. I say to myself you be pretty busy right now."

"Everyone's waiting outside. It's a big thing, Bessie. I'm hoping customers will come in after the long line of cars. Well, good for Mrs. Jones. There's a better view for the kids from upstairs. Do they know who Roosevelt is?"

"I try to explain, but I know Mrs. Jones. She's going to tell the whole about it to them."

A noise like a distant roar grew from outside the restaurant. Mama, Papa and the two men at the counter became aware of it at the same time. As it rolled closer, it increased in intensity. All four rushed to the door and out to the sidewalk. Papa, pink with excitement, remembered Uncle Charlie and the dishwasher in the kitchen. Before the glass and wood door shut behind him he went back and yelled, "Hey, Charlie. Come on. It's ROOSEVELT. Tell Harry, too."

121

They maneuvered themselves to the curb in time to see a black Chicago police car closely followed by a long white open car moving toward the front of the Austin Lunch from the direction of downtown. The immense automobile was less than ten feet away, and they saw the occupants clearly. They couldn't help focusing on the smiling man who waved warmly and enthusiastically at the throngs lining Madison from the back seat of the white convertible. The roar was at its loudest.

"That's him, Bessie."

"Waving the hat?" Mama yelled in Greek so Papa could hear above the crowd.

"Absolutely! Franklin Delano Roosevelt! The next President of the United States! And he went right by the Austin Lunch, my very own restaurant!"

"Who's the other guys?"

"The mayor was sitting with him. And the rest of them must be big shots, or politicians."

Mama had never seen anything like the unending stream of cars traveling up Madison in procession behind the enormous white convertible. "Whoo. Look at all the cars and all the peoples. Mr. Roosevelt, he got nice smile. Must be nice man. How come you so sure he's going to win, Paul?"

Uncle Charlie answered in accentless English as he and the dishwasher followed them back into the restaurant. "He's got to win. There are too many hungry people, Bessie. He's got to win because Roosevelt's the last hope for us poor people in this country."

Two hours later, Nick and I burst into the restaurant with Mr. and Mrs. Jones a few steps behind us. We rushed over to our parents who were working behind the counter; Nick shouted our news. "We saw the parade and the president guy from the front room window. There was lots and lotsa people on the sidewalk, a whole bunch of motorcycles and a whole parade of cars, more than fifty of them—real shiny ones! We could see them lined up all the way down Madison Street! There was police cars and sirens! And the president guy was waving his hat in a great big white car with no top on it!"

Mrs. Jones reminded, "His name is Mr. Roosevelt, Nicky."

"Oh yeah. And Mrs. Jones hollered, 'Yoo hoo, Frankie.' real loud at him out the window. And Mr. Roosevelt looked up at us and waved back to Mrs. Jones. He was smiling at her, too!"

Papa loved it. "That's pretty good, Mrs. Jones."

Mr. Jones explained our delay. "Went back to our apartment to listen to F.D.R.'s speech on the radio before we came down here, Paul. He's very reassuring and has a pleasant, friendly voice. He seems to care about us common people. He spoke about common sense and business sense. He even said something about 'a new deal for the American people.'"

Papa smiled. "So he's a poker player, too. I wish I could have heard him."

Mama was impressed; her face was flushed and her eyes were elated. "This things only happens in America, Mr. Jones, for us poor peoples to see the man who maybe be the president. We not doctors, not perfessors, not big shots. But he come to our poor neighborhood. He smile at us, too. And he look like he really likes us, even though we poor. We got to celebrate. We going to eat all together tonight. Sit down in the booth. This dinner's on Paul. I bring you tea with cream, the way you like it to start the celebration.

"Helen, go bring silverware and fresh napkins for Mama. Nicky, go behind the counter with Papa. He's going to give you bread and butter to bring. We going to have little party." Nick and I gladly got everything together because it was going to be fun having dinner with the Joneses. We didn't eat with company very often.

"It will be a pleasure, Mrs. Paul. We'll celebrate hope. Maybe Mr. Roosevelt will help our economy so we can visit England, someday, and so you can visit your family in Greece. I know how much you'd like that. I pray Franklin Roosevelt will bring this country out of this terrible Depression."

"Yes siree, Mrs. Jones. How about all of us we take trip and go together? First we go to England to see your folks, and then we go to the old country. You and Mr. Jones can meet our mamas and papas and sisters and brothers."

"Wonderful! Do they serve cream with tea in Greece?"

"To tell you the true, I don't know if they got cream in Greece, Mrs. Jones. I don't see too many things like cream when I was little girl in the village. But, by the time we can all go there for our trip—by that time they probably will have cream in the old country, too."

INDELIBLE 1933

We send regards to Thea Vasiliki and our little Stamata.

—Tasia to her mother, August 16, 1932

*S*udden tragedy, euphoric optimism, extra-edition newspapers about a dynamic President (an entire nation would barely be aware of his paralysis and physical handicap), five months of an unforgettable World's Fair, and the beginning of change in our family's finances sculpted 1933 into an indelible and pivotal year. Before F.D.R. took his first oath of office, an assassination attempt was made on him that felled Chicago's Mayor Anton Cermak instead. The incident occurred in Miami in February of 1933. The assassin aimed at the President-elect, missed, but hit five others. Chicago grieved for the self-made Bohemian immigrant who rose to the city's highest office; Mayor Cermak did not live to see the two-year celebration that he hoped would lift the city out of its Depression doldrums.

It was the morning of May 28, 1933, and as usual, our neighbor, George Jones, was seated at the white marble counter. He regularly ate breakfast at Papa's restaurant. Mrs. Jones's changing shifts as a nurse's aid at County Hospital usually kept her away from their apartment in the morning. Papa enjoyed chatting with Mr. Jones. He hovered near our neighbor's usual place at the counter while he took care of other customers, if there were other customers.

Mr. Jones's typical Austin Lunch breakfast began with four slices of toast generously covered with butter and orange marmalade, a spe-

125

cial treat for a special patron. George was sipping hot tea with cream when Papa brought him the rest: two scrambled eggs and a mound of American fried potatoes. In 1933, this breakfast cost ten cents at the Austin Lunch, plus a nickel for coffee, or in Mr. Jones's order, tea with cream. A typical full-course dinner included soup, entree, salad, potatoes, vegetable, six slices of bread with butter, coffee, tea or milk, and dessert; the whole meal cost a quarter. The entree for the most expensive, complete dinner on the menu was T-Bone steak: it cost forty cents.

"Big fair finally opened yesterday, George. F.D.R threw a switch all the way from Washington D.C. to start the celebrating."

"Righto, Paul. *Tribune* says the lights of our very own World's Fair were lit even more spectacularly from the rays of the star Arcturus."

"That's very impressive to a guy like me, George. You know, my village still has no water or electricity. I remember how thrilled I was the first time I saw a locomotive. That was in 1900, when I was about seven years old. That's the year the railroad was finally brought from Athens to Tripolis, our closest big town."

Mr. Jones continued studying the front page. "Politicians seem to have kept their promises, Paul. No special taxes or subsidies have been loaded on us taxpayers—yet—to put on the big show."

"Yeah, but how many taxpayers can afford the admission? Who would have guessed, ten years ago, that American citizens wouldn't be able to afford a loaf of bread in 1933, let alone tickets to the World's Fair? Anybody who would have made that prediction would have been labeled crazy. By the way, how's the orange marmalade? Bessie has it on hand for you because you told her it reminds you of growing up in England."

"Very considerate of Mrs. Paul. Thank you. Mmmm. Quite good. It's from California, I see. Must tell Iris about it... The *Tribune* says rich Chicago businessmen have kept their promise to pay for the fair."

"There must have been enough of those guys left over after the Crash."

"The paper says there was enough money to fill in four hundred acres of Lake Michigan, too. They created an artificial peninsula for the fair site."

"I don't know about that, George. I can't understand those big shots. Why do they want to fill in the lake? When I first came to Chicago in 1907, the lake shore came all the way up to Michigan Avenue. People in my village haven't got enough water to drink but over here so-called "experts" keep filling in fresh water Lake Michigan with dirt. It's a sin."

Mr. Jones nodded in agreement. "You're planning to go to the fair, aren't you Paul? It'll be wonderful for the children."

"Absolutely. I've waited a long time for this. And it's right in our own backyard. It'll probably be the only World's Fair I'll ever go to. That is, if I can pay for the tickets."

Mama walked into the restaurant during their conversation.

"Good morning, Mrs. Paul. You look refreshed and ready to tackle the day."

"Good morning, Mr. Jones. I just make ready the children to come down, eat breakfast, and go to school. You on your way to work, too?"

"My elevator awaits me."

"You not get dizzy go up and down all day in a big box? Mr. Jones, I'll be throwing up all over the place going up and down, up and down."

"After so many years, I'm used to it. And grateful to have the job."

"That's the God's true. By the way, yesterday, a customer come in here looking for rooming house to live in. Mrs. Jones tell me you looking for another roomer. This guy looks like nice man. You are interest?"

Mr. Jones readily accepted Mama's referral. "Certainly, Mrs. Paul. Anyone you've sent us so far has worked out well. You're a superb judge of character. Ask him to see Iris when she finishes her shift. Have you heard, Mrs. Paul? The World's Fair opened!"

"Yes siree, Mr. Jones. There's big doin's going on in Chicago. Paul told me about the big World's Fair. It finish in October, Paul say."

More than twenty-two million people visited "A Century of

Progress" before it closed that year. Because of its great success, the "big shots" decided to re-open and continue the exposition the following year; it closed in "October" of 1934. Mama and Papa took us once in the summer of 1933, a memorable day because we were together and away from the restaurant. Then Papa took Nick and me there again on closing day in '34. Most of our out-of-town relatives came to Chicago for the Fair during those two years. We were excited when Papa's brother, our Uncle Bill, came from Michigan with Thea Chrisoula and a beautiful new baby cousin who had the same name that I did, Helen.

Everyone who could scrape together the price of admission came to the big city to see the renowned World's Fair, the main topic of conversation for just about everyone during those two years. Chicagoans were either talking about what they had seen, or what they planned to see if they could afford the ticket. If not, they spoke of what they had heard that others had seen there.

Dr. Pugh had vaccinated me for me small pox the afternoon before we visited the fair on closing day. My arm throbbed with pain, but we had so looked forward to attending, and Papa felt that being there on the last day would be a historic experience. Indeed, Nick, Papa and I left the Austin Lunch before noon and stayed at the exposition until the lights of the fair were turned off forever. My arm, heavy with pain, dragged like a hundred pound weight. It was killing me, but I didn't utter even one complaint because I was thrilled to be there.

The Chicago World's Fair was a classy and spontaneous John Singer Sargent masterpiece, with Picasso tossed in for oddball absurdity. It lingers in my memory as joyously colorful, infinitely creative, as energetic as a two-year-old in perpetual motion and, like the Statue of Liberty, rooted in Europe but thoroughly American. Bright, colorful buildings stood out before us when we arrived inside the main gate. On the Avenue of Flags, banners of all the states and nations snapped stiffly and then crumpled again, continually energized by winds from nearby Lake Michigan. Thousands of people moved in a continuous stream because there was so much to see. The action was dizzying. A real General Motors assembly line demonstrated the amazing process of putting together an automobile. Kraft Mayonnaise's kitchen continuously filled, capped and labeled an automated moving line of jars. The Coca-Cola Company filled unending squat, greenish, six-ounce bottles that paraded by, via mesmerizing automation, in a complete bottling operation.

We were jostled in the amusement-filled Midway where Papa bypassed Sally Rand's scandalous fan dance. But we rode the Sky Ride, which dangled us so high above the earth that we breathlessly took in cobalt-hued Lake Michigan, "almost as good as God sees it from heaven," Papa said. We attended "Wings of a Century," a historic pageant performed by hundreds of actors. Our fascination never ebbed. I remember, too, old soldiers' uniforms and buckskin pioneer outfits in the life-sized model of historic Fort Dearborn, Chicago's 19th-century military outpost on the Great Lakes that helped give birth to the "City of the Big Shoulders." Papa made sure we took in as many exhibits as we had time for. Better at history than science, Papa explained things to us all day long. At night, the thousands of spectacular lights dazzled us and the myriad colors lifted our spirits like nothing else had ever done.

I realize now that the World's Fair was the one and only flash of color we experienced during the drab Depression years. Down in my basement, I still store a box with the two souvenirs Papa bought for Nick and me: a flattened penny and a walking stick, both embossed with "A Century of Progress." Despite all the house cleaning and moving we've done in sixty years, they have always been safe from the rubbish pile.

Good memories of 1933 and 1934 motivated my brother Nick, his wife Angie, our sister Connie, and me to travel to Montreal for Expo '67. In 1974, I took my niece Vicky to Spokane, Washington for that World's Fair. Our experiences at the Century of Progress in the Thirties had been so unforgettable that we wanted to enjoy the adventure again as adults, and share the excitement with our loved ones, as Papa had with us.

We don't hear of World's Fairs anymore. Technology is taken for granted, and we make pilgrimages to Circuit City instead. Epcot and Disney, inspired by the old expositions, have become substitute attractions for those exciting, heart-pounding fairs of the past that celebrated the signing of the Declaration of Independence (Philadelphia, 1876), Columbus's voyage and discovery (Chicago, 1893), the Louisiana Purchase (St. Louis, 1904) and the hundredth birthday of a great city (Chicago, 1933-34).

The great fair may have attracted tourists with money to our city because not every American citizen suffered in the Depression—but it didn't enrich our block on Madison Street. Tourists didn't come to us to spend their dollars. Mama thought 1931 had been tough, but she was to find out that '33 would be unbelievably tougher. Unemployment reached 15 million, five times what it had been two years before. Even though 1933 held glimmers of hope like the administration of a new President and uplifting color like the World's Fair, Mama's hopeless drudgery dragged on and she sensed no glimmers or flashes. She was completely unaware that, for her, change was to arrive in December. Iris and Mama may have had fun together dreaming about going back to England and Greece, but neither the Joneses nor my parents ever expected to see their homelands again. By the time F.D.R. took office in March of 1933, the Depression had just about wiped the Austin Lunch out of Papa's life forever.

My father was hanging onto his restaurant by a hair when the last of three experiments saved him. The first was Mr. Prevolos's agreement allowing my father to delay paying rent, which kept the front door open, and the second was taking my mother on as an unpaid employee to replace paid workers. Both moves enabled the Austin Lunch to survive until December of 1933 when, at long last, it started making money again, thanks to Papa's third experiment.

Word got out, then spread through the neighborhood and beyond, that the Austin Lunch's proprietor had a lead on purchasing whiskey and was going to sell it in his restaurant on the first night of repeal. Mama, Nick and I were awed on that cold December evening when the restaurant finally filled up with people after years of near desertion. A throng of patrons never seen before, who had never come to eat the good and hearty food that Uncle Charlie and Uncle Pete cooked, patiently waited for Papa to return from his whiskey buying expedition. (By that time Uncle Pete, our Thea Aphroditi's husband, was employed as the Austin Lunch's night cook.) Mama, puzzled to see so many patrons all at once, wondered to herself in Greek, "Where have these people been for the past five years?"

In a party mood, absent since hard times had overtaken them, a restaurant-full of laughing, animated, paying customers eagerly awaited the first legal alcohol available following the repeal, on December 5, 1933, of the eighteenth amendment to the U.S. Constitution. Nick and I studied the zany new set of Austin Lunch patrons as we sat in one of the booths along the side wall, having a great time with Thea Dimitra Limbers. She was as fascinated by all the commotion as we were. Her husband, Uncle George, was assisting Papa with his experiment. Chicago newspapers would be filled the next morning with stories about the return of legal alcohol. Front-page articles reported that the downtown Congress Hotel alone went through 100 cases of champagne, 75 cases of whiskey, 75 cases of gin and 100 cases of wine.

Papa couldn't lug even a single case of whiskey back to the store on the streetcar by himself, so earlier in the day he asked for a ride to the liquor supplier from Uncle George Limbers. To my father's surprise, the warehouse was mobbed with people, and by the time he got to the front of a very long line, he was informed that the whiskey supply had been exhausted; Papa had no other choice but to buy one case of gin, the only alcohol that was left. Downhearted, he loaded his investment into the trunk of George Limbers's car, worried that he had wasted hard-earned cash on a stupid case of booze.

"You know, Uncle George, when you're broke and go out to spend the few bucks you've scraped together—money you've sweated blood for—on a case of gin, you have to worry about being in your right mind. I may wind up losing my shirt."

Papa fretted all the way back to the store, breathing hard. Upon his return to the Austin Lunch he was astounded to find the unexpected crowd waiting for him with cheers and whistles. The "high class" hotels, downtown, sold gallons of booze while my father could only feature one case of gin. Yet, when those twelve fifth-bottles from a single carton sold faster and easier than food at the Austin Lunch on that icy but pivotal December night, he made the decision to sell beer and liquor with meals in his restaurant. Survival was just around the corner.

Unknown to Papa at the time was the unimaginable way in which Prohibition's repeal would impact our lives, our neighborhood and our city. After December of 1933, almost every fourth storefront on Madison Street turned into a saloon. The trend continued and by the end of World War II, the vicinity of Ogden and Madison had become part of Chicago's notorious Skid Row. The business boom that accompanied the Second World War prompted a population move toward Chicago's newer northern, western, and southwestern neighborhoods. These urban migrations left the section of the city where our family had lived in the Thirties and Forties vulnerable to decay. Its fate, for decades, was to continue in the poverty that first beset it in the Depression.

Food was still served well into the Forties at the Austin Lunch. Yet the sign boards which were a part of the facade of the old store slowly started changing in the years that followed repeal. The enamel-painted metal signs, STEAKS AND CHOPS, QUICK COURTEOUS SERVICE, DELICIOUS COFFEE, and FINE SOUPS, were gradually replaced by GOETZ COUNTRY CLUB BEER, DRINK COCA-COLA, and WHISKEY by the DRINK, BOTTLE, or CASE. Papa had witnessed many gradual shifts in business and in American culture during the twenty-five years he had been a proprietor on Madison Street. He would find the post-Prohibition changes to be the most troublesome. They were rushing toward him, fast.

MOB

"*D*emon rum," as liquor was referred to by "dry" advocates, clashed with hard times. New Madison Street characters appeared, and new problems emerged. Vagrants who slept in doorways on our block smelled, more often than not, of cheap wine or stale beer. The erratic behavior of heavy drinkers made our neighborhood feel unpredictable. One never knew when a fight would break out or a pedestrian might pass out on the sidewalk. Mama and Papa had their hands full trying to keep the store straight and as "legit" as possible.

One unforgettable incident in early 1934 brought the shady past of Tom Charlas, a fellow Greek who was Papa's closest competitor, directly into the Austin Lunch and under the white marble counter.

"Hide me, Paul. HIDE ME! Dem guys is gonna kill me if dey get dere paws on me!"

A desperate Tom Charlas unexpectedly appeared at the counter at seven in the morning, looking like he had spent the night in hell. Papa had just arrived to begin his workday. Except for Uncle Pete, the night cook in the kitchen, the restaurant was empty. My father heard the front door open. When he glanced up, he found himself face-to-sweaty-face with a terrified, unshaven Charlas, the knot of his striped necktie hastily torn away from his prominent Adam's apple. Charlas and his wrinkled white shirt were wrapped inside a crumpled dark gabardine suit. His graying hair seemed to stand on end, much like a frightened cartoon character in the funny papers. Usually ultra-neat and ever-so-flashy, Papa's neighbor had apparently spent the unseasonably warm spring night in his pinstriped, double-breasted suit. His uncharacteristic appearance so early in the morning caught Papa by surprise. Charlas desperately began pleading for refuge.

"Who's gonna kill you?" Papa asked.

"Please, Paul. I gotta hide RIGHT NOW. Ask questions later!"

Papa knew that Charlas, our local "bad guy," the only fellow country-man I can remember who Papa did not like, had been a bootlegger with mob ties during Prohibition. Papa turned his head toward the front window to check if anyone was following Charlas. He spotted two ominous looking men outside, nervously pacing the sidewalk east to west, heads turning every direction in a frantic search for something or someone.

"Here. JUMP IN HERE." Papa felt mixed emotions as soon as he said it. His first inclination was not to help Charlas at all, but a second later he felt a pang of sympathy for his rogue neighbor. When Papa spotted the two suspicious characters lurking outside, he thought of the space under the counter.

Charlas followed Papa's directions, falling belly side down over the white marble and painfully stuffing himself into the only cabinet under the counter without shelves. The instant Charlas squeezed his overweight bulk into the small cabinet, Papa hastily forced the dark, sliding wood door shut, even though Charlas's mass resisted from within. If it had been any later in the day, the space would have been stuffed with restaurant paraphernalia and dirty dishes waiting to be returned to the kitchen.

The operation was accomplished so quickly that even Papa was surprised at its speed. He looked up and froze when he saw the two men opening his front door. They were dressed in dark business suits, white shirts, dark ties, and black fedora hats.

"My God," Papa said to himself. "It's the Syndicate."

They didn't come all the way into the restaurant but shouted at Papa from inside the doorway. "You seen Charlas?"

"Who?" Papa stalled.

"Charlas. TOM CHARLAS."

"Not for a while. His bar's just a few doors down from here." Papa's mouth went suddenly dry from tension. Trying to make conversation, he discovered he couldn't get words out glibly or quickly enough and decided "the less said the better."

"Stay calm," he advised himself. "They're gangsters."

One man eyed Papa coldly, then studied the narrow spaces of the empty restaurant. "Just seen Charlas on da street. I t'ink he came in dis joint." He inspected the store with his piercing eyes, pivoting his head as he hunted for his prey. The second thug also searched the Austin Lunch's dim corners. The two men moved around nervously, like jackals, ambling more deeply into the store.

"I'm the only one here. Just got here myself. Tom must have gone into one of the other places on either side. Doors are so close together you can't tell one store from the other when you walk down the sidewalk." As he spoke, Papa could hear Charlas's heavy breathing emanating from his cabinet. At the same time, he prayed that Uncle Pete wouldn't emerge from the kitchen after he had lied about being there by himself. He wanted the hoodlums out of his store as quickly as possible, and decided not to say anything else. Papa didn't like telling lies, under any circumstances. He reached over to turn on the small, black oscillating fan that was on the counter, a few feet away. He hoped the noisy fan would muffle the sounds issuing from under the counter and from his own chest where his heart was beating loudly.

The mobster who had asked the questions backed up and gestured toward the door with his head. The second thug obeyed his signal. They exited together and then my father, paralyzed with fear and dry-mouthed, watched them run toward Ogden Avenue. Papa didn't budge and tried to warn Charlas without moving his lips. "Stay put. I want to see if they come back in."

Alarmed and red with anger, Papa felt sick to his stomach. The thumping in his chest boomed like an artillery barrage. Determined to appear casual, in case they came back, Papa issued orders to his refugee.

"If and when I say 'go,' stay crouched down and run out the back door of the kitchen into the alley. They went west; YOU GO EAST TOWARD DOWNTOWN." Papa's voice exploded with a rage that even he realized was ear-shattering, so he toned it down after his first, thunderous outburst.

"Don't you ever do anything like this to me again. You pal around with scum, with chiselers and killers who can kill me, too, if they find out you were in here. You owe them money or what?"

Papa needed to get rid of Charlas as soon as possible, but pulling him out of the cabinet wasn't easy. When he tried to open the cabinet door, it resisted. But fear motivated Papa to yank at it with all his strength. "They haven't come back. I'm watching the other side of the street, too. Get out right now. Go east. RUN."

"Sorry, Paul." That's all Papa heard Charlas say as his hands emerged onto the restaurant floor. He sucked in his ample belly and pulled the rest of his crumpled self from under the counter. Crouched, he darted into the kitchen and disappeared.

Papa told Nick, years later, that the incident had preoccupied his thoughts for days. He related it to Charlie, Uncle Pete, and Harry so they'd be on the look-out for questionable activities in the neighborhood. He had mixed emotions about telling Mama. It was important for her to be cautious, but he didn't want to frighten her.

A week after the early morning incident, Nick and I were on our way to visit Papa at the store and happened to pass Mr. Charlas on the sidewalk; he was usually friendly, a neighbor on our street who always stopped to talk to us. On that particular morning he gave us a warmer-than-usual greeting and insisted on taking us into Popper's grocery store. Inside, he led us over to the fragrant fruit bins and asked which were our favorites. Then he filled a brown paper bag for each of us, paid Mrs. Popper, and accompanied us into the Austin Lunch.

"Look, Pa, Mr. Charlas bought us fruit at Mrs. Popper's. Whatever we like. Helen got all kinds. But I got only apples. I love apples."

"You almost made them orphans a few days ago. Now you're buying them bags of fruit." Papa was not smiling.

"Hey, Paul, I like your kids. And you saved my life. Dis is my way to t'ank you. Ain't no other way which I can repay you. Dat dere was a business misunderstanding. An' dats all over wit'."

Papa interrupted Charlas's chatter by glaring at him over his eye-glasses. Nick and I knew Papa's "look" as well as Mama's, and we quickly retreated to the kitchen to show our fruit to Uncle Charlie. It was no fun hanging around when it looked like Papa was going to yell.

My father was trying hard not to be heard by a pair of customers in the nearby booth. "I don't want to know anything about your business, Tom. It's O.K. with me that you're my closest competitor. Now that Prohibition is over there's plenty of business for all of us. I don't even mind that you advertise a free lunch at your bar while I'm over here trying to sell food.

"But don't get me mixed up with your Mob connections. I avoid those people. I don't do business with them. When they come in here to eat or have a beer, I serve them politely. But I don't get chummy. Purposely. They want to be pals with me, but I know who they are and I keep my distance, thank you." Papa caught himself getting louder. He leaned his reddened face and neck over the counter toward Charlas to keep the conversation confidential, then lowered his voice. "Listen, you know I run a straight business here. I don't want any of the advantages your so-called 'business associates' can offer. Their advantages are full of disadvantages. My wife works in here with me, and my kids are here all the time. I want all of us to be safe and straight.

"You know yourself the street changed after repeal. We've got more vagrants, drunks, street women, gangsters. You name it. We've got to live and work here. I've got no other choice, and I'm trying to insulate this place the best I can to keep out the worst elements of society because they go by that door all day long. I don't want to have anything to do with guys like the hoods who were chasing you the other day. My place is going to stay completely legit. PERIOD." Papa meant business. His face was flushed, and his eyes were boring holes into Charlas over his eyeglasses.

"Paul, I didn' wanna bring you no harm. I was just scared stiff. I'm sorry. I appreciate whatchou done for me. How else can I say t'anks?" He lowered his heavy eyelids to show remorse.

"Listen, Tom, I was scared, first for me and even for you. My heart was jumping right out of my chest. Hey, I don't even want to talk about it anymore. But remember, no repeats—Ever!"

"I'll shake on it, Paul."

The sale of beer and liquor brought problems to the Austin Lunch that were never experienced when it was exclusively a restaurant, but business did indeed pick up. Sales rose above the twelve dollars a day Papa might take in, if he was lucky, before repeal. So, he decided to advertise his bargain ten-ounce stein of beer and attract even more customers. Papa invested a lot of money in a small red neon sign, had it connected to electricity, and proudly hung it in the front window. It glowed on Madison Street with its message of cheap libation: BEER 5 CENTS. It shined, but not for long.

A few days after the sign had been installed, Papa went down to work in the morning and was alarmed to find the front window in pieces on the sidewalk. His unaffordable red neon sign had been crushed to tiny bits.

"My God, what's going on here? Somebody used a baseball bat to do this good a job." Then he addressed himself. "Well, Paul, it could have been your own noggin smashed on this sidewalk instead of the sign and window." Blood rushed to his head, but he kept his thoughts to himself. "Who did this? Charlas's buddies? Maybe Charlas himself."

Papa never learned the answers. He never found out if his enemies didn't care for his catchy advertising, or his cheap prices. But he didn't raise the price of a stein of beer or that of his ten-cent, twenty-ounce schooner. After the window was fixed with two pieces of glass instead of one, because repairing it with two was cheaper, he didn't have enough money to replace the neon sign. From then on, Papa touted bargain prices by printing signs himself on butcher paper with black crayon, which he personally taped to the front window. Eventually breweries and liquor companies provided all the bars, up and down the street, with flashy colored neon signs, at no charge to the owners. At night, the bright electric colors that emanated from the vast collection of buzzing signs blended together, and cast a pinkish neon glow on Madison Street pedestrians as they passed saloon after saloon after saloon.

LIFE AFTER REPEAL

*S*ometime during the spring of 1934, Papa realized that the more beer and liquor he sold, the greater the need for him to provide a place for customers to belly up to.

"When are you going to get a bar in here, Paul?"

"Don't know, Mike. To tell you the truth, I can't afford one. A salesman from Country Club came in to sell me draft beer, but I need a bar to hold the spigots and barrels. You know what a bar costs? A used one that's only six feet long costs forty bucks. I haven't got that kinda moola."

"Get a loan, Paul. Lots of beer drinkers go for draft. It tastes better. A bar brings more business."

"Who's going to loan me forty samolians, Mike? I don't even have a savings account."

"I could."

"You've got forty bucks laying around? You'd lend me that much money? What are you, a banker?"

Mike was a regular customer who worked as an engineer for the Edison Company. He lived in a rooming house on Monroe Street and came to eat his meals at the Austin Lunch. Through their daily encounters Mike came to know and trust Papa. As a result of this faith in my father, he loaned him the money. The forty-dollar loan and tiny bar it paid for replaced six feet of white marble counter, the second step in turning the Austin Lunch into a saloon. Mike was repaid with interest, even though interest hadn't been in the original agreement. When he achieved his professional and personal goals, Mike moved away from the neighborhood and we never heard from him again, but his trust and generosity have never been forgotten.

Gradually, my mother found herself working behind that bar. It was a role that never properly suited her personality or personal precepts. Yet, in spite of her mother-superior attitude, the customers liked and respected her. The newly installed bar caused her to become even more watchful of what was going on around her. Whether talking to Papa or chatting with customers, Mama closely observed activity in the Austin Lunch while she washed glasses, waited on tables, picked up dirty dishes, or carried orders out from the kitchen. A secret service agent couldn't have done better.

Mama was especially suspicious of a frequent customer named Hazel and, more than once, shared her observations of the woman with Papa. "That Hazel over there. She's got no shame. She's no lady. She's a no good moocher. The worst one of all. Comes here with a different man every night. Where in the devil she finds them? I don't like to see a woman drink too much because when she does, she lose her dignity. There's nothing worst than a drunken woman. I try to ignore this Hazel, Paul, but watch and see. I'm going to kick her out of here pretty soon."

Mama got practice for carrying out her threat on a busy night at the Austin Lunch when "bouncer" was added to Mama's already extensive job description. Working behind the counter together, my mother drew my father's attention to a loud-voiced customer on the other side of the restaurant.

"Listen to that guy over in the booth, Paul. He's too loud. It sounds like he's had too much to drink tonight."

Mama shook her head with disapproval. "We never had a problem with customers eating too much. How come it's so easy for them to drink too much? They drink and drink and have to go to the toilet all day and all night. And they think they're having a good time. Haven't got money to eat, but more than enough to drink. I can't figure it out."

Mama turned her attention to the boisterous customer again. "That guy's too loud, Paul. He's going to bring trouble."

"I'm going over there to tell him he's had too much to drink, Bessie."

She warned him in Greek, "Be careful, *kakomoiri* (unfortunate one). Remember what happened when you broke up a fight."

Papa put down the towel, nervously tightened the white apron around his waist, and walked to the middle aisle of the restaurant. He hesitated, then approached the rowdy customer. The store was full of people. The man was wearing a greasy fedora and sitting across from a woman in an old fur coat that was frayed at the sleeves and along the buttonholes. She wore a black velvet hat decorated with a pin that made her look like she had a pair of scissors sticking out of her head.

"Barten'er! Bring us another roun' o' the same."

"I'm sorry sir, you've had too much already. It's time for you to go home."

"You tryin' ta tell me I'm drunk? I'm not ya know. I'm perfec'ly sober. Bring us 'nother roun'." His words were slurred, his tongue stuck to the roof of his mouth, and his eyes couldn't quite focus on Papa. His lady friend covertly winked at Papa and seemed relieved that he was refusing them another round.

"I'm sorry, sir." Papa shook his head, trying to speak softly and not cause a scene.

"Hey, barten'er! You jus' bring me 'nother roun' NOW."

The man's voice instantly turned nasty and louder. He grabbed the edge of the table, pulled himself up on his unsteady feet and confronted my father, face to face. Papa could see reflections of the light bulbs that framed the Austin Lunch's front window in the customer's watery eyes. Papa unavoidably inhaled the stink of alcohol coming from the man's breath.

Keeping a sharp eye on the confrontation, Mama quickly went to my father's side. The first time a fight broke out between two customers after repeal, Papa had stepped in to stop the fray and wound up on the floor with a bloody nose and bruises which ultimately turned into painful black and blue swellings on the side of his face. From that first encounter with trouble, Mama learned that heavy drinkers are often unpredictable. She stiffly smiled at the couple in the booth and whispered to Papa in Greek, "You want to get punched in the face again?

141

This drunk is ready to cause trouble. See? He's ready to take a swing at you. Let me talk to him. You go behind the counter. He won't try that with me."

"How do you know?" Papa asked in English as Mama forcefully maneuvered herself between him and the drunk.

"Sir, my husband just telling you that the next drink is on the house—but it must be Seven-Up. He's going to bring it for you and your lady friend. No more beer tonight. You come another time to drink beer. But no more tonight." Mama shook her right index finger from left to right as she repeated the word "no" in her best mother-superior manner.

The unexpected arrival of a short, dignified woman giving motherly advice instantly calmed the drunk and he removed his fedora when he realized a lady was addressing him. The lights in the front window were still dancing in his bleary eyes, and the stench of alcohol emanated from his mouth with every fuzzy word.

"Yes, ma'am. I'm sorry, ma'am. Wasn' gonna make no trouble. I'm a gen'elmun. You can see… I'm a gen'elmun. Ask my frien' here. She'll tell you… a compleet… gen'elmun."

The lady with the scissors in her hat agreed and tossed a grateful look of relief at Mama.

"Oh, I know you a gentalaman." Mama nodded sympathetically. "I bring you and your friend a couple cups of coffee, too, when you finish drinking your Seven- Ups. It's all on the house."

Smiling uncomfortably, Mama returned to the counter to fetch two glasses and two deep green bottles of Seven Up. Both she and Papa kept their eyes on the couple in the booth until they nodded "Good night," and went out the door.

"Looks like you're our new bouncer, Bessie," Papa teased.

"What means 'bouncer?'"

Papa was always adding words to Mama's English vocabulary.

She came to know the word "bouncer" and became adept at avoiding confrontational situations with heavy drinkers. Papa never forgot the time he wound up on the floor writhing in pain after his first-ever fist fight at the Austin Lunch (yes, there were others), so he left dealing with customers who had imbibed too much to Mama's no nonsense approach. She became an expert at distinguishing the fine line between sobriety and intoxication and the drink that caused the crossover. She could approach and advise a customer about to step over the line that enough had been consumed, and it was time to stop. "Period." Customers who respected her when they were sober followed her counsel, not wanting to be disrespectful to "Mrs. Paul." Mama repeatedly remembered, in later years, that the worst kind of drinker to reason with was female. "Nothing worst than a drunken woman."

Mama's generous figure revealed her enjoyment of good food, but she was a virtual teetotaler and quite honest with customers who offered to buy her a drink. "No, thank you. Don't tastes good. Remember that too much alcohol is no good for your insides—and worse yet—sometimes it keep you from being decent person. You better be careful."

Once in a while Papa enjoyed a glass of wine or a cold beer with his dinner at home, whenever he had a chance to eat out at home, but never at the store, even when a customer offered to buy him a drink. I often heard him say. "If liquor companies depended on me or Bessie to drink this stuff, they'd go broke in a minute."

With the exception of a few sips of wine to toast good luck on special occasions and holidays, Mama did not care to partake of anything stronger, even a mouthful. She instinctively knew that something so vile tasting must do harm to a person's health when consumed in excessive amounts. She had the same views about smoking, decades before the surgeon general's official warnings.

People of all kinds, sober and not, continually streamed in and out of the Austin Lunch; some weren't even customers. Hordes came looking for jobs; others came to sell their wares and beg for food or money. Shoeshine boys brought in boxes full of brushes and polish ready to shine a customer's shoes on the spot. Newspaper boys went in and out all day, as the newest editions hit the streets. Mr. Friedman, the father of our friends Jackie and Ethel, who lived upstairs from Mrs. Popper's grocery, was one of many vendors who routinely came in to sell caps and shoelaces out of a cardboard box. Some entrepreneurs were not honest like Mr. Friedman.

Mama told me that when Nick and I were quite small, Papa naively bought a box of new children's clothing very cheaply from an unknown vendor who had stopped by the restaurant. Shortly following his purchase, he was embarrassed to find himself at the local police station politely explaining how stolen goods had come into his possession. After that, Papa was suspicious of most vendors he didn't know personally and never bought anything peddled in his establishment again. Mama said men often came in with merchandise that my parents suspected was stolen, but she and Papa were too busy running a restaurant to sift out those earning an honest buck from the riff raff; there was no way of knowing. Times were tough, cash was short, and "buyer beware" was good shopping advice.

A regular Madison Street sight was the man who always wore dark glasses under his black fedora, carried a white cane, and was led around, begging, by a young girl with long blond hair. They periodically walked through every bar and restaurant on the West Side. At night, the beggar returned to Papa's restaurant (without glasses, cane, or girl) to exchange his coins for paper money. Sometimes Papa didn't have enough bills in the cash register to accommodate the transaction. Incredibly, the "blind" man took in as much as forty dollars a day.

Many destitute men came into the Austin Lunch begging for something to eat; Mama and Papa never turned them away, always serving bread and a bowl of Uncle Charlie's hearty soup. Once, I was eating at the counter and left my place to take cash from a customer at the register. When I returned, I found a hungry man sitting on the stool that I had occupied. He was finishing my partially eaten meal.

Those with a weakness for alcohol found the Austin Lunch attractive; in those days, we called them "drunks" instead of "alcoholics." A destitute drunk came in begging for a free drink one day, and Papa politely turned him down. "Be happy to give you a bowl of soup and some bread, but no alcohol."

The man refused free food, but made his way back to the men's room before leaving. When he stumbled out the front door onto Madison, something large was tucked under his coat. Mama alerted Papa to the drunk's curious getaway, but Papa commented, "Don't be so suspicious, Bessie. There's nothing worth taking from this joint." An hour later, when he went to clean the men's room, Papa discovered the missing item and shuddered. "That guy's in pretty bad shape if he thinks some bartender's going to give him a drink in exchange for a very used toilet seat."

The mix of characters and bizarre happenings played themselves out daily in the Austin Lunch. A dull moment meant the cash register wasn't ringing, but my parents could relax their shoulders, take refuge in the quiet, and even enjoy a Coke or a hot cup of coffee together at the counter. But when that front door opened, they straightened their backs, held their breaths and, with experienced eyes, looked past the window's glare to size up the volatility of the next customer.

THE BELOVED "MAGAZI"

We thank God that Apostoli still has his store.

—Vasiliki to her father, late 1931

*M*ama continued her inspection of the old Greek letters. She read to me from a fragment, guessing it had been written shortly after she went to work at Papa's place.

"Apostoli's restaurant has taken over my life. It is good that we live close so that we have our children near us. It could be worse, so we thank God that Apostoli still has his store. So many we know have lost theirs."

"You know, Helen, I don't think my family in Greece could understand what we was going through during the Depression. They was poor, too, but I don't think my father had as much weighing on his shoulders as your Papa did. They could not understand all the responsibilities and obligations we had. Life here is more complicated. Life was simpler in Greece back then. We tried not to write complaints to them, even though my brother asked about our Depression problems in his letters to us.

"You know what else I remember, Helen? Lots of people who don't own their own busyness think that if you own a *magazi* (store) you must be rich." Laugh. "Just goes to show you that some people don't know nothing. They don't know what it's like to be the other guy."

Magazi was the Greek word my parents used to refer to Papa's restaurant; it was a special word for the immigrant who was in business for himself. The translation is "shop" or "store," and it is used to describe almost any retail business—a bar, confectionery, restaurant, grocery, shoeshine parlor, furniture store, even a department store like Marshall Field and Company. Limited by newly learned English skills, Greek immigrants without higher education or technical abilities were proud to own a *magazi*. The word was pronounced with reverence when applied to one's own enterprise. No matter how inadequate receipts were, the store was supposed to be the source for making a living, supporting a family, sending money back to dependents in Greece, saving for the future, and even having the ability to be a small time benefactor.

Fifty years later, Mama shook her head in disbelief as she remembered being co-proprietor of a *magazi*. "Just because you got your own store, people is alloways coming in to ask you for money. They want it for their clubs, for churches and for themselves. They got lots of reasons for you to give them money. And, of course, it's okay if you're making lots of money to help the other guy out, if you can. Yeah, you got a store, but they're not asking first if you can afford to pay the rent or if you got any customers coming in or if you can afford to pay the help that's working for you. They not asking how many hours you spend standing on your feet to make five cents. They don't ask, 'When was the last time you get to stay home and rest? Do you ever got time to go to church with your family?' They just think that if you got a *magazi* you must be making money for them, too."

The long work hours that most shop owners put in made the *magazi* an extension of the Greek owner's home, the only place where he had time to meet people and greet visitors. Most *magazia* (plural) were closed and locked up at night after closing, but not Papa's restaurant. It was always open and always watched over, like a frail, forgetful grandparent. Uncle Pete, Mama's brother-in-law, was the short order night cook and tended to the restaurant during the night shift.

When the traditional *Vasilopita* (sweet bread with a good luck coin baked inside) was sliced by the head of the house on New Year's Day, the family's place of business was part of the ritual in many Greek homes.

Making the sign of the cross over the round loaf, the father repeated a centuries-old tradition of allocating each slice as he cut it. "The first piece is for Jesus who is always in our home, and the second for his Holy Mother. The next slice belongs to our house that keeps us warm and dry. The next one's for the father of the family, that's me, and this one's for Mama. Helen, you're our oldest child so your piece is next, and here's yours Nicky. And the last slice is for our *magazi* that makes it possible for us to have this bread today. It provides our bread and butter all year long." Good luck for the entire year was to be enjoyed by the finder of the coin, and when discovered in the piece for the *magazi*, it was a sign business might improve. There's no doubt the *magazi* was an esteemed, beloved member of the Greek immigrant's family.

Papa treated the Austin Lunch like the hallowed halls of Congress, in fact Congress should be so revered and so efficient. He stubbornly insisted a *mousteris* (old fashioned word for "customer") or *pelatis* (updated version) had to be served quickly, cheerfully, efficiently, and politely; prompt, competent workers were supposed to be on the premises every minute the *magazi* was open. When a *mousteris* came through the door, one had to stop immediately whatever one was doing for as long as necessary to serve the customer well, and at the same time gladly minister to patrons who were already inside. Mama and Papa were sticklers for attentive service, as were most Greeks in business. Restaurant owners have a saying that a sure-fire way to bring customers through the door is to try to sit down for a quick meal or cup of coffee. Millions of cups of coffee and dishes of food were consumed ice-cold by storeowners and employees in the name of good service. An owner whose philosophy was "I'll get plenty of rest when I'm dead" preferred waiting on customers to relaxing with a hot cup of coffee in an empty store. Good service was a *magazi*'s most important commodity: the customer was always right; the owner needed to be the most devoted laborer of all. Many preferred to use the word "slave" rather than "owner," but all were grateful for the opportunity to own their own businesses, an option not open to poverty stricken farm boys who remained in Greece.

All Greeks were not poor. There was a wealthy class in Greece who had no need to emigrate to America, and they did not. We didn't know any of those people. From 1890 to 1921, the overwhelming majority of Greek immigrants in the U.S. were impoverished men who planned to make money in America and return to the old country. Once they returned home, they planned to pay off family debts, provide dowries for their unmarried sisters (generous enough to allow their womenfolk to marry above their socio-economic status) and comfortably remain there for the rest of their lives. Some did return, but economic necessity kept most in the U.S. for life. Those who stayed, slowly grew to appreciate their new homeland, and eventually realized a fierce, loyal attachment to the U.S. "Why should I go back? This is my *patrida*. God bless America!" The realization developed slowly, long after hardship and bigotry had been endured.

It is a fact that in the U.S., deplorable prejudice is inflicted on racial, ethnic, and religious minorities; the most recent newcomers become recipients of the most fear, suspicion and hate. They are treated like outcasts. From the end of the nineteenth century until World War II, Greeks were newcomers in the tide of immigration, and like a painful passage through diabolical initiation rites, they, too, suffered the ordeals of discrimination.

The Ku Klux Klan was after them in the South, some places in the Midwest (notably Indiana) and in the West. During the early Twenties, the estimated three million members of the Klan dominated politics all over the U.S. Crosses were set on fire in front of Greek homes and rooming houses; Greek men were beaten up. KKK members openly attacked and/or threatened patrons of Greek-owned businesses to force them out of business. Speaking publicly in Spokane, Washington, a Klansman proclaimed that to preserve white supremacy and the purity of America, Greeks should go back to where they came from. In Utah, seating in movie theaters for "no good Greeks" was restricted to the balconies. Bigots in Chicago couldn't tell Greeks from Italians, so Mediterranean immigrants, descendants of the birth-givers of western civilization, were all lumped into one undesirable group, and collectively and demeaningly called "Wops."

One reason Greeks suffered intolerance was because they belonged to an unfamiliar religion. A majority of Americans didn't relate to someone being Greek Orthodox and had no idea that Greeks were Christian. Curious questions asked of me through the years about my faith have made me wonder. Do they picture us in some restaurant backroom worshiping Zeus on a pseudo-ancient altar of sorts because we are Greek? Or do they consider us a Jewish sect because we are Orthodox? Few outside our faith in the early days knew that Greek Orthodox Christianity began with Christ's Apostles: Paul spent much time and effort preaching to the unruly Corinthians; John wrote the Apocalypse on the Greek island of Patmos; Andrew spread the Gospel while he lived in a house, in what is now the city of Patras, in northwest Peloponnesos.

Discrimination was also heaped on Greeks because of their dark hair, dark eyes and swarthy complexions; because they had unpronounceable first and last names; and because they were poor and employed in low-paying, low-skilled jobs, and unable to speak English well. Even though they were hired to work in mines and build the railroad out west, the option of working in a factory was not open to most Greek immigrants in Chicago. Prejudice against hiring men from the southeast Mediterranean usually kept Greeks out of good paying factory jobs, so they were forced into the only employment left: the service industries. All Greek immigrants were proud of the scant few who were able to earn degrees of higher education. By the Thirties there were doctors, teachers, engineers, and lawyers among the immigrant Greek population.

According to Papa, he and his fellow newcomers were often denied rental housing and were forced to live in the cheapest quarters. They often subsisted on a cheap diet of beans, bread, cheese and olives (the lucky ones worked in restaurants)—and they saved money like misers. I remember Papa's smile when he revealed that one of his first expenditures, after a few years of working, was for a new outfit of clothing. He wanted to have his photograph taken and sent back to the village to relieve his parents' anxiety about his welfare. He felt compelled to show them that he had grown, that he was healthy, and that he was becoming successful, even though, in truth, he was an overworked shoeshine boy at the bottom rung of American society. A sepia print adheres to a fading page in our family album of a dignified and unsmiling quartet of teenagers: Papa, his brother Bill, and two first cousins, all shoeshine boys from Mercovouni (group pictures were cheaper because the cost was shared). Before individual camera ownership was affordable, newcomers had formal studio photos taken to send back to the old country. Each time a portrait from America was shown off by proud parents, a spurt of hope and a great naïve buzz erupted in the village.

"Did you see that picture of Asimakos's boys? They're wearing European style suits, neckties, and white shirts with starched collars. I thought they were shining shoes, but they look like bankers. If Asimakos's sons can be successful in America, so can mine. We have found our salvation." Stoic black and white portraits enclosed in thick cardboard frames, name and city of photography studio imprinted in a distinguished logo at the corner of each matting, were mailed from Chicago, New York, Lowell, Atlanta, Salt Lake City, Sacramento, Hibbing, Mason City, Detroit, Philadelphia, and everywhere else there were hard working kids with parents in Greece. When the portraits arrived in the old country, they spurred more immigration to America.

Working beyond exhaustion as water boys in the mines, dishwashers, waiters, cooks, candy makers, hot dog sellers, bartenders, bakers, fruit and vegetable hawkers, hat cleaners, flower sellers, shoeshine boys, etc., etc., immigrant teenagers endured the burden of being family "saviors." They conscientiously strove to live up to the high hopes and financial expectations of relatives back in the village. At the same time, most tried to learn as much English as they could, and tried to be as American as possible. Working seven days a week, from six in the morning until nine or ten at night, with no time to take regular classes, Papa learned his new language on the job. At night he read the daily newspapers with the help of a Greek/English dictionary.

Ironically, discrimination forced Greek immigrants into becoming good entrepreneurs; deprivation and sacrifice eventually earned them ownership of stores. Owning one's own business became the American dream for most, even though the Great Depression brought serious impediments. Some men carried the responsibility of sending money back to Greece for an entire lifetime, years beyond the deaths of their parents and the marriages of their sisters, well after the Second World War, the Fifties, the Sixties, and the Seventies.

"My brother back home, he never asks me if I'm going to get through this damn Depression. In the village they don't know nothing about paying rent, or mortgages. He never writes, 'Dear brother, how many hours are you working everyday? Do you ever get a chance to go to church? Do you ever take a nap in the afternoon like we do?'

"Of course I don't because I'm stuck in this damn *magazi* (store).

"He tells me what he wants me to do for HIS kids, but does he ever ask about my hopes for my kids? Am I going to be able to send them to college or are they gonna be slaves to a *magazi* like I am? Am I ever going to be able to take my family and move out of this tenement to own a house with a yard someday? All my brother knows is, 'Dear brother, SEND MONEY.' I'm getting sick and tired of it.

"Next time I write to the old country, I'm going to tell my brother that I've never been able to find those glorious streets paved with gold here in America because I'm too busy working in a two-bit restaurant to go looking for them. My working hours are seven days a week and sixteen hours a day because I have the privilege of owning the two-bit restaurant. He either still believes that old fairy tale about gold in the streets of America, or maybe he thinks I've turned into Santa Claus."

Wish lists from Greece never stopped arriving in the mail. Even decades after sisters were married, nieces' dowries were to be provided by the American uncle. First, second, and even third cousins in the old country had reasons for American relatives to send money, and families in America compassionately complied whenever possible. Sometimes, promises made in childhood became unfair priorities that were allowed to take precedence over the needs of the immigrants

AUSTIN LUNCH

themselves and the needs of their own hardworking, self-sacrificing
wives and children in the United States.

At the same time, most immigrants, male and female, generously
gave up their rights to property in Greece, not by signing legal papers,
but by not demanding a due inheritance. "Let my brother have it. He
needs it." Then, when the immigrant died, sixty years after emigrat-
ing from the old country, leaving wife, children and grandchildren in
the U.S. to grieve his absence, some Greek relatives, a continent away,
absurdly expected to get a piece of the old *magazi* for themselves in
the old man's will.

With Mama's hard work and able help, Papa struggled to keep his
magazi open in the Thirties, and was delighted when business improved enough after repeal to hang his hand-lettered WAITRESS
WANTED sign in the front window. He taped it to the glass, in the
middle of the frame of electric light bulbs in late 1934; unemployment was at 21.7%. A stream of applicants followed the posting of
the sign. In fifteen minutes as many as twelve women applied for a
job that paid one dollar per day. Most applicants were teenage girls
who had left farms in Tennessee and Kentucky. It became Mama's
responsibility to interview, hire, and train new waitresses.

"You already in America. How come you leave your mama and
papa to come to Chicago, all by yourself? You too young!"

Ultimately, she began to understand that poverty caused migra-
tion from farm to city in America, for the same reasons she left Greece.
Eventually she saw many American migrants return to farms because
poverty in big cities was unconquerable.

"They lucky they got places close enough to go back to. For us
poor Greeks to go back home is too, too far away and cost too much
money."

Mama demanded efficient work, personal cleanliness, and quick-
ness in serving customers. When there were no customers, workers
were not to stand around idly, but find something that needed cleaning and clean it. There were always cloth napkins, returned from the
laundry flatly pressed, that needed to be folded. Sugar bowls, cream

pitchers, and salt and pepper shakers had to be washed and filled. Mama was organized, and her list of instructions was endless.

"Alloways something needs to be cleaned. I'm talking about ketchup bottles, ashtrays, counter, tables, chairs, coffee urns, and everything else. Work in this place, it never end. Use your finger to clean corners with a damp towel. As long as you're doing a job, do it right. Don't use dirty towel, alloways use a clean one." Mama was a master at giving directions; she repeated them to all of us as a priest chants a litany.

As tough and demanding as she was to work for, Mama was respected and liked by most farm girls who became waitresses at the Austin Lunch. First and foremost, they knew she respected them. With Mama, it was never a situation of imperiously giving orders to others and expecting them to do the work; she worked as well. Not all waitresses put up with her demands. Those who lasted longer than a few days marveled at how she could do several things at once, all well. Mama didn't realize that everyone around her didn't have that gift, but she was patient, most of the time. Strict in her work ethic, she tried to be an understanding employer because most waitresses had no previous experience, except working on a farm. Mama pointed out what they had in common.

"I'm farm girl, too. Nobody is born to know everything. Time comes when we all got to learn something new. We never too old to learn."

They respected Mama so much that some waitresses who smoked (smoking women were still a shocking sight in the Thirties) didn't smoke in front of Mrs. Paul. She never told them not to, but they assumed that because she had such high standards for everything, she would disapprove of smoking, too. Mama's natural investigative talents turned up clandestine tobacco habits when she found forgotten cigarette butts with lipstick marks in the pockets of waitress aprons at the end of a shift. Surprisingly for Mama, even then she never told them not to smoke; it was very unlike her.

As temperamental as Uncle Charlie could be, he never minded having Mama around his kitchen, although he wouldn't let her or anyone else cook. Mama watched him carefully, picking up ways to make her own work more efficient. Even though she was a terrific cook in her own right, she was never too shy or too proud to ask questions. Mama, Papa and Uncle Charlie were the managers who made the *magazi* (store) work. As night cook, Uncle Pete did not do extensive food preparation, serving whatever meals had been prepared by Charlie early in the day, and when that food ran out, Pete prepared short orders on the grill. If leftovers had not spoiled after a night in the steam table, we, the family, ate them the next day.

Daily, Charlie cooked two or three soups, a couple of stews, and five or six special entrees, as well as salad dressings and several varieties of potatoes and vegetables. In addition, he made desserts, except for pies that were purchased from John the pie man. Creamy rice pudding and rich bread pudding were two of Charlie's specialties that used up leftovers, stale bread and cooked rice. The variety of food that came out of his kitchen was endless and the menu changed everyday. I remember that on Christmas he would prepare dishes that perfectly complemented the turkey, goose, pheasant and beef that he roasted on that very special day. Cooking in the job description of his day meant complete food preparation, from cutting meat to cleaning vegetables, although he allowed Harry, the dishwasher, to clean onions and peel and mash potatoes. Incredibly, our Uncle Charlie even made his own soap using lard and other fats, the kitchen's castoffs.

One thing Charlie Kingos knew for sure was that he had job security. Even though times were tough and Papa couldn't pay much, a measly three dollars a day, my parents knew they had one of Chicago's cleanest and most talented chefs in their kitchen. Charlie labored under primitive conditions to produce superb meals that made most other menus look meager. Charlie was responsible for all serious cooking and had to burn sooty, black coal to do it. He carefully watched and continually kept a fire burning in the old coal stove, where he cooked everything, either on the range or inside the oven with no temperature control dials. There was no running hot water in the kitchen. There was no electric refrigeration. Charlie kept foods cold by storing them in a walk-in cooler stocked with large blocks of ice that melted quickly because of heat emanating from the uninsulated but sizzling kitchen stove. Water from melting ice had to be emptied throughout the day. New blocks of ice arrived every morning as reinforcements.

The iceman parked his horse and wagon on Madison to make his daily delivery. Using sharp tongs and a strap of leather over his shoulder, the iceman hauled the heavy blocks of ice through the restaurant and back into the kitchen. In summer, the huge chunks left a trail of water from his horse and wagon on Madison to the icebox back in the kitchen.

Every day, the Barnes Coal Company on Laflin Street sent a sack of shiny ebony fuel for the big black stove in the kitchen. The deliveryman, almost completely covered with coal dust, came in from the alley entrance. After depositing the sooty sack next to the stove, he walked from the kitchen to the cash register at the front of the store to collect his money. Papa gave him twenty-five cents, the daily payment for the kitchen fuel bill.

Harry the dishwasher worked at the Austin Lunch for fourteen years. Born in Menominee, Michigan, three of his grandparents had been Ojibway (Chippewa) Native Americans. Like clockwork, Harry mopped the restaurant floor everyday after the lunch shift. Because there was no water heater, water was continually heated over a gas flame in two huge tubs in the kitchen, one for soapy water, the other for rinsing. All day long, Harry added cold water from the sink to the tubs, and helped Uncle Charlie with very basic preparations, like cleaning onions and potatoes. During the bad years, Harry earned one dollar per day plus all his meals, ending his twelve-hour shift at 7 p.m. by walking up to the cash register where Papa gave him his dollar. Purveyors, waitresses, cooks and dishwashers worked long and hard for little pay to prepare and serve the meals in Papa's *magazi*. A successful day for Papa was one in which there was enough money in the cash register to pay them all, and turn a small profit, after he paid his debts.

"ALL THE ADVANTAGES"

When my friend comes, he will explain the conditions in America.

—Christ Ganas to his father-in-law, (date missing)

*M*ama held a letter fragment and studied it. "This was written by my brother-in-law, your Uncla Christ Ganas. Looks like somebody he know, I don't recognize the name, was taking a trip to Greece. Christ says here," and she read in Greek, "'Politimi, the boys and I wanted to send you a gift with my friend, but we aren't able to do that at this time. When my friend comes, he will explain the conditions in America now.'

"People was suffering in the Depression like we never see before in our lifes. I never see nothing like it in the old country before I come to America. Christ Ganas had lost his restaurant and times was tough for Politimi and her family. All of us was having tough times. Remember Thea Stavroula who live upstairs from our old Madison joint? Her Papa never should have send her to America. He had a good job and didn't have lots of kids. She come from a good place in the old country and wind up raising Chris all by herself in Prevolos's lousy apartment. She lose her husband and then some good-for-nothing relative cheat her out of the money her husband leave them when he die. I don't remember the details, but dear Thea Stavroula don't deserve to be treat like that. And alloways she got that beautifool smile. It come from inside her. Was not fake. We do what we can for them. But she was too, too proud. She alloways refuse help."

Our friend Chris Dekazos lived upstairs from the Austin Lunch with his mother. He called my parents "Uncle" and "Thea" and we all referred to his mother as "Thea," too, out of fondness, because she was older and particularly because her husband was from Mercovouni, the village where Papa was born. That association gave us an extra-special connection. Mama insisted we refer to their adult Greek friends as "aunt" or "uncle" to instill respect for our ethnic community. Greeks were "in" people, but only among Greeks. I remember that Thea Stavroula was dressed, very simply, in widow's black throughout my entire childhood. Stavroula (Anglicized to "Viola") was a very gracious lady who, because of a physical deformity in her hip from birth, walked with a jolting limp. One leg was shorter than the other. Two sources of pride in her life were her son, Chris, and her birthplace, Sparta (the original one). She had some education in Greece, unusual for a woman of her age (older than Mama). She could read and write, but knew no English whatsoever and depended on Chris to be her interpreter. Stavroula had family in Sparta, but Chris was all she had in America. They were too poor to return to her homeland.

Stavroula, widowed when Chris was three, regularly came downstairs to the restaurant to visit with my parents who thoroughly enjoyed her lively conversation. Perhaps because she was a city girl she seemed more sophisticated and accomplished than many other Greek women I knew. In spite of bitter hardships, her face glowed with a soul-warming smile, except when she talked about surviving with little money and raising a boy without a father.

"How will we survive? At least in Sparta there was a place to grow a garden and eat vegetables. Can we plant a food supply in the back alley's concrete or on Madison Street? I come from a beautiful, green city where the sun shines most of the year and where roses and orange trees grow. What am I doing in this inhumane climate? My father sent me to save a dowry. So I was married off to a Mercovounioti with a pool hall who died at the prime of his life and mine. Then that lying, cheating hoodlum swindled me and my son out of our inheritance. And now we're dependent on my brother-in-law's handouts."

She sighed deeply. "I am grateful. I don't know what we would do without Prevolos. But, I'm from a good home and family from inside the city limits of Sparta. We are proud, tough people with an illustrious history. Spartans don't beg. We don't take charity. My father was a district attorney. I was never, never in need, until I lived in America. I went to school in Sparta, but got my real education in Chicago. I have a doctor's degree in poverty, widowhood, and the sinister influences on these streets that could destroy my son. He must survive."

Thea Stavroula had a pretty face with huge, beautiful dark eyes that filled with tears when she remembered the past, was frustrated by the present, and saw no hope for the future. Like Mama, she communicated with them masterfully, lowering her eyelids demurely, glancing out to the side with a smile, narrowing them to show anger, or closing them, dramatically, to indicate despair. Arms stretched out in front of her, fingers clasped together and troubled eyes lowered in sadness, our proud, dignified Thea from Sparta painfully whispered a request to Mama and Papa, knowing they would keep a confidence.

"I don't care about myself, but, please, once in a while, when you have extra food here at the restaurant, please feed my son."

In 1984, Mama spoke fondly of Stavroula. "May God rest her good soul. Stavroula was a good, good lady and a marvelous cook. She teach me lots. She teach me to make *koulourakia* (Easter cookies) and the chestnut dressing we make on Thanksgiving and Christmas. We had a good time cooking together. We laugh together. It was relaxing for me." Mama diplomatically provided all the groceries, insisting Stavroula's expertise was a greater contribution than flour, eggs and butter in their joint Depression cooking ventures. "When times was real bad and she's not got much food on hand, she can make plain soup taste wonnerful. Her cooking was gourmet stuff. She depend on Chris for everything and he alloways take good care of her. After he grow up, he work hard, and they move away from Madison Street. And they wasn't poor anymore. He was such a good boy. She was so proud of him. We was all proud of him."

Mother and son rattled around in a huge, sparsely furnished, seven-room apartment; its only source of heat was a lone coal stove in the kitchen at the back of the house. They occupied three or four rooms closest to the stove, leaving the rest dark, cold and vacant. Landlord Prevolos, her husband's brother-in-law, allowed them to occupy one of his vacant apartments above the Austin Lunch, rent free, for the same reason he overlooked Papa's payment of rent until better times. Prevolos needed his building to be filled with caretakers rather than have it fall into decay while he waited for the rare occupant who could pay rent. Actually, anyone who could pay good money would have looked for better quarters, but times were desperate, and Prevolos's help was appreciated.

Chris had a terrific sense of humor. His positive attitude and willingness to work hard eventually led to his financial and business success; in later adulthood he owned several McDonald's restaurants in Chicago. When Chris, Nick and I reminisced, in later years, we particularly enjoyed his telling of shaking snow off the stack of blankets his mother used in her futile attempt to keep him warm on icy winter nights.

"Prevolos's drafty windows couldn't keep out cold, especially when winds blew at forty miles an hour. The newspapers and rags we stuffed in window openings didn't have a chance. Listen, I had all the advantages when I was a kid. I didn't even have to leave my room to play in the snow."

We walked to and from school everyday with Chris. Going "home" for lunch at noon meant eating at Papa's restaurant where Mama had three hot lunches waiting on the counter. Attending to paying customers, she listened to all three of us at once after she asked, "How's school?" Chris's favorite lunch was a hot pork sandwich between two slices of fresh white bread covered with Uncle Charlie's savory brown gravy. A mound of creamy mashed potatoes, the partner of this memorable sandwich, was positioned next to it. The same irresistible gravy was ladled over the huge mound of potatoes. Nick and I loved hot sandwiches, too. We may have been poor during the Depression, but as long as Papa's restaurant stayed open, we ate well.

Faithful clientele from the Olsen Rug Factory on Laflin at Monroe would come through the door at the same time we did. Before companies started operating their own cafeterias, Papa could count on a number of workers from neighborhood factories to eat lunch at his place. Mama placed napkins, silverware, bread, cups and saucers at tables where she knew Olsen's rug makers preferred to sit. She took food orders as soon as they entered and always served meals quickly so their fleeting free time wasn't wasted waiting around for service. Mama never gave slow service. She and Papa missed Olsen's employees when the company's headquarters, showroom and factory moved to the North Side.

After lunch, we washed up and walked back to school with Chris and our friends Jackie and Ethel Friedman, who lived upstairs from Popper's Grocery. The Friedman kids didn't join us for lunch because their Mama kept a Kosher household; hot pork sandwiches didn't fit in. Whenever it was raining, snowing or simply freezing, Mama tried to find a ride for us back to school after lunch, asking this kindness from someone she knew and trusted completely. Our favorite ride was with John, the pieman. "John, it's blow zero outside. Can you please do me a favor and give these kids a ride back to the school? I don't want them to get sick and catch ammonia. School's just few blocks away. I appreciate very much."

"Sure, Mrs. Paul." John, glad to have the Austin Lunch on his sales route, would have taken Paul's kids and their friends to Evanston if it meant keeping the pie account.

"Alright, kids," he instructed while we blew our breaths at each other to see who could produce the biggest puff of frigid "smoke" through our mufflers. "I don't have any seats inside my truck, but you can sit on the floor in back."

In the deep freeze of winter, Chris, Jackie, Ethel, Nick and I were always bundled up by our Mamas and tightly wrapped in wool, like five unshucked ears of corn. Even though our pals, the Friedman kids, ate different foods and anticipated Passover while we waited out Lent and Holy Week, our parents raised us with the same set of rules, high expectations, and strict discipline with a strong emphasis on the preservation of childhood innocence. Our collective Mamas and Papas were poor in money but rich in integrity. Mama came to know Mrs. Friedman because she was her pal Mrs. Popper's sister. The three women spoke in different forms of broken English, but they were able to communicate and agree with each other better than any Washington congressmen of the same party.

We entered the narrow center aisle of the pie truck through slender double doors at the rear. Pies filled the truck's interior, from floor to ceiling, on racks that were specially built to hold pie pans. Delectable, aromatic, freshly baked, uncovered pies lined the walls of the truck in front of, above, and on both sides of us, completely enveloping us in golden flakiness. A little hole on top of each pie allowed us a peek at the luscious fruit baked inside. Papa sold the same pies in his restaurant, but they didn't look as desirable in the pie cabinet at the store as they did amassed inside the tiny truck.

We knew we could examine these delights by sight only; no touching or sampling was allowed. Anyway, our teeth and tongues were safely tucked behind lips sealed shut by wool mufflers that kept out the cold. Our tongues were not even available, to our chagrin, for catching the millions of crytal snowflakes that floated down on us out of the winter sky. Southeastern European mothers simply didn't comprehend the delights of Chicago winters.

Woolen knit hats were pulled down to our eyebrows and itchy, thick scarves reached up to the bridges of our noses, strangling our necks and clamping our mouths shut, all in the name of maternal love. Only our ten bright brown eyes were visible. Pathways for sampling pie were closed off and hands were so deeply stuck into mittens that to hold anything in them was impossible. Nick, Jackie and Chris's eyes grew larger as they inspected the myriad luscious crusts surrounding us. Mouths sealed, Ethel and I remained silent.

"Wha' flavor d'you like best?" The tightly pulled scarf, immobilizing his lips, impaired Nick's pronunciation. "Alla them," was Chris's muffled answer.

As we traveled to school in snow, either on foot or in back of the truck, we spotted kids grabbing on to rear bumpers of passing streetcars, trucks or automobiles for thrilling slides along snowy streets. Dragged along by unaware drivers, childish limbs and young heads perilously approached rolling tires and rear tailpipes. Mama and Papa warned us of instant disaster if we attempted the stunt. "If the car don't run you over—and cut you in half," (Mama knew how to get our attention) "then I'm going to spank until you not able to sit on your behinds for a month." We knew, first hand, this would not make any joy ride worth the risk. As we approached school, John the Pieman checked his truck mirror to make sure "no damn fool kids grab on and then slide under my wheels when I stop. I don't wanna be killin' any kids. I still got pies here to deliver while they're still fresh. Don't you kids do anything stupid like that dumb stunt because it's too easy to get hurt, real bad." John parked, opened the back doors of his truck, and we filed out onto the windy street in front of Brown School remembering to thank him, like our Mamas told us to do, because we looked forward to John's pie truck ride again.

School accounted for the time Nick and I were not in Papa's restaurant, sleeping at home, or at our aunts' homes. We attended Brown Public School on Warren Avenue, kitty-corner from the massive gray Chicago Stadium. To my knowledge, Brown was a peaceful melting pot. Even though unofficial segregation was the norm in Chicago's neighborhoods, Brown was integrated. It felt perfectly normal for African-American students to be in classes with white students of all ethnic groups, from kindergarten through eighth grade. The same was true when I later attended Lucy Flower, the all-girls public high school near the Garfield Park Conservatory.

Nick and I walked four blocks to school, twice each day, in the company of Ethel, Jackie and Chris. We crossed Ogden at Madison, where Pixley and Ehler's Cafeteria filled the corner space. The Reliance Bank had vacated the corner building when it closed its doors, capturing neighborhood money within, at the start of the Depression. Frustrated, furious and terrified neighbors learned the hard way that Reliance was neither reliable nor sturdy, even if it was housed in a stately, granite building that appeared as impenetrable and trustworthy as the Field Museum. A Thom McAn's store sold dozens of unaffordable black and brown shoes for men, on Madison, next door to the cafeteria. Passing the dull array of footwear, we glanced, in an equally uninterested way, at the men's haberdashery that came next. Dark fedoras, moth ball scented wool suits, starched white shirts unsuccessfully jazzed up with ultra-conservative dark ties, bland underwear, and prosaic socks were marketed by a sales force of two serious, but well-dressed old men who stared out the window in high hopes of spotting a paying customer.

Our collective childhood adrenaline didn't start pulsating until we reached the block's last enterprise, the "dime store," a large F. W. Woolworth that took up the northeast corner of Madison and Ashland. No variety store will take the place of those Woolworths we knew before 1960. Housewares, china, toys, sporting goods, candies, tools, plants, paper goods, cosmetics, books, greeting cards, ribbons by the yard, a lunch counter/soda fountain, and so much more were offered to customers for five and ten cents, with few items costing more than a dollar. Products were presented on a human scale with plenty of salespeople to give immediate service. That store was far more user-friendly than today's huge nationwide chain stores featuring hermetically sealed merchandise placed on shelves that only the Chicago Bulls can reach comfortably. Woolworth's, with its distinctive potpourri of "dime store" smells rising off warm salted nuts and lunch counter specials, was "the" store for kids. If there was time, we peered into the windows for thrills.

At Woolworth's, we turned north up Ashland, toward Warren Avenue. The marquee of the American movie theater enticed us from across the street. We thrilled to see glamorously posed movie stars on posters in front of the building. The aroma of fresh popcorn whetted our appetites in the afternoon when we used the "show's" side of the street to return home. A respectable college for chiropractors loomed over Ashland next to the theater, but since it was not in the least fascinating for us, we ignored it, continuing our deep discussion of movie attractions instead. Union Park, the Congregational Church with its tall steeple, and the stately brick and stone Spaulding School, referred to in the Thirties as the Crippled Children's School, awaited us in the distance. At Warren Avenue we crossed Ashland to travel west, passing residences for two more blocks. Some had been elegant, single family brownstones in their heyday, but the arrival of poverty transformed some of them into rooming houses and tenements. A formidable, mahogany colored brick mass, as imposing as the pyramid of Cheops, met us between Hermitage and Wood: Brown School.

Brown's brush with fame was Tad Lincoln's attendance in the late 1860s. After Abraham Lincoln's assassination, his widow, Mary Todd Lincoln, moved to Chicago with her sons Robert and Tad where they lived in a brownstone on Washington Boulevard in what was to become our neighborhood. A plaque affixed to the sturdy brown bricks proclaimed our association with Illinois's most esteemed son, through his own son, Tad. We, Brown students, were proud of our link to American history.

The only benefit I recall of being a poor kid in our school (most of the student body qualified) was free admittance to a circus held at the stadium across the street each spring. Our alderman arranged the freebie for his constituents' progeny, making sure all qualified voters knew of his magnanimity. Nick, our friends and I joyously participated. The first act began in a huge cage filled with a dozen wild animals ferociously opening their mouths to growl and reveal immense, pointy teeth. I prayed for the survival of the lion tamer, dressed as if he was on an African safari instead of Madison Street, praying he would not be torn and eaten as he angrily snapped his beasts into submission with a whip and kindergarten-sized chair. I hoped his growling creatures would not escape their cages to devour the audience, either. My shoulders relaxed and I began breathing again when aggravated tigers and lions were replaced in the center ring by a rainbow of outlandish clowns and the circus band's snappy music.

When elephants the size of Chicago streetcars paraded through the cavernous stadium, bringing a stench that displaced all the breathable air, the entire student body of Brown School held their noses. The elephants seemed like amiable animals, in spite of their monstrous size, and we couldn't help but like them, in spite of their overwhelming stench. After the elephants, acrobats sailed from one tiny perch to another so high above us that we all stretched our necks to watch the breath-stopping daredevils who didn't always reach their swings or platforms in time. Thank God there was a net to catch them. Yearly attendance taught us the finale was near when clowns scattered in comic fear, stadium lights dimmed, and a lone spotlight rested on the immense cannon at the far end of the expansive floor. To our amazement a scantily clad woman shot out. Of course, she always survived, but with fingers stuck in my ears, I wondered how I could survive the stadium-shaking boom—the only sound I knew that was louder and sharper than Papa's angry reprimands.

For years, I thrilled to see those circuses. But by the time I became a high school freshman, I was tired of them; they had become too much of a good thing, courtesy of our magnanimous alderman.

MR. KARAMITSOS

*I*n 1935, unemployment in the U.S.A. fell a percentage point below 1934's levels; 20.7 percent of the work force was still unemployed. Throughout the Depression, men streamed in and out of the Austin Lunch looking for work. Many of them were Greek men who knew the restaurant business inside out. Papa listened to their stories and viewed each distressful account as an important chapter in Depression history. Occasionally a lasting friendship started with a handshake over the white marble counter.

Early one morning, a neat looking gentleman dressed in a gray business suit, crisp white shirt, dark tie and gray felt fedora entered the restaurant carrying a well-traveled, small, black suitcase. He carefully placed it on the floor, close enough to his worn but polished shoes to check its safety with his foot. A case full of diamonds wouldn't have been better tended. Papa noticed the man's green eyes when the new customer removed and parked his hat on the empty stool next to him. Papa stared at the identical sag of exhaustion in his very own eyes every morning when he looked in the mirror to shave. The gentleman was fair skinned with light brown hair, like my father's had been before it started turning gray. He asked for coffee with cream and a sweet roll. When Papa brought him the steaming cup, a brimming creamer, and an apple danish as big as the dinner plate that held it, the gentleman asked, "Need a cook? I'm looking for work. I used to have my own restaurant. I've got lots of experience."

Papa recognized the accent. "You must be Greek."

"You, too?" the stranger asked.

Papa smiled. "And proud of it. But I'm sorry I haven't any work for you. My former partner's my day cook and my brother-in-law takes over at night. They both lost their own places. So, what else is new? I'm Paul Limberopulos. I don't believe we've met." Papa reached over the counter and they shook hands.

"I'm Nick Karamitsos. No, we haven't met. I just moved back to the city from Geneva, Illinois. Ever hear of it?"

"Sure have. What brings you to Chicago?"

"I lost my restaurant."

Papa nodded with understanding. He confided his own predicament. "I wouldn't have this place if my landlord, a *patrioti* (fellow Greek) from my own village, hadn't put off demanding rent for a while. Selling beer and liquor helped. My wife came in here to work to replace a cousin who was supposed to be making five dollars a day. I couldn't even scrape up a buck to pay him. What part of Greece are you from?"

"Peloponnesos, a village outside Megalopolis called Turkoleka. I left in 1906. Nikitaras, the Turk fighter, was from our village. Ever hear of him?"

"Absolutely. He was an Arcadian hero of the Greek Revolution. I'm from Arcadia, too. From Mercovouni—the closest village to Tripolis. I came in 1907. You beat me by a year."

"We're practically neighbors. Megalopolis and Tripolis are pretty close compared to distances in this country. I used to be a section foreman on the railroad, the Denver and Rio Grande. This is a gigantic country. I worked in Colorado, Utah, and Wyoming."

"So you helped build the railroad. Lots of Greeks worked on the railroad."

"I met many. Greeks are in every part of America. In small towns, in big cities—every place there's work. We aren't afraid of work, are we? We know the only way for us to survive is with plenty of sweat, back-breaking labor, and aching feet. Whether we're slaving away in a restaurant, on the railroad, or in the mines, we have to work like mules."

"And it ain't easy," Papa agreed. "When I stopped shining shoes back in 1917, I went to Western Electric in Cicero, Illinois to apply for a factory job because I heard they were hiring immigrants. I didn't realize you had to be Polish, German or Bohemian. I didn't know Western Electric didn't hire Greeks. Period. And I was, after all, just another 'Goddamn Greek.' Factory man took one look at my long last name and said, 'Nothing right now. We'll call you.' I amuse my customers by saying this restaurant here is just temporary work for me because I'm still waiting to hear from Western Electric about a real job." Both laughed and Papa went on.

"I've only been as far west as Kansas City. Worked there for a short time as a hat check boy in the Muehlebach Hotel. That job came between shining shoes and working in this place. I hear Geneva's a nice little town."

Nick Karamitsos sipped his coffee and started sharing his own history. It felt good to be off his feet. "When I first came to America, I worked on the railroad and made good money. I mean, of course, good money for being an immigrant. I wrote the news back to Greece and, sure enough, my father and two brothers came here. I got them jobs on the railroad, too. My father was a watchman. Well, they filled their pockets and went back to the old country. And I came to Chicago to learn the restaurant business.

"I went to Geneva in '28, the year before everything went bad. Opened my restaurant on State Street, in downtown Geneva, right next door to a movie theater. It was a great location. I had the first neon sign in town. The day my *Fox River Cafe* opened, there was a parade in town to celebrate. We were doing terrific business—then the Depression hit me right between the eyes. The WPA finished me off."

Papa was confused. "The WPA?"

"The WPA came to Geneva to fix streets and started right in the middle of town, on State Street, where I was located. They closed off State and that was the end of business for me. Business slowed down as we got deeper into the Depression but came to a complete halt when they closed State Street. It was impossible for customers to get to my place.

"Of course, I couldn't pay Mrs. Johnson, the landlady, so she made me a deal. She and her husband—the pharmacist who ran the corner drugstore—owned the building. Mrs. Johnson suggested I turn my restaurant over to her, as long as there were no customers. Then, when things picked up again and the restaurant made enough to pay rent, she would return my *magazi* (store) to me again.

"So, I cooked all the food for the day, and left her all the equipment, dishes, stove, tables, chairs. I had paid for all of it. I left everything, including the money I had in the cash register. I presented the store keys to Mrs. Johnson and walked home to the wife and kids." He shook his head, "My wife will never get over my leaving money in the damn cash register."

"Never heard from your landlady again, right?" Papa suggested.

"Right. There were no places in Geneva to get a job. How do you pay rent and feed three kids? When it was going good I said 'This is paradise!' I was living in a wholesome small town, renting a white frame house with a big back yard. It was a great place to raise kids. Now we're forced to come back here. My wife has a sister in Chicago, and other relatives, too."

Papa interrupted, "It's good to have family around. My wife has sisters here, too. But, it's almost impossible to find work, Nick. Restaurants have closed by the dozens. Two of my brothers-in-law have lost theirs. I know you're familiar with those tragic stories."

"I know all about it. I spend my days going from restaurant to restaurant carrying my carving knives and flints here in this suitcase. My feet are killing me. I'm lucky to get a job for a day or two, as a substitute. It's impossible to pay rent on time. Sometimes I think we'd be better off if we went back to Greece."

"Nick, when I came to America, I was sure I'd make lots of money, go back to the old country, and live like a king. We were so poor, my father couldn't afford to send me. He borrowed money at thirteen per cent interest to pay for my ticket. And yet, before this lousy Depression started, two of my father's brothers went back to Greece, not once but twice. They made their bundles and lived out their dreams of going back home rich. It wasn't in the cards for most of us. Who expected poverty like this in America?"

A man entered the front door as Nick Karamitsos rose and reached for his hat.

"What do I owe, Paul? You've got a customer, and I got to find a job."

"You don't owe anything. Sometimes I feel like a prisoner in here and depend on nice guys like you to come and give me a social life. Sit down, stay off your feet a little longer. This guy's not a customer. Let me introduce you, Nick.

"This is my cousin, Alkibiades Kallimeras. When he came through Ellis Island, a bureaucrat couldn't pronounce his name. So he gave my cousin a new one. Thanks to his American godfather we call him "Al." We used to shine shoes together and he worked here until I couldn't pay him anymore. But the lucky guy went out and found another job."

Shaking Al's hand, Mr. Karamitsos said his good-byes. "You are, indeed, quite fortunate, Alkibiadi. Sorry I can't stay to chat because I really have to be on my way. I've got a family to support, with no time to waste." Nick lifted his suitcase and retrieved his hat from the stool. "Thanks, Paul. Hope we meet again."

Papa reciprocated. "Al, Nick here is a good patrioti. Make sure you come again, Nick. I'm always here. Where else would I go? Like the counter and the coffee urns, I'm one of the fixtures." It was an inside joke restaurant men understood, and all three laughed. "Sorry I can't help you. Good luck."

With purposeful stride, Nick walked out the door of the Austin Lunch carrying the black suitcase in which he proudly carried the precious tools of his trade. More often than not, the suitcase symbolized a dashed hope, but his scuffed black valise also represented the dignity and assurance that he was, indeed, a master of his craft. It demonstrated he could make an honest living, when given the opportunity. Nick Karamitsos slowed to a weary stride once he was out on the sidewalk. He trudged down Madison Street, like thousands of others, looking for work.

FAMILY TIES

*E*xcept for Mama's sisters' families whom Nick and I visited on weekends while our parents worked, having friends and relatives drop in at the restaurant was the only way we had to visit with loved ones. My parents always offered our visitors food: breakfast, lunch, dinner, coffee, pie. If payment was offered, none was accepted. Uncle Jim Limberopulos was a frequent and welcome visitor at the Austin Lunch.

Stephanos, George and Jim Limberopulos were our paternal grandfather's younger brothers who sponsored Papa and Uncle Bill's U.S. arrivals and gave them their first jobs. Of the three, I only remember bespectacled Uncle Jim. A full head of gray hair, a smartly trimmed but small mustache, portly stature, and expensive three-piece suits gave Jim the aura of success. His distinguished apparel was purchased at Marshall Field and Company's Store for Men. He was married to Koula, a petite, stylishly dressed, refined woman who, more often than not, was attractively attired in fashionable hats from Field's huge millinery department. Jim married her in Greece in 1914 and disembarked at New York with his bride on the snowy New Year's Day of 1915. Koula always recalled the magic of seeing the lights of Manhattan when she first glimpsed America.

Jim, Stephanos and George owned the shoeshine parlors/hat cleaning establishments that had employed Papa, Uncle Bill and their cousins. The three brothers had four siblings who remained in Greece: Papa's father Nicholas (my grandfather) who was the eldest, Ioannis, and two sisters, Maria and Athanasia. An inconceivable family reunion took place in 1912 when Jim and his two partner brothers re-

turned to Greece as part of a volunteer army to fight for their homeland in the Balkan Wars (military conflicts between the Ottoman
Empire and the Balkan League, of which Greece was a member). A
call went out in the American Greek-immigrant community for men
to return and battle the Turks in 1912. Surprisingly, large numbers of
young men from the United States returned, enough for a battalion
from the Chicago community alone. Stephanos, Jim and George returned to Mercovouni as prominent American businessmen, wealthy
enough to pay their own fares. Their parents were proud beyond measure that their loyal, patriotic and successful sons loved Greece enough
to travel thousands of miles to fight for her. It was a high point in
Limberopulos family history. Their father Panagiotis Limberopulos
and mother Asimina (my great-grandparents) slaughtered a fatted lamb.
They prepared a feast to which the entire village was invited to celebrate the glorious return of their sons. In the evening, at the end of
the jubilant feasting, singing and dancing, old Panagiotis, smiling
proudly from his place at the head of the family table, bowed his head
and died. The villagers said it was from overwhelming happiness.

Jim Limberopulos and his wife Koula lived with their three daughters and two sons on the North Side of Chicago, a world away from
our Madison Street address. Their children, considerably younger than
Papa but older than Nick and me, weren't our childhood playmates
like our other cousins. In the Thirties, Sylvia, Theodora and Evelyn
became the first women in our family to graduate from high school
and go to college; Theodora went on to earn her degree from Northwestern University in 1938. Peter and Socrates, known as "Sockie,"
were born after the girls. In those days, a classic and distinguished
name like Socrates was not a mark of distinction in Chicago Public
Schools, but sure-fire fodder for ridicule among classmates who had
"regular" names like "Johnny," "Mary" and "Mike." The Socrates,
Aristotles and Platos I knew were called "Sock," "Art" and "Pete."

In the Twenties, Jim and Koula's seven-year-old Peter was accidentally hit and killed by a driver who didn't see the small boy quietly
playing at the street's curb, in front of his house. The tragedy shocked

and saddened Chicago's Greek community, especially our family. Hundreds of mourners arrived at Jim and Koula's home on Winona Street to pay their respects during the heartbreaking three-day wake. Peter's premature death left his parents and siblings inconsolable for decades to come.

Curiously, we were related to this Limberopulos family through both Papa and Mama, even though my parents were not kin to one another. When our parents met, it was discovered that Mama was related to Koula, Uncle Jim's wife. Koula's mother and Mama's maternal grandmother were sisters. This family connection was vital for Mama and Papa, who lived so impossibly far from their parents and still felt like strangers in America. Uncle Jim was Papa's most respected elder family member in America, and Mama, who took comfort in his warm, amiable nature, looked upon him as a father figure. We were separated from that North Side Limberopulos family by miles and miles of city blocks, and separated by our lifestyles as well: we were their poor relations. Thinking back to the Depression years in Chicago, I can count on the fingers of one hand the people we knew who had a charge account at Marshall Field and Company, and who owned their own home, plus a car. Jim Limberopulos was one of them.

We didn't see them often, of course, because we were mostly stuck in Papa's restaurant. Nick was always thrilled to discover Uncle Jim's enormous, black, seven-passenger Lincoln with jump seats parked in front of the Austin Lunch. You couldn't miss its glistening, ebony finish with silvery chrome that caught sunlight and reflected it on Madison Street like a Fourth of July sparkler. My brother, thrilled by the sight of the stately car, dared to stand on the wide running board to peek in the windows and scrutinize its elegant gray interior and sleek, powerful steering wheel. He zeroed in on each thick, black rubber pedal and every shiny chrome button. As kids, we were thrilled to ride in Uncle Jim's car because riding in any kind of car was rare, let alone riding in a seven-passenger, polished black Lincoln with jump seats. Eventually, in 1937, the Lincoln vied for Nick's attention with the glossy, dark green Cord our cigar store/bookie neighbor, Louie

Drell, parked in front of the Austin Lunch. Nick, we were soon to realize, was car crazy.

In addition to Uncle Jim's visits, we also looked forward to seeing our dear Uncle Al. It was Al who stretched our family ties in America; he was the first to join the melting pot. Al found work in a candy store on the North Side of Chicago after he left his non-paying job at Papa's restaurant. Then he moved out of our apartment to live in a rooming house close to his work. Al made a point of coming to visit us at the restaurant on his day off, and we looked forward to seeing him. He arrived one day in late summer of 1935, while Nick and I were at school. We heard details of the visit from Mama when we were older; she repeated her account of the encounter throughout her life.

Standing at about five-foot-seven or-eight and better looking than Valentino, Al Kallimeras was quiet, almost shy. He impressed the ladies with his slim physique, full head of straight, chestnut brown hair, handsome dark eyes, strong chin, and straight, well-shaped nose. He would assuredly have captured the attention of countless female eyes had he appeared on the cover of a movie magazine. Young, attractive, eligible Greek women wanted to be introduced to him, but he advised local matchmakers that he wasn't in a position to marry yet because he wasn't earning enough to support a wife and family.

"Look who's here. Great to see you again, Al. What's up? You're dressed to kill. "

It was early afternoon; lunch was over, and it was too early in the day for the dinner crowd and drinkers. There were no customers in Papa's store. A minute after Al entered, Mama yanked open the heavy door and marched in. She was muttering under her breath in Greek, "*Mnistheti mou, Kyrie.* (Lord, remember me) I'm going to chase that woman away from this place. Once and for all."

The proximity of former bootleggers, an illegal bookmaking parlor, the Syndicate, and the erratic behavior of customers contributed to a negative electricity that bounced off the drab walls of Papa's establishment. When Mama wasn't smiling, you knew she disapproved of what she was observing.

"Who are you talking to?" Papa teased. "We're way over here."

"I'm not talking to either one of you. I'm talking to God. That no good moocher, Hazel, is back. She's hanging around outside the door. I know she's waiting to pick up some strange, unsuspecting man. She's looking for suckers again. I don't like having that streetwalker around here, and I don't want our children running into people like that in this store. I've got to chase her away. For good!"

"She's bad for your temperament, too, Vasiliki. Did you see Al here?"

"Of course. I'm sorry, Alkibiadi. I'm upset with that woman hanging around outside the door. She has no respect for herself whatso-ever. Look, she's coming inside. The nerve! Let me see what she wants. It's my chance to tell her to go to the devil and never come back. Hah! She's wearing white, like a bride. Wonder what poor sucker bought her that outfit?"

Mama's least favorite customer, Hazel, was standing well inside the doorway. She was a slender woman with dark red lips and well tweezed, arched eyebrows. Her brown, less-than-shoulder-length hair was flatly combed in waves under her white hat, in the fashion of the Thirties. Her reedy figure was attired in a narrow white suit. She was a Depression-tainted, Madison Street version of Wallis Simpson, the American companion of England's young Duke of Windsor. Mama's resolve carried her to the door in a micro-second to challenge Hazel's questionable habits with a well aimed "Who you looking for? It's not nice for womans to hang around like you doing." But Mama heard Al's voice in Greek before she was able to utter the first syllable of her fiery inquisition.

"Wait, Vasiliki. She's with me."

Al was on the verge of blurting an explanation when out of nowhere, Tom Charlas lunged through the front door. He made such a commo-tion, charging past Hazel and Mama, that all four of them froze in place.

"You goddamn bastard! You son of a bitch!"

Charlas's distorted face was red; his Adam's apple bulged with every hateful word. Adrenaline started pumping through both my parents when it looked like trouble was coming through the door, and it didn't take a superior court judge to figure out that trouble had, indeed, arrived. My parents eyed each other, signaling that neither knew what the shouting was all about. Simultaneously, they turned to Al, now pallid and perspiring, who appeared to have confronted the last person on earth that he wanted to see.

Papa innocently approached Charlas. "You trying to be a wise guy, Tom? I've told you before, I don't want you bringing trouble in here. And I don't want to hear your disgusting language eith…"

Charlas pushed Papa aside with an off-handed shove to the chest that almost knocked him to the floor; Papa's glasses flew off. Then Charlas went straight for Al, both his hairy hands aiming at Al's neck, right above Al's new necktie.

"Tom!" Mama tried to distract Charlas, but Hazel simultaneously grabbed Charlas's arm and shoved Al out of his attacker's way with her hip. She dragged Charlas away, and he continued to abuse Al in Greek and English.

"You son of a bitch bastard. You took my woman." He stopped to look at Hazel. "Who da hell do youse t'ink you is? I'm gonna break every bone in dat goddamn body!" Mama and Papa were unsure whether this promise was aimed at Al or at Hazel. "Somebody jus' tol' me you married dis bastard! Izzat true?" Charlas shouted the question at Hazel, and my parents' blood pressure skyrocketed.

"Come on, Tom. Lemme talk to you outside," Hazel ordered. Mama seized the moment to encourage their joint exit. "Sure, Tom. Go outside with Hazel. Calm down and talk to her about what bothers you."

All four were relieved to see Charlas comply so quickly. He moved toward the exit with Hazel, but his eyes were still riveted on Al. He shouted one more threat before the door closed behind him. "If dis is true, I'm gonna kill you. You bastard, I'm gonna kill you!" Hazel's white hat fell off before the door closed behind them.

"Good riddance to both," Mama exhaled in Greek.

"Hey! What's going on, Cousin?" Papa's face was flushed and his voice was shaky.

"Paul…" Al didn't know how to begin so he turned and checked the door to see if Charlas was coming back.

Papa examined the window, too. "She's walking him down to his bar."

Mama repeated, "Good riddance! May they both go to the devil."

Al eyed my parents, sheepishly, like a kid confessing a misbehavior to his mother and father because he knew what he had come to say wouldn't be easy. The emotional exchange was primarily in Greek with English expressions like "moocher," "sucker," "banana oil" "pulling my leg" and "barfly" thrown in for clarity.

"Hazel and I, well, we just came from downtown—from City Hall. Ahhh, well, we just got married," he said, quickly adding, "and we're moving down to Florida."

Mama and Papa stopped breathing and stared at him with disbelief. Papa suffered an invisible stab to his heart and soul more powerful than Charlas's clumsy punch. "Banana oil! You did no such thing. What kind of a joke is this, Al? Why are you pulling my leg?"

"Nothing funny about it, Paul."

Mama's cheeks and ears sizzled and bloomed scarlet while her eyes shot invisible, lethal, arrows at Al. She directed a stinging "WHAT?" at him.

"Yes, Vasiliki," he nodded. Then Al checked the window again.

Mama's eyes bored into him. "Of all the women in the world, all the decent, clean, good Greek girls for you to marry in Chicago—you picked Hazel? What's the hell's the matter with you? Hazel's a streetwalker. I'm trying to get rid of her—like I'm trying to get rid of the scummy rats downstairs in this rotten basement. And you married her?"

Papa picked up when Mama stopped for breath.

"She's a barfly, Al, and worse. Maybe you don't know it. Did you hear Charlas call her 'his woman'? Charlas is no good either. He's a married man with grownup children. He's got no business being with her and she knows he's married. Hazel hangs on him like a feedbag on a horse. She's got other suckers, too. She's absolutely no good."

Eyes turned heavenward, Mama addressed God. "*Mnistheti mou,*

Kyrie" (Lord, remember me). Then she riveted her stare on Al. "You married Hazel? Or you just took out the license? Please tell me you didn't really marry her."

"She'll change, Vasiliki."

"DID YOU HEAR CHARLAS SAY HE'D KILL YOU?," Papa bellowed. His eyes drilled into Al over his spectacle frames. "Charlas is connected with some pretty SHADY CHARACTERS." Then Papa leaned his face directly into Al's and modulated his voice to a whisper. "The mob!" Al and Papa were nose to nose. When Papa's voice got loud again, Al jerked back with a grimace. "You SHOULD be worried. He's serious. Hazel and Charlas were VERY chummy. And I'm not talking platonic."

"Listen, Paul. Hazel and I came here so I could say goodbye. I didn't want to leave town without letting you know. You're my family. We're leaving for Florida in an hour. Hazel was waiting outside for me when you came into the store, Vasiliki."

Frustrated, Mama tore into him again. "How did you meet the woman? Did Satan, himself, introduce her to you? She picked you up off the street, or what? Why in God's name didn't you ask around about her?"

"Vasiliki and Paul, my time here today is measured. I have train tickets in my pocket. What's done is done. I can't afford to miss the train and lose my money. We're going to a new place for a new life. Only the two of you know about this. Charlas won't find out because you won't tell him."

Papa was still bright red. "BANANA OIL! He has sources. Dangerous ones. You're going to wind up stone dead in a river, or floating face down in Lake Michigan, or maybe crippled for life if you're not careful. There won't be enough left of you to have a funeral, and I'll be the poor sap that has to write news of your early demise to your poor, grieving, old father back in the village."

"Paul, when we get jobs, or maybe when Hazel and I can open up a business together, I'll write and tell you where I am."

Papa tried to be calm, but was still glaring at Al over his glasses. "Cousin, I'm going to put it in English words you'll understand. This is a real long shot, a million to one. I'm going to handicap it for you, too, Al. This horse will finish LAST."

"My soul is aching, Alkibiadi, my heart is broken. Your wedding? We should be dancing and eating Jordan almonds. Alleluia on the bum. What have you done?"

"Don't worry, Vasiliki. I have to go. We've got to catch the train. Didn't expect this. Listen, before Charlas can plan my funeral, we'll be gone. Don't worry. But I have to find Hazel."

"For God's sake, how do you plan to do that? You can't go into Charlas's bar. When he promises to kill, Al, he ain't joking. You're not using your head at all. WAIT. There she is." Looking out the window again, Papa cautioned him, "Let's see if she's alone."

After their haranguing, Al tried a defiant, self-assured tone. "I know what to do. I worked around here long enough to know how to be invisible. We'll go through the alley."

"No, no, NO." Papa accosted him again. "Charlas knows all about the back alley. Get away as quickly as possible, but for God's sake, don't use the alley."

"WAIT!" Papa's warning shattered the air. "Let me go first."

Mama and Al watched my father through the window as Papa exchanged words with Hazel. Then he signaled with his arm for Al to go outside.

Al started for the door then turned to look at Mama. "Goodbye, Vasiliki."

"Wait a minute, Alkibiadi. You left her new hat behind."

The snowy hat with its little polka dot veil, innocent victim of the afternoon skirmish, lay stylish but impaired, on the grimy floor. Al paused to scoop it up while Mama checked for Charlas through the window. When she turned to say good-bye, Al was gone, the door shut firmly behind him. Its thud broke Mama's heart.

When Papa re-entered, he found her crying. "*Pos?*" (How?) she asked.

Papa exploded with frustration. "Might never see the guy again and didn't even have a chance to shake his hand."

"I feel so much pain, Paul, like a streetcar has run over me. I'm so sorry for him. She'll look for suckers in Florida, too. She's that type of woman."

"She won't have to look too far, Vasiliki. Al, himself, will be right under her nose. What a chump."

"Paul, evil outside influences can destroy us. I expected Al to marry a good Greek girl, a lady, and he went and found this tramp. I can't understand how she hooked him. Life's all about having common sense and good self-control. Self-discipline is so important. We cannot allow our children to get involved with people who will ruin them."

"We're trying, Vasiliki. All we can do is try."

Charlas's bar, a few doors from Papa's place, didn't last as long as the Austin Lunch. His bootlegging past caught up with him and the City of Chicago permanently shut down Charlas's bar. After that, we lost track of Tom Charlas.

Distance, time and circumstances weakened our relationship with Papa's first cousin and former shoe shining buddy. Yet, Al and Hazel stayed together as man and wife until death parted them sometime in the Sixties. Through the years, we exchanged annual Christmas cards. It was exciting to receive their holiday wishes from tropical, faraway Florida signed, "Hazel and Al."

LIVE MUSIC

Sometimes I wonder if I am the same person you knew.

—Vasiliki to her mother, March 1935

*G*reat American music emerged from the Thirties because so much talent, now classified as legendary, lived on our planet at the same time. Ella Fitzgerald cut her first record in 1935, the same year Gershwin's *Porgy and Bess* debuted. America's most popular recording featured Fred Astaire singing *Cheek to Cheek.* Sigmund Romberg, Cole Porter, Irving Berlin, Oscar Hammerstein, Richard Rogers, Lorenz Hart and many other musicians were writing songs that would still be sung all over the world in the 21st century. Igor Stravinsky guest conducted the Chicago Symphony Orchestra. Besides the ability to "tame the savage beast," music also had the power, momentarily, to lift the downtrodden out of the Great Depression. In 1935, live music debuted, of all places, at the Austin Lunch.

"Guess what, Mama? Guess what? Papa's coming down Madison Street with a piano." I ran into the store to bring Mama the news. She was busy at a barrel tap; her left hand gripped three, thick glass handles, all at once, as her right trimmed off foam with a straight edge made of plastic that advertised "Country Club." It was a motion she repeated so often that Mama probably saw herself filling beer steins and trimming foam in her sleep.

Fifty years later she recalled, "Papa and me we got calluses on our feet from standing twelve, sometimes sixteen hours everyday. On top of it, we got calluses on our hands, too, from steins and schooners we was filling up and carrying from one end of that old store to the other. I could carry three in each one of my hands. Six at one time."

Shouting was out of character for me; I had startled Mama. "What's the matter, Helen?" She often sounded impatient when she was fatigued. It was no time for whining, nagging, or even pleasant conversation. The exhausted "leave me alone" look showed in Mama's face, too. It endured when she longed to be off her feet and someplace else. Seeing that I was unharmed, Mama continued her usual motion of carrying the steins to their final destination. Three day-laborers, sitting on high stools at the new second-hand bar, with faces and heavy denim overalls still encrusted with clay and dirt, waited for foamy refreshment. Mama stared at me, bewildered by what she thought she had heard. "Who's come down Madison with Papa?"

"A piano, Mama."

"I don't know him. What's his first name?"

"Not a person, Mama. A piano! You play music on it."

"Excuse me, that's five cents each one, sirs."

As Mama collected a total of fifteen cents, the front door of the restaurant opened. She stopped, turned and squinted to make out the shapes coming in from outside.

"See Mama. Here's Papa. He's with men pushing a piano down the street. Papa's holding the door open for them. See. It's a piano!"

"My goodoness! Here's come a piano and your Papa, too."

Papa was smiling. "Bessie, look what we got here. Set it up along the back wall, fellas. How do you like it?"

She was too exhausted to be elated. "What's it for? This place? Who's play piano in here, Paul? Nobody know the first thing about play music. Those things cost lots of money."

"Two bucks, Bessie. I couldn't pass up buying a piano for two dollars. I was at an auction looking for chairs. I bought some good cheap ones and this piano, too. Another joint closed down, east of Ada Street. Somebody's trying to pay off his creditors. Here, fellas.

Thanks for the help." Papa paused to tip the two deliverymen. Both enthusiastically shook his hand for the generous silver quarter they each received.

"Some joints around here have entertainment now, Bessie. That guy, Smitty. You know, the customer who sits on the end stool when he eats breakfast at lunchtime. Remember? He's a drummer. He told me music brings more business. That's why I bought the piano for two bucks. It's an investment."

"Is Smitty playing piano? Money is wasted, Paul, if nobody can use the damn thing." Mama was in no mood for Papa's gimmicks.

"Bessie, a woman musician came in last week looking for a job. She told me she sings and plays at the same time but the place has to provide a piano. She can't carry one around like a violin player."

Nick ran out of the kitchen and spotted the new acquisition. "Hey. Where'd this come from?"

"It's our new piano, Nicky. Papa bought it for two bucks. It's just like the one at school." My brother and I immediately began fingering the keys of the scuffed old upright, pretending we were playing music. In an instant, four little hands precipitated a loud commotion.

"My head's exploding from a two-day headache, Paul. More noise in this joint is going to kill me. I can't stand it."

Papa lowered the wooden piece that covered the keys. "Maybe someday you can take piano lessons, kids, but I bought this to bring more people into this joint, not scare away the ones we already got. When nobody's in here you can play with it again, when Mama's feeling better."

Within a week, a trio was bringing live music to delighted customers. Musicians were set up at the back of the store, against the wall that separated the restaurant and bar from the kitchen. Good thing that Papa had purchased more chairs because he needed them to hold additional, music-loving customers.

· Melodies like *Night and Day, How Deep is the Ocean?*, and *You're An Old Smoothie* were standards in the repertoire of Kitty Humphries, an accomplished pianist with a lovely voice. Kitty was accompanied by Smitty on the drums and Raymond Sylvester on the clarinet. Mr. Sylvester, who moonlighted at the Austin Lunch, had come to America from Spain. His real job was performing as the clarinetist for the NBC Orchestra. The trio played regularly at Papa's restaurant, routinely adding new hits like *Cocktails for Two*, *You're the Top*, and *Blue Moon* to their stock of popular songs.

My brother Nick, who was constantly whistling and singing, enthusiastically added new music to his repertoire. *Isle of Capri* was one of his favorites. We became devotees of popular American songs and Tin Pan Alley through the musicians at the Austin Lunch. Tragic, timely lyrics combined with minor strains in the melody of *Brother Can You Spare a Dime?* evoking melancholy and loss. A less remembered song also emerged from the Great Depression:

> *"Oh, why don't you work like other men do?*
> *Oh, how can I work when there's no work to do?*
> *Hallelujah, I'm a bum! Hallelujah, bum again!*
> *Hallelujah, give us a handout, to revive us again.*
> *Oh, I love my boss, and my boss loves me,*
> *And that is the reason that I'm so hungry.*
> *Hallelujah, I'm a bum!"*

Mama began using her own version of a phrase from the song, interjecting the words whenever she felt heavenly intervention was needed. She recognized *Hallelujah* as the *Alleluia* in the church's song of praise, and she knew the slang phrase "on the bum" meant something wasn't working properly. Mama added the words from the Depression song, as she understood them, to the traditional shout of glory. Her rendition turned into "Alleluia on the bum" a "Mama-ism" she repeated when she felt something wasn't going well.

Musicians were each paid a dollar a night. Business increased, even though seating was limited. Customers were content to sit on beer boxes and whiskey cases to eat meals, hear uplifting music, and most of all, relish the camaraderie that accompanied a nickel's worth of beer. The old joint was finally packed with people, and Papa shopped for more used chairs.

Late one Saturday afternoon, five hillbilly musicians came in to ask for a job. Mama watched as Papa explained to them that a trio performed Tuesday through Thursday nights, but that the hillbilly group could play on nights when the trio was absent. The musicians found a dollar per night agreeable, but Mama interceded before Papa had a chance to finalize their agreement.

"Wait, please. One minute, please, fellas." She made one stipulation before they set up their instruments by the piano at the back of the store.

"Yes, ma'am?"

"Remember to put on your neckties before you start to play your songs."

"Neckties? Ma'am we don't got no neckties."

"No siree. You must be wear neckties to play music in here."

Any musicians Mama had ever seen wore neckties. Grown men, no matter how poor, wore neckties, whether they were sitting at the counter in Papa's restaurant or at a picnic in the park. Men by habit and custom wore neckties most of the time. Mama certainly wasn't going to showcase musicians who were not classy enough to wear neckties in her husband's restaurant. Papa had worn a tie and white shirt to work when he was a shoeshine boy. If a bootblack got all dressed up to shine filthy shoes, the very least a musician could do was attire himself in a necktie. "But, ma'am, we're a hillbilly band. Us'n hillbillys—why, we ain't never wore no neckties."

"I don't care if you hilly billys. That's alright with me. I'm not prejudice. I'm Greek. Is that alright with you? But you must be wear neckties to play in here."

"Ma'am, we don't even own neckties."

"Look at everybody in this joint, fellas. Except for workers doing hard jobs like digging ditches, everybody else he's got a tie on. Playing music not like digging ditches."

"But, we're hillbill…"

"I already tell you, it don't bother me that you fellas is hilly billys. I got nothing against your nationality."

"But, ma'am—"

"No siree. Don't start because you are not hire to play here until I come right back. One minute, please."

Mama whispered something to Papa. He nodded and she exited the front door, almost running the half-block west on Madison to our apartment at the corner of Ogden Avenue. She raced up and down three flights of stairs then speeded breathlessly back to the store. Still panting for air, Mama approached the band members and passed out one of Papa's old neckties to each musician.

"O.K., ma'am. We ain't gonna argue. Thar's a Depression goin' on and we need this here job. Boys, this here little lady wants neckties— and we wear neckties." Papa officially hired the group after Mama's dress code was agreed upon. His was the only saloon in Chicago with a "hilly billy" band dressed in dungarees, plaid flannel shirts and neckties.

A year or two later, somebody down at city hall realized city revenues would increase if an entertainment tax was levied on businesses featuring live entertainment. Papa understood that to cover the new city tax he would have to raise prices. Even in good times, Papa feared raising prices would lose him customers.

The entertainment tax brought an end to live music at the Austin Lunch. At the end of the Thirties, a brightly lit red, yellow, blue and green jukebox was introduced. The very old, two-dollar upright piano remained at the back of the store, untuned and unplayed. Still, Mama always tended to it. In the Forties, before Mama began dusting, she had to shoo away Patsy (the cat that adopted Papa) because Patsy preferred the scratched piano top next to the warm kitchen as her cozy sleeping place.

CHILDREN, UNIFORMS
AND CALLUSES

*T*he unexpected was constant in the dim but lively Austin Lunch; having two small children underfoot heightened tension. Nick shared his memory of parental patience lost when he was five or six years old. Desperate for attention, he followed Mama around, tugging at her uniform skirt, whining and complaining. She was so overwhelmed with work that she didn't have time for a private moment with him. But Nick didn't take her "look" seriously. In fact he completely ignored it.

When Papa tripped over him a third time, he grabbed my brother by the arm, dragged him back into the kitchen and pushed him into the large, walk-in cooler. Mama's heart sank when she caught a glimpse of Nick, dumbfounded and dazed, staring out of the cold storage unit an instant before Papa slammed the huge and heavy door to seal him in; the bang weakened her knees. Mama instinctively knew it was best not to contradict an angry, impatient Papa and decided not to free Nick herself. Minutes dragged like hours while she waited on customers, trying to figure out a way to get Nick out of the cooler without undermining his father's authority. Then she remembered Charlie and speedily made her way back into the kitchen with a plan.

"Charlie, please get that kid out of the iceboxi before he's get sick and catch ammonia. My God, Charlie, he can suffocate in there!"

"Don't worry. He's fine, Bessie. Go back to work and I'll take care of it."

Uncle Charlie unlatched the door to the cooler and found Nick crying.

"Well, well, look who's here. Whatchou doin' in here, Nick? Tryin' to cool off?"

"Waaaah! Pa stuck me in here, Uncle Charlie," Nick sobbed.

"Whatever for? A nice quiet kid like you? Well, come on out. Or should I close the door again so you can spend the rest of your life in there?"

"No. No!"

"Then for God's sake, get outta there. I'm not gonna hold the door open for all my ice to melt. Shake a leg. It's too damn hot in here. Why'd your Pa stick you in the ice box?"

"I dunno, Uncle Charlie. I didn't do nothing."

"Maybe because a big kid like you is acting like a great big baby. Listen to that crying. You're making more noise than a vaudeville show. Shame on you, Nicky. You're a big boy now, so for God's sake—shut up and get the hell out of here until your Pa cools off. We all got work to do. There's enough noise in this joint without your nasty bawling. Go play outside."

Disheartened, Nick slouched his way out the alley door, slowly dragging himself to Madison's sidewalk. With a small, makeshift hammer in his hand that he had fashioned from wooden clothespins in his pocket, Nick leaned against the lamppost in front of Papa's restaurant. He was troubled, but singing plaintively, like a Thirties torch singer. My brother never stayed angry or sad for long. He'd snap out of his doldrums, then whistle or sing softly; he still does. That day, a professional photographer, one of Papa's regular customers, spotted Nick on Madison Street leaning back on the lamppost and took a picture. The candid black and white photograph of my melancholy brother and the street lamp still hangs on the family room wall, sixty-five years later.

Nick and I were underfoot at the restaurant more times than can be recalled. I tried to camouflage myself inside a booth and read books when Papa didn't need my services at the cash register. My brother was younger; he thrived on being in the middle of the action. Nick remembers one of those many days after Prohibition at the Austin Lunch when Mama was overwhelmed with customers. The waitress hadn't shown up for her shift. The dishwasher hadn't arrived. And Uncle Charlie complained to her about late coal delivery, as if delivering coal for the kitchen's fuel supply was one of Mama's responsibilities, too.

"Mama. Mama."

"What's the matter, Nicky? You hurt?"

"Mama."

"Hey, Kiddo, what happen to you? Tell me and get it over with. I don't want to hear no more complaints today. I'm sick and tired of them. Can't you see Mama's busy?"

"Vernon hit me."

"Who hit you? And why?"

"Vernon. You know him Mama. He lives around the corner on Bishop Street with his gramma and his Uncle King. Mama, I didn't do nothing to him. He hit me for nothing, but I still want to go out and play with him again."

"Go ahead, Nikolaki. Go play."

"I'm afraid. Maybe he's going to hit me some more."

Mama balanced an immense tray loaded with a mass of dirty dishes in one hand and added to it with the other. Even as she cleared tables of used glassware and soiled china, customers demanded her attention. An order was ready for her to pick up in the kitchen at the distant back of the store. To top it off, a little kid with a runny nose who was feeling very sorry for himself stuck to her like a nasty mosquito. Mama whispered, "*Mnistheti mou, Kyrie*" (Lord, remember me), then issued a command. "Nicky, come back in the kitchen with me."

Mama and her heavy tray arrived in the kitchen first. When Nick reached her, she had put down the dirty dish load and was waiting for him with a stick in her hand.

"Mama, don't hit me. Please don't hit me. I didn't do nothing! Vernon hit ME."

"Alleluia on the bum. I'm not going to hit you, Kiddo. You go back outside and play. If that kid—whatsizname?"

"Vernon."

"Vernor? If Vernor try to hit you again, you take this and hit him first. Period. That's all. Let somebody be afraid of you for a change. But first blow your nose. Take my handkerchief out of my pocket and blow hard."

Nick wiped his nose and reluctantly went outside with his Mama-sanctioned stick. As soon as my brother returned to the alley, Vernon spotted it.

Nick glowered threateningly. "I'm suppose to hit you with this if you try and hit me again. I'm gonna get you first!"

Mama's "enforcer" helped Nick and Vernon settle their differences peacefully. She never realized that her advice echoed Theodore Roosevelt's counsel, "Speak softly and carry a big stick."

I always picture Mama in her uniform when I recall my childhood. She didn't exactly wear it twenty-four hours a day; she wrapped herself in long pink flannel nightgowns to go to bed. The rest of the time, however, Mama wore that uniform, a wrap-around beige dress with a green collar that becomingly framed her face. The combination of beige with green complimented her very dark brown hair and olive complexion. Mama always looked well-groomed in her uniform. She was obsessed with keeping herself spotless and presentable.

Each and every afternoon, when she went home from work to rest, Mama washed her work dress in the kitchen sink with very hot water and a bar of Fels Naptha soap. It took a lot of elbow grease to coax lather out of Fels Naptha. Gripping the fabric with both hands, she vigorously rubbed out greasy spots and dirt that the thick cotton dress had absorbed at the restaurant. She labored at the chore with her teeth clenched and her lips pursed, as if washing that dress meant survival itself. She always dissolved starch into the final rinse water so that when she ironed the dress, it stiffened. After rinsing it out, she wrung it, nearly dry, with a twist that could have crushed a boa constrictor. Mama hung up her uniform on the back porch to dry everyday, except when the weather was bad. Then it hung, dripping, on a clothesline in a corner of the kitchen, over some of Papa's old newspapers.

On most afternoons of the year, Mama's wrap-around work dress, blown by Windy City gusts, floated like a flag in homage to her work ethic. I never thought of it as a flag back then, of course, because it was just Mama's uniform hanging out to dry. But now, more than a half-century has passed, and I see it differently. The indelible image of her uniform blowing in Lake Michigan's winds from a dull gray porch reminds me of that old colonial flag emblazoned with a snake that warned, "Don't tread on me." Like the Star Spangled Banner it resisted and survived. None of us realized then that Mama's unfurled banner, a well-laundered, beige and green work dress, flew in defiance of the Great Depression.

In winter, she dried her uniform by spreading it out on the radiator in our kitchen. The radiator brought steam heat up into our apartment from the immense coal-burning boiler system in the building's dark basement. The responsibility of tending the boiler fell to Mr. Yakaitis, the janitor. Radiators were bulky, grayish-silver, iron contraptions that felt dead cold when they were not conducting heat, and sizzling hot when they did. They added excitement to a room when unexpected hissing erupted into bursts of steam. Those special effects were credited to an internal safety system of sorts.

When Mama finished laundering her uniform, she cleaned our small apartment; once a week she scrubbed the kitchen and bathroom floors during her break from the restaurant. When Nick and I were home on school holidays or in summer, she spent time with us as we helped with housework or watched her doing chores. "When you do something, do it the best you can. Then try doing it even better the next time. No matter if it's washing the floor or cooking or singing, and most especially if it's your schoolwork. Little by little, you are going to get better at doing it. Since you got to do it anyway, and everybody got to work until he die—do your work first class."

Mama was never afraid of hurting our feelings when correcting our efforts. She was as blunt as a shark's jaw. "When did your hands get paralyze? Or was it your head?" "You want to be dummy all your life? Well, don't expeck me to co-operate." "I see your long face. No use being sad because if I don't tell you the truth, who you going to hear it from, the iceman? He don't give a damn about you. See? It's up to me because I'm your Mama. It's my job to criticize you and turn you into a good, clean person. Someday you're going to thank me. Right now you're still too dumb to appreciate it."

When she finally rested from work in the afternoon, Mama stretched out on the old maroon living room couch, purchased in better times, second hand, of course. Twenty minutes later, she was up again. Then she would typically take the still damp uniform off the clothesline or radiator and arduously iron it. Mama always began pressing her work dress by poking the nose of the hot iron around the two large white buttons on the back belt. She finished by carefully smoothing the green collar. The dampness that had soaked into the uniform's thick cotton fabric steamed and sizzled as she ironed. Dozens of Austin Lunch tablecloths, napkins, aprons and uniforms were laundered, weekly, by Mickey's Linen Supply. They charged twenty-five cents to launder a woman's uniform. Mama washed her own to save a quarter.

I remember watching her freshening up in front of the mirror in our small bathroom before returning to the restaurant. An electric light bulb hung down on a black wire from the ceiling above her head. Mama washed her face with a washcloth soaked with lather from a bar of green Palmolive soap, always rinsing afterwards with handfuls of warm water. She rinsed and re-lathered the cloth, washing her neck and arms, and rinsed again. After she scrubbed herself dry with a scratchy clean terrycloth towel, she reapplied a very light dusting of Coty face powder with a worn, pink puff. Then she combed her dark brown hair neatly into the bun at the back of her head, put on her freshly washed uniform, and returned to the restaurant. In Mama's life, even much needed repose was integrated with labor.

Washing her uniform was one of two rituals Mama performed as a result of working at Papa's restaurant. The other was trimming the painful calluses that formed on the balls and heels of her feet from spending so many hours on them. For good support, Mama religiously wore Red Cross shoes to work everyday. They were black chunky oxfords, which she tightly secured to her feet with "shoestringia." Mama believed in good shoes that firmly supported the foot. She said her Red Cross oxfords provided the support she needed for long hours of walking from the kitchen, at the back of the store, to the front counter which was almost out on Madison. Serving customers from morning to night killed her legs and feet. It's no wonder that Mama suffered from deforming arthritis in her knees later in life.

Despite her sturdy shoes, Mama suffered from calluses. So she regularly took a single-edged razor blade and attacked the thick, amber colored growths on the soles and heels of her feet, systematically slicing away layers of hard skin. I dreaded watching her self-inflicted surgery. She always kept a small bottle of crimson iodine nearby in case she cut herself by mistake. When she did, she would dab on some iodine, cover the cut with a wad of tissue, then put on her hose and shoes and go back to work. She performed the ritual for years, switching to bright red merthiolate when she heard it worked better than iodine.

Mama's day began at six o'clock in the morning when she woke and got ready to go to the restaurant to serve breakfast. When Nick and I came from school at noon, Mama was still working. If she was lucky, she went back up to our apartment around two in the afternoon to wash her uniform, do housework, and catch a few minutes of rest until four-thirty when she returned to the restaurant. Mama worked through the dinner shift, until about eight at night. When bar business increased, she stayed much later, sometimes returning home on Saturday night at two in the morning.

With this work schedule, it was no wonder Mama had calluses.

TEGEA

"*O*ur Tegea is specialist in growing two kinds of cherries," Mama boasted in her eighty-first year. "Sweet ones and sour ones. The sour cherries, they call them '*visina*,' are terrific, too. You add sugar and you cook wonderful preserves, with a delicious syrup. When your aunts and me was growing up, we don't see too many desserts like you eat in this country. No candy bars, no pies and cakes. Just during the holidays, if we was lucky, we eat a couple Greek cookies that our mama bake. So in the summertime, when the fruit turn ripe and sweet, we was getting our fill. For us, cherries, both sweet and sour, was what you call "gourmet" dessert. The best." Then she reflected on my siblings' visits to Greece with their families that summer of '84. "Too bad the kids missed seeing the trees full of cherries when they was in Tegea this summer. It's really something to see. Beautifool. Unforgettable. And they came home too soon to eat the tasty apples and most delicious grapes in the world.

"Helen, I got a good idea. Open the jar of cherry preserves your cousin Eleni from Tripolis send us with the kids so we can have a little taste of Tegea ourselfs today. Bring a couple of glasses cold water, too."

If Tegea ever had a Chamber of Commerce, Mama deserved to be its president. Perhaps then it would be as famous as Athens, even Paris. Tegea, too, has chestnut trees blossoming in April, and cherry trees for which Mama's favorite Arcadian township enjoys regional fame. In spring, its villages are exquisitely dotted with small orchards of stunning white blossoms, blushing with the slightest whispers of pink. The delicate flowers contrast with the rough, red tile roofs and graying stucco of village homes.

After sixty-three years of living in America, Mama was still proud of Tegea and fond of the modest house by the ruins of Alea Athena's temple where she was born. My mother and her sisters glorified the place. Their nostalgia instilled it with so much life it seemed immortal. My brother, many cousins and I, immersed in Chicago's inner-city version of the Great Depression, thought that *Papou's* (Grandpa's) house, surrounded by fruit trees, grapevines, ancient ruins, lambs and donkeys, must have been paradise. I couldn't fathom a town without sidewalks.

We called it Papou's house even though it also belonged to *Yiayia* (Grandma), too. Men tend to dominate Greek possessions. Our grandfather, Dimitrios Krilis, was born in the house, sometime before Abraham Lincoln became President of the United States. It became our grandmother's home when she married him and remained so until she died in 1947. Our Yiayia, Eleni Tsirikou Krili, had been born in Piali, too. Papou was a widower with two children when she married him. She gave birth to his eleven additional offspring in the house, which was overrun with their children in the late eighteen hundreds and early years of the twentieth century. Even though by 1984 it was a wreck, in Mama's memory it remained a lovely homestead.

"Just a little stone fence separates our house from the temple of Alea Athena. They call the temple 'ancient' because it's too, too old. Just the pieces is left. We have a nice house. Alloways neat and clean. The sweetest grapes in the world is growing on a grapevine around your Papou's house. Some of those bunches of grapes is bigger than your head. Papou's grapevine was growing and spreading over our porch like a roof. It give us cool shade in summer and beautifool grapes in Octomber, the best in the world. Sweet as sugar. So sweet, you can never forget them."

The Chicago branch of the Krilis family sprouted and started to grow after Mama and her siblings left the tiny house at the beginning of the twentieth century. In addition to Konstantinos (Kostas), the son in America, Papou Krilis had one remaining male child in Greece, Nicholas. There would have been nothing left of Krilis property for

Nicholas to inherit upon Papou's death if all seven daughters had been dutifully provided with adequate dowries. Sending the unmarried daughters to America, where they could be married without dowries, was the family's bittersweet solution.

Listening to stories about Tegea, Piali, Grandpa's house, and the people who lived in it, had been delightful entertainment for us when we were kids. Without even a radio of our own to grab our attention, we took pleasure in our adult loved ones' tales about Greece, both real and mythological. Besides seeing an occasional movie or listening to the radio at the Jones's apartment, hearing Papa explain the past in plain words that even we could understand was our fondest entertainment. Mama always reminded us that her Peloponnesian village had been part of a great city-state in ancient Greece. Its tough and exalted history made Mama proud to be called a *Tegeatissa* (woman of Tegea). The ancient ruins in Piali are the remains of the fifth century temple to Alea Athena, built during the Golden Age (approximately 594 B.C. to 429 B.C.). Alea Athena's temple is not as large, well-preserved, shining white, erect, and dramatic as the Parthenon in Athens. In fact it's in shambles. Yet those of us who have our roots in Tegea are proud of our classical wreck.

Tegeans are as fiercely attached to their birthplace as are the Spartans, the Athenians and the Irish from County Cork. Tegea was as inexorably tied to Mama's psyche as Mercovouni was to Papa's, and as Brooklyn is to die-hard Dodger fans. Unlike many landlocked villages of southern Greece, the tiny hamlets of Tegea are not rocky and mountainous, but located in a relatively flat, fertile valley surrounded by mountains. Orchards of fruit trees, grown as cash crops, do much to beautify the Tegean landscape all four seasons of the year. Even though our family is still in the habit of calling it "Piali," Mama's village is officially called "Alea." The name was changed at the beginning of the twentieth century.

Papa explained it well. "They wanted to wipe out all Turkish names forced on Greek places during four hundred years of Ottoman Turkish occupation. To give you an idea of how long that was, the Turks had taken over Greece by 1456, almost forty years before Columbus discovered America. It took until 1832 to get rid of them, and the Greeks had to fight a bloody revolution to do it. In fact, the last piece of Greece to get out from under the Turkish yoke was Crete, and that didn't happen until 1913. That was six years AFTER I came to America. This enslavement of the Greeks began before Columbus and ended after I left Mercovouni to discover America myself. Four hundred years of having those—Turks…" (Papa never said "damn" but I always got the feeling he wanted to when he talked about the Turks) "…telling us Greeks what to do and torturing or killing us when we didn't follow orders. All of this was going on in our own homeland. ON OUR OWN SOIL, not theirs. Certainly names like Ibrahim Efendi and Piali were horrible reminders of the Turks. Hundreds of Greek villages officially changed their names, but sometimes the old names stick and locals still call a village by its old name, Turkish or not.

"Alea, the new name for Mama's village, comes from Aleos, the name of a very ancient Greek king of that area. This king lived way, way back in antiquity. His name was King Aleos, just like the king of England is called King George. Well, during the Golden Age they named the temple in Tegea 'Alea Athena' to give credit to the old king and at the same time to honor the goddess, Athena. Athena was a popular gal with all the ancient Greeks so lots of temples have got her name on them.

"Tegea has been around for a very long time. Homer wrote about it in *The Iliad* and said it was one of the Greek city-states that sent an army to fight in the Trojan War. You know how long ago that was? History experts say the Trojan War took place about 1200 B.C. That's so long ago, it's even possible that Moses, from the Bible, was still alive in his part of the world when the Trojans and the Greeks were battering each other at Troy. That shows you how long Tegea has been around.

"Tegean armies showed up at almost all the important Greek wars. Powerful forces, like the ancient Persian armies, like the Ottoman

Turks, and like modern day Nazi Germany have been trying to take over Greece for thousands of years. You hardly ever hear anybody talk about the old Persian Wars anymore. If you're lucky you'll learn about them in history classes in high school. But those old Persian Wars had a big impact on the civilization we know about now. Our life is the way it is now thanks to the outcome of the Persian Wars. Those dusty old wars stopped the east from taking over the west, way back when.

"The ancient Persian Empire tried to conquer the ancient Greeks by taking over pieces of Greek land, little by little, until they'd have the whole kit and caboodle. But we Greeks kept fighting them off. That's what the Persian Wars were all about: a series of great battles fought, over many, many years, to stop the Persians from taking us over. A real famous one was fought at a place called Thermopylae (480 B.C.) where Tegeates died alongside the Spartans. But we lost at Thermopylae. You see, the Persians were smart and brave, too. On top of it all, they had a terrific army. There were tens of thousands of Persian soldiers. That's why they were so hard to defeat. But, we won the battle at Marathon. It took place in a town called Marathon about twenty-six miles from Athens. That triumph, by the way, inspired our modern Olympic sport, the Marathon. It was followed by a sea battle at a place called Salamis where the ancient Greeks wiped out the ancient Persians. The Greeks strategically trapped the whole Persian navy in a narrow strip of water so they couldn't get out. It finally looked like it was all over for the Persians, but they were hard to shake off. Greece looked too good to them.

"Here's where the Tegeates came in again. The last major land battle took place at Plataea, on a plain in the Greek province of Boeotia, far north of our Arcadia. The Greeks wiped out the Persian army once and for all time at Plataea. Real brave soldiers from Tegea and Sparta started a slaughter that so terrorized the Persian general, that he died in battle. Tegeates are proud that their army played a vital role in bringing the Persian Wars to an end.

"Here comes the good part. With the Persians out of the way, there was time, money and energy for the Greeks to develop western civilization. That's what they were best at. Instead of fighting wars, Greeks had time to think up terrific ideas, like democracy. Democracy started in Greece. It's a Greek word. With the Persians gone, the Greeks built the Parthenon and the other buildings on top of the Athenian Acropolis. They built them out of marble to replace the wooden ones up there that the Persians had burned down. And down in Tegea, around that time, the temple of Alea Athena was built. This was an extra special time in the world's history. Outstanding. It's known as the Golden Age of Greece. It took place about 450 years before Jesus was born. That's when the Greek philosophers asked all their smart questions and got people thinking better than they ever had before. Plays were written way back then that are still acted in theaters today. After more than two thousand years, they still keep audiences entertained. Will they say that about Andy Hardy movies two thousand years from now?"

Mama's and our aunts' closest encounter with the illustrious Golden Age of Greece was through their proximity to the remnants of Scopas's temple of Alea Athena as children. (Scopas was a renowned 4th century B.C. architect and sculptor, famous for expressing emotion in marble.) When archeologists weren't there digging, the ancient site served as their childhood playground. From the back wall of their home, they curiously watched French archeologists carefully excavate and measure the ancient, gray stones and fallen columns. Mama said it was especially exciting to watch the comings and goings of fashionably dressed Europeans who visited. She remembered her old playground with a smile and a wink. "Ladies in beautifool long dresses and fancy hats with feathers and flowers was coming to Piali from France. Good looking Frenchmans in good suits and tall black hats was coming to see the ruins in back of our house. But, when the fancy visitors finally went away, it was the best place for us kids to play hide and go seek."

The ruins were the cultural and historical pride of Piali, as was their museum. At the beginning of the twentieth century, the economy of Greek villages was based on a never-ending struggle to eke out a meager living by farming worn out and unyielding soil. Ancient sites, that abound in Greece, were ignored by struggling farmers, even when they were a part of their own landscape. Few villages boasted of having a museum. Knowing Papa's fascination with ancient history, Mama proudly reminded him that she came from a village "with class—because it has a museum."

Mama never forgot the hysteria in her village when thieves stole Scopas's marble head of the goddess of health, Hygeia. She was the prize of their ancient site and the jewel of their little museum. At one time, Hygeia had been a complete and exquisite statue of a woman symbolizing health in the pantheon of ancient Greek gods. Conquerors, uncompromising nature, and the intervening centuries have taken their toll on her. In the early years of the twentieth century, some covetous city slicker, with an eye for pretty heads and sophisticated knowledge about priceless antiquities, kidnapped Hygeia in the dead of night from Piali's unsecured village museum. Papa enjoyed Mama's special way of combining two events from her childhood into one story, which she related comfortably in Greek; one involved the museum and the other a renowned natural phenomena.

"There was as much commotion when they stole Hygeia as when villagers heard that Halley's Comet was going to crash down on us. I was a little girl then…" (Mama didn't know the year, but all the books say 1910) "…and I remember the horrifying noises that penetrated our house one night during the weeks when the comet was expected. Frightening sounds roused all of us from sleep, and my poor, terrorized father gathered Mother and all of us children together, not really knowing how he could save us from extinction. Running behind us, he steered us out of the house, like a moving herd of sheep, into the village street. There, we found similarly terrified neighbors. It was the only time in my life that I ever saw my father panic. I don't know where he thought we could escape to. But I do remember how enraged and embarrassed he and our neighbors became when they learned high-school-aged pranksters had terrorized us all, taking advantage of our fear and ignorance about the comet by making the awful commotion in the silent, middle of the night by banging pots and pans together and shouting, 'The comet is falling! The comet is falling! We'll all be destroyed!'

"Piali survived the comet and Piali survived the theft of Hygeia when she was stolen in the middle of the night. The morning after, news spread through all of Tegea and everyone was shocked and outraged. 'They've stolen our Hygeia!' 'Scoundrels have robbed us of our beautiful head.' It took weeks for Tegeates to calm down. When Hygeia was finally found, they didn't bring her back to us. The poor thing has to live in Athens now." (She can be found, securely under glass, in the Archeological Museum.)

Happy times in Piali came back to Mama during the drudgery of work at the restaurant, or in her rare, quiet moments alone, and always when she was in the company of her beloved sisters. Both Mama and Papa enjoyed sharing with each other, and with us, their memories of family in Greece and village life. Both were so proud of their *patrida* (fatherland) that, although they deeply loved America, their adopted patrida, there was an umbilical cord of the heart, never cut, which connected them to Mercovouni and Piali. The two village names have been in my vocabulary since birth.

We used to tease Mama by asking who appointed her Tegea's unofficial ambassador to America when she continually reminded us about its fine cherries, good people, and status as a great ancient city-state. Mama believed that next to the United States, Tegea was the finest place on earth. She even bragged about their abundance of wells that provided a never ending water supply, allowing Tegeates to grow better crops and keep cleaner homes. Ample water in a hometown has always been a great source of pride for Greeks. At this point, Papa would interject that Tegeates had their township's Lake Taka to thank for their water and that Tegea would have been nothing without it because Taka's underground water table continually supplied Tegean wells.

Papa was fascinated with the subject of fresh water because he was obsessed about the severe shortage of it in his Mercovouni, only eight or ten miles northwest of Tegea, on the other side of Tripolis. He always reminded us of how lucky we were to live in Chicago with Lake Michigan for a backyard and a source of water that never ran dry.

Papa loved history; he read it, discussed it, and reveled in it. Tegea's glorious past was always of special interest to him and while Mama imparted her hometown pride, Papa supplied the historic details.

"I told your Papa so many times that he should have been a perfessor because he know so much about all that stuff. Too bad we got no choice for a job except to be slaves in a rickety old restaurant."

FAMILY ROOTS

Venerable father, send Thanaso here to America.

—Kostas Krilis to his father, March 16, 1911

By 1935, the sale of beer and liquor brought longer weekend work hours, but also actual profits. The Austin Lunch filled with customers on Friday and Saturday nights, and our parents worked to exhaustion. We began seeing more of Mr. Prevolos, who was pleased to be collecting rent again, including installments toward back money we owed him.

Charlie and Pete were paid more per day and, with enough reminders from Mama that she was "working for nothing," Papa began giving her ten dollars a week, which she saved, of course. When anyone asked what she did with her meager earnings, Mama replied it was her business. "I'm saving my pay for good uses. Period. I'm not feeding damn horses, that's for sure." In the late Thirties when the Depression appeared to be over for our family, the first purchase Mama made with her savings was a set of Noritake china that she used for holidays and graduations. Unmatched, re-cycled, thick restaurant cast-offs made up our set of everyday china. Purchased from Wieboldt's Department Store at Ashland and Monroe, the "good dishes" included twelve six-piece place settings, one large platter, two serving bowls, a cream pitcher, sugar bowl, and even a soup tureen. Mama paid thirty-seven extravagant dollars for the entire set. The creamy Noritake china set, with its green background, deep yellow border, and pink floral accents, continues to grace our china cabinet. I still use it for special occasions.

Having two children underfoot, installed in the back booth or stuck in the kitchen until two in the morning, wasn't what Mama and Papa considered good parenting. They didn't want us upstairs in the apartment, a half block away, without good adult supervision, either. Sometimes Mr. and Mrs. Jones spent Friday and Saturday nights with us until Mama came home, exhausted but there.

On weekdays, after school and until Mama came home at night, we spent hours in the restaurant, doing homework and chores. Sometimes we were allowed to play on the sidewalk in front of the restaurant or in the back alley with our friends who lived on the same block. Mama's rule was that we had to remain well within our parents' voice range. "I'm not going to be hollering all over Madison Street for you. I'm not an opera singer. Stay close."

Neither my parents nor Mama's sisters or brothers-in-law owned a car or real estate. Even though each of them longed to buy a house with a backyard for a garden, none of them could afford one. Economic circumstances demanded we live in the least expensive housing available, and we all lived in low-cost apartments. Still, my parents respected and cared for the rented space they lived in because it was home, plain and simple; landlords were spoken of in polite terms.

Mama and Papa always reminded us to be considerate of our neighbors. "Don't yell! What will our neighbors think of us?" "Stop running! The lady downstairs is sick." "Keep quiet! The baby next door is taking his nap." "Don't touch that! It doesn't belong to you." "Pick up that piece of paper and carry it to the garbage can. What do you think this is, a barn?" By example and admonition, children were taught to be respectful of landlords, neighbors and property, even when it was not your personal possession; we had few personal possessions.

Most of our weekends between 1933 and 1938, however, were spent in the company of our four aunts, Mama's sisters, whom we loved to visit. There were no others our mother trusted more with the care of her children than her sisters. We always called our aunts "Thea," usually referring to our uncles in English as "Uncle," perhaps because these men all spoke and understood English. Greek-American children slipped back and forth between both languages. During our visits to their homes, our aunts regaled us with family history for entertainment and to keep us in touch with our extended family abroad, just like Mama and Papa did. I wish I had written all of it down because so many details are lost forever now. What is it the Pennsylvania Dutch say? "Too soon old, and too late smart."

Our aunts spoke to us about their brothers and sisters who died tragically in very early childhood. Our grandparents suffered the loss of four children, aged six, four, two, and nine months, within a forty-day period, during a diphtheria epidemic that infected Greece unmercifully during the last decade of the nineteenth century. The devastating deaths caused our grandparents to be even more loving and protective of their children who survived and those yet to be born. Perhaps this tragedy precipitated the strong desire to nurture that was characteristic of each member of the Krilis family: our grandfather, Dimitrios, our grandmother, Eleni, and their children: Konstantinos (known as Kostas), Athanasia (called Thanaso), Aphroditi, Politimi, Nicholas, Vasiliki (that was Mama), Anastasia (Tasia), Garifalia, and Stamata. Nicholas and the two youngest sisters, Garifalia and Stamata, never emigrated from Greece.

Thanaso and her older brother Kostas were children from our Papou Krilis's first marriage. Mama and our aunts often related the story of how our grandfather married our grandmother. Grandpa's first wife, Garifalia (he named a daughter from his second marriage in honor of his first wife), lay sick and dying, but aware that a neighbor girl, Eleni Tsirikou (our grandma-to-be), kept watch over the two Krilis children as they played in the village streets during the months of her illness. Knowing she was soon to die, Garifalia suggested to her husband that after her death he marry the caring Eleni. She wanted her tiny children to be brought up by someone who already showed affection for them. After Garifalia died and a year had passed, Papou asked Eleni's mother and brother for her hand in marriage.

Eleni may have shown compassion for the two small children, but our future grandma didn't want to have anything to do with our future grandpa. She was eighteen years old with no interest in marrying an "old" widower, except that she wasn't in a position to make that decision. Her father was dead and a dowry large enough to satisfy a younger, unmarried man was difficult to provide. Eleni's brother Panagiotis and mother, Stamata Tsirikou, prodded her into marrying Dimitrios Krilis. Thanaso was two when her father remarried, and never remembered a mother other than Eleni; Kostas was six and resented another woman taking his mother's place. When he was old enough, probably in his teens, he found an opportunity to emigrate and went to Chicago where his first cousins lived and worked.

Decades later, when the family had settled in Chicago, Thanaso was looked upon as sister-matriarch by her female siblings. She was widowed early in her marriage. Our cousins Ann, Helen and George were orphaned when their father unexpectedly died of pneumonia in 1928, while our aunt was still in her thirties. Thanaso's husband's death was the first great tragedy to hit the family here in America. The task of running her husband's South Side shoeshine parlor fell on a sheltered Greek immigrant woman, who spoke no English, wore widow's weeds for years, and who was left with the responsibility of raising three small children in a male-centered American society, still very foreign to her. George was three when his father died, but his kind-hearted mother could not bring herself to explain his father's absence, so for several years the child was told that his father went to Greece for a visit.

Soft spoken and gentle Thanaso, the tallest, quietest and slimmest of all the sisters, lived at 35th and Wallace on the "far away" South Side in a flat above a candy store, which we found terribly exciting even though money was rarely available for sweets, even the penny variety. Since going to their house was an all-day excursion, we were rarely sent there. When we did go, Nick and I left home very early in the morning and returned after dark. Our cousin Ann rode streetcars to the West Side to pick us up, and Nick and I rode back to her house with her. Following the return trip, Ann stayed overnight with us and returned to the South Side the next day. Thirty-fifth and Wallace was a short distance from old Comisky Park at Thirty-fifth and Shields. Although we couldn't afford to go to baseball games, we could spend an exciting afternoon outside our aunt's house watching all the people walking to and returning from the White Sox games. People-watching was an absorbing, cheap diversion when we were kids.

More excitement awaited us when we walked with our cousins through a spooky, two block-long viaduct tunnel to the Case-Moody Pie Company. When we arrived at the factory, cousins Ann and Helen bought a delicious pie at the outlet store, and we excitedly carried the delicacy back, again traveling speedily through the long and scary tunnel. The adventure ended by enjoying pie together. It didn't take much to keep us entertained, and the ever-watchful parents and adults in charge of us made sure our fun was ethical, moral, lawful and cheap, very cheap. We were the offspring of parents who had never been entertained as children. If we had only one toy, Mama and Papa reminded us they never had any. It took very little to keep us happy as kids, not because we were dim-witted, but because we were unsophisticated and poor. We drew childish enjoyment, cheaply and creatively, from our immediate surroundings. Of course, the whole family derived enjoyment from good food, sparingly during the Depression and in greater abundance after.

During the Thirties, when they were barely in their teens, all three of Thanaso's children found jobs and worked hard to help their widowed mother. The candy store building where they lived was located next door to a factory that provided jobs during the Depression for Helen and George. Ann traveled on several city buses, five days a week, from 35th Street to Grand Avenue and Austin on the Northwest Side to her job at the Zenith Corporation. Zenith was a radio factory in those days. When Americans started buying radios, Zenith needed workers to produce them, and Ann was pleased to be hired, regardless of the daily commute.

Coming from such a large family, Mama and her sisters were accustomed to being involved in family life, seeking advice from one another, and heeding such counsel. They were comfortable with the hierarchy of respect that was owed to the family's elders, including older siblings.

By the fall of 1984, all of Mama's siblings in Chicago had died, but she remembered them daily. A letter she dug out of the old burlap sack with her yellow rubber gloves surprised and fascinated her, then inspired memories of a very special family celebration that had taken place in 1912.

"Look here, Helen. My oldest brother, Kosta write this letter in 1911. He write and ask my father to send Thanaso to America. How about that? I never know this before. But I guess my papa didn't go for it because that's not how Thanaso got here."

The letter written by Kostas, Papou's eldest child, was mailed to our grandfather from Chicago in March of 1911, asking him to send Thanaso to America in the company of Tryphonas Krassakos, a man they knew well. Kostas's intent was to marry off Thanaso in America, but Papou did not follow his son's advice because Thanaso was still in Greece in 1912 when she married Jim Koliveras.

Koliveras was introduced to Mama's oldest sister in Greece following his first trip to America, at the turn of the century. He and his brother had been partners in a shoeshine parlor (Ellis Island records show Youngstown, Ohio as his U.S. residence prior to 1912), but Jim decided he missed Greece too much to live in America. He sold his share of the business and returned to the old country to buy land, marry and settle down in his native village for the rest of his life.

In the strongly patriarchal Greek society of that era, a prospective bride's mother was not expected to be included in the traditional pre-matrimonial meeting. Grandma Eleni would not participate in the primary introductions of the eligible man interested in the step-daughter she loved as much as the eleven children she had given birth to herself. Being left out of the loop, however, didn't prevent Grandma from advising her husband and eldest daughter as they set out atop Papou's horse-drawn wagon to meet the suitor in Tripolis.

"Thanaso, if, for any reason, you don't like the man, quietly whisper to your father that it's time to go home. Father will then know you aren't interested in marriage with the American. You hear that, don't you, Dimitri?"

During the formal introductions at Thanaso's aunt's house in Tripolis, Thanaso and Jim only exchanged hellos. She helped her aunt serve traditional sweets, certainly Tegean cherry preserves, Greek coffee, and glasses of cold water to their guests, while her father and the younger man conversed together. Thanaso never suggested to her father that it was time to go home. Grandpa liked Koliveras, interpreting Thanaso's silence as approval and, without consulting the prospective bride, the two men agreed on a marriage. Mr. Koliveras said he would not negotiate a dowry, accepting whatever Papou wanted to give. Koliveras was an authentic U.S. citizen and in America dowries were neither expected nor given. Papou, however, gave Thanaso a dowry because in those years to marry her off in Greece *apriki* (without a dowry) would have brought shame upon him and his family. Thanaso's stepmother, sisters and brother did not meet the bridegroom until the formal engagement in their home the following week. The bride herself did not see her future husband for a second time until her own betrothal, appropriate for a Greek bride-to-be in 1912. As Mama reminded me, "There was no such thing as dating." The week between Thanaso's introduction to Jim and their betrothal was quickly consumed by cooking a great feast and preparing for an engagement party to which the groom could bring any number of guests; the hosts would not know the number until everyone showed up. Mama was nine years old when Thea Thanaso was betrothed, and she loved remembering the event.

"We was working all week making sweets. Remember, we didn't have no electric Mixmasters. All the beating was done by hand. We was whipping butter for hours, whipping so hard with our shoulders and arms in such pain that we was ready to fall down and faint because the butter had to be light and fluffy.

"Your Yiayia and Papou, *Aionia tous i mnimi* (May their memory be eternal), kill almost all the chickens and rabbits we had running around our yard. They kill the pig, too, for the celebration dinner. Yiayia cook them all in the big clay oven she had outside in our yard. We make big loaves of bread in round shape, like a circle. Had to sweat to make good bread, kneading and kneading long, long time. Need lots of wood. Oven was working night and day. We had lots of potatoes in our village because we grow them there. We roast pans and pans of potatoes with lemon and good olive oil that Papou bring from Sparta.

"Your Papou was a farmer but he was a merchant, too. He was like a traveling salesman. He let Yiayia be in charge of the fields and every week from Thursday morning to Sunday afternoon my Papa travel back and forth from Tegea to Sparta with his horse and wagon. He go as far as Hrissafa in Laconia. Laconia is a state in Greece, like Illinois is here. Sparta's in Laconia state and our Tegea is in Arcadia state. Down in Sparta, he trade the stuff we grow in Tegea like potatoes, lentils and garlic for olive oil and beautifool lemons and oranges and other things they grow in Sparta, but that we can't grow in Tegea. We use everything we had for the big party."

Thanaso's engagement was the most memorable event of Mama's childhood.

"We had big doings going on, Kiddo. Boy oh boy! Was lots of excitement at our house. Big day finally come. Our whole family, Mother, Father, my Yiayia Tsirikou, aunts and uncles and all us kids, we wait outside the big wood door that open up into our courtyard from the street. Us girls, we can't wait to see who was the bridegroom our Papa pick out for our big sister. Then, boy oh boy, black carriages start coming down the road from Tripolis into Piali. The busynessmen and politicians in Tripolis hear that Koliveras make lots of money in America and they want to do busyness with the "American." Koliveras, he invite them all to come to his engagement party. Well-dressed people start getting out of the carriages in front of our house—even big shots with tall black hats.

"I couldn't see nothing. Who's the bridegroom? I couldn't see nobody because all the tall grownups was in front of me. So I get down on my hands and knees and I crawl under all the legs and long skirts that was blocking me. When I look up, I see I'm in the front, right between my mama and my papa. They was standing at attention, all quiet, serious, waiting for the bridegroom like he was the King of Greece. My Yiayia Stamata Tsirikou, may God rest her good soul, she see me on the floor and she bawl me out. 'Where you going, Vasiliki? Not nice for girls to crawl on the floor under everybody's legs like that. Shame on you!'

"I stand up between my mother and father just in time to hear my mama whisper a question to my papa, 'Is he the one?' She try to pick out Mr. Koliveras in the big group because she don't know him yet.

"My father stand still, just like a statue. He shake his head little bit to say 'No.'

"'Is it the man with the tall hat?' I hear my mama ask him.

"Again, my papa just shake his head, 'No.'

"'Which one is the bridegroom?' My mama couldn't stand not to know who is it.

"My father finally point to a short man with reddish brown hair. My mama took one look at him and say, 'Dimitri! You pick out that little short guy for our beautiful Thanaso?'

"Before I know it, I see my father slap my mother on the face. I was shock! Everybody was so busy looking at all the big shots that they don't see what my father do, but my Yiayia Tsirikou and me, we see him do it." Mama whispered her re-telling of the slap she witnessed and never forgot. Seventy years later, she still felt a need to maintain a secrecy about it. A flush came to her cheeks, embarrassment and shock were still evident in her fiery eighty-one year old eyes. "Not suppose to criticize husband like that.

"All the Tripolitsiotes enjoy themselfs at the big party. They eat and eat good food. They sing and dance. The old wood floors of my papa's house was bending because of all the people dancing and having a good time. We was afraid the floors maybe going to break. Us kids laugh and whisper to each other that all the fancy Tripolitsiotes with their top hats maybe wind up falling down to the first floor on top of the horse and donkey we was keeping down there."

Thanaso and Jim's engagement became the most joyful and exciting remembrance of the family for years to come. That extra-special occasion and their wedding at Piali's small St. Nicholas Church, where our grandparents had married, were the only major happy events the entire family ever celebrated together; the only one absent was Papou's oldest child, Kostas, who had already immigrated to the United States. When many members of our huge family left Piali to live in Chicago, Thanaso's engagement and wedding celebrations were joyfully recalled on both sides of the Atlantic.

"Jim Koliveras is think he can stay in Greece and be farmer again after he live in America for such a long time. No such thing. He was fooling hisself. He build a house in Tzivas, his village. It's in Tegea, close to Piali. But he find out he can't make crops grow. Farming is tough busyness. He find out he's not tough enough to be good farmer. So, two years later, he decide to take Thanaso and go back to America, this time go to Chicago because brother Kostas was already there. Having family around is a good thing.

"Before they leave for America, Koliveras suggest to Papou that they take Aphroditi with them to America. She's next oldest daughter. That way Papou don't have to give her a dowry when she's get marry and Thanaso can have her sister for company when she's so far away. My mama and papa they don't want to see them both go and they don't want to give away their daughter. But, my papa, he can't afford to give six dowries for six more girls in the family. Jim Koliveras, God rest his good soul, he and Thanaso bring Aphroditi with them to America. Good old Uncle Koliveras—*Aionia tou i mnimi*. Thanks to him we all come here."

Koliveras, Athanasia and Aphroditi departed from the port of Patras on January 31, 1914, on the good ship *Ultonia* that arrived in New York on February 25th. (The *Ultonia* would disastrously end its Cunard service in 1917, during World War I, when it was sunk off the Irish coast by a German submarine.) In 1914, two days after their first American Christmas, Aphroditi was married to Panagiotis Kuchuris, a fine Greek man from Rizes, another of Tegea's villages.

Panagiotis, more often than not, was called Pete. The wedding took place in Chicago, without a dowry.

Two years later, both sons-in-law wrote to Papou encouraging him to send his next daughter to Chicago. Despite the First World War raging in Europe, Politimi arrived in 1916, traveling in the company of two other girls from Piali. Three years later, she married Christodoulos Ganas in Chicago. Christopher, or Christ, as he was known, was an admirable Greek man from Piali. Two dowries had been saved.

When the Twenties arrived, Jim Koliveras reminded his two brothers-in-law that the old man in Piali still had four more marriageable girls, which meant four dowries. He encouraged his brothers-in-law Pete Kuchuris and Christ Ganas to write and request their father-in-law to send the next two daughters. Jim assured them that between their three families they could house and feed the girls until suitable husbands could be found. Vasiliki and Anastasia disembarked July 4, 1921.

Thanaso's arranged marriage in 1912 changed the history and future of the Krilis family forever, Mama's included. Gratitude for five of Papou's seven daughters coming to the United States is always given to our uncle, Dimitrios (Jim) Koliveras, who died too soon to watch his children grow to adulthood, to enjoy grandchildren, or to know all the nieces and nephews who were taught by his devoted sisters-in law to love and revere his memory.

CHILD CARE

Nick and I delighted in visiting our relatives for mini-escapes from Madison Street. Aunts and uncles were different from parents, but we were taught to consider them extensions of Mama and Papa. Each Thea had a distinct personality, yet the sisters shared traits that made one seem like the other. Thanaso lived on the South Side, and the other three lived on the West Side. The three lived close enough to walk to each others' homes. Our parents taught us to ride the public transportation by ourselves when we were quite young. Mama put us on the streetcar, we paid the three-cent fare, got a transfer if needed, and our relatives awaited our arrival, reluctantly or not. A refreshing change of pace and scenery, fun with cousins who were more or less our age, and a gladly anticipated visit with our aunts and uncles awaited us at the end of the streetcar ride.

"You go to the toilet and wash your face and hands?"

"Yes, Mama."

"You got carfare ready?"

"Yes, Mama."

We knew what came next in Mama's oft-repeated litany.

"Don't lose it and be careful. Don't get hit by the streetcar. Watch the traffic. Mind your own busyness. Don't talk to nobody. Be good. Behave. Don't get dirty. Alloways do what your Thea and Uncla tell you to do. Helen, watch your little brother and help Thea around the house. *Ta matia sas tessera.*" The litany always ended with her daily admonishment, "Use your eyes like you have four eyes, two in front and two in back."

Going to Aphroditi's, Politimi's and Tasia's homes by ourselves on the streetcars of the West Side became a weekly excursion, with visits to Thanaso sprinkled in occasionally so we wouldn't wear out our welcomes at any of the four. Our parents put three pennies in each sweaty palm and sent us off to a waiting Thea. Mama or Papa watched us clutching our paper bag of extra clothing, boarding the trolley at Laflin, without fearing that we'd be mugged, kidnapped, shot at or molested. Poverty was widespread but so were ethics and morals.

Aphroditi Kuchuris had the most positive attitude of Mama's sisters, always seeing the sunny side of every situation; she meted out warm encouragement as often as she offered healthy treats. Thea was into health food decades before it became the rage. Each moment spent with her was a pleasure because she was very easy to love, without physical displays of affection, of course. Her name was that of the ancient Greek goddess of love and beauty, but among her neighbors she was known as Frieda, easier for all concerned.

Aphroditi, like the goddess, was a pretty woman with high cheekbones, a beautiful mouth that smiled easily, and a well-shaped attractive nose. In retrospect, I think she resembled Audrey Hepburn in the actress's late years, except that our aunt weighed considerably more than the lissome Audrey. Like Mama's, Aphroditi's eyes were expressive and scintillating. She had beautiful, shiny, dark brown hair that she usually wore up in thick braids that crowned her head like a tiara. Thea's melodic voice was familiar to all her neighbors. When she went out on the back porch to summon her children from play, Aphroditi's singsong call had a strength, clarity and tone that the great soprano of the time, Amelia Galli-Curci, would have coveted. "Gee-ooor-geeey!" "M-a-a-r-reee!" Thea Aphroditi's calls were part of the music of her Italian-American neighborhood. My aunt should have been in show-biz.

She was married to Uncle Pete, a balding, pleasant-looking man of average height and slender build who, more often than not, had a cigar in his mouth. After he lost his restaurant and before he came to work at the Austin Lunch, he had a job with the WPA laying streets and sidewalks in the outlying parts of the Chicago area that became the city's suburbs.

There were four children in the Kuchuris family. Helen was a quiet, thoughtful and very religious girl, eldest of all us girl cousins. George, their only boy, was Uncle Pete's special source of pride. Bubbly Mary loved to laugh. And Dorothy was the adorable baby everyone loved to play with. When we went to stay with them, Mary heated up the curling iron on the old coal stove in the kitchen and practiced hair styling on Nick. When my brother was old enough to realize that only girls had their hair curled, he was careful not to be caught by Mary when she was brandishing the hot iron and approaching him from the direction of the spotless kitchen. Aphroditi, like all her sisters, was a meticulous housekeeper.

The only subject I can remember that Aphroditi and Pete disagreed about was his cigar smoking. She protested, but he persisted. In the Fifties, their daughter Helen brought home a parakeet. They repeated words over and over again trying to get the tiny bird to mimic them, but we never figured out how Thea trained the pretty little blue thing to chirp its complaints when Uncle Pete lit up his cigar.

Our uncle was a great storyteller. He knew all the ancient myths and related them for hours, in Greek. His young listeners didn't understand all the Greek words he used, but we enjoyed the stories anyway. Pete Kuchuris was the only Greek immigrant man we knew who was an avid baseball fan. While he was in the restaurant business, he was known to take off his apron in the middle of the afternoon, don the brown tweed cap he always wore, lock the door of his restaurant, and go to a baseball game. Perhaps it was both the Depression and his devotion to baseball that caused his business to collapse.

One of his dreams was to go back to the "old country" for a visit. For years he saved the foil from cigarette packages so that when he had collected enough, he could have the foil weighed and sell it. He planned to use the money to buy a ticket and return to Greece. Indeed, when he retired in 1950, Uncle Pete traveled to Greece with a baseball, bat and mitt to teach the great American pastime to the boys in Rizes, his village. Cigarette foil had nothing to do his ticket; he and my aunt were hard workers, frugal shoppers and careful savers.

In the summer, Thea Aphroditi always grew her own vegetables in a garden at the back of their house. She proudly grew the freshest produce in town, "like I did in my father's house in Piali." These small backyards, squeezed between rows of narrow two-and-three-story houses, invariably had a green space for playing catch and hitting a ball with Uncle Pete who cautioned, "Be careful. Let's not disturb the neighbors or break any windows we can't afford to replace."

LAKE STREET

Our crown prince is growing and loves to play.
—Christ Ganas to his father-in-law, December 1933

Stirring memories, some bright, some dark, come to mind when I recall staying with Mama's sister Politimi Ganas during the Thirties. The people we visited and the proximity of Garfield Park had everything to do with our stays being so enjoyably lively. Refreshing, fun outings to Garfield became an integral part of a visit to the Ganases. Our Uncle Christ regularly escorted us to the Garfield Park Conservatory at the distant western end of the huge city park. The immense, glass greenhouse (the largest plant conservatory in the nation) contained plants from all over the world. Visitors were admitted to study and admire the indoor garden, for free. When immense globs of ice and pointed icicles formed on the outside of the huge glass building in winter, tropical plants defiantly thrived inside the giant hothouse.

I remember trying to look at the gorgeous city park from the Ganas's living room window, a difficult task, even though Garfield was located kitty corner, across the street. The "El" train tracks obstructed the sunshine and view from the living room window, prison camp style. Only snippets of Garfield's green showed through, like a cubist canvas whose colors are confined by slashes of geometric black. The back kitchen window barely allowed any light in either because it was shaded by the gray wooden roof of the north-facing back porch.

A twenty-minute trip from the Austin Lunch took us to visit our

Thea Politimi on weekends. Nick and I boarded the Madison streetcar in front of the restaurant at Laflin Street and rode the clanging conveyance until we got off at Homan Avenue. The eastern edge of lush and green Garfield, which has successfully uplifted urban souls on the West Side of Chicago for decades, welcomed us as we stepped down from the trolley onto the pavement.

On our left, as Nick and I walked toward our final destination, lay blocks and blocks of the queen of Chicago's parks. Spreading out for acres beyond Homan Avenue were beautiful expanses of trees and grass dotted with flower gardens, lagoons and bronze statues by famous artists we hadn't heard of yet. One of my favorite sculptures was of Lincoln, the rail splitter. Through decades of blinding blizzards, sweaty heat waves, and torrents of autumn leaves, a young, clean shaven Abraham Lincoln tirelessly and immortally chopped logs in Garfield Park. I also remember a bandstand in some far-flung section of greenery and even a boathouse close to the lagoon. The shallow lake provided rowboat rental in the summer and a firm surface for iceskating in winter. Our Ganas cousins learned to ice skate on the frozen lagoon.

I have known Garfield Park since babyhood because Mama, her West Side sisters, and many Greek immigrant women used to push their buggies and walk their toddlers to the park for daily outings. Before I was seven, we lived in the neighborhood with trees and grass that Mama described as "beautifool." Getting out of brick apartment buildings and walking the kids to Garfield everyday was considered the healthy way to raise children. Overheard, quietly spoken Greek sparked friendships between Greek mothers that resulted in lifelong attachments; all originated on the benches of Garfield.

When Nick and I reached Washington Boulevard on our journey to Lake Street, we were smack dab in the middle of what I considered the West Side's most elegant location. I always made a point of admiring the singular elegance of the Graemere Hotel on the east side of Homan Avenue. The luxurious Graemere had a circular driveway bordered by manicured green lawns and flower gardens, quite a contrast to our Madison Street environs. In all the years of going to visit our relatives, we never went inside. Still, we knew from its elegant exterior that the Graemere was, as they said in the Thirties, a real "classy joint."

Several blocks north of the hotel, at Lake Street, Nick and I crossed under the towering, rusty steel girders of the elevated trains. We continued our walk in the grim shadows of the raised "El" tracks to the shaded door on Lake Street marked 3348. Climbing almost blindly to the second floor in the dark, sooty hallway, we were relieved when the door at the top of the stairs opened and light came out to scare away the spooky shadows. On the shallow landing, we were always greeted with smiles and kissed by Thea Politimi or Uncle Christ, one of the rare places in our childhood where we were welcomed with kisses. When I think back, I realize that there must have been times when our aunts and uncles weren't so eager to have two more children underfoot while our own parents worked, but Nick and I never knew if they ever felt that way. We were always welcomed warmly.

When I remember dapper Uncle Christ Ganas, I picture him in front of the Garfield Park Conservatory spiffily attired in his dark three-piece suit, cane in hand, sporting a small, neatly trimmed mustache and polished eyeglasses which glistened below the natty fedora that covered his glossy, balding head. A shiny, gold watch fob and chain usually decorated his vest front, just above his ample tummy. I can see him pointing to flowers and trees with his cane as he conducted my brother, my cousins and me on his personal tours of his neighborhood's main attraction. My uncle loved the place so much that he inspired everyone else to love it, too. He should have been a botany professor. Once a month, he would take us on a tour of the four-and-a-half acre "flower house," as my aunts called it, between Central Park Boulevard and Independence, north of Lake Street. Five thousand species of plants thrived there in a structure composed of 83,760 panes of glass.

Politimi Ganas was the third of Mama's older sisters. The name Politimi, literally translated from Greek, means "one of much honor." As appropriate and noble as it was for her, she had an English name, too. Outside of Chicago's Greek immigrant population, our aunt was called Pauline. She enjoyed good food and was a gourmet cook. Her figure showed it; her legs (plagued with arthritis in later years) were exceptionally round and heavy. Politimi's shiny, long, chestnut brown hair was always pulled into a bun that she wore knotted at the back of her head. Fair skinned, her face was attractively pleasant, round, and usually smiling. But that lovely face, more often than not, looked fatigued when she was at home. A never-ending Everest of drudgery faced her at home, with absolutely no help from her men. Life was tough and her complaints about enduring hard times with an unemployed husband were often imbedded in a thick wrapping of jocular, and sometimes biting, humor. Politimi and Christ raised three boisterous boys in the dark flat on Lake Street. Harry, the eldest, had been born prematurely and was babied by his mother for as long as she lived. Jimmy, the middle child, born a few months before me, overflowed with energy and was always willing to please everyone. The youngest, Gus, who came into the world during the depths of the Depression in 1931, was another darling and playful baby in our vast family of cousins.

Politimi lived in an all male world. She survived by having a warm, loving nature and an eternal sense of humor. Beauteous Garfield Park, though a few steps from the rusty "El" tracks outside her door, might well have been as distant as the Parisian Tuileries for Politimi. She didn't get there very often because she was constantly and single-handedly caring for four males without any help or conveniences. She was forever cleaning, cooking, washing, ironing, doing dishes, and comforting whichever of her sons was being disciplined by Uncle Christ with the cane he used to help him walk. Our Uncle referred to baby Gus as the *diathogos* (crown prince). We all knew he favored Gus, perhaps because he was the youngest. Harry, because of his premature birth, was declared off-limits for physical punishment by his mother, even though Christ easily overruled Politimi's edicts. Therefore, when there was mischief, no matter who the culprit was, the brunt of Uncle Christ's blows fell unfairly on Jimmy. Although our uncle was delightfully charming most of the time, none of us liked being around when he was angry; he usually carried out his threats. "If you kids don't quiet down, I'll come in there with my cane and I'll get everyone of you!"

Politimi was overwhelmed with housework. Mama and her sisters let their daughters know that they were expected to do whatever possible to make life easier for their aunt during Lake Street visits because Politimi "doesn't have daughters." The worst chore was doing laundry—a drudgery that took all day. Politimi laundered all her family's clothing by hand, as well as the heavy cotton sheets, pillow cases and towels. She would bend over the bathtub, illuminated by the only generous source of natural light in the entire house. Installed high above her, over the toilet with the overhead pull-string tank, was a skylight. It made the bathroom the sunniest and best-lit room in their apartment. When her back ached, Thea knelt in front of the raised, claw-footed bathtub. In the hot humid summer, she wore a white handkerchief around her neck and sometimes around her forehead to absorb the rivers of perspiration pouring off her hair and flushed round face.

Politimi vigorously rubbed the clothes on a metal and wood scrub board with a stubborn bar of brown American Family Soap or Fels Naptha. She would soak towels, sheets and whites in hot water with bleach, wash them twice, rinse them three or four times, then wring them out each time by hand. Finally, when the last of the suds were rinsed out, Politimi added a few drops of bluing to brighten them. Whenever hot water didn't run from the apartment's faucets, Politimi, like other women, heated it on the stove in the kitchen, then carried it to the bathroom. From the early morning hours until late afternoon, from the first soaking to the final rinse, she lugged steaming hot water in large portable basins, and spilled it into the bathtub until the laundry was done. Her hands were always raw and chapped, especially in winter. A waxy/greasy product with the strong odor of camphor, called Camphor Ice, provided some relief, and it could be found in each of our medicine cabinets after Mama and her sisters discovered its healing properties.

In spite of all their exhausting labor, Politimi and her sisters considered American washdays an improvement over the ones in their homeland. Back in Piali, they had to gather enough wood to heat water for an entire day of laundering. Then they would draw water from Papou's well, across the street from their village home, and transport it to their courtyard where they would do the washing. They even needed to make their own soap. The women of our family knew through personal experience that housekeeping was far worse for women "back in the old country." Mama and our aunts were thrilled with American innovations like indoor toilets, inside kitchens, and apartments with running water, especially hot running water. Mama's "God bless America. Period," was a sincere supplication, one also offered by all her sisters.

When Politimi had finally finished wringing out the clothes, she hung them out to dry with wooden clothespins. If the weather was warm and it was not raining, she would string cotton ropes out on the back porch to hold the laundry. On rainy days and during winter, she strung clotheslines back and forth through the apartment's kitchen, bathroom and hallway, leaving the clothes to dry. In Chicago's characteristically humid weather, that meant the next day. Children were constantly darting in and out of rooms, brushing up against damp clothing, sometimes knocking clean laundry down on the floor, but Politimi had great patience with the little boys in her family. I recall with a sense of solace that sometime in the Forties her son Jimmy bought her a Maytag washing machine with a wringer and a self-moving agitator. Politimi was, deservedly, the first of the sisters to own this breakthrough labor-saving appliance.

Uncle Christ, a disabled veteran of World War I, was an excellent chef. A U.S. Army cook while in the service of his country, he opened up a restaurant when he was discharged, but lost it in the Depression. I don't know how he became disabled in the army since he was not one of the "doughboys," as soldiers were called in World War I, who went overseas. For almost as long as I can remember, he walked with a cane in his right hand and a crutch under his left armpit.

Though the family loathed going on relief, they were forced to, during the Depression. Harry got a job in a small grocery store. Dynamic Jimmy regularly took his shoeshine box filled with polish, brush and buffing rag to the streets of the West Side. He faithfully brought his mother the money he made shining shoes. When he was fourteen or fifteen, Jim got a job as an usher for the Senate movie theater, at Madison and Kedzie, helping patrons find seats in the darkened theater. He went to work wearing a dashing, well-starched uniform with bow tie, a glistening white shirt ironed by none other than his devoted mother, and an exciting battery-operated flashlight. The need to bring money home to help the family's financial straits made many teenagers leave high school to go to work. The Depression drastically reduced the number of high school diplomas that should have been awarded in the Thirties.

Turbulence was a permanent condition in the Lake Street flat thanks to colorful Uncle Christ. Visitors came and went all day long, many of them Christ's old, unemployed buddies who dropped by to eat the exceptional meals Politimi created out of food received from "relief." Uncle Christ's bachelor friends longed for home cooked meals, and occasionally helped out by bringing over grocery bags filled with food for Thea to cook. Impromptu visitors, constant activities, a kitchen as productive as the one at the Palmer House with none of the famous hotel's conveniences, and permission to go across the street to play in Garfied Park made the weekends we spent at the Ganas home pass quickly. Our boy cousins knew "The Park" by heart. Jimmy had, no doubt, climbed every tree.

In addition to the noise and activity of our cousins and Uncle Christ's friends, the Lake Street El trains clamoured past the living room window, day and night, ten to fifteen minutes apart. When we were supposed to quiet down and give our aunt a few minutes of peace, we enjoyed calmer fun by staring out the front room window at the noisy trains. We watched steel cars and passengers whiz by the window, less than seven yards away. Some riders got off at Lake and Homan to walk toward their destinations, and we innocently followed their movements until they were out of sight. When trains weren't raucously speeding by, blurring our vision, we watched the diverse assortment of men, in various stages of sobriety, streaming in and out of the saloon on Lake Street beyond the elevated tracks, across the street from the Ganas apartment. But wobbly drunks, a standard sight on Madison Street after repeal, were nothing new to me. I preferred to twist and strain my neck at that window to search for my own refreshing peek at green Garfield basking in the sun beyond the shadows cast by sooty girders and monster-sized platforms.

When we weren't watching the trains or the drunks, we loved to study the enormous, framed sepia-tone photograph of Uncle Christ's World War I army regiment that hung over the sofa in the dimly lit living room. The game was to see which one of us would be the first to pick out Uncle Christ from the rows of tiny uniformed doughboys. Of course, the Ganas boys were experts at that game.

Sometimes Uncle Christ, himself, took us out of the house to give Thea Politimi a well-earned break. He attired himself in a starched white shirt, tie, three-piece suit, and dark fedora hat, carefully draping his gold chain and pocket watch in front of his vest, as had been the rage in his youth. Whether he was going to church, out with his cronies, or to the park across the street with little kids, he always polished his shoes and dressed up. Our uncle's lively eyes emitted energy right through the lenses of his eyeglasses. His mustache was neat, his shoes were glossy and, in spite of the cane and the crutch, his walk was spritely.

When he took us to Garfield's greenhouse, he used the red rubber tip of his cane to point out a rare flower and then, switching the cane to his other hand, to point out a shrub. Invariably, he brought our attention to plants and flowers he had known as a kid back in the fields and gardens of Piali, proud that they were elegantly growing under glass in his neighborhood's magnificent American conservatory. Afterward, if we had been good children, he treated us to a bag of warm, buttered popcorn purchased for pennies from a fellow Greek countryman whose horse-pulled popcorn wagon was usually stationed in front of Garfield's renowned greenhouse. The rig, which perfumed its environs with the enticing aroma of freshly popped corn, was parked with the horse's nose facing the wagon instead of toward the street, so that the old steed wouldn't be tempted to run away. The animal became known in our family as the "Upside Down Horse."

Customarily, Greek men celebrate the day dedicated to the saint for which they are named by attending church the night before and then having a small get-together with friends and family. Uncle Christ was baptized Christodoulos, (literally "servant of Christ"), which he translated to "Christopher." Our uncle decided that since his nickname was Christ, he should celebrate his name day both on Christmas Day and on St. Christopher's Day. Uncle Christ was the only person we knew with two name days. If his name had been Apostolos, like Papa, who celebrated on the June 30 feast of the Holy Apostles, Uncle Christ would surely have celebrated twelve name days.

Our clan usually celebrated Christmas at Thea Politimi's house so we could celebrate Christ's birth and one of Uncle Christ's name days. Nick and I were the only representatives from our immediate family because even on Christmas Day, Papa and Mama worked at the Austin Lunch. Mama always took time to decorate a small tree for us on Christmas Eve after we had fallen asleep. The four of us celebrated Christmas together in our apartment at breakfast, before Papa walked down to the restaurant.

On Christmas Day, our aunt and uncle had a present ready for each child. We were thrilled with it: a sock filled with an orange, an apple, a tangerine and unshelled nuts. None of us kids knew anything about making lists for Santa Claus because that had not been a part of Greek Christmas tradition in our parents' villages where Christmas was a holy day, without gifts. It was exciting to receive our aunt and uncle's extraordinary present because the sock filled with fruit and nuts was a new American addition to our holiday. Every Christmas without fail, I recall the thrill of receiving those simple but extra-special gifts of the Depression, bestowed on us at the Ganas's celebration.

Christmas dinner was special because the entire extended family celebrated together. Both Politimi and Christ were great chefs who concocted fabulous, memorable desserts. Thea, who today would be referred to as a gourmet cook, always made her specialty, *diples*, at Christmas. These are crisply fried pastry strips, dipped in warm honey and sprinkled with finely chopped nuts. Thea Politimi's diples were exceedingly delicate and delectable. After she kneaded and thinly rolled out the dough using a clean broom handle and much expertise, she painstakingly shaped each dough strip to look like a giant flower, then fried it in bubbling hot oil. Each one of Thea Politimi's unforgettable diples was a delicious work of art. Uncle Christ was not to be outdone by his wife's exquisite desserts on Christmas Day. He had a specialty of his own. He would present his guests with a shimmering bowl of layered red and green Jello, interlaced with fruit and walnuts. Jello dessert was new to us, and we were fascinated and delighted with the colorful, jiggly "American" dessert. Uncle Christ's surprise became a family Christmas tradition.

Thinking back to Depression years from the perspective of our gadget crazy era, I stand in awe of the women of those economically depressed times, Thea Politimi in particular. She summoned up the energy and made time to create *diples* and other labor-intensive Greek delicacies and staples throughout the year, always cooking "from scratch," while taking care of four somewhat helpless males, and doing laundry every single week. In spite of this, Politimi felt sincerely fortunate to have labor saving electricity, running water, a gas stove, ready made soap, and a flushable toilet. Some men figuratively spit on Columbus and hated Herbert Hoover because the Depression made them poorer than they had been in Greece. At the same time, Greek women, who were not expected to engage in political rhetoric, asked God to bless America because conveniences, as primitive as they appear from the twenty-first century, made their housekeeping easier.

Our uncle so enjoyed holidays that he assigned his wife a birthday. Politimi had been born at a time in Greece when dates of birth were not accurately recorded. In the case of baby girls, the dates were quite often forgotten altogether. When Politimi married Christ and needed to fill out her date of birth on the Cook County marriage license form, she announced that she didn't know it. Uncle Christ immediately assigned her the fifteenth of August because, as the commemoration of the death of the Virgin Mary, it was the third most important holiday on the church calendar. Thanks to Christ Ganas, Politimi had a birthday.

BABIES

Beloved Mother, our daughter has been named Eleni.

—Tasia to her mother, February, 1933

*C*ousin Helen Antonopoulos came into the world very quickly one extremely hot Father's Day during the Depression, born in the kitchen of the Antonopoulos apartment on Huron Street. As soon as Tasia went into labor, she knew they could not arrive at Norwegian-American Hospital in time for her to give birth there.

When Tasia realized she didn't have time to go to the hospital, she asked her husband Paul to hurry downstairs to fetch their neighbor Mrs. Sowa and use her telephone to call Dr. Pugh to ask him to come as quickly as possible. While Mrs. Sowa watched over Tasia, Paul and their seven-year-old Georgia ran three blocks in steamy humidity to fetch Aphroditi, the closest sister. Georgia stayed with Aphroditi's family on Kedzie Avenue while our aunt and Paul rushed back to the apartment. In the meantime, Mrs. Sowa contacted Mrs. Novak, the neighborhood mid-wife. Helen's quick birth was attended by a melting pot of assistants: Polish Mrs. Sowa, Jewish Mrs. Novak, Welsh Dr. Pugh, and Greek Thea Aphroditi. It was a truly American event.

By the time little Georgia returned home that very hot June 18th evening, she found that *Panagia* (the Holy Mother of Jesus) had delivered a heavenly package, a brand new baby sister. It was so suffocatingly hot and humid that Georgia and her father walked to Walgreen's Drugstore at Madison and Kedzie, on that very same evening, to buy an electric fan. It cooled the family every summer until Georgia's own son was born in 1958. Paul and Tasia took good care of everything, electric fans and children included.

Most Greeks were excellent parents. They loved children and took parental responsibilities seriously, well into their children's adulthood. However, many Greek immigrant parents in America were not openly affectionate. Maybe it would have helped if bumper stickers asking, "Have you hugged your kid today?" had started showing up on the rear ends of Greek donkeys during the nineteenth century. Greek villages at the time of our parents' childhood were places where debilitating hard work yielded little economic stability. Parents, eking out a sparse living to survive, had no time, example, or inspiration to give praise, play games and share "quality time," hugs and kisses with their offspring. Demonstrations of affection were signs of weakness and raising kids to be weak during those tough times was considered bad parenting. No "talk shows," newspaper articles, or child rearing books with advice by renowned child psychologists advised parents that good self-esteem begins with healthy hugs and verbal approval, an alien idea to our collective family.

Demonstrations of physical affection and expressions of "I love you" were uncommon to our brood, yet I would still describe ours a warm and loving family. I felt a tinge of embarrassment when Papa gave Mama a peck on the lips in front of us on Christmas Day; he kissed us then, too. The only times we witnessed unembarrassed and lavish demonstrations of love was when they were directed at the always-welcome infants in our family. Babies were squeezed, cuddled, cooed at, sung to, played with, and kissed—Mama advising, "never on the mouth," declaring it unhealthy for a baby. The arrival of a tiny new cousin was a joyful event, and three were added to our family during the early Thirties. I never heard complaints about more mouths to feed during the Depression from any of my adult relatives.

"Only the Evil One doesn't fit at our table," was said often. There was always room for brothers-in-law, sisters-in-law, cousins, friends, *patriotes* (fellow Greeks), unemployed cronies, nieces, nephews, new babies, and the rest of the world. When we children wondered aloud where babies came from, Mama and our aunts matter-of-factly explained that *Panagia* (the Holy Mother of Jesus) brought babies into the world because babies were a gift from God. Birth, therefore, like the Holy Trinity and the Eucharist, was a matter of faith. Case closed. No additional questions were entertained. No further explanations were necessary. Period on top of period. Pregnancy wasn't discussed or even hinted about. Women discussed secrets of "expecting" in whispers, when children and men were out of earshot. Polite people did not discuss pregnancy in mixed company or around children, and never used the word "pregnant."

Every blessed event was greeted with a joyful, congratulatory wish, "*Na sas zisi to neogennito*"(May your newborn live), a wish that originated during the centuries when Greece suffered high rates of infant mortality. Since early times, a profound love for life has permeated Greek culture, a love that reaches far back into pre-history. While the ancient Egyptians were making such a big deal about celebrating death, the Greeks came along and put their hearts, souls and hopes on life.

Traditionally, Greeks bring new born infants a gold coin, symbolizing their hope that the infant be as strong and as precious as the metal in the coin. When bestowing it, the giver says, "*Siderenio na einai*" (May the child be as strong as steel). The "life wish" is evident in many other Greek benedictions. "Wear it in good health." "May you live to enjoy it." Even the wedding wish for a bride and groom, "*Na zisete*" (May you live), has at its core the life wish—the desire for the couple to exist happily, in peace, love, good health and prosperity. "*Hronia polla*" on a name day means "May you live many years." "*Na ta ekatostisi*" (May you live to be a hundred) is a birthday sentiment."*Kai tou hronou,*" (And again next year) can be heard at every annual celebration, expressing a hope for survival so the event can be enjoyed again. The desire for life is even integrated into death rituals. "*Syllypitiria kai zoi se sas*" (Sympathy and life to you) is murmured to the bereaved when a loved one has died. It conveys sympathy, and wishes life to survivors so the memory of the deceased will endure.

U.S. silver dollars were the Greek-American baby gift of the Thirties. Hard times contributed to the scarcity and hoarding of gold coins when the United States went off the gold standard; their circulation became illegal. Letters happily mailed to Piali announced the births of four Chicago grandchildren by the end of the Thirties. The first Depression baby, Aphroditi and Pete's Dimitra, was named in honor of Papou Dimitrios Krilis. She has always been called "Dorothy." The second baby was Constantinos Christophoros Ganas. His patron saint is St. Constantine the Great, but everyone calls him "Gus." Traditionally, the first boy and first girl born to a family are named after their paternal grandparents; the second boy and second girl are named in honor of their maternal grandparents. Dimitrios Ganas, our cousin Jimmy, was named for Papou Krilis. We had many Helens in our family, named in honor of Grandma Eleni (Helen) in Piali. I myself was named after Papa's mother, Eleni; both my grandmothers had the same first name. The custom was well followed by the Greek immigrant community in America. Even though Greek names provided emotional ties to the old country, most immigrant parents learned that having an American name was also important. Greek parents wanted their children to fit into their American culture. *Athanasios* became Tom, *Haralambos* usually became Harry. Mama's younger sister Tasia, whose baptismal name was *Anastasia*, was known as Anna among her American neighbors.

TRANQUILITY

Venerable father, your grandchildren kiss your right hand.

—*Tasia to her father, May 10, 1935*

"*I* miss my Tasia. *Aionia tis i mnimi.*"
Mama's voice broke and tears streamed down her cheeks as she gently patted a letter from the sack written in her younger sister's hand. "Tasia was my best friend," she half-whispered. Thea Tasia had died of throat cancer six years before, a debilitating loss for Mama. She ached for the visits and long telephone talks they enjoyed together after Thanaso, Aphroditi and Politimi had passed away, leaving them the sole survivors of the Krilis clan in Chicago. I, too, miss her and our other aunts, who were like second mothers to us, sharing their homes and love of family, providing refuge to two kids growing up in a restaurant.

"Tasia's letter here gives advice to my Mama and Papa. She tells them not to worry about any of us because we all got our health. She says, 'Even though you hear all about the poverty we have in America, none of us are begging in the streets. All of us are strong and have good health. Venerable father, your grandchildren send kisses for your right hand.'"

Many of our weekends were spent with Thea Tasia and Uncle Paul Antonopoulos, tranquilly and safely in their bright apartment on West Huron, east of Homan and just south of Chicago Avenue. Unlike our apartment on Madison and the Ganas's on Lake, sunlight poured

233

through the curtained windows which framed the glorious trees that lined Huron Street. Our own windows on Madison street framed sooty brick, rusty fire escapes, and the starkly brown Flatiron Building.

I still find comfort in memories of the restful and quiet security I enjoyed in Thea Tasia's comfortable presence. She was married to Paul Antonopoulos who, unlike most Greek immigrant men we knew in Chicago, was not in the restaurant, grocery, confectionery, or bar business. During the Depression, he actually had a regular paying job with days off at the Santa Fe Railroad repair yard at 22nd Street and Wentworth, near Chinatown. Paul was proud to work for Santa Fe, which he pronounced "Santa Fee." Our warm, loving aunt and uncle were practical and sensible people. Very generous, they were always giving of their time, their goods, and themselves. Life in Greece and the Great Depression taught them to be thrifty in order to survive, but innate generosity prevented them from ever being stingy. Tasia knew how to get the most out of Paul's hard-earned paycheck and put money into savings, too. He was the only brother-in-law who had a steady, relatively secure job during the Depression. When Papa needed a twenty-five dollar loan during the early Thirties, Uncle Paul lent it to him; the amount was considered big money in those days. Our parents paid it back and never forgot his trust and generosity.

Paul was a quiet, gentle man born in the village of Kalogeresi in the Greek province of Messinia, the only brother-in-law who wasn't from Arcadia. In his youth he had cut down redwoods in the lumber camps of Northern California and Oregon. Like Uncle Christ, he had been an American "doughboy" in World War I. An old-fashioned black-and-white photograph of him in uniform, framed with American flags and other symbols of U.S. liberty, hung in their living room. We could tell that he had started losing hair early in adulthood, because a thinning crown was evident in their wedding picture, which also hung in the living room. He was a tall, dark, and handsome man, over six feet tall. His commanding height contrasted with my aunt's petite frame.

Tasia, like Politimi and Mama, wore her long hair parted in the middle and neatly pulled into a simple bun at the back. She had a loud voice, but she never said anything mean or unpleasant. I remember her amiable, square and sturdy face; it could have been Irish or Polish, German or Italian. The very best of being Greek came from within Tasia. She was warm and hospitable. She was our family's "Martha Stewart" sixty years before the world encountered the "really McCoy." Tasia prepared her years' supply of *hilopites* (Greek noodles) and *trahana* (Greek porridge) by hand, passed on countless helpful hints to Mama, put up yearly fruit preserves, baked specialties for each holiday, crocheted, embroidered, and grew a small vegetable garden every summer. A gifted cook and meticulous homemaker, her household was as pure and squeaky clean as her warm and giving soul.

Youthful years working in the American West strongly influenced our uncle who enjoyed reading paperback Zane Grey cowboy novels when he wasn't working with his hands, expertly using the wonderful tools that he kept well-organized in a large metal box. His treasured implements were always in good working order and only a reach away. Nick and I admired the way he could build and repair things because our Papa didn't know anything about tools or how to use them. (The latch to his store's huge walk-in fridge once broke and until he could be convinced that it needed professional repair, Papa kept the door closed with multiple layers of Scotch tape.) Tasia, our aunts, and Mama could always depend on Paul to fix whatever was in disrepair. He quietly persisted at his projects, studying them through wire-rimmed eyeglasses, while puffing on handmade cigarettes. Paul rolled them himself, using cigarette paper and Prince Albert tobacco. When the tobacco was used up, he saved the bright red tins with the dapper figure of Queen Victoria's prince consort etched on the front, to store nails and screws.

Tasia always spoke of her husband with reverence, and Paul was gentle with her. It was a quiet, loving relationship, unlike the equally caring but more boisterous marriages of our family. She woke up every workday at four in the morning to make breakfast for him and prepare his lunch. His large black lunch pail carried a sandwich, a piece of fruit and a tall thermos filled with coffee. Tasia brewed it every morning in an aluminum pot over the wood-burning kitchen stove.

She was the first of our aunts to wear eyeglasses; hers were wire-rimmed. Sadly, in later years, Tasia lost most of her sight because her optic nerves had not received adequate nourishment when she was growing up. An ophthalmologist said the condition was prevalent in Mediterranean-born women of her age. Our aunt's eyesight may have dimmed, but her sharp memory never failed. Without written records, she remembered the date and time of each niece and nephew's birth and the weather in Chicago on that day. She was a devout Orthodox Christian and knew all the holy days without looking at a calendar. I can still hear her admonishing Mama for not keeping a special feast day holy.

"Vasilo, you should be fasting today, it's the first day of lent."

"You're doing laundry today, Vasilo? Shame on you. It's Saint George's Day."

"Remember, it's a sin to eat meat today, Vasilo."

Mama often replied, "Tasoula, I didn't kill anybody, did I? I don't have a calendar at the store to keep track of church holidays. I get so busy I don't know what day it is. Besides, there are 365 holidays in the year. If I kept them all holy, we'd be in the poor house."

From the Thirties to the Sixties, Tasia and Paul lived at 3304 West Huron Street, in a two-story, eight-flat building of dark, reddish brown brick with two attractive entrances on Huron. Trees lined Huron and a tidy patch of grass landscaped the front of the building; Spaulding Avenue intersected at the corner. Neighboring yards were planted with flowers and vegetables in spring and summer.

Small and large factories were located on nearby streets. The Rockola Company produced jukeboxes at Chicago Avenue and Kedzie. The beautifully landscaped grounds of the Bunte Candy Company at Homan Avenue and Franklin Boulevard produced delectable confections, notably chocolates and individually-wrapped hard candies. Wilson-Jones, a manufacturer of paper office supplies, was located closest to the Antonopoulos's apartment. These factories, along with hundreds of others scattered throughout the neighborhoods of Chicago, provided jobs in the Twenties and Forties (but perhaps not in the Thirties) that gave credence to the saying, "If you can't find a job in Chicago, you aren't looking hard enough." The Wonder Bread Company at Lake Street and Sacramento, between the Ganases and the Antonopouloses, was the home of Wonder Bread and the birthplace of Twinkies. Enticing aromas of things baking continually emanated from the factory, filling the surrounding streets. At the Wonder factory store, a small day-old, loaf of spongy white bread sold at half the regular nickel price. The bread was wrapped in eyecatching waxed paper covered in big red, yellow and blue dots and featured an innovation—it was sliced. A package of Twinkies (the original filling was banana flavored) could be purchased for two-and-a-half cents at the discount "day old" store. If we had a nickel, we left the Wonder store with a package of Twinkies and a small loaf of bread. Mama and our aunts claimed Wonder had none of the nutritive value of the heavy and firm village bread that nourished generations in their native Piali. "It really fill your belly up good." We kids preferred smooth and squishy Wonder, the bread you almost didn't have to chew.

Local factory whistles blew at noon, Monday through Friday, to announce the lunch break and again at four to mark the end of a workday. Employees poured out of factories and rushed passed Huron and Spaulding toward streetcar lines at Chicago Avenue and nearby Kedzie. They headed for homes in other parts of the city providing us, as they did so, with daily free entertainment. Workers' faces became familiar to us as we played outside in the warm weather, marking hopscotch and roly-poly grids with chalk on the walkway at the front door of the small apartment complex. When employees filled the sidewalks, our aunt called to us in Greek, "Move over and let the workers pass. They're in a hurry to get home." Then we'd stop, sit on the low metal fence that separated the grass from the sidewalk, and watch them.

Six years older than Helen, Georgia was a watchful and caring big sister. She took Helen to school when she was old enough and supervised her homework when necessary. My aunts and most of the Greek women we knew spoke very little English. As with most children of immigrants, the oldest child assumed the responsibility of being mother's interpreter and link to the neighborhood. Tasia spoke English better than her sisters, Thanaso, Aphroditi and Politimi, perhaps because she had a fourth-grade education, albeit a Greek one, and functioned very well in her community with the neighbors and storekeepers she dealt with daily. Georgia, however, was her mentor and guide. When they bought their first radio, Georgia listened to all the Cubs' games in the sunny kitchen of their four-room apartment. She became an avid Chicago Cubs baseball fan and knew the usual line-up, players' names, numbers, and positions by heart.

Descending to the basement to do laundry with Thea Tasia on Monday mornings was a weekly adventure. Excitement came in exploring the dark corners and discovering what neighbors stored down there: folding card tables, bicycles, tools, suitcases, paint cans, electric fans—all fascinating to curious kids who had few possessions. The basement had an area set up for doing laundry. A sink with two deep wash tubs and scrub boards was provided. Several single light bulbs dangled from the ceiling; one hung over the double sink. Daylight filtered in from high windows that were level with the sidewalk outside. Sometimes we would watch multitudinous feet walk by, then try to guess who they belonged to.

Each flat had a wood and coal burning stove in the kitchen to provide heat for cooking and for warming the house; there was no central heat in the building. Coal was stored in individual tenant bins in the basement and brought up to each apartment, as needed, in a bucket. The basement smelled distinctly of coal dust combined with soap, bleach and wet, clean clothes hanging from clotheslines. We kids delighted in being in the basement when a coal truck made its delivery. We watched and listened in awe to the rush and roar of a Niagara of falling black coal as it tumbled down a chute running from the coal truck to the bins through the basement windows.

"Thea. Thea! The coal truck's here. Look at all that black stuff coming through the cracks in the closets." Tasia did not share our childish delight. "*Poh. Poh*. I started washing before the sun came up and now the clothes are getting dirty again." Every day, except Sunday, Tasia's basement was colorfully decked with hanging laundry. When it wasn't raining in spring, summer, and fall, tenants hung their clothes on ropes attached to pulleys at the back of the building. Like scenes from the American realist painter George Bellows, white sheets, colored towels, work pants, shirts, dresses and underwear festooned the air.

Within view of Tasia's living room window was the Samuel B. Morse Elementary School on Spaulding Street. Georgia and Helen attended it through eight grade. In the morning, at lunch, and again at three, children, shouting and laughing, crowded the sidewalk in front of the apartment house. Thanks to Morse School, we participated in exciting Halloween parties held, after school, on the playground. Our parents related to masquerading because of *apokries*, carnival time before the start of Lent in Greece. Dressed in homemade Halloween costumes, we were allowed to celebrate the fun American holiday. Playing with Georgia and Helen in the security and love of Thea Tasia and Uncle Paul's apartment in their peaceful neighborhood was a special and memorable treat away from the noise and tobacco smoke of our semi-confinement at the Austin Lunch.

Mama and her sisters had one more sibling in Chicago, their eldest brother Kostas. He was the first member of the Krilis family to immigrate to Chicago, sometime after the turn of the century. Kostas and his wife, Thea Marigo, and their four children lived on the West Side, too, near Austin and Grand Avenues. Uncle Kostas's sons, Peter and Louis, were the eldest of all our cousins. Their two daughters, Jenny and Clara (their Greek names were Dimitra and Garifalia in honor of Papou Krilis and his first wife) were younger than me.

Kostas and his sons were in the wholesale produce business. They were successful enough during the Thirties to own a Packard sedan and a truck for hauling fruits and vegetables. Our uncle was much older than his sisters, so they looked upon him as a brotherly patriarch. A huge, bushy mustache coupled with his serious demeanor gave us kids the impression that he was gruff, but perhaps we were misled by his size and patriarchal standing in the family. Most of his nieces and nephews were afraid of him; yet his sisters continuously assured us that he was a good man who was not to be feared. With our family involved at the Austin Lunch, and our uncle and his sons industriously running their produce business, we did not see as much of Uncle Kostas as we saw of our aunts; nor did Nick and I go to his house very often. In our Greek culture, as in so many others, it is the mother's sisters and female relatives who help with taking care of children.

NEW WORDS IN A NEW WORLD

Our children are learning to read and write in Greek

—Tasia to her father, May, 1936

*T*here's an old saying, "The Greeks have a word for it." I have heard at least three different Greek words for sister-in-law: *kouniada* (which means my husband's sister), *nymphi* (my brother's wife) and *synyphada* (my husband's brother's wife). This is just one example. Greek immigrants appreciated the richness of their language, and a visceral desire to preserve it conflicted with their urgent need to learn and use English. My parents were determined that Nick and I would learn both languages.

Life in America forced them to invent words for which they knew no Greek equivalents. "Pineapple," "strawberry," "grapefruit," and "sandwich," to name but a few, were unknown in the Greek villages they left behind. As a result, newly arrived immigrants at the beginning of the twentieth century became as capable as the ancients in creating words; by necessity they produced new additions to their Greek vocabularies, creating a sort of "Gree-lish." "Hospital" became *spitalia*. "Grapefruit" was *grayfrou*. "Strawberry" and "pineapple" were *stromberri* and *pie-nappla*. A sandwich was referred to as a *sammetsa*. "Overcoat" became *vrecoto*. Lake Michigan was called *Lakey Michigah*. An electric refrigerator was an *iceboxi*. "Elevator" became *eleveta*, and the same word was used for the elevated train in Chicago. Overalls were called *ovrahallia*. Television, which hadn't even been invented when Greeks started arriving in the U.S., became *televizio*. And I love this one, *tsintzerella*, was Gree-lish for "gingerale." I also heard several words coined to describe the bums on Madison Street: *bum-ides*, and the more colorful *chewntabakia* because many vagrants used to chew tobacco and spit all over the *siyeevori*, Greelish for sidewalk. Greek and English were often combined by adding the Greek suffix "ides" to an English word to make a new plural noun. For example, lousy people were known as *lous-ides*. Then there was the one for which children got their mouths washed out with soap: *son-ava-bitch-ides*. The list is endless. It wasn't until travel to Greece became easier after World War II that those of us who had assumed that our Greelish words were really Greek, realized from the puzzled looks on our relatives' faces that we were speaking a strange tongue. We also learned that Greeks did indeed "have a word for it"—for the pineapples and strawberries and other things our parents did not know. I believe that the newly coined Gree-lish words sported a capriciousness that neither their Anglo-Saxon nor Greek equivalents convey. Those anonymous wordsmiths were poets.

The first language spoken by most children of Greek immigrants was Greek. Incredibly, certain words still come to me more easily in Greek than English, especially those I learned while helping Mama in the kitchen. *Katsarola, tigani,* and *koutala* come to my tongue more quickly than "cooking pot," "skillet," and "large mixing spoon." As children, we learned to speak the language of our parents, a language shaped by their lives in the village and by their levels of education. Once they came to America, most Greek immigrants held on to the language they knew. Yet Greek, as spoken in Greece, continued to evolve. Most immigrants, so distant from their homeland, could not keep up with the subtle changes. My own spoken Greek is a combination of circa 1907 "Mercovouni Greek" and circa 1921 "Piali Greek" colored with Chicago Greek and, of course, English.

I didn't speak a word of English when I was enrolled in school, and I was completely lost and embarrassed during my first days of kindergarten. As I learned the language of the United States, I added and mixed English words with the Greek ones I learned from my parents. Of course, I was sent to Greek school. In order to keep their language alive in the new country, most Greek parents tried to send their children to Greek language schools. Most of them were administered by the Greek Orthodox Church. No matter how difficult it was, parents did their best, even during the Depression, to save the meager tuition for the lessons, plus the streetcar fare when the classes were not within walking distance.

Cousins Georgia Antonopoulos, Harry and Jimmy Ganas, Nick and I were enrolled in a Greek school by Uncle Christ Ganas who was the friend of a pastor of an Orthodox Old Calendar Church. Uncle Christ always tried to find pupils for the priest because his church had few parishioners and needed the business. The conservative church adhered to the old Julian calendar, which celebrates Christmas on January 7th. Most Orthodox Christian churches adhere to the Gregorian calendar—and they had many more parishioners. Therefore Uncle Christ's priest friend, with few parishioners of his own, was grateful for the tuition paying students my Uncle brought in.

Several times a week after school, Nick and I climbed onto the red Madison streetcar that headed south at Fifth Avenue. We descended at California Avenue, and walked south toward Monroe Street and tiny St. John's Church. Classes were held in a small room off the frankincense-fragrant sanctuary. The bearded, black-robed priest, Father Vouvounas, was a strict disciplinarian. If for some reason homework wasn't done or misbehavior erupted, he meted out punishment.

Little girls followed rules, answered politely, and brought completed homework. Little boys tended toward mischief after a full day of classes at "American" school. My brother Nick towed the line pretty well because no form of mischief was worth having Papa shout at us for not acting properly at school. As far as Mama was concerned, no matter who the instructor was, if you had to be disciplined by any teacher, it was your fault and Mama disciplined you, too. Cousin Jimmy Ganas, always lively and aggressive, used Greek school to act out in his own creative manner, making preposterous, irreverent comments in Greek and English, uttering obscenities in both tongues to get attention. In fact, Jimmy spoke Greek very well. After one outburst, the priest calmly sent him and his partner in mischief on an assignment. "Ganas and Katsoubas, I want each of you to go outside and bring me the best tree branch you can find." When both boys returned with their specimens, Father Vouvounas passed judgement. "Excellent. Ganas, you've got the best one." Pleased with himself and grinning smugly, Jimmy glanced back at his classmates and winked. After all, he had climbed every tree in Garfield Park; if anyone knew about branches, it was Jimmy.

"All right, Ganas. Put out your hands for your reward."

Jimmy's smile disappeared when the priest began walloping him with his prized branch. After school, when the priest told our uncle about Jimmy's mischief, poor Jimmy got it again at the end of Uncle Christ's cane. Shortly after that incident, Jim left Greek school forever.

One song taught during Greek classes (many of us had learned it at our mother's knee) was the Greek National Anthem. The words come from *Hymn to Liberty,* a beautiful allegorical poem by Dionysios Solomos that contains 158 verses. It is played at every Olympiad no matter which country hosts the games. Gratefully, we only sang the first verse. Just as we didn't know what we were supposed to be looking for at daybreak when we first sang, "Oh! Say can you see by the dawn's early light," most of us ignorantly parroted "*Se gnorizo apo tin kopsi tou spathiou tin tromeri,*" (I shall always recognize you by the dreadful sword you hold.) Solomos's poetry reached way over the heads of eight year olds. Our parents were proud to hear the patriotic words in our childish voices. Did they ever realize we didn't know what we were singing about?

To our astonishment and glee, St. John's Church and Greek school caught fire and burned down after six months of our attendance—answer to a schoolboy's prayer? I was saddened by news of the sanctuary's destruction, but relieved at not having to attend classes in addition to those I attended at daily public school. Following the fire, a second-floor hall was rented for religious services and Greek classes at Kedzie and Fifth Avenue. When the lease terminated, Greek school was held at the priest's house (a true example of dogged determination). Cousin Georgia continued to attend, but Nick and I were allowed to drop out because we had increasing responsibilities at the Austin Lunch, plus "American" school. I had learned enough to read and write Greek in a rudimentary manner, but never got "the hang" of diphthongs and the proper placement of aspirates. But I can still sing the first verse of the Greek National Anthem.

MAXWELL STREET

*S*hopping for clothes was a rare event in the Thirties. I don't remember Mama shopping for herself until the Depression years were over for us. If Nick or I needed shoes or clothes during hard times, Mama waited until a holiday like Easter, the religious "season of renewal," to go shopping. She always shopped in an area near the infamous Maxwell Street, where she could find the best prices. Old Maxwell Street is gone now, and I can't say I'm sorry because I was scared to death of the place when I was a kid. Teasing older cousins had confidentially given me the low down: children were kidnapped and sold there by Gypsies who tore offspring away from their mothers and peddled them along with other merchandise.

What, besides false rumor of wholesale abduction, frightened me about Maxwell Street? The noises and shouting made me uncomfortable. Menacing hawkers and shadowy Gypsies alarmed me. Even the smells turned me off. To make matters worse, I was disquieted by Mama's comfort in the place. How come she took all the strangeness in stride, and I, her own flesh and blood, felt so uncomfortable? Maybe being different from Mama is what really scared me. I realize now that Maxwell Street and its surrounding neighborhood is where I received my first lessons on how not to be intimidated. I learned from Mama, of course.

Even though Wieboldt's department store was closer to home and to the restaurant, Mama preferred shopping at the open-air bazaar of intriguing Maxwell Street, a scary place for a timid little girl. A massive, forbidding, brick building loomed over the corner of Halsted and Maxwell; it was the local police station. A semicircle of letters, carved into the cream-colored stone arch over the front entrance, identified it as the 7th District Police Headquarters. The need for a whole station full of police made me uncomfortable.

Maxwell Street was a conglomeration of drab yet multi-colored buildings. On both sides of the street, torn and faded awnings stretched from crumbling storefronts toward the sidewalk's edge where the curb dropped into the street. Hastily suspended old canvases sheltered wooden stands and flimsy card tables where a mishmash of items were offered for sale. Dresses, socks, winter coats, boys' sailor suits, fur muffs, long underwear, galoshes, and all varieties of apparel were displayed on wire hangers, which were hung off awnings, stands, and ropes that swung high above me. Rugs, chairs, towels, and myriad other items were displayed along the street.

A cacaphony of sound and color assailed shoppers on Maxwell Street. A forest of signs accosted bewildered customers announcing owners' names, prices, and brand names. The signboards, many of them rudimentarily scratched out in black crayon, competed with all the merchandise that hung every which way. Wire rug beaters were sold next to silk nightgowns, denim overalls, and shiny silver plate tea services. Food stands were interspersed between dry goods stalls. Smells ranged from coffee to mothballs to rotten fruit to hot dogs, mustard, and pickle relish. Acrid, greasy smoke evaporated from the back kitchens of small delicatessens smelling of sauerkraut.

A rainbow of languages could be heard on Maxwell. Haggling was carried on in Yiddish, Italian, Polish and Greek, but predominantly in loud broken English. Gypsies lurked in the shade of awnings waiting to tell fortunes. Their children ran back and forth playing games with each other amid the stands and tables. Mama held on tightly to her purse, and I held on tightly to Mama. I was not surprised to hear her cautioning whisper, "*Ta matia sou tessara*" (Make your eyes into four eyes).

"Let's go home now, Mama!"

"Yes, my little bird," she answered in Greek. "But, first, let's go see what they've got over here."

She was undaunted by the actions around us. Mama bravely forged ahead in curiosity while I shrank back in fear of the suspicious looking Maxwell Street denizens surrounding us. Of course, there were housewives there just like my mother, and little girls, just like me, hanging on tightly. Were they afraid, too?

Pedestrians, stray dogs, pushcarts, wagons, horses, trucks and cars caused traffic gridlock on Maxwell itself. This was where "Raksolion" lurked—men who Mama warned might take us if we didn't behave. Later in life we learned these men were shouting "Rags, old iron!" from the top of their horse-pulled wagons and were out buying old goods to re-sell so they could support kids of their own. They really weren't interested in adding us to their list of dependents. I wonder if "Raksolion" men ever knew that many parents kept their children in line with the warning that junk men took and sold misbehaving children.

What scared me most, I think, were the hawkers who followed shoppers down the street, trying to badger prospective customers into buying what they had to sell. In the Thirties, the Chicago City Council passed a law making these "pullers" illegal. These were salesmen who literally dragged customers into their places of business and prevented buyers from leaving without a purchase. With her most powerful mother superior attitude, Mama handled those guys with a simple but tough, "Leave me alone, willya!"

When she found it necessary to buy dry goods, Mama headed for a neighborhood she called "*stous Dodeka*" which meant "at Twelfth." These were old fashioned, plain, and sometimes shabby stores which lined Chicago's Halsted Street between Taylor and Maxwell. Twelfth Street, or Roosevelt Road as it is now called, intersected somewhere in the middle. Her sisters began shopping there when they first arrived as new immigrants. Even Papa (who only enjoyed browsing and shopping in bookstores) had purchased Mama's wedding dress in that shopping district. I can't really picture him shopping for any kind of female apparel by himself, and assume he merely paid for the dress that Mama and her sisters shopped for together. The merchants, predominantly Eastern European immigrants who owned stores along this strip of the city, encouraged haggling, and Mama joined in, enthusiastically.

I remember holding on to Mama's hand and boarding the old red Madison streetcar to go shopping during Holy Week. We rode the short distance to Halsted, transferred to its trolley, and were on our way. While I quietly sat next to Mama on the streetcar, enjoying the subtle fragrance of her Coty face powder and her always clean Palmolive freshness (she called it "Palmalla soap"), fear of arriving at Maxwell Street began gnawing at me. I fretted over the bargaining tactics Mama would employ when she became joyfully involved in the drama of getting a good deal. I still remember the adventure of shopping for shoes.

"The shoes fit the little girl beautifully, lady."

"How much?"

"Two dollars."

"Don't fits that good. Too much money."

"They feel good, Mama."

She turned to me and said in Greek, "Don't say anything my little bird, only when Mama asks you. I'll do all the talking to the man."

"See lady, she likes them."

"What she know? She's just a little kid."

"I have a store full of shoes for the little girl, lady. Let me bring something else."

"Bring me anything you want. I got to have the best price."

"Lady, I gotta pay the rent here. Can't give this stuff away free."

"I ask you for nothing? I don't want anything for nothing, Mister."

"Here's a cute shoe for a cute girl."

"Too cute. Not enough support. Fall apart in two weeks. No good for her feet. She's a growing child."

"Certainly you're concerned about your child's feet. How about this pair?"

"Alright, let's try them on."

I whispered in her ear. "These hurt Mama."

Shadowed by the brim of her hat, Mama's perfectly shaped eyebrows wrinkled over lively brown eyes riveted on the salesman. "Wrong size, Mister. I told you size four. See, the kid she can't even walk in them." Mama then yanked one shoe off my foot and peered inside to read the size. "This is wrong number. You try to fool me? I'm not as dumb as I look, you know. This is crooked busyness."

"No, no! Of course not, Madam, I brought it out by mistake."

"Anyhow, I got to go back to work. I don't have time try on all the shoes in here. What's your best price for first ones?"

"Two dollars."

"Whooo. You think I'm a millionairy?"

"What the matter, Missus?"

"Too much. I already told you, that's too much money for little of pair shoes like this. Hardly any leather in them." She tugged the other shoe off my foot, scrutinized it, then tossed it to the floor like a piece of trash.

"For you, lady, because you got such a nice little girl here, a dollar eighty."

"Come on, Helen. Put your shoes on. We going to go to the next shoe store, or we go to Wieboldt's." Mama took my hand and headed for the door. "Lots of shoes for little girls in Chicago, Mister. This is a big city."

"Not this quality, Lady. You'll be sorry if you leave this store without them."

Her back was to him. "I not sorry for nothing, Mister." We were at the store's threshold.

"How much you wanna pay, lady?"

"Seventy-five cents."

"You must be kidding."

"I'm not laugh. Got no time for jokes, Mister. I got to go back to work."

"You have a nice little girl. She wants the shoes. You can have 'em for a buck sixty."

"Whooo. Still, too much. You want my husband get mad at me?"

We were further out the door, almost in the warm, spring sunshine on the sidewalk.

"O. K. Lady, take 'em for a dollar and a half."

"I give you one dollar. Take it or leave."

"Lady, you drive a hard bargain. Give me a dollar and thirty cents and you can take them home."

"Let's see how much I got in my purse. Here's a dollar and—here's a quarter. No more. I need the other nickel and pennies for our car fare to get back home. Got no more money and I'm too late for work. How about it? I'm in a hurry, Mister."

"Let me put a string on the box for you to carry them, little girl. Like I said before, your Mama drives a hard bargain."

We left the store smiling. I was thrilled that the haggling was over—and I owned brand new shoes. Mama smiled because she had enjoyed making the deal. As I looked back, I could see the salesman shaking his head, but he was smiling, too. He didn't know that besides our car fare, Mama had one more nickel in her purse.

Then one day, Mama discovered radiation and began buying shoes for Nick and me at Wieboldt's Department Store. In the shoe department on the first floor of Wieboldt's, there was an impressive X-ray machine that took pictures of the skeleton of our feet in the shoes we were trying on for size. Mama and a bald-headed salesman named Leo could see how well shoes fit and if there was room to grow. The machine was as tall as I was and twice as wide. Nick and I delighted in peering down through the special viewer into the black cavern of its insides. Our flesh disappeared on the dark screen, and we saw the bones of our toes and feet wiggle in the eerie green light which we flicked on and off with the touch of a button. It was as close as we ever came to playing what are now known as "video games." Mama preferred this scientific method of shoe buying to the enjoyable haggle. She always insisted on good sturdy shoes with enough support to prevent foot problems. Consequently, the shoes she chose for us were usually inflexible and took several weeks of constant wear before they bent comfortably with our feet. Scientifically trying to better our lives, our Mama didn't suspect the dangerous effects the X-rays may have been inflicting on our tender little bodies.

I was always relieved when we left Maxwell behind and walked toward the Twelfth Street Store at the corner of Halsted and Twelfth. Mama shopped there when she was finished bargaining but still needed something. It was an unadorned department store; there were no elegant displays or beautiful mannequins; haggling was not tolerated. My favorite department, the busiest in the store, was located in the basement. The aroma of freshly baking waffles floated throughout the lower level. If it wasn't a time of fasting, like Holy Week, and if I had been a very good girl, Mama would treat me to the store's specialty, an ice cream sandwich made with freshly baked waffles. Waffle machines were lined up in full production on a back counter. After orders were placed, employees dressed in pristine white uniforms sliced squares of ice cream from frozen bricks of exciting, multicolored neapolitan and placed them on still-warm waffle squares. Then more waffles were laid on top and the greatest ice cream sandwiches on earth were served on white paper napkins. It was the treat of treats that soothed the discomfort of a quiet young daughter shopping on Maxwell Street with her never bashful Mama.

MAMA AND GOD

*M*ama removed the yellow rubber gloves and washed her hands with soap and hot water, three times, up to her elbows. She advised me to do the same before we took a late lunch break in our yellow kitchen, away from the rat-nibbled letters. The September afternoon was beginning to wane, but Mama's concentration and curiosity were winning over fatigue. Even as we ate cottage cheese, Ritz crackers, and sweet, seedless grapes, her brain buzzed with recollections, colored by a spectrum of emotions. Before she donned the yellow gloves and we delved into the letters again, she recalled some rumors she had heard about herself after she went to work at the Austin Lunch.

"One Greek woman was talking about me behind my back. She go from one house to the other and tell people I don't go to church hardly because I don't believe in God. Can you imagine a big lie like that—about me? I was working, with no day off, for sixteen hours, each and every day. I didn't have time for lots of things I like to do when I was working in the store, include going to church. But what I could do about it? Nothing. I try to mind my own busyness, be nice, not hurt nobody, raise good kids, be good wife, not talk lies about nobody and keep my family together. But people don't know nothing about you when they can't stand inside your shoes. Thank God, everybody don't believe that crazy woman. One thing I know for sure was that God understand the whole about it. God's much nicer than people is. God knows I love Him and in those days I got no choice but to work for my family and to keep them together like He want. He know I hadda do what I hadda do." Mama dabbed away tears of frustration with a crumpled Kleenex.

Mama had an individual relationship with God. She loved Him with all her heart and soul and taught us to love Him, too. When I was a kid I was sure Mama knew God personally, like she knew her father. Mama inevitably had real inside info on what God expected of us. Loving and respecting each other, and telling the truth, were highest on the list, she said. She listed what He disapproved of, too. Disobedient, dishonest children were big losers. Sticking out your tongue disappointed and angered God so much, Mama said, that he was likely to cut your tongue off completely. She had true, nitty-gritty data.

Since both the Lord and Moses had overlooked specific rules about chewing gum in church, Mama issued her own commandment. It was one hundred percent forbidden. Period. God did not like to see children chewing gum during religious services. "What kind respect is that to be chewing like a goat in God's house?" Crossing one's legs when seated in church was a sign of disrespect, and forbidden, too. Did God drop in on our Madison Street apartment for a consultation with Mama in the kitchen before we went to church and prior to her leaving for work every morning? A kid had to wonder.

Of all the holidays we celebrated, Mama loved Easter the most. She believed that on Good Friday it was important to sacrifice by fasting, just as Jesus had sacrificed his life for us. It was important, she said, not to complain about fasting because then it did us no good. Mama didn't parade her fasting or engage in ostentatious demonstrations of devotion because these were private communications with God and the whole world didn't need to know about them. She added, "*Kai to poli kyrie eleison to varietai kai o Theos,*" ("And even God tires of hearing too much Kyrie Eleison.")

Even though we had to work at the store on Good Friday, Mama still found her own way to keep it holy. Known as *Megali Paraskevi* (Great Friday—the word "*megali*" or "*megalo*" means great or large), Mama referred to the somber holy day with her own special English translation: "Big Friday." Whenever it rained on that day Mama explained that the very heavens were crying "'because they remember what Big Friday's all about. It's the most saddest day in the year."

Every Good Friday Mama burned incense in the tiny brass censer that rested on the shelf in the icon corner of my parents' bedroom. She carefully ignited the amber colored incense with a match and tiny wads of paper. After two or three pebbles of incense started to sizzle, melt and burn, she extinguished the flame causing fragrant white smoke to billow heavenward; the smoke of burning incense symbolizes earthly prayers ascending to God. Mama made the sign of the cross with aromatic smoke in every room of the house and over each of our heads as she prayed silently, also making us cross ourselves three times and pray.

When our public school spring break coincided with Greek Orthodox Holy Week, we were discouraged from playing, most especially on Good Friday. Requests to go to the movies on that particular day off from school was met with a look of disappointment. "Today we mourn Jesus' Crucifixion. Do we go to the movies when we go to a funeral? What kind of respect is that? Jesus die and somebody want to go out to have a good time? No siree. Suppose to think about God on Big Friday. Period."

Mama knew God understood that she and Papa worked very hard to make a living for their family and couldn't go to church very often. She was certain that He knew "the whole about it." And she believed that as long as they didn't hurt anyone, didn't steal, lie or cheat, and kept their family together, God still loved them. Daily we'd hear her speak to Him in Greek: "*Doxa Si O Theos*" ("Glory be to you, O God."), "*Theouli mou*" ("My Dear God."), "*Panagitsa mou*" (a supplication to the Holy Mother of God) and her most used "*Mnisthetimou Kyrie*" ("Remember me, O Lord," the words of the thief who had faith in Jesus and was crucified next to Him on Calvary). Very early in our lives Mama taught us how to reverently make the sign of the cross and to pray. She taught us prayers, including *The Lord's Prayer* in Greek, making sure we said them before we went to sleep at night, always adding the names of our loved ones at the end, in a kind of litany, so God would keep all of us safe and well.

GOOD FRIDAY

Venerable father, we wish you a good Resurrection.

—Vasiliki to her father, April, 16, 1934

"*P*a, I'm sooo hungry. What can I eat? Mama's making us fast real strict because it's Good Friday."

"Don't complain, Nicky. In Greece they don't eat meat or dairy for almost two months before Easter. Snack on an apple and just don't think about it. Are you finished helping Harry? You've got to finish back in the kitchen before you can get ready for church. Remember, Mama's taking you to the Good Friday *Epitafios* service at church tonight."

"Are you coming, Pa?" Nick watched Papa pick up dirty dishes, place them under the counter where he had once shielded Tom Charlas, then rinse out a white cotton towel and wipe the counter.

"I wish I could, but somebody's got to stay here at the store."

We usually walked seven or eight blocks to St. Basil's, at Ashland and Polk, to attend church services. However, on Good Friday we worshiped at Holy Trinity Church on Peoria Street, close to Blue Island and Twelfth. Our neighbors in the Austin Lunch's building, Thea Stavroula and Chris, were our traveling companions as we boarded the Madison streetcar and rode east to Halsted. Although we regularly rode the streetcars, the ride to Holy Trinity Greek Orthodox Church on Good Friday evening was something special. It was the only evening of the year when streetcars were filled with Greeks traveling from all parts of the city to attend the religious services.

The building that housed Holy Trinity had originally been an Episcopal church. TEGEA, an organization of Chicago Greek immigrants from Mama's beloved township in Arcadia, initiated the purchase of the brown brick edifice in 1897, establishing the first permanent Greek church community in Chicago. Many of Mama's fellow Tegeates, some of her older cousins, and Uncle Christ Ganas were active members of the patriotic society. Mama eventually joined TEGEA, too, but since she rarely had time off from work, she attended only one meeting. Like Holy Trinity, most of the buildings that housed Chicago's first Greek Orthodox churches originated as Protestant or other houses of worship. Our own St. Basil's, with its horseshoe shaped balcony and occasional Stars of David, had been a Jewish Synagogue.

In the Thirties, almost every Greek immigrant living in the city considered the church on Peoria to be the Mother Church, an island of "old country" familiarity in the midst of metropolitan Chicago. Holy Trinity's interior walls, covered with colorful yet somber icons of familiar saints and scenes from the life of Christ, brought them temporary respite from the alien images of life in the immense Windy City. The voices of the priest and chanters intoning age-old prayers, a sound so familiar in Greek villages, also comforted the worshipers. Newcomers to America longed to be enveloped by the fragrances of smoking frankincense and melting wax candles, a spiritual reminder of the homeland.

Greeks were married at Holy Trinity and baptized their children there. As the years passed, other Greek Orthodox churches cropped up in the city, and worshipers could choose among St. Basil's, St. Constantine and St. Helen on the South Side, Annunciation on La Salle Street, Assumption at Harrison and Central, and other parishes further north and south. There were eleven Greek Orthodox parishes in Chicago by 1930. Yet on Good Friday great numbers returned to Holy Trinity where they had first worshiped God in America.

On that Good Friday in 1934, the five of us from Laflin and Madison transferred to Halsted's red trolley and headed south. By that time of night, there was only standing room on streetcars. If Nick, Chris, or I had seats, we were told to give them up to older people. We rode, standing in the aisle, tightly gripping handles built into the top of seat backs to steady ourselves against the wobbling, jolting streetcar. The brown leather straps hanging from the ceiling were too high for us to reach. All around us, we could hear people speaking quietly in Greek.

"How come almost everybody's got black clothes on? Is it like when Uncle Jim Koliveras died?"

"Yes, my little bird. We are sad because Jesus was crucified."

"Why are you whispering, Mama?"

"So the Americans won't call us greenhorns. There're too many of us together speaking Greek in the streetcar tonight." Thea Stavroula's limp slowed us down. We trailed behind the crowd pouring from the streetcar and found great numbers of people standing in front of the church. It was the tallest building in a block of old brick and wood-frame houses in a primarily Italian-American neighborhood. Several "Mom and Pop" type grocery stores were interspersed between the houses. The façade of the church rose skyward, and a Latin cross graced its apex. We joined a long line of worshipers slowly climbing the five front steps and entered the arched entrance of the church. Thea Stavroula asked the last person in line, "Will they let us in?"

"Of course, but only to venerate the icon. We'll have to come outside again after we reach the front of the church. Every space inside is filled already."

Mama assured us, "That's alright. After the *Lamentations* are chanted, the priest and everyone else will come outside for the procession around the block. That's one of the reasons we came here tonight. We came for the outdoor procession. It reminds me of my parents and my village." Thea Stavroula agreed that the services on Peoria Street reminded her most of being home in Sparta. While every Christian Orthodox church followed the tradition of a Good Friday procession, only Holy Trinity held theirs outdoors, like in the old country

"Are we going to stand up all night?" Chris asked the question weighing heavily on all our minds. I added my own complaint, whining "My new shoes hurt."

The woman ahead of Mama turned to face us and impatiently

replied, "Remember, Jesus hung on the cross longer than we're going to stand here tonight." When she turned around again to face forward and climb the steps, Mama gave Chris, Nick and me a sympathetic wink.

"Church will empty out when everyone follows the procession around the block," Mama reassured Chris. "After that we'll find a seat inside for your Mama, Christaki, and then you can sit on her lap. It won't be long." Mama knew how we felt. She had been on her feet from seven that morning at the restaurant.

After a while, we finally entered the narthex where the comforting and familiar scent of incense surrounded us. Our Mamas gave each of us nickels to deposit into the tray on the counter next to a stack of orange candles with fresh white wicks. Seeing us reach up to deposit our nickels, a gentleman wearing a badge embossed with a cross leaned over the counter and gave each of us two candles.

"How come we gots two candles, Mama?"

I answered my brother. "One to light now and make our cross in front of the icon over there. And the other one is for after, when we walk around the block in the big procession." Mama smiled approval.

"How do you know?" Nick challenged snippily.

"I remember from last year," I snapped back. Mama "Shusshed" both of us with the mere raising of an eyebrow.

We each lit a taper using a flame from one of the hundreds of lit candles standing in a shallow container of sand built into a section of the high counter. Guided by Thea Stavroula and Mama, we squeezed our way through the crowd to the closest of two huge glass encased icons installed on either side of the entrance to the church. It was a large icon depicting God the Father, with a long white beard, and Jesus, both sitting on thrones. A white dove, the symbol of the Holy Spirit, hovered over them. We three were too small to reach the image so our mothers lifted each of us, one at a time. Hoisted by our armpits, we were held close to the holy picture until we had finished making the sign of the cross. As Mama had taught me when I was very young, I joined my right thumb, index and middle fingers together to touch my forehead, chest, right shoulder and left shoulder, three times. Suspended off the floor by Mama, I completed my veneration of the earthly representation of the Holy Trinity with a quick kiss.

We joined the line again as it slowly continued down the middle aisle and finally entered the nave of the church. I was surprised to see a mass of people packed into the church's interior, jammed into every available space. As we entered the back of the nave, I heard more clearly the three chanters who continued their Byzantine chant. Only the priest's readings and prayers interrupted them. Worshipers, crushing in around us, were solemn. The icon depicting the Holy Trinity and the all-seeing eye of God looked down on each of us from the top of the iconostasion.

Nick tugged on Mama's skirt and when she bent down to see what he wanted, he whispered in her ear, "Are we there yet?"

"Not yet. We have to get to the very front of the church." Mama picked up Nick, as she had done in the narthex, and held him as high as possible so he could see above the line in front of us.

"Look in front. See a table with a roof of beautiful flowers over it? Look quickly. You're heavy."

When Nick was back on his own two feet, Mama bent over to whisper.

"The canopy of flowers you saw up there is supposed to be like the place where Jesus was buried. On the table, under the flower roof, is a velvet cloth icon with Jesus' picture on it. When we get to the front, we'll make the sign of the cross again and kiss the cloth. Then each one of you will scoot under the table for a special blessing from God, and then come back. My Mama made me and my sisters and brother do the same when I was a little girl. Then we'll go back outside to wait."

I tried to imagine Mama as a little girl crawling under a table at church with a long line of siblings waiting their turn behind her. But I was distracted from my thoughts by familiar faces in the crowd. "Look Mama, there's Thea Tasia and Georgia and little Helen." Then I searched for uncles in the crowd of men on the right side of the church.

"Shhh, we'll talk later," she whispered. "The other Theas and Uncles and cousins are probably here, too. God doesn't like for us to talk in church, only pray. Look ahead and don't be turning around. Jesus is up in the front." I saw the icon of God's eye staring down and decided to keep my thoughts to myself.

We reached the flowered bier minutes before the priest began chanting the *Lamentations*. We hurriedly kissed the velvet cloth embroidered with the image of Jesus in the tomb, scooted back and forth under the table that held the icon tapestry while making the sign of the cross three times. Fresh spring flowers covering the canopy seemed to float above us. In an instant, we were outside on Peoria Street again in a crowd that had grown while we were inside the church. The adults around us began singing the *Lamentations* as soon as they heard the familiar words through the doors and open windows of Holy Trinity.

"Thou O Christ the Life, was laid in the tomb, and armies of Angels were amazed, and they glorified Thy condescension."

"All generations offer adoration to Thy Entombment, O Christ."

Both Mama and Thea Stavroula knew most of the stanzas, recited in a Greek that we did not speak at home, and I wondered how Mama knew them. "Maybe in school," I thought to myself. "Same way I learned *America the Beautiful*." When the *Lamentations* were completed, four men appeared outside the front door of the church. They carried the floral canopy by four posts that held it high. My eyes followed the canopy as it slowly moved down Peoria Street. Looking between people in the crowd ahead of me, I caught a peek of robed altar boys carrying icons, large candles and the smoking censer in solemn procession. Then came the priest in his purple vestments, carrying the gold-covered Book of the Gospels. Chanters and worshipers followed, their somber faces shining in the warm glow of the candles. In later years, probably in the Fifties, a band of musicians joined the procession, filling Peoria and Halsted Streets with the plaintive melody of Chopin's *Funeral March*.

We reverently proceeded around the block in a long candlelight march, eventually turning toward Jane Addams's Hull House, which had vigil candles glowing from all its windows in honor of Greek

Orthodox Good Friday. The famous settlement house, where sociology was practiced, was the first Chicago institution to recognize the worthiness of Greek immigrants in America and to respect their holidays. Jane Addams was very much in the news of the Thirties because in 1931 she had received the first Nobel Peace Prize ever awarded to an American woman. Her death in 1935 brought her posthumous recognition for everything she had done to help the city's immigrants. Businesses in "Greektown" closed on the day of her funeral to mourn their loss and to show esteem for the American who respected their humanity and contributions to society. During the first years of Holy Trinity's Good Friday procession, most non-Greek Chicagoans watched the ancient commemoration of Christ's sacrifice with respect and quiet curiosity. Yet I do remember hearing about certain Good Fridays when raw eggs were thrown at the worshipers and shouts of "greenhorns," "Grease balls," "dirty Greeks," "greasy Greeks," "Wops," even "God damned Greeks" were hurled at them. But no one ever came to blows. After all, it was Jesus' funeral, just as Mama said.

At the end of the service, we filed through the church again to receive one of the fresh flowers, that had graced the canopy, from the priest's hand which we kissed reverently as he wished us "*Kali Anastasi*" (Good Resurrection). We took our flowers home to place on top of the icon of the Crucifixion in our parents' bedroom until the next year's Holy Week when, dried and shriveled, they would be replaced by fresh Good Friday flowers.

Worshipers were less somber as they exited onto Peoria Street at the end of the long service to seek out relatives and acquaintances. We, too, found my aunts with their families, and we all visited in front of the brown brick church. Nick, Chris, our cousins and I pestered our parents for pennies to buy the small round anise-flavored breads that were called *kouloures* from the elderly man who sold them. Each and every Good Friday night, we looked for him and his delectable treats, which he peddled from a huge straw laundry basket.

GREEKTOWN CHICAGO

*M*ama, what's this word?" I spelled it out for her in Greek. "P-a-n-t-o-p-o-l-e-i-o-n."

"My goodness. You're a schoolgirl, Helen. Use your head and figure it out. Look in the window and see what the guy's selling." My eyes searched the store window for clues, but before I had time to answer, I heard Mama say, "See? Means grocery store!" She may not have known the term "deductive reasoning," but my mother was an expert at it.

"Mama, I thought grocery store is "groceria."

"Yeah, in America we saying 'groceria,' but the really Mc Coy Greek word for it is *pantopoleion*. Means they selling little bit of everything in there."

The exotic, dowdy stores of Greektown were walking distance from Holy Trinity Church. Everyone we knew at Good Friday services used public transportation to return home. We traveled Halsted Street's tiny business district together, chatting in animated groups, until we arrived at our respective streetcar stops. It was the only place in the city where I could practice Greek by reading the words printed on signs and store windows. Struggling to unlock each word, letter by letter, I turned to Mama when I didn't know its meaning. My word puzzles were fun to do without a teacher breathing down my neck.

Several Greek restaurants, a travel agency, a newspaper office (the *Greek Star*, still in print, dates back to 1904), book and music stores, a photography studio, a pharmacy, Greek doctors' and lawyers' offices, sweet shops, grocery stores, the Washington Dairy, and Collias's Funeral Parlor comprised the Greek ethnic neighborhood, also known as "the Delta," near Holy Trinity. Blue Island Avenue, Harrison and Halsted formed a triangle of streets at the focal point of the Greek neighborhood. Stores were open after church, even at night, to serve a hoped-for influx of shoppers. More often than not our mothers dallied at the small grocery stores that smelled like oregano and vinegar-cured olives. They stopped to buy staples that could only be purchased in Greektown: feta cheese, dried figs, olive oil, dandelion greens, kalamata olives, Corinthian raisins and yogurt (forty years before it became a supermarket staple). Shopping, comfortably transacted in Greek, became a metaphorical trip back to the "old country."

While the grocers in Greektown and other ethnic neighborhoods brought comfort to immigrant families, the foods they provided were a target of ridicule. Olive oil, garlic, yogurt, pasta, tortillas, lamb, squid, pizza, dandelion greens, pierogi, bagels, blintzes, pilaf, feta and Parmesan cheeses, first brought to America in cheap suitcases and homespun sacks, were looked down upon by many Chicagoans as low class, peasant fare. Being ethnic was definitely not "in."

During our visits to Halsted Street, we would inevitably urge our parents to visit the *zaharoplastia* (sweet shops) that displayed luscious desserts inside glistening glass cases. Othon Spiropoulos, who first began working in the U.S. with Papa as a bootblack, was a gifted confectioner, and our favorite. His spotless, aromatic shop, which graced Halsted Street for decades, offered mouth-watering, freshly baked Greek sweets. In Spiropoulos's shop, we could find *Baklava* (the accent is always on the last syllable); *loukoumia* (jellied sweets flavored with extracts of rose, mastic, or bergamot, and dusted with powdered sugar) and *galactoboureko* (a creamy custard wrapped in crispy filo layers sprinkled with just enough honey syrup). But his *koulourakia* (plain butter cookies) and *kourambiedes* (butter cookies covered in confectioner's sugar) couldn't hold a candle to the ones Mama made at home. Customers sat on wire-backed chairs at small, marble-topped tables to enjoy Spiropoulos's treats, always served with glasses of cold water.

Beside the sweetshops, bookstores were another important feature of Greektown. They sold Greek books as well as up-to-date Greek language newspapers from New York and stale ones that had traveled ever so slowly by ship from Greece. They were also the only stores in Chicago where the newest recordings of popular Greek music could be found. They also sold candles for weddings, baptisms and Easter, and wedding stephana and white baby clothing for baptisms. The cluttered Kentrikon Bookstore was prominently located at Halsted and Blue Island Avenue. The proprietor, Michael Hatsos, eventually launched a Greek radio show that aired several times a week. News of local weddings, engagements, baptisms and funerals was announced between commercials aimed primarily at restaurant owners. Recordings of the latest music from Greece were aired between the news and commercials, sometimes in honor of a bride and groom. When our families finally bought their first radio sets in the Forties, Thea Tasia and Thea Politimi became avid listeners, and shared local Greek news with Mama who was too busy at the Austin Lunch to listen herself. About half-way through Hatsos's show, our aunts would "Shhush" us with solemn expressions and hushed voices demanding our silence as the announcer read the obituaries, while melancholy bells chimed in the background. My aunts would murmur, "*Aionia tou i mnimi*" after each sad notice, whether or not they knew the deceased.

Off limits to us in Greektown were the several *kaffeneia* (coffee houses) that functioned as the Greek immigrant equivalent of men's clubs. I remember watching Greek men, most with cigars and cigarettes hanging from their mouths, sitting at tables drinking coffee, playing cards and backgammon, or engaging in vociferous political discussions. A fog of thick tobacco smoke made it difficult to see beyond the plants growing out of coffee cans in the *kaffeneia* windows. The leaves of miniature orange and lemon trees (grown from the seeds of fruit eaten in Chicago), sweet basil and mint plants turned away from the pervasive tobacco fumes and reached outward toward the sun shining on Halsted Street. Barely discernable through the smoky haze were framed maps of Greece and sepia etchings of 1821 Greek Revolutionary heroes that hung on dark, bluish-green walls. Each coffee house was associated with a particular area of Greece:

Arcadia, Lakonia, and Messinia. Greek men would frequent the coffee house associated with their birthplace. Papa never spent time in Greektown's *kaffeneia*.

The business which Nick and I most assiduously avoided in Greektown, however, was the Collias Funeral Parlor on Halsted. Our cousins, Nick, and I had all had to go inside with our parents to pay respects whenever someone we knew died. Collias' windows were shrouded in morbidly gray, forbidding drapery; the suffocating smell of drooping cut flowers, perhaps chrysanthemums, hung heavy in the air. From a child's perspective, mourning Greek women of that generation were downright scary. Dressed completely in black, they wore hats with heavy black veils that obliterated their faces. The tragedy and woe expressed in their apparel was sobering enough, but their heartwrenching keening gave me the shivers. Our parents encouraged us to shake hands and say *"Zoi se sas"* (May you live to remember him) to them. We also had to convey our condolences to the stoic, grim, and silently grieving men of the family who wore black armbands that matched their black neckties. I felt sad, but uneasy. Worst of all was the casket. We shuffled over, ever so slowly, to make the sign of the cross, kiss the icon, and say a prayer over the "sleeping" deceased whose face wore layers of garrish pancake makeup that made him look neither like his natural living self nor a Hollywood star.

I also remember paying painful condolence visits with Mama to the homes of the bereaved where I found mirrors and pictures covered with black crepe fabric. Sweets were not served to guests, only coffee, *paximadia* (Greek biscotti), and a bit of cognac sipped in memory of the departed, accompanied by "May God rest his soul" and *"Aionia tou i mnimi."* Mourners were expected to be thoroughly somber (sweets and smiles were for happy occasions), and the bereaved were expected to be disheveled. Household mirrors were covered for forty days because the sorrow was supposed to run so deep that the mourners were not expected to want to do anything but mourn—not even comb their hair. Forty days following the death, a traditional Greek Orthodox memorial service was held at church by the departed's family. Mourning practices "lightened up" after the first forty days, but most widows wore black for seven years, and many donned black for the rest of their lives. I deeply dreaded Greek wakes, funerals, and eerie condolence calls. A mere glance of Collias's undertaking establishment in Greektown when I was a kid, brought uncomfortably morbid sensations, chilling remnants of childhood "visitations."

Before boarding our respective streetcars at the end of our Halsted Street walk, we exchanged wishes: "Happy Easter," "And again next year," and a "Good Resurrection." We looked forward to being reunited with our families and friends, twenty-four hours later, at the midnight Resurrection service. Returning home from Holy Trinity Church on "Big Friday" night, Chicago streetcars were again filled with Greek conversation, softly spoken, so we wouldn't be called "greenhorns," "God damn Greeks," or worse.

CHRISTOS ANESTI

We miss you most especially at Easter.

—Tasia to her mother, April 16, 1934

*H*oly Saturday was always a hectic day for Mama. Scurrying from kitchen to booths to counter all day, she waited on customers at the front of the restaurant while back in the kitchen she dyed dozens of eggs scarlet red, a Greek tradition. She dyed enough to give away for good luck at the restaurant, too. Non-Greek customers were always impressed by the pure crimson color, but they were surprised that Mama's eggs appeared well after most of them had celebrated Easter. Easter Sunday for Eastern Orthodox churches usually falls a week, two weeks, and sometimes a month after the date commemorated by most Christians.

Customers, who had already celebrated Easter, wondered why our family was just getting around to it. Papa explained that our church calendar originated in the days when all of Christianity was one religion. He said that Orthodox Christians faithfully adhered to rules established before the Great Schism of 1054 split Christendom into Eastern Orthodoxy and Catholicism, and centuries before Henry the Eighth started the first Protestant church. He further explained that church laws set up "way back when" ordained that Christian Easter had to follow Jewish Passover in order to be historically accurate. The Orthodox Church adhered to the rule. Papa's explanation completed, Mama assured Nick and me that "Our Easter day is the really Mc Coy one."

While she was in the restaurant's kitchen coloring eggs, Mama also began preparing the traditional Easter soup, *mageritsa*, made of lamb heart, liver, lungs and entrails. This delicacy was not destined for the Austin Lunch menu but lovingly prepared for her family's Easter celebration. Nothing edible was ever wasted in the old country she reminded us "because people don't got so much meat to eat. So they use up everything, even the guts. But you got to clean them real good. I don't eat that soup unless I know the guy that's cooking it is a real clean and particular cook."

Mageritsa, Mama style, took hours to make. She began by using a pencil to turn all the lamb intestines inside out so she could clean them. Then she finely minced the yards and yards of squeaky-clean intestines and sauteed them with finely chopped lamb heart, lungs, and liver along with a blend of onions, garlic, parsley and dill. The soup was left for hours to absorb the flavors of the herbs, and it was finally ready in the early hours of Easter morning, right after the Resurrection Liturgy. It was then that Mama cooked rice in the savory lamb broth and folded in a freshly prepared, frothy, thick, and tangy egg-lemon sauce.

With great anticipation around eleven o'clock on Saturday night, Mama, Nick and I walked to services at St. Basil's Church with Thea Stavroula and Chris. The most exciting part of the Resurrection service for a child is the darkening of the church minutes before midnight. All lights are turned off and all candles are snuffed out. Most people beyond the crowded church are at home, sleeping, while the Greek kid stands in a building packed full of hundreds of wide-awake worshipers, quietly waiting in darkness. Except for the sound of breathing and an occasional cough, the entire congregation is silent. At twelve o'clock sharp, the priest emerges from the darkened sanctuary holding a tall, white, candle. A tiny flame atop his candle is the only light, yet its miniscule flame sends out a glow that seems to illuminate half the church. The colorfully robed priest, his face bathed in yellow candlelight, approaches the congregation and chants, "Come receive light from the unwaning Light; and glorify Christ, Who has risen from the dead." His taper touches one candle with fire, then two, then three.

Worshipers turn and light their neighbor's tapers with their own. In minutes the dark church is aglow with hundreds and hundreds of candles. At the end of the Gospel reading, the worshipers accompany the priest in the most joyful, best-known hymn in Orthodoxy, "*Christos Anesti*" (Christ is Risen). The worshipers sing it over and over again throughout the early morning Liturgy, and in every church service for the next forty days: "Christ is risen from the dead, death trampling down death, and bestowing life to those in the tombs."

Close to two o'clock on Easter morning, after the priest had distributed bright red eggs and *antidoron* (bread representing the Eucharist), services were over. "Christ is Risen" and the response "*Alithos Anesti*" (Truly He is Risen) could be heard up and down the sidewalks outside St. Basil's. We invited relatives and acquaintances who didn't have other plans to join us on our hike back to Papa's restaurant for an Easter party.

In Greece it was a custom to bring home a burning candle from the Resurrection liturgy to re-kindle the vigil light in the icon corner. In the middle of the night, Chicago streetcars were filled with Orthodox faithful returning home with candles aglow. Mama, Thea Stavroula, Chris, Nick and I feebly illuminated the dark sidewalks of the West Side as we carefully transported our glowing Easter candles, bringing the "new light" back to our apartments. For people who were trying hard to blend into the American environment and not appear foreign, we must have attracted questionable attention. Anyone, not Greek, who saw us walking against the wind, protecting candle flames on the dark streets of Chicago after two in the morning, surely assumed that we were "greenhorns." Fiercely outmatched by sharp Windy City gusts, we used our hats, handbags, hands, and even opened our coats to shield the consecrated fire from extinction. Mama and Thea Stavroula complained that bringing Easter Fire home was a greater challenge in America than it had been in the old country. We considered ourselves lucky to get just one of our candles, still burning, back to the Austin Lunch where Papa enthusiastically greeted us with, "*Christos Anesti.*"

Before the door closed behind her, Mama took off her hat and coat and put on her apron. Then she disappeared into Uncle Charlie's kitchen to whisk together the luscious egg-lemon sauce destined for the *mageritsa* soup that she had prepared earlier in the day. After chanting three more rounds of "*Christos Anesti*," we broke the Easter fast with Mama's superb soup, red eggs, fresh sesame covered bread, and *koulourakia* (traditional Easter butter cookies). We had great fun playing the traditional egg cracking game to see whose red egg would remain unbroken after it had been tapped, point to point with everyone else's egg. "*Christos Anesti*" was repeated before each hit; the reply was always "*Alithos Anesti.*" The owner of the uncracked egg was winner of good luck for the year. We were annually reminded that a cracked Easter egg also symbolized the opening of the tomb in the miracle of Jesus' Resurrection.

A succulently roasted, traditional Paschal lamb was sometimes added to our midnight feast when Mama didn't plan to serve it in the middle of Sunday afternoon. Some years she was too exhausted after dying eggs, making soup, attending church and working all day at the restaurant to prepare lamb, potatoes and the rest of the feast for our midnight get-together. On those occasions, Mama finished cooking the long anticipated Pascal meal on Easter Sunday afternoon.

These Easter gatherings, whether they were held after midnight service or on Sunday afternoon, were an occasion for grown-ups to reminisce about *Pascha* (Easter) in Greece. Thea Stavroula proudly described the sumptuous Easter dinners served in her native Sparta. Mama remembered *Pascha* in Tegea. There was no doubt, however, that Papa was the best storyteller of all.

REMEMBERING PAPAPETROS

When he was in a jovial mood, Papa told the most entertaining stories, often ones he had heard from his father about Papapetros, the priest of Bedeni, a village next to Mercovouni. The Easter holiday especially inspired him to recall legends about the colorful old cleric, and we reveled in hearing the tales again and again.

"Father Peter, or Papapetros as he was known from one end of Peloponnesos to the other, lived at a time when priests in Greece were very active in the life of the country. These were the years after Greece's independence from Turkey after four hundred years of occupation.

"Our *patrida* (native land) had done very well for itself in ancient times. Greek philosophers had opened up the mind of Europe. Eighteen hundred years later, when the Turks were through with us, we were a backward, impoverished country. Greece never participated in the European Renaissance because it took place at a time in history when our Turkish captors were keeping us blind, deaf, and dumb.

"I never heard whether Petros's decision to become a priest was based on his devotion to God or just the need to survive during especially impoverished times. Something in his spirit, however, enabled him to serve God and his village, which before his ordination had a church but no priest. Once in a while Papanikolas, from Mercovouni, would go to Bedeni to say the Liturgy and preach to the Bedeniotes. Bedeni didn't have a teacher, either. Kids from Bedeni walked two miles to Mercovouni to go to school.

"Petros didn't have much education, but he knew how to read and write. It was not uncommon for Greeks to be illiterate after the Revolution because for four hundred years the Turks had forbidden them to learn how to read and write in Greek. Petros left Bedeni in his youth and journeyed to Russia to make his fortune. America hadn't been discovered yet by poor Greek immigrants like me. I don't know how long he stayed in Russia, but after a few years he married a Russian woman. He had promised her that if she married him, he would take her to the best place on earth.

"What did Petros consider the best place on earth? Bedeni, of course. He loved his village that much. So, after they married, Petros and his bride began their journey to Greece, traveling the entire distance from Russia in a horse-pulled wagon. When they reached Constantinople, the great city on the Bosphorus, his bride asked, 'Is this Bedeni?'

"'No,' Petros answered. 'Bedeni is much better than this place.'

"They traveled hundreds and hundreds of miles and finally arrived in Athens. Stopping to admire the white, marble treasures of the Acropolis shining brightly above them, his wife asked, 'Is this Bedeni?'

"'No, no,'" Petros replied. "'Bedeni is better.'

"They journeyed south of Athens into the Peloponnesos and finally reached the plain little town of Tripolis. Again she looked at him inquiringly, but before she could get the question out of her mouth Petros shook his head. 'Not yet. Bedeni is still better.'

"A half hour later they pulled into a small, dusty, almost treeless village. A cluster of tiny stucco houses with red tile roofs lined the narrow, rocky path that led through the unadorned town. Petros tightened his horse's reins, stopped the wagon and gazed around him. Pride and love filled his face. He lifted his hand and with a sweeping gesture introduced his village to his bride.

"'This, my dear wife, this is the very best place on earth. This is paradise. This is Bedeni!'

"Still seated atop the wagon, his wife looked around at the impoverished little village. Then she looked directly into his eyes and said, 'If this place is pleasing to you, then I will love it also.'

"After a few months, Petros decided to become Bedeni's priest. In those days there was a shortage of priests. In fact, churches were desperate for clergy and the required training in a theological school was often overlooked when a likely candidate showed an interest in the priesthood. In the case of Petros, who had no money but who could read and write, a theological education was overlooked altogether by the Bishop at Nafplion. By the way, did you know that right after the Revolution, the first capital of modern Greece was not Athens? It was Nafplion." Papa slipped a history lesson into his narrative whenever possible.

"Theological training was overlooked out of a dire need for priests, but the fees for ordination were not, and Petros had no money. Not being able to pay the expenses didn't dampen his desire. He walked 150 kilometers from Nafplion to Athens to beg the Bishop there to ordain him. Petros's powers of persuasion must have sharpened during his long journey. When he left Athens, he was a duly ordained priest with paid, return transportation to Bedeni.

"When Petros returned, he wore black robes and a *kalymmafhi*, the tall, black, brimless hat that an Orthodox priest in Greece is required to wear. He was called *Papa*petros and his wife was addressed as *Presvytera*, the title of respect for a priest's wife. They settled down in Bedeni, raised a fine family, and did God's work the best they could. It is said that in his prime, Papapetros was known from one end of Peloponessos to the other. He was already famous when I first saw him, a huge, robust man, and so very full of life. I went to school with one of his sons but heard the stories about him from my father, my uncles, and older men in the village. I remember one story my father told me about a particular Easter when Papapetros made village tongues wag.

"A short distance from Bedeni and Mercovouni, there's a small church on top of a mountain dedicated to St. Elias. The little church has no congregation or assigned priest. It's only opened a few times during the year. One of those times is the day after Easter, a big holiday in Greece.

"It's traditional for all villagers from Bedeni and Mercovouni to make the short pilgrimage to St. Elias on Easter Monday. They pack up all their day-old Easter leftovers: the lamb, Easter breads, red eggs and wine and carry them up the mountain. When services are over, they picnic together. A few musicians are brought along for singing and dancing, too. This all takes place on the mountaintop, right outside the little church of St. Elias.

"The priests from Mercovouni and Bedeni celebrate the Liturgy together. Because the tiny church can't accommodate all the people, more worshipers stand outside the building than can squeeze into the church. And, you know, it's easy to become inattentive and noisy while standing outside during a three-hour service.

"My father told me that before the Liturgy had been completed during one such celebration, some easily distracted young men from Bedeni, impatiently standing around outside St. Elias, challenged a few equally distracted young men from Mercovouni to a shooting match. There's always been a friendly rivalry between the neighboring villages and it came to a head that particular Easter Monday. The young men found a huge rock a short distance from the church and set a red Easter egg, their target, into a crevice near the top of the rock. One guy volunteered to be the scorekeeper. He wanted to see which marksmen were best: those from Mercovouni or those from Bedeni. Each side started taking turns shooting at eggs while some other fellow continuously replaced the shattered targets with more Easter eggs.

"As Papapetros chanted the sacred words of the Divine Liturgy, he heard a sudden burst of gunshots, shouting and commotion. He abruptly stopped his prayers, went behind the altar, and called someone to his side to ask what was going on. When he heard it was a shooting contest between Mercovouni and Bedeni, he became very agitated, then whispered a question into the gentleman's ear.

"'I don't know, Father,' was the reply.

"'Find out and come back immediately,' the priest demanded.

"Visibly irritated, Papapetros resumed the Liturgy, taking his accustomed place in front of the altar with his back to a buzzing congregation of distracted worshipers. A few minutes later, the messenger returned and whispered his reply into the priest's ear. 'The Mercovouniotes.'

"Papapetros stopped chanting, grabbed the shotgun he always kept behind the altar and raced outside in the direction of the commotion. He owned a shotgun because those were the days after the Revolution when thieves and scoundrels threatened the population. Kind of like the old West in America.

"Everyone left the church in a frenzy when shouts of 'It's Papapetros' were heard coming from the direction of the contest. His colorful vestments flowing luminously behind him, Papapetros aimed his shotgun and joined the shooting match on the Bedeniotes side, finally winning the competition for his village because he was such a good marksman. When they had used up the red Easter eggs, the contest was declared to be over. Papapetros returned to complete the Divine Liturgy with the dumbfounded, trembling priest from Mercovouni.

"When services were over, foods carried to the mountain top in baskets and roasting pans that morning were set out on the ground over tablecloths, and the picnic began. Food and drink were shared, and the two villages ate together as one, happy, united community. After lunch, musicians started playing beloved old songs and traditional folk dancing, part of every happy Greek event, commenced outside St. Elias Church. Papapetros, himself, joined the dancing and moved to the front of the moving circle to lead the dancers. This shocked most of the villagers because they had never seen a priest dance before. You can imagine how strange a sight it was in those days—even now in our own modern times of 1934, we never see priests dancing at weddings or celebrations.

"The Mercovouniotes, bothered by their defeat that day, began to tease Bedeni's cleric. One man in the crowd needled the proud priest by shouting a question at him.

"'Papapetros, are priests permitted to dance?'

"In reply, Papapetros removed his *kalymmafhi*, you know, his priest's hat. He walked over to a boulder and carefully positioned his black hat on top of the huge rock. Then he rejoined the dancers and shouted to the crowd.

"'Over there, on the rock, is the *Papa* (priest). Over here, in the dancing, is Petros. And Petros is going to dance all day long!'

"The villagers cheered with shouts of '*Yiasou*' (To your health), 'May you live a thousand years!' and '*Kai tou chronou*' (And again, next year), Papapetros!'"

When Papa finished his story, we were well into Easter's early morning hours. All of us were exhilarated by Papa's tale and full of Mama's terrific soup. Outside Papa's restaurant on the Madison Street sidewalk, exhausted but still struggling to keep our Easter candles lit, we wished each other "Christ is Risen." As we dragged ourselves home, we passed the dark silhouettes of two or three men under newspapers, snoring in the doorways of stores between Papa's place and our apartment a half block away. Retired for the night, they snored away, oblivious to the gracious, centuries-old Easter rites being enacted, a few steps from their concrete bedrooms. Our neighborhood's colorful neon signs had been extinguished. Except for Papa's restaurant (open 24 hours but no liquor sold after 2 a.m.), all the saloons on Madison Street had finally turned off their lights and locked their doors for the night.

UPSTAIRS AND DOWNSTAIRS AND DOWN THE STREET

*H*ey, Pa! Guess what I just seen!"

When Nick ran in from the front door, he found my father sitting on a counter stool working at keeping his accounts in order; he did his own bookkeeping. Wrapped in numbers, Papa's brain concentrated on entries in the heavy black ledger book on top of the white marble surface. But he played along with my brother's riddle with little thought to the childish question before him. "What?"

"A stiff!"

"A what?" Blood rushed to my father's head.

"A stiff."

"Did you say a stiff?" Papa asked cautiously. The alarming image of a corpse slumped in front of the Austin Lunch jarred my father's senses. After all, this was West Madison Street.

"Yeah, a stiff. Some guy died upstairs in one of Mr. Prevolos's apartments and they had a wake up there last night. That means they stay up all night to watch the dead guy. Chris told me all about it, Pa. The dead guy was in a big box in the living room. Chris says he was all dressed up, looked the best he ever seen him. People came over to visit and sat around the guy in the box, but he didn't move or nothing because he was dead."

Relieved, Papa said, "Yes, I heard about the gentleman's death. His funeral is today."

"That's right, Pa. That's the exciting part. They just left the apartment upstairs to go to church, but they had a big problem."

"What was that?"

"They was leaving the apartment with the guy all closed up in the box, but the stairway ain't wide enough for the box. So Chris and me, we saw them take the stiff out of the box and carry him downstairs, outside the box. They brung the box down sideways and put the dead guy back in when they was on the sidewalk. He really was all stiff and everything. I don't think he could bend at all, Pa."

"Well, they say there's more than one way to skin a cat."

"Guess so, Pa. And speaking of cats, I just remembered something else. I went down to the basement with Uncle Charlie this morning. Boy oh boy, Pa, this basement's pitch dark and real spooky. It's gigantic. Goes all the way under the Madison Street sidewalk and winds up, I don't know where."

"Been working at this store a pretty long time, Nicky. Remember? I go down there all the time. It's dark as a cave, damp and cold."

Nick was anxious to share what he had seen. "Yeah, Pa, but when Uncle Charlie turned on the lights, I thought I saw cats running around down on the floor. But Uncle Charlie told me to be careful because they weren't no cats. They were great big rats. He said someday he's going to bring a gun to work and go down there and shoot them. Pa, I want to go down to the basement again when Uncle Charlie goes to shoot the—"

"Banana oil. Uncle Charlie isn't going to shoot any rats, Nicky. That's bunk. We try to control them with traps and poison because they're a menace in this neighborhood. A rat bite can make you real sick so we all have to be careful. There are cats around but the problem's too big. That's why we keep the door to the basement closed up tight and we keep our eyes open real good when we go down there."

"Yeah, Uncle Charlie says they'll eat anything."

"And Uncle Charlie's right. I had to call a plumber to fix a leak in the basement a couple months ago. He told me the rats bit right through the lead pipe."

When draft beer was introduced at the Austin Lunch, the only space to store beer barrels was in the dark, smelly basement. Papa, and Nick, when he was older, had to go down there all the time to replace empty barrels with full ones. I marveled at their courage and kept my trips down to the basement at a minimum. I'll never forget the dank, moldy stench of that spooky, black basement, and how I looked forward to seeing light again as I hastily climbed to the top of the stairs.

Gradually, Nick and I were allowed to spread our wings and cross streets on our own, carefully of course, with multiples of eyes. Our joy was amplified when our personal boundaries finally stretched far enough to include two local movie theaters. Thrilled as we were to be allowed to go to "the show," Nick and I argued about which theater to attend. Our parents mandated that we had to go together or not all, only on Saturday mornings and only after our chores at home and store were finished. Nick's favorite was the Century movie theater on Madison, a block east of Papa's restaurant, which showed cowboy movies with Tom Mix and Buck Jones. The Century also featured Buck Rogers and Flash Gordon, the great-grandfathers of Luke Skywalker and Hans Solo. These adventure films were made into serial movies which drew us back every Saturday because we were desperate to know if our heroes had survived or perished.

I preferred the American Theater, on Ashland a half block west of Madison, because it featured movies with the "swell" dancing of Fred Astaire and Ginger Rogers. Great musicals plus wonderful dramas and comedies with Clark Gable, Claudette Colbert, William Powell and Myrna Loy played at the American along with films starring six-year old Shirley Temple, the rage of the Great Depression. She was introduced into America's hearts and minds in 1934. Even Mama, who was not a movie fan, loved Shirley Temple.

Adult admission was fifteen cents. Nick and I qualified for a child's ticket. It cost a dime. The price included a double feature: two full length movies, a cartoon, and a newsreel. Occasionally movie theaters offered promotional gimmicks to draw customers. Sometimes a glass dish was given with an adult ticket. Whole sets of dishes could be collected by devoted motion picture fans while they were entertained by their favorite stars, all for fifteen cents. Cousin Jimmy Ganas brought green glass dishes and serving pieces home to Thea Politimi when he worked as an usher at the Senate Theater, pieces which are now known as "antique Depression glass."

PAPA'S DAY OFF

*T*he frame of electric light bulbs that outlined the front window of the Austin Lunch gave Papa an excuse to take a break from the restaurant on Mondays, a habit that he religiously adhered to well past his retirement, decades after the light bulbs had vanished from the window and the building was gone. It became known as "Papa's day off."

When light bulbs burned out in the Thirties, the utility company provided free replacement bulbs. Papa had to travel downtown to return burned out bulbs at the Commonwealth Edison Company where he traded them in, without charge, for brand new ones. He started running this errand on Mondays because it was the least busy day of the week at the restaurant. While he was downtown, he took in a movie, and when Nick and I were out of school, he took us with him.

He liked to frequent a movie theater called "The One Hour Show," which exclusively ran 60-minute newsreels. In the days before television, the only place to see moving images of news was in the local movie theaters, on newsreels shown in between the cartoons and double features. The One Hour Show specialized in these projected newsreels.

Trading in light bulbs also led to Papa's habit of going to the Loop every Monday, even when he didn't go to Commonwealth Edison. The "Loop," the center of downtown Chicago, is so named because elevated train tracks loop around the main business section which is crammed with shops, restaurants, sky scrapers, department stores, government buildings, hotels, and theaters. The movie theaters were exceptionally inviting to Papa on his day off, as were visits to several of his *patriotes* (fellow Greeks) who had offices or businesses down-town. Eventually, Monday became Papa's official day of leisure.

When business picked up after repeal, Papa raised Uncle Charlie's salary and began paying Mr. Prevolos back rent. He also started going to the race track. "Vasiliki, tomorrow I'm taking the day off. I'll be back by dark. You, Charlie, and the waitress can handle everything. Mondays are slow."

"Where you're going? If I can ask."

"Taking a ride into the country."

"How?"

"On the train."

"Alleluia on the bum. Are you going to go feed the horses, Paul? There's a Depression going on."

"Bessie, do you know that the race track has been busier than ever during the Depression?"

"So just because lots of people want to throw their money away, do you have to do it, too? If everybody jumps in Lake Michigan, are we going to go follow them? You know how people get to Hades, Paul? One guy he follows the other one. Now that we're making a few nickels you don't have to throw money away at the racetrack. I know I'm not going to stop you. I just want to make you think about it. And how about Helen and Nicky?"

"What about them?"

"You not going to take them with you for fresh air and sunnyshine? Are you going to leave them here under my feet all day? They got summer vacation from the school. Give them day off from Madison Street, too."

"OK. That's all right with me. I'll take them."

Nick and I were delighted to accompany Papa on his day off for a change of scenery. Mama could see how excited we were as we twirled around on the counter chairs, listening to her traveling instructions, while we waited for Papa who was in the kitchen with Uncle Charlie.

"Make sure you hold on tight to Papa's hand, wherever you going. Keep an eye on each other and on Papa. Don't talk to strangers. In case you have to go to the bathroom, don't touch anything and wash your hands with soap, real good. Nicky, you only go in the bathroom with Papa. And Helen, you make sure Papa and Nicky is staying outside the ladies bathroom door when you go inside by yourself. Don't eat no junk because junk is going to make you sick. You going to have a good time, my little birds. It's a beautifool day to go out in the country."

"I wish you could come, too, Mama."

"Me, too. Not to see the lousy horses, but to be together and see some sunnyshine and breathe some fresh air without smoke in it. But somebody got to be here at the store. Here's Papa. All set?"

"Charlie gave me a couple of bucks to play a horse for him."

Mama shook her head. There wasn't much she could do about their fascination with the sport of kings; she still hadn't figured out its lure.

We waved good-by to Mama, who watched from the restaurant's front window, as we boarded the Madison streetcar heading for the Loop. After a few minutes, we passed a large, elegant store on the south side of Madison. A uniformed man was stationed in the shadow of the store's classy green-and-white striped awning that shaded the building's distinguished front door.

"Who's that guy, Pa?"

"The doorman to the fanciest furniture store in town, John M. Smythe & Company."

"Is that where our furniture came from, Papa?"

"Afraid not, Helen. Mama and I bought our furniture from a second-hand store before you were born."

It was a warm summer day in July of 1935. I wore my floral print cotton dress, Nick was in his usual short pants, and Papa was dressed in his regulation white long sleeved shirt and dark tie. He looked just like he did at the restaurant, except he had left his long white half-apron behind; he wore a suit jacket instead. Part of the morning's *Chicago Tribune* was folded and stuffed into his coat pocket; a jaunty straw hat shaded his eyes and forehead. When he was outdoors in summer, Papa always wore a "boater," a stiff hat with flat crown and a brim of pale yellow straw set off by a black band. The hat shielded his fair complexion from the sun, but tiny spots of sunlight reached Papa's face through gaps in the braided straw.

Nick and I jumped off the streetcar step, thrilled to be downtown. Less than two miles from where we lived, downtown was excitingly remote and enchanting for two sheltered Depression kids. The streetcar had deposited us across the street from the Chicago and Northwestern Railroad Station, just west of the Civic Opera House and the bridge over the Chicago River. Each of us tightly held on to one of Papa's hands as we crossed the busy street and entered an enormous gray railroad station on the north side of Madison Street. A large clock attached to the front of the building showed us it was still well before noon.

"This place is gigantic. It's even got a different sound in it."

"Those are echoes of all the sounds being made in here, Nicky." Except when he was real busy at the store, Papa explained things to us.

We walked across the shiny floors and passed dozens of benches filled with people, some stretched out and sleeping on the hard, polished wooden seats. Suitcases, bundles and brown shopping bags were clustered around waiting passengers.

"How come they're sleeping here, Pa? Why don't they go home?"

"They're waiting for trains to come and take them where they want to go. This is called the waiting room. Lots of people change from one train to another here in Chicago and sometimes they have to wait a long time between trains."

"Are we going to sleep here, too?"

"No, our train is waiting for us, Nicky. But we have to buy our tickets first."

We entered another cavernous room with light streaming in from windows high above the floor close to an unreachable four or five story ceiling. Papa guided us to a wall in which an endless row of little windows had been installed, with a man in a tiny office behind each opening. Papa approached the man at the window.

"Three roundtrips for Arlington Park. One adult and two children, please."

I only saw the man's lips move. The window was far above our reach and noisy echoes prevented me from hearing his voice. I watched Papa respond to what the man said by pushing money through a large slit under the glass. The man pushed back three tickets. My father checked them and asked, "Which track does it leave from?"

The man's lips formed "two." Papa thanked him, took Nick and me by the hand, and led us outside through an immense door. A towering black roof above us was attached to the huge building we had just left, but further on I could see daylight. Gigantic black trains were lined up along the terminus of uncountable sets of railroad tracks. Each track was labeled with a very large number. Papa led us to track two.

Uniformed conductors were stationed along the string of train cars, near the doors. Smelly steam escaped from underneath the tremendous steel wheels of a black locomotive on track three. Nick and I, at eye level with the giant hubs, were startled by a loud hissing noise and a powerful gush of steam that squirted out at us as we walked by. Papa laughed when we jumped.

Nick strained to look ahead, to the front of our train so that he could check out its black engine, but Papa tugged him toward the door. A conductor helped us up a portable set of stairs which led us onto the train's own steps, then Papa ushered us into a railroad car.

"Let's sit by the window," Nick said, choosing one of many unoccupied seats.

Papa grabbed the back of the seat and reversed it so two seats faced each other. "Now all three of us can sit together and you each have a window to look out of."

"Can't do that on the new Green Hornet streetcars," Nick complained.

"This trip is longer than a streetcar ride and costs more so we get other benefits."

The short tufts of dark green horsehair-like fabric on the seats irritated the backs of my legs when I sat down.

"The seat's itchy. It pinches," I whined.

"All abooooard!" came the conductor's call.

"That's the signal that the train's about to leave the station. We just made it!" Papa said.

As the car began to move, I remembered that we had taken the same trip in the past, prior to hard times and Mama's employment at the restaurant. "We did this before, Papa, a long, long time ago."

"Yes, but I think Nicky was too young then to remember."

Nick was noticing everything now. "Hey, we're passing people down in the station. Wow, Pa, we're moving." The immense train began one of its daily runs from downtown Chicago to the suburbs in the northwest of the city.

"We're out of the station. Look at all the tracks. There's thousands of them! Look at the big buildings. Hey, Pa, does Uncle Paul work here?" Nick faced the open window and already had a speck of soot on his cheek.

"No, Uncle Paul works for the Santa Fe Railroad at another train station. This is the Chicago and Northwestern line."

After we pulled out of the railroad yard, the train picked up speed and we watched our city speed by as Papa took the newspaper out of his pocket, unfolded it, and turned to the *Tribune's* sports pages. He began reading up on the day's races at Arlington Park, the racetrack in Arlington Heights, Illinois, where we were headed.

Nick watched the cheerful conductor as he bounced through the speeding car to check tickets. Nick's eyes were riveted on him as he lurched into the adjacent train car through connecting doors.

"Pa, isn't he afraid he's going to fall off the train? He's outside between the doors!"

Papa didn't look up from his newspaper. "He's got to be real careful."

The first stop was at Clybourn; no one got off or on so the train moved again. City apartment buildings with brick fronts in various shades of brown came into view. Row after row of brick buildings, studded with rectangular windows, raced by the train's window as we clipped past them. Wooden porches, with crisscrossing wooden stairs, painted an industrial gray, seemed to lunge at us.

While Papa intently read his newspaper, Nick stared out the window and quietly sang about the Isle of Capri under his breath. Fresh air from the Northwest Side of Chicago mixed with the noises and soot of the moving train. I concentrated on the scenery. Single-family homes with front porches, trees, flower gardens and vegetable plots moved into view.

Our locomotive pulled into the Norwood Park station, a neat little brick and frame building, typical of small midwestern railroad depots. Staring out the open window, I noticed two children with bikes. Straddling shiny two-wheelers, a boy and a girl were stopped at the signal crossing waiting to get to the other side of the tracks when the train pulled away. I noticed that Norwood Park was full of trees bearing heavy limbs and branches, thick with millions of shiny green leaves. I had never before seen so many trees in one neighborhood. Even Garfield Park didn't have trees that big, that beautiful, and that densely planted together.

Lovely lawns stretched in all directions from beautiful, well-kept homes. Most were two-story, white-frame dwellings with picket fences; others were brown brick bungalows. The train slowly began moving, but my eyes stayed glued on the children playing in the front yards of some of the homes and in the backyards of others. Those lucky kids lived in houses with pleasant front porches, not in city apartments attached to so many other apartments with dingy, dark hallways. They lived surrounded by trees, not on busy streets too far from city parks. I closed my eyes and dreamed. I pictured Mama and Papa and Nick and myself living in a single-family house with a yard, like the ones I saw close to the Norwood Park station. It would be so quiet a neighborhood that little kids could ride bikes and cross streets at anytime without their mamas and papas worrying about them being hit by monstrous streetcars. Suddenly, I was startled out of my daydream by a shout, "Park Ridge!" Papa explained we had left Chicago. Park Ridge was an independent town that was not a part of our city. It looked so different from where we lived, I felt as if we had left our native land and were traveling through a foreign country.

"Des Plaines is next." The conductor again interrupted my fantasy and stark reality pierced my dream. I knew I would never live in a house like those I had seen in Norwood Park. My secret wish of living in a beautiful, tree-filled neighborhood was too good to ever come true. The voice of the conductor returned me to our train ride and I realized that Papa was talking. "Des Plaines is older than Chicago. See that sign over there where it says "Sugar Bowl?" That's a candy and ice cream store owned by a Greek man. We're in downtown Des Plaines."

Papa always pointed out businesses or buildings owned by fellow Greek immigrants. He never envied them if they were more successful than he, or put them down if they were less prosperous. Papa was genuinely proud of the accomplishments of immigrant boys who, like himself, shined shoes, washed dishes, checked hats, worked in mines or on the railroad, and struggled to own their own businesses, no matter how big or small. He hated the Depression knocking them down and always assured us, "It's temporary. We'll make it when the country's in better shape. Even the big, big tycoons are hurting. Immigrants like us are on the bottom rung of the ladder."

Nick looked out at Des Plaines while we were stopped at the brown brick railroad station. "This is downtown? How come there's no big buildings, Pa?"

"Des Plaines is a tiny city compared to Chicago. There are no skyscrapers here."

We began moving again. Mount Prospect was next. The stop was brief and before we knew it, the conductor announced,

"Arlington Park Race Track!"

ARLINGTON PARK

*P*apa jumped off his train seat as soon as he heard we were about to pull into the Arlington Park station. He stuffed the *Tribune* sports pages back into his jacket pocket, grabbed the back of the seat to steady himself, and herded us down the swaying aisle. Even though the train was still moving, he hustled to get to the door. Wobbling, we stood near the steps in a tiny alcove that smelled like coal. "Hold on tight because we're going to lurch forward when it stops. Be careful. Stay close to me."

The racetrack had its own special stop on the railroad line. Mama always said she knew the reason. "Takes the suckers directly to the door. Got them where they want them."

Papa was anxious to get inside the vast fenced area.

"Why are you walking so fast, Papa?"

"We don't want to miss the Daily Double."

"Oh. What's that?"

"I'll explain after we get in and settled. Come on, shake a leg!"

Crowds of excited people rushed from the train stop toward the immense grandstand in the distance. When we reached it, Papa stood in line at a tiny stand to buy a program. The seller gave him a thick green pencil, too. Papa let Nick hold the pencil and gave me the book.

"What's this for?"

"It lists the names and numbers of all the horses running in today's races. Don't lose it. Look through it when we sit down and pick out a winner."

I opened the book as we walked close behind Papa and immediately spotted a name I liked. "Blueberry Pie? A horse is named Blueberry Pie. That's Mama's favorite."

"We'll get inside first and then study the book."

"What are those guys selling over there, Pa?"

"Scratch sheets."

"What's that?"

Papa explained as we sped to keep up with him. "The guys that write those pieces of paper want us to think they've got exclusive information on each horse and that they can figure out the winners. If we pay them and buy the sheet, we'll win."

"Does it really work?"

"They're just selling guesses to make a living. If they really knew the winners, they'd be rich guys. They wouldn't be standing out here everyday in the heat and sometimes in pouring rain, screaming at the top of their lungs to sell sheets of paper. Nobody knows the winner until the race is over and everybody sees which horse comes in first."

By then Papa had bought our tickets and was handing them over at the turnstile to a man wearing a blue uniform. We entered Arlington at basement level, under the grandstand. All around us racing fans were intently studying programs, newspapers and scratch sheets. The back wall of the immense room was studded with a row of small windows similar to those at the railroad station. A food concession was located in the center of a sprawling area where fresh popcorn was perking and spilling out of a machine. The place smelled like cigarette smoke, hot dogs and popcorn.

"Pa, do we buy our tickets to get back home over there by those windows?"

Papa looked up from the program he was scrutinizing and gazed toward the back wall. "No, Nicky, we already have return tickets. Bought them at the train station downtown. Those windows are for placing bets. I'm going to do that first and then we'll have some hot dogs for lunch."

Nick and I looked at each other with smiles. Papa had not forgotten it was time to eat, and we'd be eating hot dogs, a rare treat for us because Mama and our aunts disdained the all-American frankfurter. It had something to do with not knowing what kind of "old meat scraps" were used to produce them. The women of our family were suspicious of sausages they didn't make themselves. The tantalizing aroma of steaming hot wieners, onions, pickle relish and mustard rising off street push carts always tempted us, but Mama forever rejected our suggestion of buying anything from these outdoor food vendors, hot dogs in particular.

"You tell me if you really want to eat this guy's hot doggies. You see him? He blows his nose and worse—he wipes his behind, too. But where he washes his hands? Do you see a sink and soap anyplace? You want to eat from somebody that got no place to wash his hands? No siree." Mama's arguments were always pursuasive.

Papa headed for a window with a "Daily Double" sign hanging over it. He spoke to the caged man who had a cigarette dangling from his lips and a green visor shading his forehead. Papa pushed money into the opening at the bottom of the bars. In return he received a colored ticket that he slipped into his shirt pocket.

"How come your hands are shaking, Pa?" Nick was naive and blunt.

"My hands aren't shaking. See!" Papa stretched out both of his short, substantial hands in front of Nick's face. Flushed and excited, Papa was half-angry and half-embarrassed. "Let's get some hot dogs now." The invitation distracted Nick from any further behavioral study of our father.

After lunch, we strolled into a green park between the grandstand and race track. We reached the chain link fence in time to see and hear a bugler dressed in a black velvet cap, bright red coat, white riding pants and high black boots. A white scarf was elegantly tied around the neck of his fancy white shirt, like a movie star. He turned toward the grandstand, paused, and blew into a shiny bugle. Papa told us the man in the red coat would play a bugle call before every race because his job was to announce the arrival of the race horses and jockeys on the track. As Papa spoke, a line of beautiful horses slowly ambled onto the dirt track and began parading before the crowd. Atop each horse I observed a tiny rider, no taller than myself, arrayed in a brilliantly hued shirt, tight fitting white pants, and high black boots. The gloriously bright colors of the jockeys' shirts matched their caps; they wore goggles, too. The trappings on each horse were the same colors as its rider's apparel. Each immense, lanky horse wore a huge number printed on a white piece of cloth that hung from beneath a simple black leather saddle.

"Those saddles aren't like the ones the cowboys got in the movies."

"No. They try to keep everything on a racehorse as light as possible, so he can run better and faster. That's why jockeys are such small men. It's almost time for the race. Look, they're heading for the gate."

"What gate?"

"That moveable metal contraption over there. See? It's got numbers on it. Each horse fits into a space under its number, closed in by a door. When the race starts, they automatically open all the doors at the same time, so all the horses start off together. Then they run all around this track, and whichever horse gets to the finish line first is the winner. See this wire right here in front of us, above our heads? This wire is the finish line. Winning money is paid for horses that come in first, second and third place."

We admired the big signs with numbers in the infield that were surrounded by colorful flowers and vast green lawns. The signs had something to do with odds, Papa said, but it was too complicated to follow. I suddenly remembered the most important question of all. "What's the name of the horse you bet on, Papa?"

"Greek Fire. It's number four. I liked it because it's got Greek in its name. But the experts like it, too. It's got good odds."

"They're off!" A bell rang at the same time the announcer's voice startled us in a blast from the public address system. I looked around and noticed that the place was packed with yelling people. Horse players in back of us began pressing forward and before we knew it we were pinned to the fence. The announcer shouted the running order of horses, but it was difficult to understand his rapid litany. Pushing adults were yelling names and numbers, and the combined shouts mushroomed into a roar that kept getting louder as the race progressed. Papa's face was red and the short gray hair that showed from under his boater hat looked even whiter in contrast to his very pink complexion.

"Come on Greek Fire!" he shouted. Papa was so involved in the running of the horses he seemed oblivious to the world around him. People crushed in around us and pushed us into the fence under the rail. Nick and I cowered under the press of humanity, but Papa didn't notice. His eyes were riveted on the horses fast approaching the finish line under a cloud of dust. As the horses roared passed us, I barely caught a glimpse of jockeys bent over flat, leaning toward the heads of their horses. They seemed to be hitting the animals, but they passed so quickly I wasn't sure if I had imagined sticks in their hands or not. Suddenly it was quiet; everyone had stopped screaming. Confusion and dust prevented me from seeing what was going on. Papa looked disappointed.

"What did we win, Pa?"

Nick's voice startled him back to reality. Papa had forgotten we were there.

"Nothing this time. The big board says Greek Fire came in fifth. That means we lost the Daily Double, too."

Papa looked too disappointed for me to ask what the Daily Double was all about, so I left the question for another outing. He looked at the little colored ticket in his shirt pocket and turned it over to Nick.

"Here, you can have the ticket. It's no good now."

"Gee, thanks, Pa. You mean if you lose we get to keep the tickets?"

"It's better to win, Nicky. You can have your pick of all these other losing tickets."

Discarded blue, yellow, red and green tickets were scattered all over the ground. "Looks like lots of people lost, Pa."

In no time at all, we went back to the little windows and Papa pushed more money under the cage. Before the second race, he took us to the paddock area to see the horses, up close. We watched them being walked, saddled and petted by men who, Papa said, were trainers and owners. The men were quiet and calm, but a few of the horses were jumpy and nervous.

"That horse gots a wild look in his eyes, Pa. Is that good or bad?"

"Who knows?"

We watched the third race from high up in the grandstand where we viewed the entire track. Flat but verdant fields and farms studded with neat rows of green corn stretched for miles beyond the boundaries of the racetrack. Before each race we heard the bugle announce the arrival of horses on the track, and during each race we witnessed the surge of excitement in Papa followed by quiet disappointment at the end. Nick and I added more colored tickets to our collection before we traveled downstairs to the little windows again.

Papa held up the latest paper purchase for us to see. "Experts don't pick it, but I bet on it anyway. This horse is number five, Blueberry Pie."

"Mama's favorite!"

"Let's go downstairs again so we can see Blueberry Pie better. The gate's set up close to the fence."

We admired the horse and the beautiful scarlet and royal blue colors of his jockey. The big animal resisted as its trainers tried to prod him into a gate position under the number five. "Looks like Blueberry Pie doesn't like the gate."

The horses were finally trapped behind the swinging doors and the announcer's voice blasted over us again announcing that they were "off." Suddenly over the din we heard him say, "And Blueberry Pie is moving up."

"Come on Blueberry Pie!" Nick was shouting this time.

In no time at all, the sound of hoof beats approached from the left again. The thunderous noise from the crowd around us made it impossible to hear the announcer as a cloud of dust and horses raced by in front of us. We had been pushed into the chain link fence again but were instantly released when the race was over. "I think I saw Blueberry Pie's colors go by in the front."

Papa bent over to pick up his straw hat, knocked off in the crush of excitement. Bright red and stiff with tension, he looked over at the huge sign in the infield. Then my father relaxed and smiled. "He did it! Blueberry Pie came first! Well, how do you like that? Let's go get our money!" Papa's grin widened and his eyes sparkled. "And he was a long shot, too."

Papa grabbed each of us by the hand and led us to the payment windows. Nick and I dragged our feet through a sea of colored tickets all the way to the payoff. Still smiling, Papa collected his winnings and peeled off two singles from a clutch of bills.

"Here's a dollar for you, Helen, and here's one for you, Nicky. We'll save these five for Mama, who likes Blueberry Pie, and now we'll play with the track's money."

We were thrilled with our share of the winnings. "Can we bet, too?"

"No, no, Nicky. That's not a good idea. It's against the law for children to bet. You save your money for something good. Don't lose it. Put it deep in your pockets. I'll hold it for you if your pockets aren't good enough. It's a lot of money. Come on. Let's go have some ice cream."

We stayed at the track until the end of the last race, and Papa added to our colorful ticket collection after every running following Blueberry Pie's triumphant victory.

WINNING AND LOSING

"*D*id we win, Pa?" Nick asked the loaded question as we searched for window seats on the crowded train heading southeast to Chicago.

"You, Helen and Mama are the winners. Good thing we bought return train tickets this morning."

Papa was not as cheerful on the way home as he had been in the morning. Over the years, we learned to read what kind of a day he had had at the track by the mood he was in at the end of the day. When he won, Papa was animated and in good spirits. When he lost, he was unapproachable, unless you wanted your head chewed off, figuratively speaking, of course.

Mama was busy delivering meatloaf and mashed potato dinners to a couple at the counter when we walked into the smoky Austin Lunch after our day at Arlington; she smiled when she looked up.

"Look at all the sunburns. I see rosy noses and rosy cheeks all over the place. You got lots of sunnyshine today, Kiddos."

Papa went behind the bar to put on his apron, and Mama quietly heckled him in Greek.

"Did the horses get enough to eat today, Paul, or did they treat you for a change?"

"Bessie, here's five dollars from me and the horses because you like blueberry pie. Helen and Nicky will explain."

She teased more. "Should we sell the store and retire?"

"Not yet. Looks like we'll have to stay a little longer."

"Well, Paul, I see you're still wearing your pants. At least you didn't lose them to the track. Did Charlie feed the horses, too?"

"Charlie didn't win anything, either. Hey! Someday I'll figure out a system and you'll see all kinds of winnings, my dear wife. We're not busy, so why don't you take the children and go home?"

As we walked to our apartment, our sunburned skin glowed pink under the neon beer signs that shined on us from both sides of Madison Street. I was glad to be holding one of Mama's hands knowing we'd have time together with her at home. Nick and I always relished the time we could spend with both of our parents away from the store.

"So, you had a good time, my little birds?"

"It was fun, Mama. We saw little kids playing in their nice backyards. We saw them from the train."

Nick interrupted, "We ate hot dogs and pop corn and ice cream and Papa gave us a buck when Blueberry Pie winned the race. And, Mama, the people that sell hot dogs over there have clean hands."

"What does blueberry pie have to do with horses?"

"The only horse that winned for Papa today was called Blueberry Pie and he played it because it's your favorite. When he winned that race, the first thing he did was give us money, five bucks for you and one buck for me and one for Helen."

"He lost all the other races?"

"Yep. But after he winned, Papa said he was using the track's money. Every time a race was over I heard lots of people say cuss words, but not Papa. He got real 'xcited. He even turned red. But he never cussed."

"Nicky, you know Papa never says bad words, but he gets too excited about horse races, for sure. He wasn't using the track's money. That was money we work real hard for, money that we need to make sure we can have a more secure future. But your Papa is a good man."

"And he's smart, too, and lots of people like Papa!"

"Nobody's perfect. Papa's smart about everything in the world except one thing, betting on horses."

Mama met an array of people at the restaurant, including bookmakers. Louie Drell, his son, and the bookies who made up the supposedly secret second-floor bookmaking operation above Drell's cigar store were regular customers. Mama felt a sickness in her stomach when Papa placed a bet with them. She never kept her feelings about gambling secret from Papa and always hoped that something she would say would, somehow, change his habits. Those heated discussions with him took place in Greek.

"I'm not working for horses, Paul. You know that. I've got thick calluses on my feet that hurt—like hell. I sacrifice time at home with our children to work here, with no time to even see my sisters. I'm working for us, for our family—not for bookies."

As much as she resented Papa's gambling streaks, she didn't blame Papa's behavior on Drell or the bookies. "Those guys don't force any-one to do business with them. They're trying to make a living just like everybody else on this street. Stay away from it, Paul. Be strong. Put your two dollars away for our children when you think about going to Drell's. Gambling is flushing money down the toilet. You think I work and go home dead tired every night to flush it all down a toilet? I'm no sucker, and you know it."

When Mama first went to work, she was appalled to learn that Uncle Al and even Uncle Charlie played the horses. The only other men in her American life, her brothers-in-law, never gambled. My uncles played card games, like pinochle, but not for money. So Mama could not fathom an exhausted Papa staying at the store, at the end of his day, to play cards with his poker playing *patriotes* (fellow Greeks) until three or four in the morning.

"Doesn't make sense, Paul. You're wasting your time, your health and your money. You can't afford to lose any of them. Your friends may have nothing better to pass their time, but you do."

Mama remained puzzled for decades. She knew the only sure way to win anything in her world was to be patient and to work hard. Mama and Papa argued loudly about this weakness of his all their lives. Sometimes Papa would yell that he was working hard and could do anything he wanted with *his* money. His words deeply wounded Mama. She angrily countered that they were "slaving away like hell together" and she dared to consider it "their money."

Papa kept his gambling under control during the Depression. After business improved in the mid-Thirties, he started gambling more frequently. He avoided bookies but was drawn to the race track all summer long because it was legal, open, available, and offered an escape from the Austin Lunch. Decades later, when Papa retired he began going to the track six days a week during racing season (the track was closed on Sunday). Mama never gave up trying to talk him out of it.

Fifty years later she mused, "Was a sickyness, I guess."

LOST ON MADISON

May your new grandchild be as strong as steel.

—Vasiliki to her parents, October 1934

*I*t was the autumn of 1934 and a cool day in Chicago. Mama was reading a letter from her brother in the village, which she had received at the Austin Lunch in the first of two daily mail deliveries. In those days the Post Office delivered mail twice a day, six days a week, fifty-two weeks a year. As deeply interested as she was in her letter, Mama glanced up from reading to study a bearded old gentleman, dressed in black, who walked through the door. The old-timer looked dazed. Instead of making his way into the restaurant, he hesitated by the cigar case at the front of the store. The confusion on his face and the slump of his narrow shoulders told Papa that the slight, elderly stranger was in unfamiliar surroundings.

"Who's the little old guy? You know him, Paul?"

"No. I've never seen him before. Looks a little shaky. Let's see what he wants."

Standing in the dim light of the Madison Street windows, the old man was wearing a large black hat and matching coat; the lower part of his face was hidden behind a white mustache and short white beard. Papa thought maybe he was a Jewish rabbi since few men wore beards in the Thirties. The gentleman approached Papa over the glass cigar case and uttered one word. It came out in a half whisper, more exhausted than confidential.

"Greek?"

It was the way he said it that instantly told Papa that his response should be in Greek. "*Nai* (Yes)," Papa answered.

The old-timer looked relieved.

"I'm looking for Louie and Angelo Panagiotaros and I was told they live on this street somewhere," he said in Greek. "But streets here are too long, too busy, too fast. You must excuse me. I've walked a long way this morning. I'm very tired. Do you know the Panagiotaros brothers?"

"Yes, I do. They live right across the street."

Glancing heavenward, the old man made the sign of the cross three times over his upper chest. "I've been looking all morning. My prayers have finally been answered. My son, would you please take me to them?"

Papa smiled and imagined that his own father, if he were to see him again, might resemble the little old man. "Of course. I can get away for a few minutes. Let's go right now." He told Mama to keep an eye on everything while he took the stranger across the street and that he'd be back in ten minutes. Mama was curious, as usual.

"Who he is?"

"Don't know. He's looking for Louie and Angelo, across the street. Looks confused and I'm sure he's lost. So I'll take him over there myself."

Papa escorted the small, silent gentleman out the door, and the two merged with the foot traffic on the narrow, busy sidewalk. As they passed Louie Drell's cigar store, Papa steered the stranger to the left, pointing to the place where they would cross the street. He grasped the old gentleman's arm tightly as they stepped off the curb, making sure he didn't trip over the streetcar tracks. They crossed Madison where Laflin ends, quickly reaching the other side as a monstrous red streetcar, heading east toward downtown Chicago, clanged behind them. Simultaneously, a long and menacing fire engine rounded the corner, turning left from Laflin, sirens screaming and bells clamoring as it sped west. The old man remained silent, but his eyes widened at the sights and sounds of the iron trolley and fiery red truck. Papa sensed his fear and reassuringly smiled at him.

Papa wondered who this old man might be. But the man was silent and tired, not interested in making conversation, so Papa kept quiet as they rushed across the street together. A few steps past a small grocery store, Papa turned into the narrow doorway of the two-story brick building directly opposite the Austin Lunch. He opened the marred wooden door with its dirty glass inset and ushered his companion into a tiny vestibule. Four tarnished brass mailboxes with button-sized doorbells were installed in the wall to their left. A stairway in front of them led to the upper floors. Papa pushed one of the bell buttons. But he wasn't sure if it had rung upstairs, so he started climbing the grimy wooden steps in the constricted, sooty hallway, looking back several times to make sure the stranger was following him.

By the time they reached the dimness at the top of the steep stairway, the old man was out of breath. Papa knocked on the first door. After a few seconds, it opened. "Good morning, Angelo. This gentleman is looking for you—"

Before Papa could finish his sentence, Angelo smiled and began talking to the old man in Greek, grabbing him by the shoulders to hug him. "Uncle Papou! Welcome. Welcome."

Tears welled in Angelo's eyes as he ignored Papa and warmly embraced the small man, kissing him on both cheeks as was the custom in the old country. The exuberant welcome brought Louie to the door, and while Louie embraced the old man, Angelo thanked Papa for helping to bring him upstairs.

"Who is he?" Papa asked.

Angelo smiled again. "This is Papapetros."

Mouth agape, Papa took a quick look at the visitor, a look so incredulous, it verged on being rude. "This little old man is the priest from Bedeni?" Papa asked Angelo in English so as not to embarrass their elderly guest.

"Hard to believe, isn't it? The years have really eaten away at him. Uncle Papou is nearing ninety now, Paul. The poor guy's been through lots of sickness. It's a miracle he's still alive."

Louie then introduced Papa to his uncle, explaining that Papa came from Mercovouni, the village next to theirs in Greece. Louie added that Papa and Papapetros's son had been in school together. Then Angelo and Louie thanked Papa for escorting their uncle to the door, and invited him to return in the evening to have a bite to eat with them. My father accepted without hesitation.

"You have my blessing for your help, young Mercovounioti," the exhausted visitor whispered as Papa bent to kiss his right hand, a traditional way of paying respect to a priest and his holy office.

Still smiling and incredulous, Papa flew down the steps and ran across Madison between moving cars. He burst through the door of the restaurant and found Mama serving late breakfasts to a couple in one of the side booths. Mama looked up at him quizzically.

"Bessie, it's Papapetros."

"Calm down, Paul," she answered in English. "Take it easy. It's no good to get all excite like that. What happen? The old guy fall down or something?"

"Bessie, the old guy is Papapetros."

"The priest from Bedeni? That old man? He's the priest from Bedeni you're alloways talking about?"

"Absolutely. I can't believe it. Papapetros is in Chicago, on Madison Street. In my store!"

With no other customers to tend to, Mama suggested they sit down in a booth so Papa could calm down. My father's fair skin was flushed and his hazel eyes danced as he peered above his eyeglasses, now further down on his straight nose, to look at Mama. His voice was loud with excitement. "The guy's a legend. But he's so small. I remember a big man. Bessie, I never recognized him."

"You was a little kid back then and he looked big to you. Looks like he cut his beard and his hair, too. How you suppose to recognize him? All the priests in old country got long beards and long hair. His hair was probably black last time you see him."

"Angelo says he's been sick, and he's almost ninety."

"Maybe he's shrink. Happens when people get old. Why he's in America?"

"I don't know. They invited me back for dinner tonight. I have to go, Bessie."

"Of course you have to. Didn't you tell me he got sons in America?"

"Yes, but in Texas."

"Maybe he's going there."

"I'll find out tonight."

Papa was excited for the rest of the day. Mama sensed he was reliving his youth and remembering Papapetros stories as he went about his Austin Lunch duties. At one point when they weren't busy, they sat down at the counter, each sipping a cup of coffee with cream and sugar and Papa told her more.

"It took a while for Tripolis to become a diocese after the Revolution because there was too much confusion in the government and in the church, too. My father told me that when Tripolis finally got a bishop and became a diocese, all the priests from nearby villages were supposed to pay their respects to their new boss, the new bishop in town. He arrived at Easter, so each village priest brought his best fattened spring lamb as a gift for the bishop, and Papapetros did the same."

Mama knew the familiar story, but Papa was having such a good time telling it that she listened as if she was hearing it for the first time.

"After Holy Saturday morning services in Bedeni, Papapetros mounted his donkey and rode to Tripolis with a tiny lamb under his arm. At the bishop's house he dismounted and found a pen for the animals at the side of the house. He looked inside, saw the pen was full of fattened white lambs, and correctly assumed they were Easter gifts from his fellow clerics. He placed his small gift in the pen and went inside the house to meet the bishop.

"His visit went well. They enjoyed a cup of coffee together, and the bishop was impressed with Bedeni's priest. When their meeting was over, Papapetros kissed his superior's hand and went outside to mount his donkey and return to Bedeni. But Papapetros paused and thought for a moment before he left the bishop's courtyard. Then he returned to the animal pen where all the new lambs had been left. He studied the animals, thought some more, then reached over and picked up the fattest lamb in the bishop's new flock. He placed it securely under his arm, climbed on to his mount, slapped its haunches, and started for home.

"A shocked caretaker, who had been watching Papapetros's comings and goings, shouted 'Stop!' as he chased down the mounted priest, donkey and bleating lamb. Papapetros reined his mount and paused to listen.

"'Hey, where do you think you're going with His Grace's lamb?' the caretaker called out.

"Papapetros was smiling. 'How nice of you, but there's no need to thank me, my good man. The bishop is unmarried. He has no wife and children to help him feast tomorrow. I regret my family and I can unburden him of only one lamb to reduce his oversupply.' Papapetros then called out '*Kali Anastasi*' (Good Resurrection) over his shoulder, nudged the donkey with his foot and with a healthy and chubby white Easter lamb bleating under his arm, raced back to Bedeni, richer for having met the Bishop."

UP CLOSE AND IN PERSON

*S*everal of Papa's old friends from Bedeni dropped by the restaurant to bring news that the legendary priest was in Chicago. They informed my father that Papapetros would only be in town for two days because he was on his way to Texas to join his sons. Papa assured his friends that he, too, had been invited to spend the evening with Papapetros and would see them across the street within the hour.

By the time my father arrived, Angelo and Louie's small apartment was filled with Chicago Bedeniotes asking the old man for news of their families back home. Papapetros, who had rested and looked ten years younger than he had in the morning, wanted to know about their lives in America. The old priest was alert and animated. Under the glow of a single light bulb hanging from the ceiling in the otherwise gray and grimy room, the huddle of men reminisced about sunnier days in Bedeni when they were young boys and Papapetros was their priest.

Not wanting to take even a few minutes away from the fellow villagers' precious time together, Papa waited quietly and listened with interest. He was anxious to ask a question of the guest of honor. When there was a lull, Papa spoke up.

"Papapetros, we've all heard so many accounts about the things you've done in your life. However, there is one story I would like for you to verify. It may not even be true, but if it is, I think all of us here would like to hear it in your own words. The story is about a butcher who was a terrible bully. I had heard he worked in Tripolis and was taking disrespectful advantage of a young, unmarried woman. Do you know the story? Is it true?"

The other men had also heard about the bully butcher and they all turned to the old priest awaiting his reply. "Oh, it is very true, my boy. In fact, that butcher became one of my best friends."

Papapetros sipped his wine and looked around at the men in the room. Basking in their interest and attention, he began to reminisce.

"Two young men from Tripolis came to Bedeni one day to ask my spiritual advice. They explained that both their parents had died and they were living in the family home with their unmarried sister. As good brothers should, they felt responsible for their sister's welfare. It was evident to me that they were a very close-knit family. The two men told me that their sister took care of them in the manner of a mother, and they watched over her as paternal big brothers.

"On Saturdays she walked to the *agora* (marketplace) in Tripolis to buy food which they were unable to produce in their own fields and household. On her weekly trips to the *agora*, she met and fell in love with a young man who worked as a butcher in one of the meat stalls. The brothers described him as a huge fellow, quite muscular and very menacing. They told me he was so attracted to their sister that after one of the couple's meetings in the *agora*, he followed her home to see where she lived. From that day on, the butcher came to see her regularly, after dark, and even spent the night.

"The two men told me that the brute completely ignored their protests to his staying overnight and that he had not yet broached the subject of marriage to their sister. They said that the girl loved but feared him. It was obvious to me that both brothers, small in stature, were scared to death of the butcher. They begged me to keep our conversation confidential because they were afraid their sister's reputation would be ruined. I asked what they wanted me to do.

"The older of the two said, 'Father, please go to him and tell him he must marry our sister. Since you are a priest, he will not harm you when you demand this.'

"On the following Saturday, I went to the marketplace in Tripolis, walked through the meat stalls, and finally spotted a good looking hulk of a man with a full mustache. He was wearing a bloodied apron and was chopping a lamb carcass into pieces with a sharp cleaver. Since he fit the brothers' description, I was sure he was the man I was looking for.

"I walked up to him and asked for a kilo of lamb. He wrapped the meat and gave me the package. While I was getting money out of my pocket, I asked his name and he told me. I knew for sure, then, that he was the man. So, I invited him to have a glass of wine with me and told him there was something I wanted to talk to him about.

"'I don't socialize with priests,' he warned. 'But I'm curious about what you want from me. I accept your invitation.' We walked a block away from the *agora* to a basement *taverna*. After we were seated and served, I told him what I knew about him and the girl and added that I had heard it all from a concerned neighbor of the family. Then, of course, I encouraged him to turn his life around and live according to God's commandments. I finished by telling him to marry the girl. The butcher listened to me intently as he sipped his wine, but remained silent. Even up to the time we finished our drinks and emerged into the sunlight from the dark basement, he said nothing. So, I decided to see what his reaction would be if I were silent, too. Without saying good-bye, I turned away and walked toward the road that leads to Bedeni. I was ten steps away when I finally heard his gruff voice.

"'Hey, Priest!'

"I turned around. He was gesturing me back with a wave of his arm.

"'What village did you say you come from, priest?'

"I answered, 'I'm from Bedeni.'

"'Are there any good looking girls in your village?'

"'Many,' I answered. 'And they're all the marrying kind.'

"'Who said anything about marriage?' His tone was sarcastic.

"'Is that the kind of scoundrel you are?' I asked him. 'I'll fix you. Remember one thing. I am Papapetros, and don't you forget it!'

"'So what?' he bellowed back at me. Then he turned to trudge back to the agora.

"The next day, the older brother came to see me again. I asked if he was quite sure his sister wanted to marry the big oaf. But the brother assured me his sister had proclaimed her love for the butcher and could not be convinced otherwise. Then I told him my plan. He promised me that he, his younger brother, and their sister would do whatever I advised. I asked him to let me know the next time the butcher came to spend the night in their house.

"Three evenings later, I spotted a man running toward my house from the road that leads to Bedeni from Tripolis. As he came closer, I could see it was the eldest of the brothers. He had run the entire distance and collapsed at the door to my tiny courtyard.

"'The butcher is at our house right now!' He was panting for breath and could barely get out the words. 'It looks like he won't be leaving until morning.' The fellow was half dead.

"'Good.' I was elated with his news. 'Where does he usually sleep?'

"'In the room on the upper floor of the house. My brother and I stay on the ground level.'

"He was still panting for breath, but I urged the poor fellow to run back so that both he and his brother would be at home when I arrived. I told him to expect me in a couple of hours. When he left, I got myself ready to carry out the plan I had worked out in my mind after meeting the butcher. First, I loaded my shotgun and pocketed 'Giannoula,' my pistol. Years before I became a priest I decided that a pistol was a necessary and trusty companion for me to have, and decided to name my weapon because I couldn't imagine having a friend without a name." Papa and the men in the Panagiotaros's apartment laughed.

"My trusty Giannoula and I have been through much together.

"I set out on foot in the light of a full moon and decided to take the back roads to Tripolis so I wouldn't be seen and attract any attention. When I arrived in Mercovouni, I stopped to say hello to my friend Zagenis, and he treated me to a glass of wine. On finishing it, I accepted a second glass to help build my courage. When Zagenis asked where I was going, I told him I was on my way to Tripolis to bless a house.

"At the outskirts of Tripolis, I stopped at a basement taverna to fortify myself with additional courage and by luck I ran into a friend who is a constable. 'You're having good luck, Petros,' I said to myself. 'You've found yourself a helper.' I took the constable aside and in highest confidence told him of my plan. Then I asked if he would do me the favor of coming along to help me.

"'Yes, I will, Father. But, I won't be much help because I am unarmed.'

"'Here, you can use my shotgun,' I told him, 'and I'll have trusty Giannoula here in my pocket under my cassock. That's all we'll need. But first, let's have another drink. You'll need courage, too.'

"When we arrived at the girl's house, I found the brothers waiting for me outside the door. I introduced them to the constable and told them he would play a very important part in my plan.

"'Where's the butcher?' I asked.

"'Upstairs with our sister.' They eyed the shotgun and pleaded, 'Please be careful, Father.' At that moment I knew for sure they were cowards.

"I looked around and realized the only light available to us was an oil lantern burning to illuminate the ground floor room where the two brothers had been waiting. I grasped Giannoula in my right hand and gestured to the older brother to take the lantern and lead the way. We began following him up the stairs until he stopped, petrified with fear at the sight of a second firearm. 'What's the matter?' I asked. Since I had already determined these brothers were men of little courage, I was not surprised by his reply.

"'I'm afraid.'

"'Why?' I probed. 'Is the butcher armed?'

"'No, I'm afraid to go first.'

"'Then, give me the lantern and I'll walk first. You, my friend the constable, follow right behind me, and then you boys follow the constable into the room.' I was whispering. 'We must all be very quiet so that the fellow doesn't know about us until we have him surrounded.'

"I arrived at the top of the stairs and pushed the door open with my elbow. The lantern was in my left hand and Giannoula in my right.

"The upper level of the house was one large room, completely dark except for a shaft of moonlight coming through the open window. The lantern helped to illuminate my path. When I arrived at one corner of the room with the lantern, I spotted blankets spread on the floor and in the dim light made out the forms of two people under the covers. I moved in the direction of the blankets, quietly signaling for the others to follow me and form a circle around the two motionless forms on the floor.

"The girl was awake because she knew that I was coming to help her, but the butcher was snoring and sound asleep. The girl suddenly sat up and asked, 'What's the matter?'

"I answered that I had heard she was ill and had come to read some prayers and blessings to give her the strength for a speedy recovery.

"'Yes, I haven't been feeling well lately,' she agreed.

"'What's that on the floor beside you?' I asked her.

"'Oh, him?' She lowered her eyes with embarrassment but her determination to bring dignity back into her life spurred her to gently shake him awake.

"The butcher stirred, opened his eyes and was dumbfounded to find us surrounding him in the lantern light. Spotting firearms, his first reaction was to nervously twist his mustache. Squinting, he searched the darkness for a way out.

"'What do you think you're doing here?' I demanded.

"'What business is it of yours what I am doing here, priest?' he snapped.

"Using Giannoula, I motioned to the constable to be prepared with the shotgun. I looked over toward the terrified brothers and demanded them to be ready for anything that may happen.

"'Stand up,' I ordered the couple on the floor. The girl shot up to attention, but the butcher stood up slowly. I could see he was looking around for a chance to escape.

"'Don't make any stupid mistakes,' I warned. 'We'll shoot if you try to get away. Stand still and don't move.' He took a longer look at

Giannoula, then at the shotgun, and stood motionless. I gave directions to the girl.

"'Come over here, my daughter. Stand right here, next to the bridegroom.'

"'Bridegroom?' he shouted. 'What do you think you're doing, you crazy priest?'

"'I'm going to marry you to this lovely girl. I know you think she's lovely, too, that's why you've been spending so much time with her. You're a lucky man, with good taste in brides.'

"'You're going to force me to marry her?'

"'Of course,' I replied. 'Since you won't agree to do it the usual way, the marriage will have to take place by force. Remember me? I told you, I'm Papapetros! No one fools with me. This perfectly beautiful girl will make you a fine wife. And you had the nerve to ask me if we have beautiful girls in my village. You scoundrel.' I looked around at everyone and asked, 'Are you ready? The holy sacrament of matrimony is about to begin.'

"I gave Giannoula to the oldest brother and asked him to keep her constantly aimed at the groom while I chanted the sacred words of the ceremony. He was shaking so much I was afraid he'd shoot someone by mistake, but I had to do what I had to do. I put the lantern down on the floor, took two rings out of my pocket, and began the first part of the sacrament, the betrothal.

"'The servant of God, Giorgios, is betrothed to the servant of God, Persephone, in the name of the Father and of the Son and of the Holy Spirit. Amen.'

"As I slipped the rings on the fingers of the couple, I looked down and saw the trembling hands of the bridegroom. The bride was visibly nervous, too.

"'We will need a best man.' I said to the others. My friend the constable, stepped forward.

"'I would be honored to be best man,' he volunteered. 'But, Father,' he reminded, 'I see you remembered rings, but we have no *stephana* (wedding crowns). Stephana are the most important part of a wedding.'"

"'You're so right my friend. But the stores in Tripolis that sell stephana were closed when I came here tonight. We'll have to substitute something else for pretty white crowns. I know. We'll use the shotgun, instead.

"'Now listen to my instructions. When I say, "The servant of God, the groom, is crowned to the servant of God, the bride, you, best man, lightly tap the groom's head and then the bride's head with the tip of the shotgun.'

"They all looked at me in disbelief, but I had God's work to do, so I continued performing the sacrament.

"When I finished the crowning, we began the highlight of the wedding ritual, the traditional *Dance of Isaiah*. Now you all know that in this part of the ceremony the priest holds the Gospels in front of the couple and leads the bride and groom around a small table. The best man walks around with the couple, his hands touching the stephana while the bride and groom take their first footsteps together as a married couple, following the Word of God symbolized by the Holy Book, as they should throughout their lives, as all of us must do.

"But these weren't usual circumstances. Out of necessity, we had to use substitutes for the usual symbols. The bed covers, still scattered on the floor, took the place of the small table, and I led the couple around the mound of sheets, pillows and blankets at our feet. I was chanting the beautiful hymn of Isaiah and about to begin the third walk around the bed linens when the bride interrupted me.

"'Father, pardon my mentioning this, but you've left out so many of the prayers which are an integral part of the wedding ceremony. You haven't even read the...'

"At this point, I interrupted her.

"'Yes, my daughter, but I've been a priest for many, many years and by now I know all the words of this sacrament by heart. Don't be concerned, because nothing has been omitted from this ceremony. This is a complete and binding marriage rite. You see, to save time I said the other prayers on my way over to your house tonight.'

"Quickly continuing the ritual while the best man rested the barrel of the shotgun on the bridegroom's shoulder, I led the couple around the bed covers for the third and final walk, symbolizing the happy couple's journey through life together.

"The ceremony ended with the traditional prayer, and I directed that the weapons be put down. I congratulated the bride, the groom, the best man, and the brothers. As I wished the couple a long and happy life together, the bridegroom made a dash for the stairs and, in seconds, he was out on the street in front of the house.

"I ran to the open window, stuck my head out, and shouted down to him from the second story.

"'Hey. Where do you think you're going? You're a married man now. You've got responsibilities.'

"When I visited them a few days later, the butcher had returned. They were all very happy and the butcher and I became good friends. I was even invited to baptize their children."

Papa and all the Bedeniotes laughed and applauded, ending a perfect evening on West Madison Street. They had delighted in being temporarily transported to their beloved homeland through an unforgettable tale told by a man who had become a legend in his time. When Papa went home that night, he wrote down all the stories he could remember about the priest in a little black notebook. He told Mama,

"I'm going to write it all down before we all die and nobody knows anything about what happened before us."

A few days later, Papapetros left Chicago for Texas to visit his sons and their families. He returned to Chicago again in early 1935. He surprised my parents at the Austin Lunch on the sixth of January, the Greek Orthodox feast day of the blessing of the waters. On that day, parish priests traditionally go from house to house bestowing blessings with holy water.

When Papapetros arrived on Madison Street that evening, the small bar at the Austin Lunch was crowded with animated patrons, as were the restaurant counter and booths. Papa glanced up as he was serving a customer and was surprised to see the old priest come through the front door. A narrow brocade shawl embroidered with Byzantine crosses, part of a priest's ecclesiastical garb, adorned Papapetros's neck and reached down to his knees over his black wool overcoat. Before Papa could even say hello, Papapetros spoke.

"Apostoli, I am here to bless your place of business." He made the announcement in Greek and immediately went to work.

Papa watched Papapetros pull a glass baby bottle out of his coat pocket. The bottle was filled with a clear liquid and capped with a rubber nipple. Without hesitation, the priest began chanting in a loud melodious voice as he moved down the middle aisle of the Austin Lunch toward the back of the crowded store. Papa realized the bottle was a substitute holy water dispenser and he watched the old priest generously sprinkle holy water to his left and to his right, on the fixtures, walls, back bar full of whiskey bottles, and on the astonished patrons sitting at the bar, at the white marble counter, and in the booths.

Mama, busy in the kitchen, looked up from her chores and froze the instant she heard Greek chants about Jesus, John the Baptist, and the River Jordan drifting into the kitchen from the front of the restaurant. Then she rushed to the front of the store to see what was happening. Shaking her head in disapproval but also smiling, Mama watched the little priest generously sprinkling startled customers with the consecrated contents of the baby bottle. In seconds she was at Papa's side, chiding him in whispered Greek and English.

"Alleluia on the bum. Where did he come from? Your Papapetros is going to scare all the customers away."

Papa considered putting a stop to the old priest's blessing. But he stood by, powerless. "It's probably sacrilegious for him to bless a saloon. But who am I to stop Papapetros?" he thought.

When Papapetros had finished blessing the Austin Lunch, Papa slipped the old cleric a dollar. The priest looked at the bill and pushed it deeply and securely into his coat pocket. Graciously accepting an honorarium was a gesture he had perfected through the years of his vocation.

When the customers had calmed down, Mama invited Papapetros to have something to eat. After he had finished his meal, Papa asked him if he had decided to settle in Texas or Chicago.

"No, no, Apostoli, I have seen my children, my grandchildren, and the New World. In this country I am a transplanted tree. God knows I am too old to be a sapling and too set in my ways to be transplanted. In Bedeni, I am Papapetros, the tall and sturdy cypress. Papapetros is going back to spend the rest of his life in the best place on earth—again!

FORTUNE TELLIN' MAN

"*O*ne guy I remember who come into the *magazi* (store) was that fortune tellin' man. He only come once and I still remember when it was, the springtime of 1936. How that guy know what he know? I can't never figure it out.

"Papa was on his way to Indiana with his *patriotes* (fellow Greeks) and I was taking care of the front of the *magazi* by myself while Charlie was cooking back in the kitchen. I've told you about it before, Helen. Remember? I never can forget that man, because he scare me to death."

Indeed, I had heard the story from her many times. It was quiet at the store and Papa wasn't there. Very early that morning, Uncle George Limbers had picked him up and the two of them and two other Mercovouniotes began driving to Elkhart, Indiana on a matchmaking expedition. The married men planned to introduce the single son of a Chicago Mercovounioti to the unmarried daughter of a Michigan Mercovounioti. Elkhart was in the middle. The young bachelor was not with them and the old fogies presumed to check out the prospective bride on his behalf. Mama assured Papa she could handle the *magazi* while he was gone for the day, and wished him good luck with making the match. She added that it would have been a good idea to take the prospective bridegroom with them.

My father had a soft spot for Mercovouni and his fellow villagers. In the Twenties, he and the rest of the Chicago-based Mercovouniotes formed a group, The Mercovouni Society, to raise money for needed public works in the village. Some factions within the all-male club were in favor of improving the village school while others felt repairs to the church were important. Papa championed a project to build a reservoir in Mercovouni to collect rain water during winter and spring, then store it in the reservoir for use during summer and autumn when the village was dry. Papa insisted that without water, anything else they attempted in the village could not succeed, arguing that when the water shortage was solved, all other projects could follow.

The Society's meetings were always boisterous and filled with heated arguments over which project best merited the money. There must have been something in the scarce water they drank as village children that affected their lung power because most Mercovouniotes were champions at raising their voices. Had their vocalizations been musical and trained, La Scala and the Metropolitan Opera most certainly would have wooed them with lifetime contracts. As a child, whenever I attended Society meetings with Papa, I was not only frightened by the noise, I was also sure the men would never speak to each other again when the meeting was over. I feared they would come to blows like movie cowboys. Papa, of course, merited the "loudest" award.

During the meetings, insults were sometimes hurled from one Mercovounioti to another. "You're as stupid as your Uncle Aristidi who cut the tail off his donkey." "Hah, your family is infamous for being a bunch of cheapskates." "Everyone in the village knows your people are dullards."

When arguments ensued, old nicknames flew through the room with uncomplimentary epithets. Each male Mercovounioti had a *paratsoukli* (nickname) from childhood. Mr. Prevolos, our landlord, was called "*daskalos*"(teacher) because he was a very smart man. Papa's was "*houssos*," but I never understood what it meant. His father's nickname was "*Asimakos*," derived from Grandpa' mother's first name, "Asimina." Asimakos meant "little one of Asimina." Sometime in the early Twenties, an immigrant Mercovounioti disappeared from Chicago for three days. When he resurfaced, they gave him a new nickname, "*Lazarus*." Sometimes I remembered a *paratsoukli* better than a surname and often confused them, leading to my red-faced embarrassment because some nicknames were derogatory. I was never sure which were insulting and which complimentary.

When a nasty *patrioti* wanted to insult Papa, he usually did so by bringing up Mama's job at the restaurant. "You should be thankful to the Tegeatissa. You would have nothing without her." That was a hard hit for Papa. The moment he got off the streetcar after a Society meeting, we could tell from the expression on his face whether or not he had disagreed with his beloved *patriotes*. Despite their differences, Mercovouniotes actually enjoyed getting together. They forgot disputes while remembering the old days when they were boys in the village and new immigrants in America. Papa was especially proud of his hometown and said that, in spite of its poverty and hardships, he couldn't think of one crook that had been born there. Mercovouni only gave good people to the world.

Mama knew how much Papa enjoyed the company of his *patriotes* and on the day Papa joined them on their matchmaking expedition to Elkhart, Mama gladly worked the extra hours at the restaurant. She was taking advantage of a quiet moment late that Sunday morning when a deep male voice broke into her thoughts.

"Lady, I'll tell you your fortune for a glass of wine."

The man had silently entered the restaurant and sat quietly on the counter stool behind her. Startled, Mama turned to face him and found herself looking at a stranger with long black hair and a black beard, looking a bit like the icons of Jesus she had seen in church. His appearance shook her. Longhaired men with beards were rare in the Thirties. Most were clean-shaven with well-cropped hair. Even Papapetros had trimmed his priestly beard and hair in America.

"What can I get for you, sir?" Mama asked, distracted.

"Ma'am, I can tell your future. So, I'd like to make a trade. I'll give you information about what's going to happen to you, and you give me a glass of wine in return."

"There's no such thing, Mister!"

"No free wine?"

"No such thing that you can tell me what's going to happens before it happen. But I give you a glass of wine anyhow." When Mama brought a small serving of muskatel to the "fortunetellin' man," she found him looking at some unusual playing cards spread out in front of him on the white marble counter.

"Mister, move your cards over, please. I don't want to spill on them."

"Ma'am, you are going on a very long trip."

"Alleluia on the bum. Mister, don't you know there's a big Depression going on? Can't hardly afford to go downtown Chicago on the streetcar and you think I'm going on vacation?"

"Lady, you and several other people, maybe your family, are going to cross a huge body of water, like the ocean."

"Yeah?" Mama was intrigued. He wasn't anyone she knew. "And what else you think going to happen?"

"I'm sorry to tell this to you Ma'am. You are going to get some very bad news. Someone you know very well is going to be in great danger and a tragedy will occur. There will be sorrowful news about someone you know, but the person you are closest to will survive. And in the not too distant future, you will take a trip that will bring you much pleasure and happiness."

"Bad news? Who's going to make me sad?"

"I don't know that. But don't worry. Your loved one will be fine."

"Whooo. That stuff's nonsense, Mister. Like my husband say, 'Banana oil.' You don't know nothing."

"Don't be frightened, Missus. The trip will make you happy."

Mama turned and walked toward the coffee urns. "What kind of guy he is?" she asked herself. But, Mama was superstitious enough to believe there might be truth in his predictions, especially since Papa had been considering a trip to Greece for the coming summer—something only her close family knew about. Deep in thought Mama cleaned the back counter. Then Mama was once again startled by the sound of the stranger's voice.

"Thank you for the wine, Ma'am."

When she turned around, the man and his strange cards were gone. His empty wine glass was the only sign that he had ever been there. Mama was uneasy. "So what's new?" she thought to herself. "Greek ladies pretend to read fortunes in the grounds at the bottom of a cup of Greek coffee all the time." Thea Stavroula, who lived upstairs from the restaurant, foretold the future every time she and Mama visited and sipped demi-tasses of thick, black, Greek coffee. The first prediction Stavroula came up with was a trip. It was expected in the fortune telling game. But this man said he foresaw tragedy and his words unnerved my mother.

Mama was given to superstition. She believed there were meanings in dreams and even acquired a dream interpretation book, written in Greek, which she regularly consulted. Mama often saw sheep in her sleep and the book interpreted them as a bad omen. Papa tried to reassure Mama by providing an alternative interpretation: since sheep had been such an important part of her early life in Greece, it made sense that they would appear in her dream life in America. We all tried to dismiss the book's ominous interpretations and eventually Papa "misplaced" Mama's dream book. Its disappearance was not a mystery to Mama; she immediately suspected sabotage.

Mama was also a believer in the powers of the *mati*, the "Evil Eye." She assured us that not only was the *mati* real, but that the Church itself had prayers and rituals to rid a victim of the *mati*. Signs included headaches, crankiness and depression *Mati* was never suspected when there was fever, infection, or any other physical ailment. It was "known" that some individuals innocently and inadvertently brought the evil eye on their victims through excessive admiration of their talents or beauty. Therefore, whenever someone received a complement, they had to expectorate dryly, three times, and say "*Ptou, ptou, ptou*" to dispel the powers of the evil eye.

During her voyage to America as a girl, Mama learned prayers for getting rid of the evil eye from a fellow passenger. As seasick as she was on the journey, Mama memorized the prayers and their attendant rituals. Later, she used them at home. Whenever she suspected someone of suffering from the Evil Eye, she prayed silently over them and refreshed their forehead three times with water from a glass in which she had also added three drops of olive oil. She then encouraged her "patient" to sip three times from the glass. If the water and oil combined in the glass, after the patient had taken the sips, Mama knew that the *mati* was present. If small drops of oil continued to float on top of the water, Mama could be sure that the that the "patient" was free of the Evil Eye. If the *mati* was present, Mama would dump the glass's contents outdoors—never down a drain in the house. This part of the ritual was especially exciting during below-zero weather when she silently opened the door and spilled the oily water out on the back porch's ice and snow. After Mama had disposed of the liquid, the ritual was over. Then she would wait to see whether or not her "patient's" disposition improved. Sometimes, the symptoms of the Evil Eye persisted, and the family turned to Thea Aphroditi's more powerful method for dispelling its influence. Aphroditi silently intoned her prayers while she tied salt and frankincense in the corner of a clean white handkerchief. If *mati* was present, Aphroditi began yawning. The more she yawned the more *mati* was being dispelled. But if our aunt's stronger evil eye remedy failed, the "big guns" were brought in. The "patient" was sent to "Corba the *Italida*," the evil eye specialist of Chicago's West Side Mediterranean immigrant population. The *Italida* (Italian woman) was an immigrant, always dressed in black, who lived in the Italian neighborhood around Taylor and Halsted streets. I never witnessed her ritual and therefore don't know the details of her method. If, however, the Italida's methods failed and serious *mati* symptoms persisted, a Greek Orthodox priest was summoned.

Mama never got over the prediction of the fortuneteller at the Austin Lunch. "The guy with the long hair say we was going to take a trip over the ocean. How that fortunetellin' man know Papa want to go to the old country in 1936?"

As much as she longed to see her family in Greece, Mama was against Papa's plans. She argued best in Greek. "We can't afford it. Look, Paul, we've finally made a few nickels and don't owe anything to anyone. We worked like slaves to get out from under our money problems and you want to waste hard-earned money taking an expensive trip? Spend it all and then what? The Depression is still going on. People are still suffering. You travel to Greece with Helen and Nicky, if you want to go so badly. I'll stay and run the store. If we leave, even for a few months, we'll lose everything and have to start all over again."

Papa's most fervent dream had always been to visit the old country and he tried to convince Mama that this might be their only chance to see their parents again. All four were still alive, but they were old and getting older. A year or two might be too long to wait. Papa assured Mama that he would leave Uncle Charlie in charge of the Austin Lunch, even make him a partner. Papa insisted that all four of us needed to go. "Period." Mama was still not convinced.

She fretted about the predictions of the fortuneteller. Several hours after the psychic's departure, the telephone rang. Mama answered, surprised to hear Thea Dimitra Limbers' voice at the other end.

"Bessie, I just had a phone call from George. They never made it to Indiana. They had an automobile accident very early this morning. It happened on the South Side."

Mama's stomach tightened. "What? Anybody was hurt?"

"Well, Bessie, I asked George that question, but he didn't answer. He said they had to help the police make a report and would be back by tonight."

"Why police mixing up in it?"

"Whenever there's an accident, Bessie, the police have to make a report. We'll ask questions when they get back. George didn't stay on the telephone. He hung up. You know, George doesn't say much. That's all I know, Bessie. Don't worry."

It was easier for Dimitra to say because she hadn't had her fortune told that morning. Mama hung up the phone, more upset than Thea Dimitra could imagine. For the rest of the day she watched the front door for Papa to return. She kept herself busy even though business was slow. She folded stacks and stacks of napkins that had been re-turned, laundered and pressed flat, from Mickey's Linen Supply. "AUS-TIN" was machine embroidered, in red cursive letters, on the corner of each tablecloth and each heavy cotton napkin. Then she covered each booth table with a clean white tablecloth. Overflowing with nerv-ous energy, she then set out to clean the entire restaurant, to rid even its upper reaches of the soot from tobacco smoke and the coal-burning stove. Uncle Charlie found her perched on the back counter, washing walls.

"Hey, what are you doing up there, Bessie? Trying to kill yourself? Or are you going to tear this joint apart? Come down from there. Cleaning every corner of this place is hopeless."

Flushed and perspiring, Mama looked down at him and Charlie instantly saw the fear in her face. Steadfast Charlie felt a sickness in his own stomach after she told him about Dimitra's phone call. He silently wondered if something serious had happened to Papa, but tried not to show concern. In order to distract Mama, before she had a chance to fall off the counter and hurt herself, he asked her to come into the kitchen to help him. Although Charlie Kingos crammed a lot of work into a day, he never wanted help with cooking. He called it interference. In trying to distract Mama that day, he made an exception.

"The South Side isn't in the next world, Charlie. Paul should be back by now. What's keeping him?"

Charlie didn't go home at the end of his shift. Instead, he waited around with Mama for my father's return. When Papa hadn't shown up by eight that night, Charlie sent word for his wife Violet to come down to the store to be with Mama in case there was tragic news. Aunt Violet Kingos, French-American and devoutly Roman Catholic, was a quiet, kind and gentle lady. She kept very busy at home as the mother of their five children, but sometimes she dropped in to visit at the store. Violet's peaceful presence had a calming effect on Mama.

By ten o'clock, Mama had stationed herself at the front window of the restaurant. The frame of light bulbs in the window illuminated her flushed face. It was beginning to show panic. Riveted in place, she searched the area in front of the restaurant, examining the outline of every person who stepped off the streetcars and each pedestrian who approached from left and right. She finally spotted the familiar square outline of Uncle George Limbers' dark green car pulling up to the curb. When the door opened and Papa got out, Mama relaxed her shoulders and made the sign of the cross, three times.

Papa looked gray when he came through the door; Mama had never seen him look so grim. She said nothing as he approached the cigar case. He looked at her grimly and spoke in Greek.

"Vasiliki, this has been the worst day of my life," he said shaking his head in disbelief. "We were in an accident. Tassos Fotias was killed a few yards away from where I was sitting."

"What?" Mama made the sign of the cross again.

"We never got out of the city today. A drunk driver killed Tasso."

"Tassos Fotias is dead?"

"Yes, a drunk was speeding down Michigan Avenue when we stopped to fix a flat tire on South Michigan. He hit Tasso and killed him—instantly. All day we've been making police reports. We had to go tell Evangelia. What a nightmare. They have three small children."

Tears welling in her eyes, Mama looked upward. "*Theouli mou*" ("My dear God"), she whispered. She made the sign of the cross over her chest again. All day tension had been building in her, and now Papa's news brought crippling distress. He looked shaken and grief stricken at the same time. She was so crushed by the news and by Papa's grief that she couldn't talk. Violet sensed her despair and put an arm around her shoulder. Then Mama's thoughts exploded into words.

"*Panayitsa mou*" ("My dear Holy Mother"). She made the sign of the cross again. "One of their little ones is handicapped. *Poh. Poh.* My God, how could this ever have happened? How is Evangelia?"

"She is in shock. She screamed when she heard about Tasso. I'll never forget that scream. We went to their house with the police when they gave her the bad news. She couldn't stop screaming."

"Dear God, the poor woman. Were you hurt, Paul?"

"No, actually I was the farthest away when the car got hit."

"What happened?"

"Well, Uncle George's car started slowing down. The other guys all know about cars. One of them said, 'It must be a flat tire. Let's pull over and see what's wrong.' We all got out of the car. I told them I don't know anything about cars. I can't drive. I can't change a tire. I told them I'd be over on a park bench and stay out of their way while they fixed the car. I closed my eyes to get a few minutes rest while they took equipment out of the trunk; the three of them started changing the tire.

"I was laying down on the bench, half asleep, and suddenly I heard this screech and loud thump. Then, I heard yelling. I could tell by the sound that something had been hit. A speeding, weaving car had sideswiped Uncle George's car. And when I looked over in the direction of the noise, my God, one of my friends was laying on the ground. His body had been thrown by the impact. I could tell by his clothes that it was Tasso. And in the distance I saw the black car that hit him, but it just kept speeding away. We knew, by the way it was weaving, that the driver didn't know what was going on. He must have been drunk. I went to find a telephone to call a hospital and call the police. The others tried to help Tasso. But only God could help Tasso."

"Did they catch the bastard?" Charlie asked.

"Not yet. Don't know if they ever will. He was out of sight before we got our wits together. Police say they'll try to track him down. It's a nightmare." Papa was almost in tears. "And we make our bread and butter selling liquor in here. I've been thinking about that all day."

Mama, Violet and Charlie tried to calm him. Uncle Charlie advised Mama to go home with Papa. He would stay to finish out the shift until Uncle Pete came for the night.

"You both need to get the hell outta here and go home. Get some sleep!"

Everyone associated with the Mercovouni Society was shaken by Mr. Fotias's death. The Greek community wanted to assist "Tassena," as the Mercovouniotes called his widow, but no matter what help was or was not offered, the tragedy could not be altered. A young immigrant woman, who spoke little English, was left to raise three small children, one of them handicapped, without a husband in the middle of the Depression. "Tassena" saw that the only way to survive the tragedy was to help herself. Mrs. Fotias went to work in a factory, and on her own raised three children into fine, responsible adults, personally caring for her handicapped son until her own death in the nineteen eighties.

The accident on South Michigan Avenue in 1936 distressed my parents every time someone mentioned it. Starting the night of the accident, Papa suffered insomnia that Mama thought would never end. Whenever he fell asleep he dreamed of the accident and the sound of his friends' screams awoke him. Mama was fearful that Papa would become seriously ill unless he could learn to sleep again. And Papa began pressing her to go to Greece, convinced more than ever that life was too short and unpredictable for them to wait. "Don't you think Tasso Fotias dreamed of going to visit Mercovouni with his family?" He told Mama that if they didn't go back home that summer, they might forever miss an opportunity to see their parents alive again. Mama agreed to think about it—but only if they both took time from work to ask the doctor's advice together.

EXCITEMENT

It is impossible to believe that we will be seeing you again.

—Vasiliki to her brother, June 30, 1936

"*D*octor Pugh, how can we take a trip so far far away? Paul can't even sleep. He's jumping up in bed every night like he's seeing ghosts."

The doctor's advice took Mama by surprise.

"Mrs. Limberopulos, if you can afford to take a trip like that, take it. This man needs to forget what he experienced. Change the scenery. It's the only prescription I can suggest. The change will do him good. It will do both of you good. Go away. Send me a postcard."

It was old Dr. Pugh who convinced Mama that going to Greece in 1936 was the best medicine for Papa. Mama and her sisters respected Pugh in the same way they revered their father. The white-haired general practitioner brought their babies into the world, treated their ailments and always came when he was needed. Mama never stopped saying, "I wouldn't change doctors for the world. No doctor is better than Pugh!" If the esteemed doctor said, "take the trip if you can afford it," Mama knew we should take the trip.

Papa heard the Pan-Arcadian Federation was sponsoring a trip to Greece in the summer of 1936 to hold its annual convention in the "old country." Membership in the Federation was made up of Greek-Americans in the United States whose families were rooted in the province of Arcadia; the Mercovouni Society was a member of the Federation. So

Papa, with the encouragement of Dr. Pugh and the co-operation of Mama, quickly went to Halsted Street and found the office of the travel agent in charge of arranging the Pan-Arcadian tour. He immediately began making arrangements for our trip that was to begin in the middle of July. Reservations did not need to be made months in advance because it was still the Depression, even though unemployment had dropped to 16.9 percent and the veteran's bonus was to be paid that year. Most Americans were staying very close to home. The travel agent on Halsted Street prayed for customers. He was thrilled to make last minute travel arrangements for good green cash.

In preparation for the trip, Papa put his business affairs in order. He made Uncle Charlie a partner in the Austin Lunch without any exchange of money, because he was sure a partner would have more interest in the restaurant's survival than an employee. He came to school and let our teachers know that Nick and I would not return until October. The trip would take almost three months.

Mama shopped for suitcases and a trunk because we had no luggage, except for the little cardboard "grip" (suitcase) Papa had brought from Greece when he immigrated in 1907. She also bought gifts, primarily clothing, to take to our grandparents and relatives. Mama and her sisters decided that silk stockings would make terrific presents for lady relatives. Our extended family and friends were excited that we would be seeing many of the loved ones that they had left behind when they came to America. A few of our acquaintances grumbled. "What's Paul taking his family to Greece for? They sit on old, second-hand furniture, their carpets have holes in them, and they live in that tenement. Why doesn't he take care of his house first?"

In 1984, I learned that the criticism had hurt Mama's feelings.

"I know there's lot of places for that money we spend when we go back to the old country in '36. But your Papa was right. After we take the trip, things start getting bad in Europe. Hitler bring war and by the time the big war was over, then in Greece they had another war, the Civil War and by that time, all your grandmas and grandpas was dead. To see them was more important than furniture and rugs and stuff. But some people got to say that what you're doing is alloways wrong. I learn to don't pay attention to what people say because some people criticize everything. Whatever you're doing, they don't like it."

Mr. and Mrs. Jones were thrilled that we would be taking the long anticipated journey. Although we couldn't travel together as all of us had dreamed, they continued hoping they would return to England one day. England was very much in the news of 1936 and the Joneses were wrapped up in all of it, especially Iris.

In January, Great Britain's King George V died. Mrs. Jones took the loss badly and she mourned for her monarch as if he were her grandfather. When the king's oldest son David, Prince of Wales, became King Edward VIII, Mrs. Jones hailed him with "Long Live the King." News articles and pictures of the new, handsome young king excited her. Yet the more she read of his involvement with Wallis Warfield Simpson, the American divorcee, the more she prayed for them to end their relationship. Iris Jones was taking the entire royal matter to heart. She was convinced that before coronation ceremonies took place, David would break up with Wally.

One evening before our trip, while Mama was packing our new trunk, Mrs. Jones came to our porch screen door. She found Nick and me in the kitchen examining a new suitcase we had hoisted onto the kitchen table.

"I'm so glad you're at home, children. Come over tonight and listen to the radio with us. We want to see more of you before you leave on your trip because George and I will miss you while you're away." No one had ever said that to us. Nick and I were usually underfoot, never far enough away to be missed by anyone.

We invited her to come in. "Mama's in the front room, Mrs. Jones."

"Mrs. Paul, George and I would appreciate it if you'd let the children come over to listen to the radio with us tonight. You'll be away for three months and we'll miss you."

"We going to miss you, too. You and Mr. Jones is such good people. Why you want to listen to radio? Something special on tonight?"

"Fibber McGee and Molly." They're on every Tuesday night, but they'll be going off the air for summer."

331

"Don't want the children to bother you, Mrs. Jones."

"Please, Mrs. Paul. They're no bother."

"O.K. Go ahead. But come right back home when it's over. Be good. Remember, no arguments." It was so unlike Mama. She was so good at saying "no" and this time we didn't even have to beg. Mrs. Jones's saying she'd miss us must have made an impact.

We huddled close to Mr. and Mrs. Jones's floor model Philco radio that proudly stood against the wall in their kitchen. After the set "warmed up" and sound gradually became audible, we heard, "Bing" "Bang" "Bong," the NBC chimes. Then Harlow Wilcox's voice announced, "It's the Johnson's Wax Program with Fibber McGee and Molly!"

For the next half hour we laughed at the antics of the funny couple that lived at 79 Wistful Vista. We never knew where Wistful Vista was, but it didn't matter. For thirty minutes on Tuesday nights, Wistful Vista was as real as Chicago. Fibber and Molly's eccentric neighbors were delightful. By the time we had heard the program several times on the Jones's radio, we came to anticipate the characters' funny responses. We knew "Old Timer" would say, "That ain't the way I heerd it, Johnny," in retort to scheming Fibber. Old Timer called everybody "Johnny" except Molly; he called her "Daughter." We laughed at the unexpected surprise in Fibber's voice when he encountered Mert, the invisible and inaudible telephone operator who only Fibber could hear at other end of his line. "Is that you, Mert? How's every little thing, Mert?" Those were the days before dialing, when a telephone caller always dealt directly with the operator, an actual human being.

Patient, sensible Molly, Fibber's wife, never resorted to language stronger than, "Tain't funny McGee!" or "Heavenly days!" when her frustration peaked. Pompous Throckmorton P. Gildersleeve was such a hit as the McGees' testy neighbor that his character was eventually spun off into a separate program, "The Great Gildersleeve." Even the commercials for Johnson's Wax were winsome. New hit songs and oldies by the Billy Mills Orchestra began every show and a musical intermission was presented at midpoint. All this and the suspense of

Fibber possibly opening their notorious, overstuffed hall closet entertained an entire nation of avid listeners from April 16, 1935 until
1952 when television took over America's living rooms and imaginations. Thirty weekly minutes of "Fibber Mc Gee and Molly" had everything, offended no one, and provided outstanding, timely humor.
The engaging characters were as familiar to us as people we encountered everyday at the Austin Lunch.

Nick and I loved listening to the radio with the Joneses. We spent
many delightful hours in their apartment imagining the actions of "Fibber McGee and Molly," "Burns and Allen," "Amos 'n Andy," "Jack
Armstrong, the All-American Boy," "Little Orphan Annie," "The Shadow"
and many more. We sat motionless close to the set, concentrating on its
sounds. We studied the front of the radio set, admiring its shiny finish,
checking out the dials, staring at numbers on the tuner, and memorizing
the pattern of the cloth over the speaker where sounds emerged. Listening intently, we glanced at each other to laugh or nod in agreement. Our
imaginations turned sounds into pictures. Our brains gave form to unseen voices coming to us through the patterned cloth and wood cabinet.
Radio characters became familiar to all of us, yet we each had a different
image in our minds as to how they looked and acted. When we were at
the Jones's, we followed Mama's rules of etiquette. She instructed us to
listen to the programs that the Joneses wanted to hear, not play with the
dials, not argue with each other, and behave, "Period." After all, Mama
reminded us, it was their radio, and we were not to touch it. Listening to
the radio with the Joneses stretched our world beyond the West Side of
Chicago, and we liked it. When Mrs. Jones escorted us back to our apartment, we found Mama in the kitchen writing a letter.

"Good program?"

"Real funny, Mama. We should get a radio."

"When you get a radio, children, George and I will miss your
company." Twelve years of never dreaming I'd be missed by anyone,
and suddenly I was hearing it for the third time. I liked it.

"Then you can come here and enjoy your programs at this house,
Mrs. Jones. Wish I had time to listen, too. I don't even have time write

to my brother. Paul send letters to all of them but I decide I have to write to my own brother, myself. Anything you want me bring you from Greece, Mrs. Jones?"

Iris was at a loss for words. "How very thoughtful of you, Mrs. Paul. Let's see, what could you bring? I don't know what they have there."

"You know why I ask you, Mrs. Jones? A good Greek lady friend of mine, her name is Athanasia, she ask me to bring her something. My friend and her family is living over here on Monroe Street. Her husband is a fruit peddler. Maybe you see him push his wagon hisself because he's got no horse. They are very, very good people who's working very hard. Got a little boy and girl like Helen and Nicky. Sometimes she's sell ice cream in front of the hospital on Jackson Boulevard in the summertime. When the circus is coming to the Stadium, she's selling better and fresher peanuts outside the Stadium for cheaper than they selling them inside.

"When Athanasia hear we going to go back to the old country she say, 'Vasiliki, I never going to go back home because we too poor. Please bring one thing back for me. Bring me a little bag of dirt so I can touch Greek soil again before I die.' She make me cry, Mrs. Jones. God, he make it so I can go see my Mama and Papa. I thank God everyday and I wish I could take everybody who want to go back with me."

"That's very moving, Mrs. Paul. Yes, you and your friend, Athanasia, have given me an idea for what you can bring us from Greece. Helen and Nicky, are you listening? When you go up to the Acropolis, pick up a little stone and bring it back. Like your friend, we, too, will touch greatness."

FAR FROM THE AUSTIN LUNCH

A few days prior to our departure, a truck arrived on Madison Street to pick up the trunk that had been packed with our clothing and gifts for relatives in Greece. Mama had also stuffed other necessities and a first-aid kit inside. All of her sisters, Uncle Paul Antonopoulos, and most of our cousins came to our apartment the day before we left to say good-bye. Christina Fellas, Thea Dimitra Limbers, Mr. and Mrs. Jones dropped by, as did Thea Stavroula with Chris. Uncle Paul, Thea Tasia, Georgia, and Helen were going to California that summer on the Santa Fe Railroad. In the Thirties, that, too, was an unfathomable journey for unseasoned travelers like us; excitement lightened the heavy Depression atmosphere.

Most of our socializing took place at Papa's restaurant or my aunts' apartments. It felt good to have visitors in our home for a change. We even cranked up Papa's Victrola and played old records he had collected in the Twenties. We kids took turns at making it go. Most were Greek songs, but he had a couple of Enrico Carouso records, too. We ate together and visited while we packed our final things. I remember that Mama and my aunts rinsed out many pairs of silk hosiery (nylons hadn't been invented yet) that were to be given as gifts in Greece. Mama and our aunts said silk hose lasted longer if they were washed first.

Our plans were to be away until October. This would be the first time since coming to America that Mama would not be a streetcar ride away from her beloved sisters. Our farewells were tearful. Six suitcases and a trunk accompanied us. Wash-and-wear fabrics had not been invented yet, and we had to bring enough clothes to last us for a while. As a going away gift, Thea Dimitra brought us a wicker picnic basket with a beautifully matched set of green dishes, glasses and flatware, but Papa said we couldn't take them with us because there was too much to keep track of already.

We were heading for Europe at a time when U.S. radio and newspapers announced worrisome news from across the Atlantic. Earlier that year, while Papa was trying to convince Mama to take the trip, Hitler sent his troops to re-occupy the Rhineland. In late June the Ethiopian emperor, Haile Sellasie, whose African country had been taken over by Mussolini in May, addressed the League of Nations. Selassie prophetically told them, "I am here today to claim the justice that is due my people. It is us today. It will be you tomorrow."

On July 14, 1936 we left the Austin Lunch and our apartment on Madison Street for Chicago's Grand Central Station on Polk Street. Our journey was to begin on a Baltimore and Ohio train headed for the east coast. Because we were part of the Pan-Arcadian group, we were departing with other Greek-Americans. Each traveler was accompanied by a crowd of friends and relatives who came to wish their loved ones *Kalo taxidi* (a good trip). The train depot was absolutely jammed with well-wishers speaking Greek. The mass of people was so thick that if someone had fainted in the station that day, there would have been no room on the floor for them to fall down.

Reserved railroad coach cars awaited the Pan-Arcadians. Mama, Papa, Nick and I boarded the train, and I was thrilled that all four of us were going someplace together. When the dinner bell rang, the four of us sat down at a table and ate together without looking over our shoulders for a customer to serve; unbelievably, someone was waiting on us. We rode coach cars and slept and lived in our seats, next to each other, until the Pan-Arcadian tour got off at Washington D. C. We took a fast bus tour of the nation's capital city, had our picture taken in front of the United States Capitol Building, then boarded the same train again for New York.

Washington was the place where I first became aware of the possibilities of trick photography. Mr. Heracles Veros, the travel agent in charge of Pan-Arcadians, made all arrangements and was to be ever-present, at every stop along the way, to make sure our trip ran smoothly. In our group picture at the front of the Capitol Building, Mr. Veros's ever-presence occurs twice: he's the first one on the left side of the extra wide, rectangular souvenir picture, and the last person on the right.

Our final train destination was New York City. We slept overnight at the Rex Hotel, at 106 West 47th Street, probably because it was owned by a Greek-American. Other families joined our group on stops after Chicago, so by the time we arrived at the port, two hundred Pan-Arcadians were ready to board the Cunard White Star ship named for one of England's queens, Eleanor of Aquitaine. Mrs. Jones had filled me in on Eleanor's extensive resume. Queen Eleanor, the most powerful woman of the 12th century, had been queen twice: as wife of France's Louis VII, then as wife of England's Henry II. In her life-time, two of her sons became England's kings, Richard I, the Lion-Heart, and John. We were on the verge of sailing away on the good ship *Aquitania*. I'll never forget the date: July 16, 1936.

When we arrived in our cabin we found a box of candy, flowers and a telegram sent to us on ship as a surprise *bon voyage* gift from our friends and customers at the Austin Lunch. We were pleased beyond words at their thoughtfulness, not even knowing such gifts could be given long distance. Mama was sure that it had been Aunt Violet Kingos's thoughtful idea. To Papa's astonishment, Chris Stavropoulos, a fellow shoeshine boy during his early days in America, was a member of our tour. His daughter, Georgia, a year older than I, accompanied him; the rest of his family stayed home. Georgia and I became traveling companions.

We traveled third class. That meant we didn't have a private bath or a porthole in our cabin. The tiny room had four bunks, two low-ers, two uppers, and a small sink. We were living on Madison Street in the Thirties; for us, traveling third class was an undreamed of luxury, and we couldn't fathom second or first class being any more splendid. We were accustomed to rooms without windows. For the first couple of days at sea Mama and I were miserably seasick and didn't see anything but the ceiling above the bunks in our rocking chamber on the beautiful *Aquitania*. While we were dizzily stationed in our beds, Papa and Nick explored the ship and brought us news of exciting seagoing activities. Mama never fully recovered and stayed in our cabin for most of the journey; we don't even have a snapshot of her aboard ship. Eventually I was able to walk about the *Aquitania* and enjoy its pleasures.

"Don't worry about me. You have good time. Same thing happen when I come to America with Tasia. I was sick as a dog. I'm going to be alright when we get off the boat."

We brought Mama frequent news bulletins of our adventures on board, excited that there was even a free movie theater. Mama was barely able to lift her head off the pillow, but she was well enough to editorialize. "Not so free. When Papa buy the boat tickets, he pay for the show, too."

Nonetheless, we were impressed by the small theater and by a large, airy salon called The Lounge where sea goers could play games. Passengers played chess, checkers, cards, and a horse racing game where flat wooden horses moved along a track in spaces determined by the roll of dice. Again, it was hard to believe that people could play games all day long without having to return to work. At night, we went to the movies. The film I remember most was "Show Boat" with Irene Dunne, Allan Jones, Helen Morgan and Paul Robeson. Nick added "Ol' Man River" to his whistling and singing repertoire. On one of our days at sea there was even a party for children, complete with party hats and favors.

Much of the activity on the ship centered on eating. We were assigned to a table of eight and took every meal with the same passengers in the third class dining room. Crisply-uniformed waiters gracefully presented our meals. We began each day with a complete English breakfast; the perfectly round fried eggs impressed us. Papa surmised they had been cooked using a mold of some kind, and reminded us Uncle Charlie didn't have time to bother with gimmicks like that.

At eleven o'clock in the morning, beef tea was served on deck; it was a clear broth. Nick and I were not impressed. An elegantly served lunch followed. Four o'clock in the afternoon was teatime, an important daily ritual on the English ship. Two American kids of Greek immigrants had never heard of teatime, but Nick and I reveled in the wonderful goodies. We never tasted the tea but sampled all the beautiful and luscious fruit tarts, cookies, cakes, and splendid desserts that had never been part of our Depression childhood. The only familiar one was pound cake, but it too came in two varieties, with and without raisins. We never bothered with cucumber and watercress sandwiches.

Sailing the Atlantic Ocean on the *Aquitania* was an adventure we never dreamed of. Even the movie we had seen at the American Theater with Fred Astaire and Ginger Rogers dancing on board a ship didn't fully reveal the wonders of ocean travel. The film never showed the games for kids, the nooks to explore, the fascinating equipment or the crew at work. But the best part of the journey was that it gave us a chance to be together as a family outside the confines of our tenement apartment and the Austin Lunch. On the fifth and final night of our journey, the *Aquitania* hosted a farewell party for all her passengers. We attended the gala all together, although Mama ate nothing and stayed for a very brief time. "Just be glad I'm up on my feet. I'll eat when we step on solid land again," she said.

During our trip across the Atlantic, the Spanish Civil War began. Both Hitler and Mussolini sent "volunteers" to help the Fascist cause. Papa said signs were bad for the future of Europe. "Good thing we're taking this trip now. A few months from now we might have decided not to take it."

We disembarked at Cherbourg, France. Within walking distance of Cunard's dock, we boarded a train and immediately left for Paris where the Pan-Arcadian tour checked into a hotel. The first thing I noticed were the doors—the knobs were in the middle. I never dreamed there was anyplace else for a doorknob except the edge. As soon as we arrived in our rooms, our group, by necessity, took its first French lesson. The Pan-Arcadian expedition immediately learned the word for soap, *savon*, because none had been provided. It would have been so easy to include a bar, even several, in one of our six suitcases, but we were inexperienced travelers. Papa tried to tell the woman at the front desk that the rooms had no soap, and she became very angry with him, chastising him in French. So our very first activity in Paris was to go out to buy *savon*. Our stay lasted two days. My most vivid memory is visiting the Arch of Triumph and seeing the flame beneath.

Mama, alert and recovered from her five-day bout of seasickness, got wind of a very important piece of traveling information while we were in Paris. She heard a rumor that no food or dining car was being provided for the Pan-Arcadian train during its three-day journey. She knew that we would get very hungry long before we reached Athens. So she, Papa, and Mr. Stavropoulos went out in search of a delicatessan and bought French baguettes, crackers, cheeses, olives, salami, cucumbers, and tomatoes, which they stuffed into paper bags that we took on the train along with our six suitcases and the trunk. Mama reflected that Thea Dimitra's wicker picnic basket would have been very useful. Nick, Mama, Papa and I shared one train compartment with Mr. Stavropoulos and Georgia in a private train reserved for two hundred plus Pan-Arcadians going home to Greece. My very daring brother Nick climbed up onto the metal luggage rack, high above us inside the compartment, discovered he was able to stretch out up there, and used it as his own private bunk for naps and bird's eye views.

At dinner, other Pan-Arcadians searched for the absent dining car, then for Mr. Veros. He was on the train, but no longer ever-present or ever accommodating; nobody could find him. Mama started passing food out to little children who peeked into our compartment to watch us eat. By breakfast, Heracles Veros was a wanted man. When the passengers finally found him, they gave him an earful of angry, passionate complaints about how hungry they were. He let everyone know that he had wired ahead to a Swiss town and food would be provided at the Swiss railroad stop. When we arrived at the chilly Alpine station, only coffee and pound cake were available for sale. Other passengers had hoped for a more substantial meal, but the six of us enjoyed the rich, buttery cake and hot *cafe au lait* as a lovely dessert to our compartment car French picnic.

We continued our journey, gazing out of our compartment window at the exquisite Alpine beauty of Switzerland and northern Italy. It was a scene out of a fairy tale for us Chicago travelers who had never even been to downstate Illinois. Finally we turned south into Yugoslavia. By that time, hungry passengers were ready to hang Mr. Veros, so he wired ahead for food, again. It was dark when we reached Belgrade, but all two hundred plus members of the Pan-Arcadian expedition alighted the train and walked to several restaurants located near the station to enjoy hot meals, outdoors, and under the stars. Everyone on the tour was full of anticipation when we boarded the train again; Greece was the next country on our route.

The euphoria was infectious as it spread from one smiling adult traveler born in the "old country" to the next when we crossed into Greece from Yugoslavia; they were home again and feeling good. The train stopped on the Greek side of the border and Papa took snapshots of the first blue and white Greek flag he had seen on Greek soil in twenty-nine years. Officials boarded to inspect our passports, and following behind them were hotel representatives hoping to reserve rooms for us. Since we had no relatives to stay with in Athens, Papa made reservations at the Acropole Palace Hotel, the headquarters for the group's Pan-Arcadian Athens convention.

Everyone was exhilarated when we arrived in Athens. Many of the passengers were met by their families and all around us were embraces, tears, and happy shouts. Our relatives were waiting for us in Tripolis, so we took a cab to our Athens hotel.

At the Acropole Palace, we were assigned to a suite that included a very spacious living room, a huge bathroom, and an enormous bedroom with two single beds. The suite was almost as big as our entire apartment on Madison. Papa arranged for two additional beds to be brought in when Mama pointed out, "So much room for only two itsy bitsy beds?"

After traveling for ten days, we had a heap of dirty clothes in our suitcases. Mama decided to start washing them by hand, but Papa convinced her to send them to the hotel laundry. In his youth, Papa had worked at the Muehlebach Hotel in Kansas City and he knew about hotel accommodations, including laundry. So Mama took his professional advice. But she was shocked when the clean clothes arrived with a bill for forty dollars. Papa said it amounted to more than a month's pay for the average American worker. Mama, herself, washed and ironed our laundry for the rest of the trip.

The highlight of our stay in Athens was climbing up to the Acropolis under a brilliant sky that stretched out above us in an ethereal shade of blue. Papa, flushed with excitement, showed us the Parthenon and the Erechtheion. He told us stories about the goddess Athena, her father, Zeus, and her uncle, Posiedon. Greek goddesses had relatives, too, just like we did.

Papa pointed to a hill where St. Paul had preached, and to another where Socrates had been imprisoned in a cave. But what impressed me most was the quality of the light. Perhaps my frame of reference, a dreary apartment and a dim restaurant, inspired my appreciation of the Greek *phos* (light) on the Acropolis. Even an eleven year old couldn't miss its distinctive brilliance. The ancient buildings were a creamy color that I couldn't get enough of. The sunlight made everything stand out in striking detail—the trees, flowers, buildings, and narrow streets that wound through the city below us. Papa made us search for the sea in the distance, and even though it was quite far from the Acropolis, we saw it and marveled at its color. Our Lake Michigan may have been a beautiful and refreshing aquamarine blue, but Greek seas were the color of sapphires.

In those days sightseers could walk all over the ancient ruins. We stood inside the Parthenon and Papa explained that in ancient times, when the building was in good shape, a room called the "cella" existed in the middle of the temple and that an immense gold and ivory statue of Athena had stood in its center. Papa was thrilled to be surrounded by the monuments of Greek history which he loved and knew so well through his books. He had read enough history about the Hellenes to enthusiastically explain to us, everywhere we went, what we were seeing and why it was important. There was no finer tour guide than Papa. Mama reminded us to pick up a few small stones for Mrs. Jones. I was impressed that the only ones we found were real marble, and that even the sidewalks in Athens were made of marble that sparkled in the bright summer sunshine.

The child inside me remembers that I was astonished to find everyone speaking Greek. I could follow conversations, but didn't know many of the Greek words. The natives didn't speak "Greelish" as we did in America. Even Mama inadvertently scattered English into her sentences. "Sure," "O.K.," "Yes," "No," and myriad other words baffled her Greek listeners. Sometimes Papa, Nick and I had to remind her that she was speaking English and didn't realize it.

All signs were in Greek, and I strained to read them. Sometimes I gave up half way through a word because Mama told me to stop dawdling and "Shake a leg." We were so used to moving quickly at the Austin Lunch that it took time to change our habits; customers weren't waiting. Athenians didn't rush and we finally realized it was all right to slow down. There were far fewer automobiles than in Chicago, and I never saw a red, yellow and green electric traffic signal. Helmeted, gloved and uniformed policemen controlled the flow of traffic with hand signals from stationary platforms in the centers of intersections.

Athenians did and did not resemble Americans; styles of clothing were slightly different. Orthodox priests did not wear black business suits with white Roman collars. Instead, they wore the tall, black, brimless *kalymmafhi* hat, and a long, black cassock. Every priest we encountered had a long beard, longer and stringier than Santa Claus's, and very long hair that was pulled back and tied into a bun at the back of his head. The familiar and the strange were observable to us everywhere.

Restaurants spilled out onto sidewalks all over the city, like the sidewalk cafes we had seen in Paris. Waiters carried heavy trays from their kitchens to the outdoor tables; others stood at the restaurant doors inviting passers-by inside. All the restaurant workers were male. Mama observed, "I'd be out of a job here. They got no waitresses. Papa never would have hired me because I'm a woman. Right, Paul?" Then she gave Papa a glance that made him smile. We bought black and white postcards and mailed them to our loved ones in Chicago, to Dr. Pugh, and to Uncle Bill in Michigan. Each pictured either the Parthenon or the Erechtheion. Papa chose one showing the entire Acropolis hill for the Joneses.

Papa had never seen the cradle city of western civilization as an adult, and he fully appreciated every step he took; Mama had never even been to Athens. When she left Greece with Thea Tasia in 1921, they disembarked from Patras, the port city of Peloponnesos with no need to go through Greece's capital. After three days of enjoying Athens and attending the Pan-Arcadian convention banquet, we left for Tripolis. The purpose of our trip to Greece, after all, was to meet our grandparents, aunts and uncles in Mercovouni, Tegea and Tripolis. We left by train for Peloponnesos, and it took nine hours to travel the 123 miles from Athens to Tripolis. The train crept through the dry, brown-and-yellow mountainous terrain and stopped everywhere under the stupendously brilliant blue sky.

LOVED ONES

*I*t was pitch dark when we arrived at Tripolis. I descended from the train into the dense, dark night and glanced upwards. Packed together as I had never seen them before, a sky full of stars amazed my senses. I stood dumbfounded for an instant until a push from Nick and a word from Papa reminded me to keep going. Two tiny light bulbs, one at each end of the platform, with impenetrable darkness between them, were the only source of light in the train station. I followed Mama and squinted ahead in the thick night as we took our first few steps away from the immense black train. Papa and Nick were behind me.

Without warning, the thickness enveloped us. A crowd of unknown people pushed in at us from the blackness. Confused and scared by the invasion, I was afraid I'd lose my parents in the crush of humanity. My fright was amplified by the darkness and the horde that was falling on us, grabbing, embracing, and kissing us in the dark. I didn't know who was hugging and kissing me, but they seemed to know who I was. Nick and I struggled to stay close to Mama and Papa, but unknown people grabbed at them and pulled them away from us. Voices erupted out of the night calling out our parents' names in Greek. Shouts of "Vasiliki!" came from one direction and "Apostoli!" from another. The only English I heard was Mama calling to Papa, "Paul, watch out for the kids. Don't let them get step on by everybody."

Mama and Papa were finally able to get hold of us and I was relieved. Then I heard Papa say, "Boy oh boy, I didn't expect a welcoming party like this. Don't be afraid of the crowd, I think they're all our relatives."

I heard Nick ask, "Do we got this many relatives here?" The next instant, he was whisked from my side by a mustached man wearing a cap. Light from the tiny bulbs reflected off the metal in the stranger's mouth, and I could see he had gold teeth. After being mobbed by many Greek hellos, tight embraces, and garlicy kisses on both cheeks, our parents nudged Nick and me to face two other mustached men. My eyes had finally adjusted. We were told that one was Mama's brother, Uncle Nicholas, and the other was Papa's brother, Uncle Kostas. Both were handsome men with full, thick, dark hair. Uncle Kostas didn't have white hair like Papa did so he appeared much, much younger. Our parents and their brothers were teary-eyed during the introductions. We hugged the two men and were, in turn, warmly embraced and kissed by each of them on both cheeks.

Papa's brother informed us that a horse and carriage were standing by to take us to Mercovouni where our grandparents were waiting for us. Mama's brother said he understood that we had to go to Papa's village first (this was in deference to patriarchal tradition). However, he politely suggested that we first drop by the home of Thea Vasiliki, who was both Grandma Eleni Krili's sister and Mama's godmother. He said she lived less than a block from where we were standing and was anxiously waiting to see us. Uncle Kostas brusquely protested there was no time for a visit before going to Mercovouni. Uncle Nicholas apologetically reminded Papa and Mama that her godmother, an old lady, would be offended if we passed by her door and didn't stop to greet her.

Papa assured both of them that, of course, we could visit Mama's Thea Vasiliki before we continued on to Mercovouni. My parents waved temporary good-byes to people in the crowd and Uncle Kostas and Uncle Nicholas led us to a horse and carriage. The driver was introduced to us as "Uncle Stelios" and it turned out that he was Papa's older sister's husband. Another round of hugs and kisses on both cheeks followed the introduction. When we stepped up to take our places in the carriage, we found a woman in her early twenties already there. Mama smiled at her and asked Uncle Nicholas, "Who is this young lady?"

"Vasiliki, this is Stamata."

"Stamata?" Another round of hearty hugging, laughing, and crying took place as the carriage pulled away. Stamata was seven years old when Mama left for America, and our mother had not recognized her own baby sister. But as Nick and I looked at Mama, then at her youngest sister, we recognized a strong resemblance. In fact, of all our aunts in America, these two sisters resembled each other the most.

After Thea Stamata welcomed us with hugs, she took our hands in hers and held them tightly until the carriage reached Thea Vasiliki's house. In the dark, still holding our hands, she led us all through a door in a courtyard wall. Using a kerosene lamp, our aunt guided us into the dark courtyard over huge uneven paving stones. Then she directed us up wooden stairs to the second level. It was the house our mother remembered from her youth, and now Mama's godmother shared it with Mama's youngest sister whom she had adopted. Before entering the second story door, we were reminded by Mama to refer to her Thea Vasiliki as "Yiayia," to show respect for her age and her relationship to our maternal grandmother. It was the first time in my life that I had ever called anyone Grandma.

The visit was brief but emotional. The short, round, elderly woman grasped Mama in a bear hug and appeared reluctant ever to let go of her. Mama cried and hugged her back. When Papa was presented to Thea Vasiliki, whose white hair was starkly pulled into a bun at the back of her head, she embraced him warmly. Then she hugged, kissed, examined, and admired Nick and me, and ordered Stamata to bring the traditional thick fruit preserves for her guests.

Thea Vasiliki told us that since it was almost the end of July, the Tegean cherry season was over, but proudly added that the cherries we were about to be served were from the newest crop. Stamata brought out the dark red, fruit conserve, bathed in a burgundy-red honey-like syrup. My first-ever taste of the famous and luscious Tegean cherries made me an instant fan, even in their preserved state. The welcoming sweets were presented to us on tiny dishes with tiny spoons, all served by Stamata from a large silver tray. A round of cold water followed, presented from the same silver tray in Thea Vasiliki's fanciest glasses. A toast was made wishing us a sweet and happy visit.

Time passed quickly in the dimly lit room. Several kerosene lamps worked diligently to brighten our surroundings. While the adults conversed, I strained to examine the black-and-white photograph of a somber-looking couple that hung on the wall. The man was slim, mustached, bearded, and stern. The woman, also unsmiling, wore a long, elegant dress with a small bustle. I later learned from Mama that it was Thea Vasiliki's wedding picture. She explained that in the old days a bride didn't always wear a white gown and veil at her wedding. A lovely dress that could be worn again was the practical choice for wedding attire in a culture where clothes closets only held a half dozen items. After twenty minutes, Uncle Kostas impatiently reminded Papa that we had better leave for Mercovouni. As we kissed Thea Vasiliki and Stamata goodbye, they reminded us that they looked forward to seeing us again for a much longer visit.

MERCOVOUNI

*T*he open carriage ride to Papa's village took about a half hour from Thea Vasiliki's house in Tripolis. Stars shone brightly above us in profusion; I felt we were immersed in them. So many more stars were visible on this dark road to Mercovouni than I had ever dreamed were in the sky. Papa said they were multitudinous from the deck of the *Aquitania*, too, but I guess our parents made sure we were in our bunks at night and not out on the deck looking at the stars. Years later when I learned something about astronomy in school, I remembered the heavens as I had seen them in Greece and decided we must have been looking sideways, through one edge of the Milky Way. I have never experienced brighter days, blacker nights, and more brilliant stars than those I remember in Greece in 1936.

The horse, progressing at an even trot, pulled our carriage through the entrance to the village. Even though it was the end of July, the night was cool. Papa was excited and in his glory of glories. He pointed out the dark silhouette of the sole village church. As the carriage forged ahead, he explained that the school was over to the left; we could barely make out a small, one-story building in the blackness. A few hundred yards beyond the school, the horse and carriage pulled off to the left and stopped in front of a white stucco house. The windows on the second story glowed with a soft yellow light, and I could see shadows moving about. We stepped off the carriage into the dim light of a thousand stars and a crescent moon. Uncle Kostas led us to an exterior stairway and we ascended to the second story. At the top, my uncle pushed open a door and we entered a dimly lit, crowded room.

I held my breath when a small elderly couple approached us out of the mass of strangers. I had never seen pictures of them, but I knew who they were. Choking with emotion, Papa silently hugged the mustached, wiry old man and lively old lady. In that moment, I realized that my father, like me, was someone's child. They were all crying as Papa introduced Mama, Nick and me to our grandparents. Mama embraced them warmly, as if she had known them all her life, and called them *Mitera* and *Patera* (Mother and Father). Instantly I recognized a resemblance between Grandpa and my father, even though Papa looked decades younger. Papa's hair wasn't as white as Papou's, yet he had his father's nose and eyes.

They were people from the past who I knew but didn't know. When kids at school referred to their grandmas and grandpas, I felt like an orphan of sorts. Now I was in the embrace of the grandparents my brother and I had been named after; they hugged and squeezed us warmly. I was surprised that Yiayia Eleni and I were almost the same height, and that Papou Nicholas was just a wee bit taller. Papou's voice was raspy; he had a white mustache and a full head of white hair. When Yiayia smiled, even through tears, her face and eyes lit up warmly. She was lovable and familiar to us because she resembled our Uncle Bill.

While Papa and Mama answered questions about our trip and about Uncle Bill and his family, I looked around. I noticed that the only sources of dim, yellowish light were four glowing kerosene lamps. Papa had said there was no electricity in Mercovouni. Here was the first sign that little had changed since he had left for America in 1907. There was enough light in the crowded room for me to see that a double bed was placed against one wall. People, tables and small wooden backed chairs with straw seats took up the rest of the space. My eyes finally adjusted to the dimness. I was surprised to see women with scarves around their heads, tied at the back, so that only their eyes, noses, cheeks and mouths were visible. "We're indoors and it's summertime," I thought to myself. "Why are they all wrapped up?" They were older women and even in the dimness I was aware of their deeply wrinkled faces. The girls and young women in the room wore no scarves. And I remember that in the semi-darkness of lantern light, the girl that I was in 1936 observed the sparkle of gold teeth among the many smiles.

Each person in the upper-story room embraced us after we met our grandparents. Whereas most of our greeters at the railroad station were men, most members of the welcoming committee in Mercovouni were women. Papa's two sisters, Thea Panagiota and Thea Georgia were introduced to us, as was Thea Ekaterini, Uncle Kostas's wife, and their recently born baby girl, *Beba* (Baby). She didn't have a name because she hadn't yet been baptized. The other people in the room were Papa's cousins, but there were too many new faces for me to remember so late in the day. Our aunts were tending to tables on which they had spread platters with mountains of food. Obviously, the women had stayed home to prepare an immense meal while the men came to the railroad station to welcome us.

Although it was past midnight, we were presented with plates piled high with roasted chicken, potatoes and vegetables. Great hunks of heavy dark bread were added to each of our plates. Papa had always talked about how poor they were in the village and about how he never had his fill of food until he had worked in America for ten years. Now it was twenty-nine years later and there was enough food on my plate alone to feed three people. I came to understand that the feast that night was unusual in Mercovouni. We were being treated to an extra-special welcome for a son who had been sent away when he was thirteen years old, and who had finally returned with a good wife and children named in honor of their grandparents. This late night banquet was a long awaited homecoming celebration.

The four of us ate only a small portion of food on the plates laid before us because we weren't used to eating after midnight, and we were exhausted. Before long the adults decided that Nick and I needed to go to bed. Mama, Yiayia and one of our aunts took us to an adjoining room where we found another double bed.

"I have to go to the bathroom, Mama."

"That means we got to go outside and downstairs someplace. Remember what I told you, the bathroom's outside," she reminded us in English.

We had been warned by both our parents that going to the "bathroom" in a Greek village meant going outside to a spot that might or might not be sheltered by an outbuilding. It would not be located too close to the house, but not too far from it, either. Getting to it might involve some walking, so we were to make sure we had shoes on. We knew the spot might be smelly and that there might not be any toilet paper. However, Mama, who had not remembered to bring a bar of soap, did remember to bring toilet paper all the way from Chicago. It was one of the necessities she had packed away in the trunk. Mama and Papa also warned us that there would be no sink or bathtub near the "toilet," and that we would have to wash our hands in a *niftera* (tiny water basin) hanging somewhere in the outdoor courtyard. We were to locate it, use it every time we went to the toilet, and do a thorough job of washing up. Soap would be provided.

Our parents tried to prepare us to expect no running water, as we knew it, in the Greek villages we were going to visit. Grandpa Krilis in Piali had a well that provided lots of water, but it was across the street from the house, and there were no pipes bringing water into anyone's home. Papa told us that every day villagers in Mercovouni loaded large barrels on their donkeys and traveled to a well at the edge of the village to collect their daily water. He also told us that because collecting water took so much work and because water was often scarce, it was to be used sparingly and not wasted, as Chicagoans were apt to do. He added, "Now you'll know what I've been talking about when I've told you Mercovouni does not have enough water and you're so lucky to have Lake Michigan in your back yard."

We returned to the room with the double bed and Mama tucked us in. As I laid my head down on my pillow I noticed it was covered with a beautifully embroidered pillowcase. I later learned that one of the women of the house had not only done the beautiful needlework, but had even woven the white cloth. Nick had a question about our new surroundings as soon as his head hit the mattress. "What's that crunchy sound?"

"I think it came out of the pillow, Nicky."

"I never heard sounds come out of pillows before."

"Mama. Come back!" I shouted.

"What is it, my little birds?"

I squeamishly pointed to the beautiful pillow beneath my head. "Noises are coming out of here."

"Noises in the pillows?" She patted, then squeezed the object of my fear. "Oh," she explained in Greek. "I forgot to tell you. Villagers make the stuffing for pillows from dry cornhusks, the leaves on the outside of the corncob. You know, the part we throw away? Pillows don't have feathers in them here. Cornhusks crackle because they're dry and crispy. There's nothing to worry about. You'll sleep fine."

The next morning we were awakened by more sounds we had never heard before. We jumped out of bed to look for our parents and found them dressing in the living room that doubled as their bedroom. "What's that noise?"

Both of them laughed.

"Roosters crowing and donkeys braying. Haven't heard it in twenty-nine years. Better than an alarm clock, isn't it?"

During our stay in Mercovouni, we were introduced to Papa's cousin and old classmate, Andreas. Every morning he appeared at Grandpa's door and seemed to have nothing else to do but talk to Papa. He took Papa to Tripolis to see old classmates and to sit in the *kaffenion*. As in Chicago's Greektown, the coffee house was strictly for men. While sipping heavy, sweet Greek coffee from demitasse cups, patrons passed their time away discussing politics, playing cards, and engaging in backgammon matches, just like they did on Halsted Street. In Chicago, however, *kaffeneia* were always indoors while in Greece tables were set up outside as well. I came to understand, after listening to the talk of Greek women, that kaffeneia had the reputation for being the gathering place for slothful men.

One morning Nick and I woke up to a loud, complaining voice. It sounded like Papa hollering in Greek, but the voice was raspy. We went downstairs to the courtyard to find Papou bawling out Andreas.

"What do you think this is? I waited twenty-nine long years for

Apostoli to come home and I want to see him and talk to him—to my heart's content. But I haven't had a chance to do that yet because every morning you come to take him away from us. All you want to do is go to some damn coffee house in Tripolis to sit with a bunch of lazy strangers. If he wanted to see strangers, he could stay in America. I've had enough of you. Go home! Get out of here. Leave me and my son alone." The reprimand worked for a few days. Then Papa's persistent cousin came back to Papou's house, still trying to monopolize Papa's time, but this time more timid in Grandpa's presence.

Papa delighted in showing us his village. He pointed to a hill, east of Mercovouni, and drew our attention to a tiny church on top. It was barely visible. "That's St. Elias Church. It's only open for services twice a year. All the Mercovouniotes and Bedeniotes (people of Bedeni) go up there the day after Easter and on the feast day of St. Elias in late July. We arrived too late for St. Elias's picnic and celebration. They just had it. That little church is where Papapetros joined the shooting contest on Easter Monday and won for his village. Remember?"

Every time flocks of sheep or goats passed on the street below the second story window of Papou's house, Papa drew our attention to them. Sometimes the shepherd was taking them to be milked, or else he was looking for green fields so the animals could graze. Green fields were hard to find in Mercovouni in August because the countryside had yellowed and dried in the sizzling Greek sun.

"Sheep and goats are very important in Greece. There isn't much meat to eat here, especially in the villages. Cheese takes the place of meat in the diet, and it's made from the milk of goats and sheep."

"What about Yiayia's cow, Papa?"

"Yiayia's cow gives milk, too, but it's reserved for drinking. Yiayia sells milk from her cow to help support the family."

Soon after we arrived in Mercovouni, Papa pointed to a tree growing near Papou's house. "See this tree? When I was a kid, I planted it. Now I'm going to climb it."

Surprised to learn that our very urbanized Papa had planted anything in his life, I was even more astounded to see our father sit down on the ground and very uncharacteristically take off his shoes and socks to climb a tree.

He took us for walks in the low mountains that enclose two sides of Mercovouni from the north and west. We were thrilled to see the places he had explored as a boy, never realizing before that my graying father enjoyed a boyhood. He took us to watch the Mercovouniotes at work. Unlike American rural communities where the farmer's fields surround the farmhouse, in Greece homes are clustered in the village and their farms are located out of town. Mercovouniotes had to walk one hour everyday to get to fields that were located in a valley over the northern mountain. That same mountain walled Mercovouni in from the rest of the countryside.

"They walk for one hour with their animals and farm equipment just to get to work every morning," Papa explained. "And sometimes we complain about getting to the streetcar stop. Spoiled, aren't we? The Mercovouniotes skirt the edge of Bedeni, over in that direction, to get to work." Papa pointed over the mountain.

"What's a 'skirt' got to do with it, Pa?"

"Skirt doesn't always mean a piece of clothing, Nicky. It can also mean to walk around something. I'm saying the villagers don't walk right through Bedeni but around the edge of the town."

"Is Papapetros there?"

"I've already asked about Papapetros and was told he's in Texas again with his sons. Those boys must be doing very well if they can keep sending him steamship tickets."

"What's at the other end of the one hour walk, Papa?"

"The valley. It's known as Milia."

I knew that *milo* meant apple. "Do they grow apples there?"

"*Milia* means apple tree, and there are a few apple trees around and even some cherry trees. And there are fields of corn, too. I'm not talking about sweet corn. This is corn grown to feed animals. But vineyards dominate. That's where grapes are grown."

One morning, Yiaya put Nick and me on two donkeys so that we could make the trip to Milia with Papa and Papou. Our grandfather wore his big straw hat and *poukamisa*, a collarless tunic that reached to his knees which Grandma had woven and sewn. As we approached the valley, we spotted small cornfields scattered ahead of us. Papa explained that each farmer had his own fields and vineyards, but they were not necessarily adjacent to each other. Ordinarily their plots of land were scattered throughout the valley and in order for work to be done, the workers trudged from one distant property to the other.

We found the farmers in Milia watering their stands of corn with water pulled from wells. Some were bent over using trowels while others stood upright pushing hoes. Workers directed irrigation water down ditches between rows of corn with hand held tools; there was no farm machinery. In the vineyards, grapevines were being dusted with a light blue substance called *galazopetra*. Men, holding hand sprayers, pumped the chemical on the vines so that all the leaves and unripe grape clusters were bathed in a whitish blue film. Later, Papa looked up *galazopetra* in the English dictionary and found out it was an emulsion of copper sulfate.

In spite of the intense heat, workers were covered from head to foot. Men wore hats, and every woman wore a scarf that covered her head and most of her face, leaving only her eyes and nose exposed. Most of the scarves were bright yellow with tiny black flowers; others were plain black.

"Papa, how can they stand to be all dressed up like that? Aren't they dying of the heat?" I asked.

"Sure they're hot. But, they're protecting their skin from the sun. Suntans aren't fashionable here. Too much sun turns skin thick and leathery, so Greeks protect themselves whenever they are out in it."

"How come so many ladies are wearing black? That must be even hotter."

"Most women wear black for the rest of their lives after their husbands or very close relatives have died."

We found out that most work took place very early in the morning, often before sunrise, before the penetrating heat of the Greek sun sapped the workers' energy. That meant farmers woke up when it was still quite dark, gathered their animals and tools together, and walked an hour to get to work. They returned home around one in the afternoon, plodding the hour's distance under a broiling sun. Nick and I were surprised that everyone took a nap following the mid-day meal. Papa explained the purpose of the rest was to avoid working outdoors in the afternoon, the hottest part of the day. Nick and I tried, but had a hard time sleeping while the sun was shining and never got into the habit. We had to stay quiet, though, and not disturb the rest of the family.

Another morning, Papa, Papou in his straw hat, and Uncle Kostas loaded Nick, me, and all the empty water barrels on a donkey to travel to the well and bring back water for the day. The donkey knew his way so well that he didn't need steering. The *sella*, or wooden saddle, forced us to ride side-saddle. Nick wanted to ride like Tom Mix did in the movies, but the *sella* wouldn't accommodate him. Finally, to please him, Yiayia threw a blanket over the wooden saddle so Nick could play at being a cowboy.

On our way to the well, we passed a flock of large birds. "Hey, Pa, those look like turkeys." Nick and I were city kids, but we had seen live turkeys in the coop outside of Mrs. Popper's grocery store during the holidays.

"You're right, Nicky. Those are turkeys."

"They got no Thanksgiving here, so how come they got turkeys?"

"Don't need Thanksgiving to eat turkey, Nicky. But to tell you the truth, I'm surprised, too. I've never seen turkeys in Mercovouni before."

After going uphill, then downhill, and over lots of dry, barren fields with barrels and donkey, we finally reached the well. Grandpa and Uncle Kostas filled the heavy containers, and loaded them on to the animal. Papa helped, too, then turned to us.

"See how hard it is to get water? This goes on everyday, and it's been going on everyday for generations. Makes it easier to understand why everything isn't as clean as we're used to."

The next day, Grandpa and Papa found Nick in a corner of the courtyard trying to penetrate the stone hard ground with a shovel he found among Grandpa's tools.

"What are you doing there, Nikolaki?"

"I'm digging a well so you can have water here at home, Papou."

"Nikolaki, you can dig to the other side of the earth and you'll only find one thing here. Rock."

Even though Nick's project was unsuccessful, it was never forgotten. For years, Papou told everyone about his resourceful and energetic eight-year-old grandson who came all the way from America to dig him a more convenient well.

No matter which village we were in, Mama was kept busy. She helped the women of the house prepare meals and tried to make their jobs easier with some "American know-how." She also reminded them how important it was to keep everything clean. In village homes, animals were kept on the ground floor below the second-floor living quarters; this meant there were many flies to fight off. All day long, chickens and roosters roamed the courtyard. I never got used to them pecking haphazardly between the stones and around us humans, so shooing chickens away became my regular courtyard exercise. I preferred chickens in a coop, like at Mrs. Popper's grocery store, and dreaded walking through the courtyards, but they were the only way to enter and leave village homes.

The kitchen was usually a separate room, within the courtyard, in close proximity to the donkey, cow, chickens and whatever other animals were being housed on the ground level. Flies were inevitable, and there were no screens. Mama waged a futile battle as she tried to persuade the village women to cover food so flies wouldn't contaminate it with whatever germs they had picked up from the animal droppings. Papa, too, had an aversion to insects of all kinds. Before every meal, both Papa and Mama stationed Nick and me over the table with towels that we were to ceaselessly wave over the plates and food to discourage the flying pests. But the task was impossible, and our arms felt like they were going to fall off by the time the meal was served.

Mama may have been on a trip to Greece, yet she was hardly on vacation. She cooked under primitive conditions, heated water to wash clothes by hand, and ironed without electricity. A heavy, cordless iron was heated in the fireplace over and over again, and ironing was done on the kitchen table covered with layers of blankets. I never heard Mama complain. She didn't expect village women to do the work of taking care of the needs of her husband and children. "They got plenty to do around here, poor souls." Mama had only been away from Greece for fifteen years and had not forgotten village ways, but she felt compelled to improve them. One of her first projects, after our arrival in Mercovouni, was giving Uncle Kostas and Thea Ekaterini's newborn baby her first bath. Village custom dictated that infants be wiped clean with olive oil rather than soap and water. Mama told them we were never too young or too old to use warm water and soap for bathing.

Late one morning, Papa decided to take a Mercovouni stroll, but rushed back a few minutes later. Within earshot of Grandpa's house, he called to Mama in English. "Quick Bessie! Find the first aid kit and follow me."

Mama grabbed the cardboard box from the trunk and ran with Papa. Nick and I followed. "What happened Pa?"

"Old Uncle John fell off his wagon and hurt himself. Looks like he's hurt bad."

"Maybe you should call the doctor, Pa."

"There isn't any, Nicky. We'd have to go to Tripolis for one. The old guy needs help now. Shake a leg!"

By the time we ran to the home of Papou's widowed brother-in-law, two men were carrying the white-haired old man into his house. He had cuts and abrasions on his forehead, face and arms. Blood mixed with dirt covered the exposed parts of his grazed flesh. I couldn't bear to look at him. We followed them up to the second floor where the men laid him on a thick blanket spread out in the corner of the dark room near an unlit fireplace. Mama asked one of the men to bring her a pan of very hot water. While we waited for him to return, Mama and Papa talked to the old man, asking where he hurt, trying to put him at ease. He said he had slipped from his wagon and had fallen onto the street in front of his house. Papa checked him out and said nothing seemed to be broken. Mama tried to cheer the old man.

"Courage, Uncle John. You'll be fine. Before long, you'll be as good as new and asking us to find you a new bride."

Mama found a clean cloth and some soap. She waited a long time for the hot water because it had to be heated on a wood fire. When the boiling water was finally ready, she allowed it to cool a bit then began washing Uncle John's wounds, which were caked with dirt and animal dung. Mama tried to wash the filth out of his hair, too, as she tended to the cuts on his head. To disinfect his cleaned cuts and scratches, she applied iodine from her American first aid kit. Old Uncle John shuddered when the dark red antiseptic stung his sores. Then Mama finished up by covering his wounds with bandages. Her comments to Papa were in English.

"I wonder when was the last time this poor old guy had a bath? Be good idea you should tell him to take one. Tell you uncla that a bath will make him feel a lot better."

As we walked back to Papou's house, Nick asked Papa about something that had puzzled both of us. "Why'd they put Uncle John on the floor, Pa? Why didn't they put him in his bed?"

"He hasn't got one, Nicky."

"No bed? How come?"

"He never had one and never will."

"Why, Pa?"

"A bed's a luxury. Have you seen many luxuries in Mercovouni?"

"I guess not."

"It makes you appreciate Madison Street, doesn't it?"

PIALI

*U*nexpectedly, Mama's long awaited reunion with her parents took place in Mercovouni rather than Piali. Since Papa was planning for us to spend the first week or ten days in Mercovouni before going on to Piali, my maternal grandparents and Mama's brother Nicholas traveled by horse and wagon to Papa's village. They couldn't wait. For a second time, we witnessed the long awaited return of an impossibly distant child. Once again Papa, Nick and I were smothered with warm and loving embraces. Even though I was meeting them for the first time, I felt I had known them all my life.

Ten days later, we traveled to Piali for an extended visit with our maternal grandparents. Piali was less than ten miles from Mercovouni, but the locals considered it a sizable distance. When we arrived, we were greeted with warm embraces, sweet Tegean cherries, and glasses of cold water. After a few hours of getting acquainted with our maternal relatives, Papa initiated our first reconnaissance of the ancient ruins behind Papou Krilis's house, in Mama's "backyard." Each time we walked among the ruins, Papou Krilis watched us from the other side of the rock wall that separated his property from the ancient site. He stood silently on the porch of the house where he had been born and studied his new family members who were exploring the place he had known since birth. The sight of the imposing figure of Papou Dimitri Krilis observing us from that porch has never been erased from my memory. I can still see him, tall and silver-haired but bent with age, framed by the lush green of the famous grapevine Mama and our aunts remembered so often back in America. Indeed, huge clusters of green grapes, larger than any I had ever seen in any Chicago grocery store, hung down from thick foliage that shaded the house's plain concrete terrace. The vines provided grapes in early fall and tender leaves for *dolmades* (stuffed grapes leaves) in spring. Ripe, sweet autumn grapes filled Papou's barrels with enough wine to last a year. Mama lamented that we were leaving Greece before harvest and would miss sampling "the sweetest grapes in the world."

The initial awe I experienced on first seeing our elderly maternal grandfather was heightened by his strong resemblance to Uncle Kostas Krilis back in Chicago. Except for their age, father and son were identical, down to their substantial white mustaches. The invisible connection between people who looked so similar, yet were separated by almost ten thousand miles, was incredible. Mama looked like Thea Stamata. Papa stongly resembled Grandpa Nicholas. Uncle Bill's face was a carbon copy of Grandma Limberopulos's.

"Thea Garifalia looks just like Thea Aphroditi," I advised Nick.

"Yeah, they even sound the same. They use the same words when they talk and move their hands the same way. Its spooky."

Garifalia, the family's second youngest child, looked exactly like Aphroditi, the eldest of Yiayia Eleni Krili's children. They were fifteen years apart and they had never seen each other after Aphroditi left for the United States in 1912, when Garifalia was only five. Our two aunts did not know each other as adult women, yet the resemblance in their mannerisms was eerie. Thea Garifalia lived in the Tegean village of Episkopi, about a mile away from Piali. She and her husband, Epaminondas Giourokos, were the parents of four-year old Dimitri. When we met her in 1936, Thea was pregnant with their second child, who was expected in November.

To my surprise, Papou Krilis was quite old. He had been born in the 1850s, before Lincoln was elected president. The youngest of six, his father had died a few months before his birth. As a result, Papou was given his father's first name, Dimitrios. He had five older sisters and even though he was the youngest, as the only male in the family he was burdened with the responsibility of acquiring dowries for his sisters. Also by tradition, he could not marry until all his sisters were wed. Between his sisters and his daughters, Grandpa Dimitri spent most of his life preoccupied with dowries for his womenfolk. No wonder he had two occupations.

Papou and Yiayia lived in the house by the ancient ruins with their son Nicholas and his wife, also named Eleni. By the time we met our grandfather in 1936, Grandpa Krilis was using a shepherd's crook to help him walk. It was hard to imagine the young man of our aunts' descriptions traversing mountain footpaths to Sparta every week to sell Tegean produce in exchange for olive oil from Laconia. We had been told that Grandpa was a towering man, and we found that to be true, but the robust man of our family's stories was stooped and fragile, though still tall. Like our grandfather in Mercovouni, he wore a *poukamisa*, the long overshirt that reached down to his knees.

As Papa did in Mercovouni, Mama sought out her friends, relatives and the corners of Piali she knew from childhood. She reminisced about playing among the ancient ruins with her brother and sisters and about kneading bread and learning to cook in the ground floor kitchen. Mama drank water from Papou's well, across from the old house's front door and extolled its extraordinary good taste. She was delighted with the orchard of fruit trees that Uncle Nicholas planted in the field directly across the road. Mama was happy to see her brother was making improvements, and she shared a secret with him.

"I wish I could be here for an entire year, to see cherry and pear blossoms in spring, eat the world's best fruit in summer, and work side by side with you during the autumn grape harvest. We could huddle around the old fireplace in winter like we did when we were children and eat steaming hot, sour *trahana* (Greek porridge) garnished with burned butter and grated *mizithra* cheese."

Whenever we walked around Tegea's archeological excavations with Papa, we waved and called out to Papou. Smiling, he waved back, pleased that his Mercovounioti son-in-law from America was enthusiastic about the backyard relics. Once when the three of us explored, Papa started talking to us about a man called Pausanias, who seemed to know a lot about the ruins. "Pausanias said that the temple of Alea

Athena in Tegea was the best temple in Peloponnesos. Pausanias said one of the two pediments of the temple showed a scene from the Trojan War because the Tegeates had sent an army to Troy."

"What's a pediment, Pa?"

"Remember in Athens when we were up on top of the Acropolis and got our first look at the Parthenon? It was kind of like we were looking at its front door. Remember the great big triangle at the top of the Parthenon? I showed you some parts of statues still remaining way up on top, right below the slanting of the Parthenon's roof. Remember? That triangle was one of the temple's pediments."

"The Parthenon didn't have no roof, Pa."

"We didn't see a roof because it's been destroyed. It's not there anymore, but it had one when they first built it. And the roof was there up until about the late sixteen hundreds."

"When was that?"

"Sixteen hundreds, let's see. That's like forty years before George Washington was born. That's when the Parthenon had its roof blown off—almost a hundred years before there was a United States of America. The Turks occupied Greece at that time, and they were stupidly storing gunpowder inside the Parthenon. Then when the Venetians, who were trying to take over Greece from the Turks, shot a cannon at the Acropolis, the Parthenon blew up. That is how it lost its roof."

"Venetians? You mean like those creatures from the planet Venus?"

"No, no, Nicky. You're mixing up your Flash Gordon movies with real history. I mean people from Venice in Italy."

"Papa, I remember the triangles on top of the Parthenon. They were all torn up."

"That's right, Helen. They were damaged in the gunpowder blast. But then, a couple hundred years later whatever remained, after the explosion, was stolen by an Englishman whose name was Elgin. He did even more damage. But that's another story. We were talking about pediments.

"There are two great big triangular pieces, pediments, that sit on top of the columns of a Greek temple, one at each end of the building, right below the roof line. They were used to hold up the roof—when the roof was still there. In addition, they were used for decoration, so the temple would look beautiful. Figures were carved into the pediment. The figures always told a special story about the place where the temple was located.

"The pediments of the Parthenon told stories about Athena, how she was born, and why she was important to the city of Athens. Not too many people could read in those days, so when they wanted to get a story across to everybody, they showed a picture. The marble ones have lasted. Everyone can understand a picture."

"What kind of story did Tegea's pediment show, Pa?" Nick had just hopped onto the base of an old column smothered in dry Tegean weeds. The small ancient site was choked with brittle overgrowth that had yellowed in the summer sun. Segments of columns were almost hidden by parched grasses; no columns stood upright.

"Hey look at that big bug. Wow, it's got enormous legs."

"That's a grasshopper, Nicky. We don't have them on Madison Street. Let's see now, what were we talking about?"

"Pediments."

"Right. Every Greek temple had two pediments, one in front and one in back. The other pediment here in Tegea showed another famous local story the Tegeates were proud of, the killing of the Kalydonian boar."

"What's a Kallingbonium bore?"

"The Kalydonian boar was a vicious animal, like a giant pig with great big tusks coming out of the front of his head. It was a big monster, running wild and threatening the people who lived in these parts, like a ferocious lion on the loose. Everyone was in danger. And a girl named Atalanta killed the boar. After that, everyone was safe again."

"What'd she do, Papa?" I was really curious. For a change, the hero was a girl.

"The girl, Atalanta, is famous in Greek mythology because she was known to be the fastest runner in the world. Just like Jesse Owens. He's the fellow from Chicago who won gold medals for running at the Olympic Games in Berlin this summer. Remember? I read to you about him from the newspapers.

"Anyway, Atalanta was a local girl. I guess she was a Tegeatissa, like Mama is. Atalanta was able to run real fast and catch up with the wild Kalydonian boar and she shot it dead with her bow and arrow. Atalanta became the greatest heroine around these parts when she killed the boar. So the villagers had a statue carved in her likeness and put it up on the other pediment. The pediments of an ancient Greek temple were kind of like local advertising. They informed everybody about local heroes and about why the place was special enough to have a temple. Nowadays famous people are remembered with a statue in the park or in front of the courthouse. But in ancient times one of the ways that heroes were honored was on the pediment of a temple. Now, Pausanias also said that when he came here to Tegea, he actually saw the old shriveled-up hide of the Kalydonian boar. Its skin was on display here in the temple of Alea Athena."

"They must have kept it for a souvenir."

"Right, Helen. They also kept the tusks, because Pausanias said that the boar's tusks had been on display here, too. But when the Romans took over Greece, Augustus Caesar, himself, stole the tusks from this temple and took them to Rome and put them on display in his own neighborhood, at the Roman Forum, in what we now call Italy. When Pausanias saw the boar's tusks from Tegea's temple of Alea Athena, they were in Rome."

"Who's Gustis Sneezer?"

"Augustus Caesar was kind of like the king of Rome. The Romans so much admired everything the Greeks had done, that they helped themselves to the good ancient Greek art. They took their stolen goods back to Rome when they returned home after they conquered Greece. Later on, they made copies of the statues. Their own artists were good copiers but not as good at making originals as the Greeks were."

"Who's this guy Pausanias, Papa?"

"Pausanias was a Greek doctor in ancient Roman times, about two hundred years after Jesus was born. Pausanias took a tour of Greece, kind of like we're doing. That was when all of this stuff was in good shape. Imagine seven hundred years had passed from the time this temple was built to when Pausanias saw it and everything was still not broken. Pausanias kept a diary of all the art and all the temples he saw on his vacation. Just like Mrs. Jones told you to do, Helen. By the way, have you been writing down all the places we've been to and what we've seen?"

"Yes, Papa. I was doing better when we were on the train coming to Greece."

"Well, keep it up. In his diary, Pausanias wrote down the tiniest details of how everything looked and where it was located. He wrote all about the statues, the pediments, the temples, and the columns. Mr. Pausanias didn't miss a thing. Thanks to him we have a good idea of what everything looked like, way back when the temples were still in good shape, before they became the ruins we see today. Pausanias even came here to Tegea. All we have to do is read his book and know what it was like here then."

"Where's his book, Pa?" Nick hopped from one ancient stone to another searching for more grasshoppers. "In all the libraries, of course, Nicky. When Pausanias's diary was discovered, the scholars read it and realized, 'Say, this guy, Pausanias, he was an eyewitness to what the ancient world looked like before it got ruined.' After that, Pausanias's diary was made into a book and translated into all the languages that are interested in Greek history. It's famous. The Chicago Public Library has Pausanias's book."

"How did Tegea get ruined, Pa?"

"About three hundred years after Pausanias wrote his diary, some German hoodlums, they were called Goths, came through Greece and stole everything they could get their hands on. What they couldn't steal, they smashed. They were stupid and destructive villains. Their leader was a barbarian whose name was Alaric. He was kinda like Adolph Hitler, that lowdown Nazi we see in the newsreels."

"The guy with the little mustache?"

"Yeah, that guy. He's up to no good and neither was Alaric. Alaric and his henchmen helped themselves to everything that the Romans didn't get their hands on and vandalized everything else."

"Did Pausanias say that, too?"

"No. By the time the Goths came through Greece, Pausanias was dead and gone. Of course, Greece has always suffered from earthquakes and the quakes have done their share of damage to the ancient temples as well. Statues have been knocked over and broken. Columns have fallen and roofs have caved in. Pieces of ancient Greek temples have been removed to build houses and churches. The walls of the church here in Piali have been partially built with some of these ancient stones. Take a look next time we walk by.

"For hundreds and hundreds of years, powerful empires have tried to take over Greece. The Turks were here for four hundred years! Many helped themselves to glorius Greek art. When a statue was too big and heavy to carry back home, lots of times they broke off the head and took the head home for a souvenir. That's why we see so many headless statues. Lots happens in 2000 years. Greece has suffered through too much. What are you staring at, Helen? Trying to picture the ancient Tegeates walking around here?"

"I'm trying to picture Mama and Thea Tasia and Uncle Nicholas playing hide and go seek here."

Papa laughed. "That's right. It's a classical site and Mama's old playground, too!"

Yiayia and Papou enjoyed hearing Mama and Uncle Nicholas reminiscing about their childhood, as did Nick and I. As they talked, we found out about their childhood capers and quickly realized that Uncle Nicholas had a great sense of humor. "Nikolaki, see how my ears stick out? Do you know why?"

"Why Uncle Nicholas?"

"Your mother pulled them all the time."

Mama laughed.

"Why'd she pull them?"

Mama intervened. "He didn't like going to school. Yiayia and Papou made me responsible for seeing that Nicholas went to school. Papou used to travel to Sparta for oil. He wasn't home enough. Yiayia was busy with the younger children and with managing the workers in the fields. She couldn't check on Nicholas to make sure he stayed in school when she sent him there every morning. So she put me in charge. I loved school, but we had trouble with Nicholas. Sometimes I had to pull his ears to get his attention. And you're still not friends with the alphabet, Nicholas. That's why you don't write letters to us often enough. Nicky, let me tell you what happened to Thea Aphroditi once when she was a girl.

"One morning, Aphroditi went out into the garden to cut some fresh vegetables to cook our main meal of the day. While she was working, she heard a rustling sound and saw something alive and big crawling under the plants in one corner of the garden. She ran into the house screaming, 'There's a monster in the garden. It's hiding under the eggplants!' Aphroditi was scared to death and wouldn't go back outside. Our Thea Anastasia, one of Papou's sisters who lived right around the corner from here, *Aionia tis i mnimi* (May her memory be eternal), heard the commotion and came over. When they told her why Aphroditi had screamed, she laughed. 'There's no monster in the garden. It's Nicholas. I watched him fall behind the other children on his way to school this morning. He hid in the eggplants instead of going to class.'

"Yiayia went into the garden and sure enough, she found your Uncle there. She gave him a good spanking and after that she put me in charge of making sure he got to school and stayed there. I was supposed to help him with his studies everyday and verify that he finished his homework. By the way, his ears would have stuck out anyway. They were that way before I started pulling them. Your Uncle Nicholas was born with those ears."

Our uncle laughed again. He enjoyed Mama's spirit. He said he was pleased to see that Mama was not timid, that she had opinions of her own. "Your mother was my little sister, but she took good care of me. She was like an older sister and sometimes like a big brother. When we played with other kids in the village, she was my champion.

369

I was very good at marbles. Once when I won a game, my opponent started to hit me, but your mother joined the fracas and started beating him up."

"You really did that, Mama?"

"Of course I did. Nobody was going hurt my brother. They wouldn't dare. Nicholas was the 'tender young shoot' of our family tree. Yiayia and Papou taught us to watch over him and care for him."

Yiayia interrupted. "He is the hope for the continuation of the Krilis name, and so is your Uncle Kostas in Chicago. Kostas has two sons and our name will live on through them. We hope that sons will be born to Nicholas and Eleni here in Piali, too, when God wills, to continue our good name."

It was clear by the way everyone fussed over Uncle Nicholas that he had been the pampered son of the family, quite characteristic of boys raised in Greece. We had heard it over and over again from our aunts. Rejoicing occurred when a boy child was born. It was important for boys to go to school. The best pieces of meat at mealtime, the freshest cuts of bread, and the sweetest clusters of grapes were given to the sons of the family. It was expected behavior and accepted by sisters as well as parents and brothers.

I have often wondered why my mother had such terrific self-confidence. I now believe it began in childhood when her parents entrusted her with the betterment of her older brother. Perhaps Mama's sense of responsibility and self-worth took hold and flowered when she was put in charge of Nicholas, who was considered the most important child of the family.

As protected as he was by the women of his family, Uncle Nicholas turned into a caring and responsible adult. He continued to keep watch over his baby sister, Stamata, who lived in Tripolis and to keep an eye out for Garifalia, who was already married, a mother, and a resident of another village. He tenderly cared for our elderly grandparents. Nicholas had become the new head of the family.

Yiayia Eleni was twelve years younger than Papou and far more active than he was in 1936. She always wore a large cotton scarf wrapped around her head and neck when she went out, and let it drape around her shoulders when she worked at home. She looked a lot like our Thea Politimi. Most of the day she was occupied with preparing food in her ground floor kitchen with Mama as her assistant. When Yiayia finally had a moment to relax, she sat on the floor with her back against the wall to relieve chronic leg pains.

Our grandmothers were soft spoken, gentle, but hard working women. I don't remember if I ever saw either one without a scarf wrapped around her face or down on her shoulders. A scarf was traditionally part of a village woman's dress. Their hands were tough and wrinkled and they wore rough, heavy work clothes, usually a skirt and blouse shielded by a long, clean apron. Even in the heat of August, they wore long sleeves and skirts that reached their ankles. I never saw them wearing bright colors. They were always dressed in gray, brown or dark blue, but never black. That color was reserved for mourning; within the year, one of them would wear black for the rest of her life.

It was obvious, even to a child's eyes, that our grandmothers were primarily concerned with their families. They were especially attentive to their newly arrived grandchildren from "*Ameriki.*" Both Yiayias became quite worried when I came down with a fever and my skin broke out in big red blotches. The malady, whatever it was, put a crimp on my Greek travels. I never suffered a condition like that before or since, and we never knew what caused it. I felt like a leper. One pitch-black night, Uncle Nicholas hitched up his horse to a cart and rushed me to the doctor's house. The doctor said that perhaps there was too much iron in the water for me and didn't agree with my system. I spent many quiet days recovering from the fever and waiting for the red blotches to go away while we visited in Tripolis with Thea Stamata and Mama's aunt and godmother, Thea Vasiliki.

CELEBRATIONS

*O*ur midsummer visit to Greece coincided with a two-week fasting period prior to the fifteenth of August, a church holy day which honors Mary, Jesus' mother. The fast was strictly adhered to in all the homes we visited.

Brother Nick's birthday falls on the eighth of August. Whereas name days were well celebrated in Greece, no one paid particular attention to birthdays. Yet Mama wanted to have a little party for him, probably to make up for all the birthdays she was too busy working at the restaurant to celebrate. So Mama introduced a new observance to our Greek family, which they commemorated for my little brother. Lenten fare had to be served because of the fasting period. Eggless and butterless *melomacarona* replaced the traditional American birthday cake at Nick's party in Tripolis that was hosted by Thea Vasiliki. She and Thea Stamata made the *melomacarona*, wonderfully moist, spicy cookies dipped in honey and covered with nuts.

Summer dining usually took place on Thea Vasiliki's enclosed second floor porch. Her house was old and the floor's narrow planks had separated and slanted with age, like venetian blinds. Activities at ground level, below the porch, could be seen and heard from the upstairs through spaces separating the slats. The ancient wooden floor slanted toward a windowed wall that overlooked a winding grapevine that covered the courtyard like a canopy. Just beyond the window glass, large old flower boxes billowed with huge hydrangeas. Growing out of second floor planters, the enormous blue flowers competed with the cerulean Greek sky for attention. They added exquisite color to the courtyard from above and dressed up the spartan, almost decrepit second-floor porch. After years of living without flowers in Chicago, Mama reveled in the ones she found in Greek gardens. She held her breath when she spotted the hydrangeas hanging over the courtyard from the second story at Thea Vasiliki's. "Look at all the beautifool flowers. What a blue. Never seen nothing like them before." Mama didn't realize she was speaking English, but Papa provided a translation for her puzzled hostesses who eventually began to tease her when she inadvertently lapsed into "American."

Nick himself provided the floorshow for his ninth birthday party. After dinner, our relatives asked Nick if he knew any songs to sing for them. My little brother never needed prompting to sing or whistle, and he began crooning a medley of songs he had learned at the Austin Lunch. Nick's audience of grandparents, aunts, uncles and cousins was seated around the dinner table, still covered with a white cotton tablecloth sprinkled with the scattered crumbs from our Lenten meal. Partially filled water and wine glasses remained, within reach of each listener.

Nick was never shy when he sang. "The music goes round and round oh, oh, oh, oh and it comes out here…" followed by a cowboy tune, "I'm an old cow hand, from the Rio Grande…" Nick's repertoire was never complete without his rendition of *Isle of Capri*. "T'was on the isle of Capri that I met you, beneath the shade of an old walnut tree…"

Uncle Nicholas shouted, "Bravo. Bravo." The applause was enthusiastic even though his listeners didn't understand a word of what my brother had sung; Papa gave a two-sentence explanation of each song. When someone requested a Greek song, Nick's audience was astounded to learn that he knew a few of those, too. Perspiration glistened on his flushed little face and moistened the crop of straight brown hair that slanted down on his forehead. My brother belted out a song called *To Yelekaki* about a vest sewn together with sorrows and troubles:

"*To yelekaki pou foris to'ho ego rameno me pikres ke me vasana…*"

Our family then taught Nick a new Greek song, to sing for our relatives in Chicago, about a young man who is reluctantly leaving for America. Nick still remembers the words to the mournful melody:

"*Mi me stelnis Mana stin Ameriki yia' tha marazoso tha pethano 'ki. Dolaria den thelo, pos na sou to 'ipo, para psomi kremidi ke afin p'agapo.*"

The young man in the song pleads, "Don't send me to America, Mother, because I will pine away and die there. I don't want dollars. How can I tell you? I only want bread and an onion and the girl I love."

Nick was a hit on both continents.

At the end of the Lenten season, we were treated to a *panigyri*, the annual festival in Tegea. The fair, which Mama and our aunts longingly reminisced about in Chicago every August, is renowned throughout the Peloponnesos. It was and continues to be held in Episkopi, the village of Thea Garifalia and Uncle Epaminondas. It celebrates the church's name day, *Kimisis Tis Theotokou*, literally translated as The Dormition of the Birth Giver of God. Both church and festival have a very long history. The Byzantine church in Episkopi dates back to the twelfth century A.D.

To begin the holiday we attended Divine Liturgy in the morning and received Holy Communion at the celebratory church from a bishop wearing a gilded robe. Just as priests did back at familiar Holy Trinity and St. Basil's churches in Chicago, he asked my name and invoked it in the Greek prayer he repeated after I opened my mouth to receive the gold communion spoon that he held out to me. His left hand held tightly to an ornate gold chalice filled with consecrated wine and crumbs of bread that he gently ladled out with a long handled gold spoon. "The servant of God, Helen, receives the Body and Blood of Jesus Christ for remission of sins and life everlasting, Amen."

We attended the festival as a huge, extended family: Mama, Papa, Nick, Uncle Nicholas and his wife, Thea Stamata, Thea Garifalia, Uncle Epaminondas, and some of Mama's first cousins and their children from Piali. As soon as services ended in the cool interior of Tegea's famed house of worship, we emerged into the bright and hot sunshine of the fair. Instantly our senses were stimulated by music, folk dancing and odorous farm animals. Uncle Nicholas told us that merchants came to Tegea to sell their wares at the annual bazaar and celebration from as far away as Thessaloniki, Albania and Bulgaria. Bolts of men's dark wool suiting fabric, rolls of colorful dress prints, multi-hued rugs, brightly colored hand woven wool blankets, traditional black fabrics for mourning clothes, hand knits, and embroidered pillowcases were displayed alongside shovels, hoes, scythes and plows. Delectable, freshly prepared foods tempted fairgoers from every direction.

The air was filled with the savory fragrance of succulent *souvlakia* (shish-ke-bab) cooking over hot coals. Still more tantalizing was the mouth-watering aroma of whole pigs roasting on large spits over fires that constantly flared up when pork fat dripped down into the intense heat. We even discovered Gypsies telling fortunes, repairing cooking utensils and selling pots, pans and other household items. As we approached the stalls where farm animals were displayed, the savory aromas were replaced by a stench that reminded me of the Chicago Stadium when the circus came to town.

"Look at all the donkeys. How come they got so many of them in one place?"

Mama explained in English. "They are for sale. When somebody needs a new donkey, he know when he's come to the *panigyri* in Tegea, he can buy one. They selling all kinds of farm animals here, horses, mules, sheeps, goats. When a farmer he needs new animals, he wait to come here and buy it."

"Like a used car lot for donkeys?"

"Exactly!"

We all sat down to eat the grilled pork that was the culinary highlight of the fair. Mama advised us to eat the meat but avoid the crispy, well-done skin that was quite fatty but tasty. The skin, delectably marinated in lemon, garlic, oregano, and salt and pepper, was the best part of the roast pork, and Papa couldn't resist. Mama admonished him in English. "Paul, the pork's too fat. Don't eat the skin. You going to get sick."

All the merriment and commerce took place around the corner and down the block from Thea Garifalia's house. The ruins of an ancient theater lay buried in the ground beneath our feet, just a few yards away from the shadow cast by the huge dome of the Byzantine church. Papa explained that the ancient theater was located under the ground because over the years successive towns were built on top of the old amphitheater.

"That's why digging to find ancient ruins is called excavating. Over the course of the last two thousand years, houses, buildings and roads have been built over the ancient sites. Archeologists have to dig in the ground to find them."

Papa had bought a book about Tegea at the museum in Piali, a few days before, and told us about Tegea's medieval history. During the middle ages, Frankish knights took over parts of Greece. They held immense tracts of territory in the Peloponnesos, including Tegea. Papa explained that these knights, resplendent in armor, swords and colorful pennants, held jousting tournaments in and around Tegea. In medieval times, however, the township had a different name. It was called "Nikli."

"Last night, I finished reading the chapter about Tegea's part in the revolution against the Turks. In the eighteen twenties, about thirty years before your grandfathers were born, Nikitaras, the famous Arcadian hero of the Greek revolution fought the Turks in a bloody terror-filled battle on these very streets. Right here where we're standing."

During our stay in Greece, Papa continuously reminded us that we were surrounded by history. At the same time, however, we were engulfed in the real world of village life. We slipped back and forth from the Golden Age of the ancients to the early Twentieth Century of our rural relatives. At Tegea's annual festival our attentions shifted from an ancient theater—to visions of King's Arthur's knights—to a sword wielding revolutionary hero of 1821—then back to a dry field with donkeys for sale.

Dust permeated the air and flies buzzed around the farm animals. A park with trees and thick hedges across from the church accommodated throngs of people who had come from surrounding villages and far flung corners of Peloponnesos. Tegeates who had moved to Athens made a point of returning to their township in August for the annual fair. Mama met people she remembered from her childhood, years before she came to America. Within a stone's throw of our aunt's house, the ruins, and the old church, happy crowds of people celebrated the *panigyri*. The last thing on their minds was the history that had made its mark on the grounds where they danced in semi-circles on a very hot August day.

"Know what this reminds me of, Nick?" I asked my brother.

"What?"

"It's kind of like a Greek Maxwell Street—but out in the country. Instead of hot dogs and ice cream sandwiches, they're selling *souvlakia* and *loukoumia*."

"Yeah, but this is much more fun, and I'm not afraid of the strangers."

Back in Tripolis that night, Papa had a hard time digesting the fatty pork he had so enjoyed in the afternoon. We could hear him, awake most of the night, running up and down the stairs using the "bathroom" facilities in Thea Vasiliki's courtyard.

TRIPOLIS REMEMBERED

*T*hea Vasiliki and Papa came to know, enjoy and trust each other during the many days and nights we spent in Tripolis. Late one afternoon, she brought him a box and asked him to examine its contents. "Apostoli, I have some papers here. Some are written in English but I don't know what they are. Can you help?"

"Sure, Thetsa. Let me see."

Thea Vasiliki handed over her box, then stood over Papa, hands on her wide hips, while he read. He found unredeemed cashiers' checks from the U.S. dating back to 1923 mixed in with personal letters; the checks had expired. Some had been written from banks that closed in the early years of the Depression.

"What are they, Apostoli?"

"Thetsa, these are checks you should have exchanged for drachmas years ago. Let me make them good. I'll give you money for them."

Papa was willing to pay her so she could have the money, but Thea didn't realize that in return, Papa would get obsolete paper.

"Oh, no, Apostoli. Thank you, I don't want drachmas. I just wanted to know what they are. I'll just go on keeping them safe."

Hearing their conversation, I wondered why she preferred old papers to money. I asked Mama about it.

"My godmother is not able to read or write. When she and my Mama was little girls, nobody send them to school because they was girls. Female children didn't count except to clean and cook and work in the fields. It was okay to marry them, but not to educate them. And when they get marry, everybody expect them to have little boys. My big sisters, they never went to school. But the law change when I was a little girl so that's why I was the first girl in our family to go to school, then Tasia, and Garifalia, and Stamata went too. In the old days, when a baby was born you hear somebody say, 'Too bad it's a girl. Would be better if she was a boy.'"

"Why Mama?"

"Because they don't know no better. They worry about have to give dowry to the girls. A boy, when he's marry, he gets dowry and that brings money into the family."

"Did Papa say that when I was born?"

"No, no, no my little bird. Your Papa was so proud when you was born. He never said such a stupid thing. Things is different in America. Everybody knows all of God's children is valuable, boys and girls. It changed a little bit in Greece now. It's not so bad like it use to be when my Mama was a girl. Still, some people don't know no better. They ignorant.

"Thea Vasiliki is saving papers. In Greece you don't see lots of paper like we see in America. My godmother is old lady now. She never going to read or write nothing. She don't know that sometimes nonsense things is written on paper, stuff that don't matter. But she thinks every piece paper is important because it got words on it. Words is special for her because she can't read them. She's well off and feels she don't need more money. So she saves paper with writing because she thinks its more special than cash."

There was as much to discover about attitudes, customs, and living conditions in Tripolis as there was in Mercovouni and Piali. Staying in Tripolis with Mama's godmother and Thea Stamata was fun, and far less primitive than the village. I slept in the back of the house in the same room as Thea Vasiliki. Nick slept on the enclosed porch with the slanted old floor. Thea Stamata bedded down on a cot in the room off the porch that served as a second-floor makeshift kitchen. Mama and Papa slept on the double bed in the living room. There was no electricity or plumbing in the house. Running water came, indeed, through pipes in the courtyard, but at noon the city water department shut it off. The citizens of Tripolis had to get all their jugs, bottles and urns filled before the noon cut-off. Each morning, Nick and I helped Thea Stamata fill all the containers with water for the day. We rushed around the courtyard under the cool shade of the massive grapevine canopy. Compared to the daily labor of fetching water in Mercovouni, this was ultra-modern.

Mama relished acquainting herself with her "baby" sister. While Thea Vasiliki napped in the afternoon and Stamata took a work break, she and Mama visited together, quietly whispering, not to disturb our elder aunt. I enjoyed sitting between Mama and our wonderful "new" Thea during their hushed visits. Sounds, we were reminded, floated up through the open slats in the porch floor as well as they leaked down.

"Stamata, how are you getting along with my godmother?"

"Fine now, but it was hard at first."

"I've always known she is difficult. Did you want to be adopted and come here?"

"Never. I was fourteen years old. I pleaded and pleaded and cried and cried not to leave my parents, brother and sister. But everyone assured me I would be better off in Tripolis because I will eventually inherit this property. Coming here would help our family's economy. They promised to visit me often so I wouldn't be lonely. Our brother Nicholas said he'd come and see me every day."

"Did he?"

"That's what made it bearable. I looked forward to his visits every single morning."

"Our sister, Politimi, says Thea Vasiliki is the most difficult woman she has ever met," Mama said. "Politimi remembers coming to help her at holiday time."

"She can be impossibly difficult. She never had children of her own and she has forgotten what it is like to be young. But, I've adjusted. I had to adjust. As a little girl, I loved to sing and dance. When I came here, Thea told me that dancing and singing were not respectable activities for a proper girl, therefore they were forbidden to me. One day, when I was alone, I found a short rope for drying clothes down here in the courtyard. It was hanging off the post that supports the kitchen ceiling. Every time Thea Vasiliki or Uncle John, *Aionia tou i mnimi* (May his memory be eternal), sent me downstairs to bring them something, I'd grab the end of the rope, quietly sing a song to myself, and dance around the post a couple of times. It was my secret. No harm done. I wasn't disgracing the family name. It was just me and the rope and a song in my heart. My secret dance kept me going. Of course I made sure she couldn't see or hear me through that blasted old floor."

"Did you complain to Mother?"

"I did at first, but she just kept telling me to be patient, that I was helping out old people who needed me. I knew our parents wouldn't go back on their word and take me back. There was no use complaining. I didn't want Mother or Father to worry, so I kept quiet. Then I got used to my new home, to my life in a city, to my work. I even got used to brushing the horse's teeth."

"Brushing what?"

"Uncle John brushed his horse's teeth. When he got too old and infirm, he insisted that I brush his horse's teeth by myself."

Mama started laughing uncontrollably, inspiring me and Stamata to laugh, too. I lost control and giggled hilariously as I pictured Thea Stamata with a can of Squibb tooth powder in one hand and a giant toothbrush in the other, reaching into the horse's mouth. The three of us curled up trying to muffle our laughter so we wouldn't awaken Thea Vasiliki. Gasping for breath, tears streaming from their eyes, Mama and her sister cured a thousand of their ills that afternoon with their laughter. "Stamata, when I was a little girl, I had heard that Uncle John, *Aionia tou i mnimi,* brushed his horse's teeth, but I had completely forgotten it. Was it really true?"

"You're looking at the main teeth brusher of the household, an eye-witness and participant! The man didn't have children, so he aimed all his attention on that blessed horse."

"How often did you have to brush the horse's teeth?"

"Everyday. I don't know if the old man brushed his own teeth everyday. When the poor guy, may God rest his soul, got too old to come downstairs and do a dental check on the animal himself, I wised up."

"What do you mean, Thea?"

"Helen, while I was downstairs with the horse, Uncle would shout directions down to me through the upstairs window, 'Mata, make sure you get all the way back into his mouth. The uppers are more difficult. Hold his mouth open with your left hand while you work with your right. Sometimes you have to hold his tongue to get at the back.'

"'Yes, yes, Uncle,' I'd call back up to him. 'He's very cooperative today. After all these years he's finally getting used to this.'"

Naive Chicago girl that I was, I asked my aunt with a shudder, "Thea, how could you stand to do that? Hold its tongue? Euooo… that's awful."

"He thought I was cleaning his horse's teeth, Helen, but I wasn't doing anything of the kind. All I was doing was carrying on a two-way conversation with an old man who needed to give orders. I wasn't even touching the horse. What the old man didn't know didn't harm him. The horse was at peace and so was I… and so was Uncle John… *O Makaritis* (Blessed one)." Mama joined her in finishing the sentence… "*Aionia tou i mnimi,*" and then we all burst into laughter.

Years later in 1984 when we were sifting through the old letters, Mama sadly recalled the day we received news of her dear youngest sister's death almost twenty years before.

"I still feel my heart break every-time I remember when that damn telegram came to our door bringing the terrible news." Tears streamed from her eyes. "God took our Stamata away too soon. She was only in her fifties, too young and too good to die. It was a stupid doctor's fault. She had fallen and broken her leg. The damn doctor put a cast on her leg, too tight. Stamata had phlebitis and he cut off her circulation. What a tragic waste. She never lived to see her daughters Sophia, Vasiliki, and Eleni marry. She deserved to live. She deserved the best. Everybody loved Stamata. She was good to everyone. Stamata's heart and soul were pure gold."

KALI ANTAMOSI

While I recuperated from fever and skin blotches in Tripolis, Nick spent time in Mercovouni. One day, Mama and Papa left the village to visit elsewhere, but Nick didn't want to go with them. He preferred staying with Yiayia in Mercovouni so he could play at being Tom Mix with the family donkey.

In her enthusiasm to please him, Grandma put Nick on the donkey, cowboy style, and proudly led him through the narrow, rocky street of Mercovouni, up and back, several times. Then she continued her daily chores while Nick entertained himself by digging a well for Grandpa. Grandma milked the cow, cleaned the courtyard, and gathered fuel for the cooking fire. Nick watched Grandma pick up chunks of cow manure that she placed on the wall of the courtyard to dry in the hot sun. When the dung dried, it could be used as fuel to heat water on laundry days. Dung was an abundant and economical source of fuel in Greek villages where animals were plentiful but trees were not. When her chores were complete, Yiayia interrupted Nick's well digging project to ask what he wanted for dinner.

"I'm not hungry yet, Yiayia."

Nick was exhausted by nightfall, and Yiayia began to be concerned because my brother kept telling her he wasn't hungry. Our parents had still not returned.

"Please, Nikolaki, you must be famished. Are you sick? You haven't eaten all day."

"I'm fine, Yiayia. But, if you insist, I'll eat. You know what I'd like?"

"Anything, Nikolaki. What can I make for you?"

"An egg sandwich."

"What's that?"

"It's American, Yiayia. I'll show you how to make it. First we need two pieces of bread and then we have to fry an egg."

Yiayia brought out the dense, brown village bread that Nick insisted on slicing himself; he sawed off two thick, crooked slices with much difficulty, under Grandma's supervision. She marveled at the independence and ability of her American grandson. When Grandma realized that Nick's recipe required a fire, she lit branches then brought out her heavy black skillet, an egg, and some olive oil. She placed the skillet over the fire, heated it, and poured in a small amount of oil. Yiayia picked up the egg and was about to crack it when Nick begged her,

"Yiayia please let me do it. I know how."

"Be careful, Nikolaki."

By the time Grandma had said "careful" Nick had cracked the egg, aimed, and missed the frying pan; the egg wound up in the fire.

"Oh, I'm so sorry, Yiayia."

Grandma was sorrier than Nick.

"Got another egg, Yiayia?" Nick's frame of reference for eggs was the Austin Lunch; Uncle Charlie ordered them by the case.

"That was my only egg. What else can I make for you to eat, Nikolaki?"

"That's all right, Yiayia. I'll just have bread and butter. I like that."

"Is that all you're going to eat today, my child? Just bread and butter?" Our grandmother was in tears.

"It's fine, Yiayia, I eat it all the time in America."

Grandma brought out a container with a tan liquid.

"What's that brown stuff, Yiayia?"

"Butter, Nikolaki. Didn't you say we need butter for the bread?"

"Butter is yellow, Yiayia. It comes in a square. It's hard and cold."

"Nikolaki this is the only kind of butter we have."

"Okay, Yiayia. That'll be fine."

Nick fell asleep at the table, his limp, little hand half-grasping a partially nibbled hunk of coarse, brown village bread soaked with brown Greek butter. Yiayia gently put him to bed and waited for my parents. When they returned, she uncharacteristically scolded them for staying out so late. Then she reported how upset she was that her only grandson had starved all day and fallen asleep hungry.

The next morning Mama asked Nick about how the previous day had gone. "You know, Nicky, Yiayia was really McCoy upset. Why you don't eat nothing? You make poor little Yiayia worry. She feel real bad because she's afraid you going to get sick."

"Mama, I almost cried when I broke the egg and it fell in the fire."

"Nicky, they don't have lots of eggs here like we got in America. Why didn't you let Yiayia fix it for you?"

"Well, Mama. You know I love Yiayia. But you know her hands are kinda rough and…"

"And what? She's know how to fry eggs, Nicky. She try so hard to please you."

"Mama, I wanna tell you somethin' but you got to promise. You got to promise to never tell Yiayia. I don't want to hurt her feelings."

"What I got to promise?"

"And never tell Papa neither?"

"What is it, my little bird? What happen?"

"Promise?"

"I promise."

"Well, yesterday I saw Yiayia pick up the ca-ca from the cow—with her hands. I don't know why, but she put it up on the wall. Why is she saving it, Mama? What's she going to do with it? Well, I didn't see if she ever washed her hands. And I just didn't want her to touch food after that."

"I understand, Nicky. Don't worry, I never tell Yiayia."

"Or Pa either?"

"I not tell Papa, too."

A cure was finally found for the welts that accompanied the fevers that made me sick in Greece. A little old lady, who was an expert in folk medicine, was found in a neighboring village. She cut thick leaves from a green plant, then sliced them crosswise into two pieces, and tied a section of leaf onto each one of my red blotches. Within a few days my ugly blemishes were miraculously gone. Mama stopped worrying about whether I would be allowed to enter my native land again. She remembered the old days at Ellis Island when immigrants were forbidden to enter the United States and were turned back when they looked as sickly as I did during much of my Greek vacation. Papa told Mama that there was no reason to be concerned because I was an American citizen with rights to enter the U.S. that aliens lacked. He added, "That little old lady who cured Helen is worthy of the Nobel Prize for medicine."

After three months in Greece, the thick calluses that seemed a natural part of Mama's and Papa's hands and feet had softened. But it was almost the end of September and time to go back to the Austin Lunch, Brown School and Madison Street. Partings were difficult. We knew that a long time would pass before we could cross the ocean and the continents again. How many more beers had to be sold at the Austin Lunch before we could afford another trip? How many fifteen-cent breakfasts and twenty-five-cent dinners needed to be served to buy steamship tickets again? How many times would the old cash register on top of the glass cigar case have to ring to make it possible to go back to Greece? Beyond our personal limitations, Hitler and Mussolini were threatening the world. Our grandparents were very old. Mama and Papa knew it might be possible to see their sisters and brothers again, someday. But they doubted that they would ever again feel the kisses and warm embraces of our gentle yiayias and our white-haired grandfathers. Mama and Papa dreaded saying good-bye. For a second time, our parents experienced the wrenching separation of "the living death" as they had done when they left the first time in 1907 and 1921. Nick and I were also sad, but we were too young to seriously contemplate the possible death of our loved ones when we said our good-byes in Mercovouni, Piali and Tripolis.

Uncle Nicholas promised Mama that he'd write to us more often. Almost everyone in each of the villages came to say good-bye. Fondest regards were sent back to practically every Greek-American we knew from someone who loved them in the old country. The bonds of family had been strengthened and they extended love half way around the world. During our stay in Greece, Nick and I learned we had families who loved and cared about us thousands and thousand of miles away from the Austin Lunch and Chicago. As we left, we said "*Kali Antamosi*." It means, may we meet again under good circumstances, a perfect way to say "Good-bye." We wished it to each other and prayed it would come true.

The Pan-Arcadian expedition split up after the July convention in Athens, and travelers within the group were required to get back home independently. Mama took care of all the practical details, everything that didn't involve reading signs or schedules, and ably assisted Papa in returning us to Madison Street.

"Remember, Papa get to America almost all by hisself in 1907, without Mr. Veros's help. And Papa was still a little kid and a fresh greenhorn back then."

We departed Greece from the port at Piraeus. Thea Stamata, Uncle Nicholas, and Papa's brother, Uncle Kostas, accompanied us to Athens and stayed with us until we sailed away. When we arrived in Brindisi, Italy we disembarked and boarded a train to Milan. All I remember of Milan was staying overnight in a hotel and looking at an ornate cathedral. Another train took us to Paris. Mama, of course, was prepared; a bar of *savon* was ready and waiting in a handy corner of the suitcase.

A third train connected us to Cherbourg's port where we boarded another Cunard White Star ship, the *Berengaria*, named after another English queen, the daughter-in-law of Eleanor of Aquitaine, the wife of Eleanor's son, Richard I. Berengaria's vessel was not as spiffy as the *Aquitania*. We could tell that it wouldn't be long before the ship was packed away in mothballs, or whatever it is they do to rickety old sailing vessels. When we finally arrived in the United States, we stayed overnight in New York City, then boarded a train for Lansing, Michigan. Mama and Papa said it was the perfect time to visit Papa's brother,

Uncle Bill, his wife Thea Chrisoula, and their daughters, Helen and Connie who lived in Lansing; Baby Connie was our newest cousin in America. Our parents wanted to take advantage of the opportunity to visit Papa's brother because they knew that after we returned to the Austin Lunch it might be decades before we ever left town again. The prediction came true. In retrospect, Papa's two thousand dollar splurge on our trip to Greece was the deal of a lifetime. As a family, we never traveled together farther than Lansing, Michigan, ever again.

Nick and I went back to school, and our parents returned to work at the *magazi* the day after we got home. The Austin Lunch was still in its twenty-five- foot niche at 1458 West Madison, unchanged. We returned, so quickly, to our routines that within a few days our trip seemed only as real as a movie at the American Theater. Our neighborhood had not changed. The Flatiron Building still looked brown and dirty through Mama's beige organdy curtains. The one visible difference was the clump of trees in Union Park; when we left in July the leaves were thick and green. Now they were descending in a confetti of russet, gold and brown.

It was good to be back. All our Greek friends expected us to visit and bring them news of their families in Greece. We did more visiting than we had ever done before our trip. For some of Mama's and Papa's fellow villagers, we were the first people to report first-hand on the well-being of loved ones in the "old country" since they had arrived in America.

"THE WOMAN I LOVE"

*H*alloween and Thanksgiving flashed by and before we knew it, Christmas was near. In mid-December of 1936, Nick and I found ourselves in front of Iris and George Jones's floor model Philco radio anticipating an unscheduled news bulletin. Mama had given us permission to go over to the Jones's apartment when she heard it was for an announcement of historical importance, which to her meant some kind of history lesson. She had found time to stay home to prepare for the coming holidays. Mama was baking her delectable *kourambiedes*, powdered sugar butter cookies.

Mr. and Mrs. Jones, Nick and I huddled close to their radio. We heard a crackling sound; Mr. Jones said that static was quite usual for an overseas transmission. The announcer said that the King of England was about to address us and we listened closely through the static. Iris Jones held her breath through most of His Majesty's speech. When he informed the world, "I have found it impossible to carry the heavy burden of responsibility and to discharge my duties as King as I should wish to do, without the help and support of the woman I love," Mrs. Jones gasped for air. Sobbing, she realized that, indeed, David was giving up the throne for Wally. When we heard him say, "God bless you all. God save the King!" through radio static, Mrs. Jones began weeping audibly.

"He really is abdicating!" Mr. Jones spoke because his wife was carrying on like a mourner at one of those funerals we had attended. George Jones was shaken, too.

"What's the matter, Mr. Jones?" Nick was nine, naive enough to ask the question I was afraid to broach.

"Well, Nicky, our King doesn't want the job anymore. His younger brother, Bertie, will be King of England now." Mr. Jones tried to comfort Iris to no avail. "Maybe you should accompany Helen and Nicky back to their apartment, Iris. Mrs. Paul must be waiting for them."

We found Mama in the kitchen. The *kourambiedes* were out of the oven resting on large rectangular pieces of waxed paper spread out over the white and blue porcelain tabletop. With a teaspoon and the small seive she used to keep seeds out of our morning orange juice, Mama dusted a fine cloud of powdered sugar, like freshly fallen snow, over the warm crescent shaped butter cookies. The fragrance of powdered sugar and fresh, *kourambiedes* sweetened the air.

"You just in time. Come on and sample them. First we let them cool off for a couple minutes and then they be ready to eat." Mama looked up, took one look at Mrs. Jones, and panicked. "What's the matter? We got a war or something? What kind of history you hear about on the radio? What's going on?"

"Mrs. Paul, our King has abdicated!"

"What happen? Explain to me the whole about it, please, because you know my English is not so good, Mrs. Jones."

"The King has given up being the head of England. He'd rather marry that, that, brassy divorced woman—Mrs. Simpson. Our religion doesn't allow our King to marry a divorced woman, Mrs. Paul. But he'd rather have her than be our King. Imagine all the fine women in this world that he could marry, and he picked one who's been married twice—and divorced twice."

Mama's shoulders relaxed and she made the sign of the cross over herself three times in relief. "Whooo. I know all about those kind of troubles. That's just like Al and Hazel. I understand why you so upset, Mrs. Jones. I'm so sorry. You know, Paul and me feel same way about it when Paul's cousin, Al, he marry that good for nothing Hazel. All the good girls in Chicago and he pick a streetwalker. This guy is just like Al. I guess kings is people, too. He's making big mistake, just like Al. He be sorry but it's too late by that time. Not worth it for you to cry over guy like that, Mrs. Jones. So, now where England going to get another king? Prob'ly got big supply of guys who want the job."

"His younger brother will take the throne. He's married and has two little princesses." Mrs. Jones's voice was still shaking. Using her embroidered hankie, she wiped her eyes and blew her nose.

"Sound's like nice family man. Maybe he's do better job being king than the other guy. Don't worry, Mrs. Jones, everything going to be all right. Not worth it to cry for kings, Mrs. Jones. I'm tellin you the true. Is he cry for you? You are over here living on Madison Street and have to take in boarders to pay the rent—and you working hard in hospital all day long. Mr. Jones, he go up and down in his *elevata* (Gree-lish for elevator) box all day long. I get dizzy just think to about it. You think the king he cry and worry for you?

"Forget about the kings, Mrs. Jones. They not care at all about you changing bedpans in the hospital everyday. Kings got it too good. Here, eat some *kourambiedes*. Take some home to Mr. Jones and let me make tea with cream so you can enjoy the cookies better. Christmas is coming. We suppose to celebrate. It's not good to cry."

"Thank you, Mrs. Paul. I'm just too emotional about our beloved England and our royal family. Ummm, your cookies are as exquisite as ever. They melt in my mouth. I've said it before Mrs. Paul. They're the best cookies in the world. Yes, I will join you for a cup of tea with cream. By the way, did you find cream in Greece?" She had calmed down.

"Yeah, Mrs. Jones. I find cream in the old country, too. Things is getting better all the time over there."

MOURNING

S ome time in 1937 an envelope with a black border bearing Greek stamps arrived at the Austin Lunch. Mama noticed it while it was still in the postman's hand. Papa spotted it when he reached out to take the letters from the mailman's grasp. Seeing the envelope's horrid black border was, for them, like hearing the dreadful death chimes they remembered tolling in Mercovouni and Piali. My parents felt their hearts dropping to their stomachs. Color drained from Mama's face and she started to mourn as soon as she saw the envelope. "*Theouli mou* (My dear God). Where is it from? Mercovouni or Piali?" She crossed herself three times.

"From Stamata in Tripolis."

"Stamata wouldn't be writing to us about a death in Mercovouni. Something has happened to my father. Or to my godmother. Open it, Paul!" Tears filled her eyes and fear distorted her face. Papa took a knife from the counter and slit open the black-bordered envelope that announced death. Silently, he began reading. After a few seconds, he said, "Sit down, Vasiliki."

"Who is it?"

"Sit down."

"All right, I'm sitting. Who is it? Not my mother?"

"Vasiliki, I'm so sorry. It's your—"

"Tell me."

"It's your brother, Nicholas."

The letter said that Nicholas had died from phlebitis in his legs. We were all shaken by his unexpected death, but no one more so than Mama.

We all remembered that while we were in Greece, Nicholas had accidentally bruised himself and blood began gushing from his leg. My father had taken him to the doctor. "I didn't realize it could be fatal," Papa reflected.

Now that Nick and I had met our relatives in Greece, we cared about what happened to them. Nick and I were deeply saddened by the loss of our caring and warm Uncle Nicholas who had such a wonderful sense of humor. The entire family, on both sides of the Atlantic, was plunged into mourning. Mama began wearing black when she wasn't at the store and did so for a very long time. She and Papa were very concerned for Yiayia and Papou Krilis, who were devastated by the loss of their only son in Greece. On top of that, Nicholas's wife suffered a miscarriage following her husband's passing. Stamata and Garifalia were doing their utmost to console Yiaya and Papou, but they could do little to assuage the ravages of grief.

Several months later, sorrow struck Papou and all our family again when a letter tucked inside another black-rimmed envelope but mailed from America announced the death of Uncle Kostas Krilis, our grandfather's first-born son who lived in Chicago. Papou suffered the deaths of both sons in one year, 1937. Kostas was survived by his wife Marigo, two sons nearing twenty, Peter and Louis, and two young daughters, Jenny and Clara. Grandpa Krilis's sons were tragically gone forever; our aged grandfather had outlived both his male children. Our lives were filled with sadness in 1937 and 1938. For a long time, we didn't go to movies or listen to the radio, and our holidays were somber.

Years later as an adult, I reflected on the loss of our dear Uncle Nicholas who died before his parents and thus never had a chance to inherit their property. Grandpa Krilis's daughters had been sacrificed, sent to an unknown land, so that Nicholas could inherit enough property to live comfortably and so the Krilis family name could be passed on to the next generation. Did Grandpa Krilis ever regret "getting rid" of his daughters for Nicholas's sake? We'll never know. But we do know that while immigration was so painful, the exiled daughters did very well in their new homeland.

Aphroditi, Politimi, Vasiliki and Tasia married fine and earnest men who were not attracted by the economic rewards of an antiquated dowry system. And they matured mentally, socially and psychologically in ways they never would have in the old country. In spite of the harsh, traumatic experiences of immigration and the poverty of the Great Depression, they learned to love the United States. They become good and content Americans. These positive results were never dreamed of in Greece when they were blindly sent across the ocean.Eventually, they expressed thanks for all the good things they found in America: good husbands; childbirth attended by registered nurses and medical doctors; Dr. Pugh; indoor plumbing, electricity; "Lake Michigan for a backyard;" hot and cold running water; labor saving devices like washing machines, refrigerators, gas ranges, and electric mixers; telephones to soothe loneliness; the comfort and camaraderie of close family; central heat; screens on doors and windows; sliced bread; radio and television; American citizenship and the Constitution; the vote; Eleanor Roosevelt; Rosie the Riveter; greater freedom for women; education and jobs; good friends and neighbors from other religions and ethnic backgrounds; living in the land of plenty which Mama described in one word, "Paradise"; and terrifically grateful children and grandchildren. As Mama often said, "God Bless America."

CHANGE BECOMES DRASTIC CHANGE

*T*he Austin Lunch was our vantage point for watching the world's twists and turns in the late Thirties. Our rough neighborhood, newsreels at the One Hour show, radio, the newspaper stand outside Papa's place, the restaurant's gaudy jukebox, life-changing family events and the personal trials of people we knew exposed us to real life. Although Nick and I still watched and listened from the back booth, by the late Thirties we were working behind the counter and coming face to face with the real world.

The Depression and Papa's Austin Lunch had given us work experience at an early age. I was nine when I first used the cash register, took money from customers, and made change. Nick, at seven, stacked and washed dirty dishes and peeled potatoes. As we grew older, our responsibilities and work hours increased.

Nick started working a paper route. One of his stops was the bookmaker upstairs from Louie Drell's cigar store. The old mystery of how horses could be played with in that building was eventually solved for him. He also discovered that the bookies who operated over Drell's also rented three, separate apartments on our block to protect their operation when "the heat was on." That meant the police conducted raids that the bookies knew about in advance. When a raid was to take place, the bookmakers moved to an apartment over the Austin Lunch, or to an apartment in the building where we lived at Ogden and Madison. Illegal bookies with "syndicate" connections literally covered Chicago, even though most of the city's residents were unaware of it.

By law, because Nick and I were both minors, neither of us was supposed to sell alcoholic drinks. I remember one New Year's morning when we were left in charge of the Austin Lunch while Mama and Papa caught up on a few hours of sleep, exhausted from having worked working well past three in the morning. The restaurant was usually empty in the early morning hours, except for an occasional straggler in search of a morning cup of coffee. What could go wrong?

A customer came in and asked for a glass of beer, of course. Nick served him, but by the time I brought the man his change, counted back his money, and looked up to thank him, the man had disappeared. I thought our patron was gone, but Nick had watched him slip off the counter stool. We ran around toward the front of the bar to help him up, but found him on the floor, in a motionless slump. Even at that young age I knew there would be some kind of trouble if the police came and found two kids in charge of a saloon with an unconscious (or worse) man lying on the floor. Papa had said that police in the neighborhood were to be avoided because they were always "on the take." I was paralyzed with fear.

We stared at the man, hoping he'd stir, but he stayed absolutely still. I looked over at Nick. "Maybe he's dead," I shakily advised.

"Now what?" Nick was numb, too.

"Get Papa! Tell him to come right away. Now."

Nick ran the half block, up three flights of stairs, and tore into our apartment at top speed.

"Hey, Pa! Some guy fell off the bar stool and he's on the floor. He's dead!"

Papa grabbed his pants, pulled them on over his pajama bottoms, pushed his bare feet into shoes, swooped up his eyeglasses, and ran out of the house, never thinking to grab his overcoat. Nick said he never saw Papa move any faster.

Scared to death, I stood alone, riveted, for what seemed like a lifetime, to the dirty linoleum floor of the Austin Lunch, looking over a dead man who wasn't even in a casket. I had been surrounded and comforted by family when we had attended Uncle Jim Koliveras's funeral. This just wasn't the same.

With my eyes shut tightly, I prayed until Papa and Nick burst into the store and my father rushed to the stranger. We all heaved a collective sigh of relief when the "body" finally started moving under Papa's very watchful attendance. The man on the floor sat up and apologized. We had witnessed an epileptic seizure.

The jukebox at the Austin Lunch afforded Nick and me a chance to keep up with American popular culture. "Swing" music livened Papa's place during the late Thirties. For a nickel a selection, our customers listened to the "big bands" of Benny Goodman, Artie Shaw, and Jimmy Dorsey. *Sing, Sing, Sing* and *Stompin' at the Savoy* filled the air at the Austin Lunch along with the Andrew Sisters' *Bei mir bist du Schoen*. As months passed, war themes emerged from the brightly colored box.

In the fall of 1938 our Chicago Cubs won the National League championship, but lost the World Series to the Yankees in four straight defeats. Orson Welles shook the country in October with his new radio program, "Mercury Theater of the Air." On Halloween night Welles dramatized a Martian invasion in "War of the Worlds." Many thought it was the real thing, and panic gripped some of America's radio listeners. I missed the original airing but heard all the commotion about it at school the next day.

In the autumn of 1938, I was a freshman at the all-girls Lucy Flower Public High School on Chicago's West Side. I'm sure my parents felt my childhood innocence could be prolonged if there were no boys in high school. Flower was located across the street from the Garfield Park Conservatory that Uncle Christ Ganas had introduced to us when we were very small. The "upside down horse" continued his watch outside the glass-enclosed garden, and Uncle Christ's Greek friend still sold hot, fresh popcorn every day.

News from Europe was somber. The prime minister of Great Britain, Neville Chamberlain, hoped to avoid war by appeasing Adolph Hitler. In response, the Nazis helped themselves to a piece of Czechoslovakia. In 1938 the Nazis invaded Austria. Whenever we accompanied Papa downtown to the "One Hour Show" we viewed countless scenes of German cheering masses adoringly waving at Hitler and of his obedient goose-stepping armies in review. "They sure got lots of parades in Germany, Pa. That's almost all we ever see any more in the newsreels."

Papa shook his head. "It's not good, Nicky. We have to keep up with what's going on in the world, but next week, for a change, we'll go see *Snow White and the Seven Dwarfs*. It's something new. They call it a full-length feature cartoon."

With the help of a thriving bar business our family was well out of the Depression by 1939. We still called Papa's establishment by its original name, but new customers referred to it as "The Country Club." I smile when I think about it. The new name wasn't inspired by interior redecorating—we hadn't even added a new coat of paint. The difference was on the exterior. The brewery had installed a sign in front of the store that covered the lower third of its facade. The advertisement, a huge red sign placed right below the window display of whiskey in fifth-sized bottles, shouted "Goetz COUNTRY CLUB Beer" in large white letters. Newcomers thought "Country Club" was the name of Papa's place. The Depression still festered for a good portion of the population in 1939. Eight million Americans were unemployed. Although the unemployment rate had dropped to 14.3 percent in 1937, it was on the rise again and by 1939, 17.2 percent of U.S. residents were out of work. The average hourly wage, when available, was 62 cents. Even though major changes occurred in our lives during 1939, our parents still worked hard, spending long hours on their feet behind the bar and white marble counter of the Austin Lunch.

Nineteen thirty nine was a year filled with creativity, expositions and drastic change. The New York World's Fair welcomed visitors from all over the globe, at the same time that San Francisco's Golden Gate Exposition opened on the west coast. George VI and Elizabeth, the King and Queen of England, came to America to visit the east coast world's fair and were treated to hot dogs by Eleanor and Franklin Roosevelt. Mrs. Jones was thrilled and spoke to us of nothing else. It looked like David's brother, Bertie (George VI), was working out well in Iris Jones's beloved England. John Steinbeck's *The Grapes of Wrath* became an immediate best seller. *Gone with the Wind* came to the screen at the American Theater, around the corner from the apartment where we lived. Papa, Nick and I went to see it after it had opened to critical acclaim in Atlanta, Hollywood and other major American cities. *The Wizard of Oz* brought us Munchkins, Judy Garland and *Somewhere Over the Rainbow*.

In reality, the flights that soared somewhere over the rainbow were not of pretty bluebirds but war planes. Nazi troops and aircraft attacked Poland on September 1, and by September 3, Great Britain and France had declared war on Germany. The Spanish Civil War was over, but World War II had begun. One of F.D.R.'s fireside chats in 1939 advised us that the United States would remain a neutral country. That looked doubtful. The Austin Lunch was filled with the disturbing news of the war in Europe.

Papa set a cup of coffee with cream and a piece of cherry pie in front of a customer sitting toward the middle of the counter. He thought hard, trying to remember when he had seen the man before. He peered over the top of his eyeglass frames at the gentleman with the green eyes and gray hair. "You look very familiar. You've been here before. And you're Greek. Don't tell me, I'll remember. You're Nick—"

"Karamitsos."

"That's right How are you, Nick? I'm Paul—"

"Limberopulos. I remember you, too." Both smiling, they shook hands over the white marble.

"You came in looking for a job once upon a time. I bet you own your own place again."

"Well, not quite."

Papa sympathized with the gentleman. "Times are still tough. Unfortunately, they're calling this 'Roosevelt's Depression.' How's the family, Nick?"

"They're in Greece."

"Yes, sir. Our American born children need to experience the village. It helps them better appreciate what we've got in this country. But are they coming back soon? This is no time to get stuck in Europe."

"Well, they're not quite on vacation."

"How's that? I don't have to tell you Hitler's making lots of noise over there. It took less than a month for Poland to fall. Who knows what's next?"

"Tell me about it. I'm desperate to have them back. But my wife is involved in a law suit. I sent my family there because I own property in Kalamata."

"Kalamata? I don't remember that you're from Kalamata, Nick. I thought it was Nikitaras's village."

"Yes, that's true. But when my father and both my brothers went back to Greece, we agreed they would return down south to Kalamata, instead of our village, to buy land with the money we earned together working on the railroad. Land is fertile in Kalamata. It's good for growing cash crops.

"When my wife and three kids went to Greece in '37 I thought I was sending them to a piece of land that I owned. They would escape this damn Depression and work a farm that would give them good food to eat, and an income. I was going to join them, eventually."

"Sounds good, except for what's going on in Europe now."

"Hitler's causing troubles, but so is one of my brothers. He says that I don't own any part of 'his' land. He won't admit my money helped to buy 'his' land. My wife is in court on account of my own brother."

"What about your other brother?"

"He's on my side. But my wife's trying to win in a man's world without me. She writes that it's best for them to come back here."

"Your wife is right."

"I'm doing my best to get them back here but it is impossible and damn frustrating. Right now I'm thinking about leaving Chicago and moving to Ann Arbor, Michigan. I'll buy a restaurant so I can support all of us when they get back. My oldest boy will be ready for college pretty soon and the University of Michigan is located in Ann Arbor. It's one of the best schools in America. All three of my kids can go to school, enjoy professions and have nothing to do with this lousy restaurant business. At present, I'm a cook in a restaurant at Crawford and Madison. I live over here on Paulina Street. I felt like taking a walk on my day off, so I came down Madison today and remembered your place. You've made some changes."

"Yeah, I've got a bigger bar. Most of my business is beer and liquor now."

"How's your family, Paul? I remember, your wife worked with you."

"She still does, but her schedule changed this spring. We had a—"

Papa was distracted when he looked toward the front door and saw Mama entering. She paused to hold the door wide open for Nick. He was trying to maneuver a green wicker baby carriage into the Austin Lunch.

"Well, here they are now. Let me introduce you.

"Vasiliki, Nicky, this is Mr. Karamitsos. And sleeping here in the buggy is baby Constantina, the newest member of our family. She was born in June. She surprised us all."

"Pleased to meet all of you. *Na sas zisi* (May she live a long life). Congratulations."

"Nice to meet you, Mr. Karamitsos." Mama smiled at the gentleman and then at the baby in the carriage. "We've been to the doctor this morning. Since the old Dr. Pugh die, may God rest his good soul, his son take over. The new Dr. Pugh Junior is pretty young but doing a good job. He says the baby's healthy and everything's fine."

"Pa, we just went and seen an apartment in the Salvation Army Building."

"Why, Nicky?"

"Because it's for rent." Mama answered.

"Last time my wife went apartment hunting, she brought a whole new career upon herself. That was when she started working in here."

Mr. Karamitsos nodded. "You're a lucky man, Paul. I wish my wife and kids were around me. Are you still working, Mrs. Limberopulos?"

Mama smiled again. "Sure I'm still working. Baby's no bother. She bring lots of happiness. My children is a big help. When they not in the school, Nicky and his big sister are old enough to take care of the baby, but my own sisters help, too. I was working right up to the time Paul take me to the hospital. Everything is fine." Mama lowered her voice to say something to Mr. Karamitsos in Greek.

"*Ti stelni o Theos pou den ta vastai i yeis?*" Then she translated the old saying in English. "What God sends down to the earth that the earth she can't soak it up? Nothing. God, alloways knows what He's doing. He only sends just enough for us to handle. But I got wonnerful sisters. They big help to me. You got family, Mr. Karamitsos?"

"Three children. They're in Greece with my wife. I miss all of them."

"They be back soon?"

"I hope so." Nick Karamitsos stood up, put on his fedora, and pulled some change out of his pocket. "Nice meeting all of you. I've got to get going."

"Drop in again, Nick. I hope your family will return soon. Put your money away. There's no charge for good *patriotes*. Paulina Street is close, so come again."

"Thanks, Paul." Mr. Karamitsos tipped his hat, walked to the glass and wood door, and exited.

"He's looks like nice gentlaman. You know him before, Paul?"

"He had been in, maybe three, four years ago. Bessie why are you looking at apartments in the Salvation Army Building?"

"Because it's much better than the one we got now, Paul. We can afford the rent, too. It is thirty dollars a month."

"How is it better?"

"It's got one more room than what we got now. It's got more light. It's newer. We need more room, Paul. Now we got five of us. It's time to get little bit better and bigger place to live."

Indeed, the birth of our baby sister came as a thunderbolt of a surprise. Not only did her arrival precipitate our move to larger quarters, it permanently changed all our lives. Babies do that sort of thing. Mama was in the hospital for seven days following childbirth and Papa swapped shifts with Uncle Charlie so he could be with us in the evenings during Mama's hospital stay. We were only allowed to look up at Mama from the public sidewalk at the hospital; she came to the window to wave down at us. Hospital rules decreed visitors had to be over sixteen years of age. Papa took us to Riverview that week and we thrilled at being in Chicago's famed amusement park with honky tonk midway, hopeful games of chance, an immense, dizzying Ferris wheel, and breath-taking rides like the "Bobs."

One evening, before Mama and baby came home, Papa took Nick and me downtown for a very special treat, a movie and stage show. The Chicago Theater, the Oriental, and other Loop movie houses featured special attractions with live performers and a live orchestra between projections of the main feature. Frequently, famous actors, actresses, singers, and musicians appeared. I remember that once we saw an energetic, talented, and very short Mickey Rooney on stage. On that June night in 1939, the three of us enjoyed the movie together and then a full orchestra magically glided out onto the stage and the glittery live show began. After a few musical numbers by a tuxedoed band, a woman came on stage and began to sing and dance. She sang a couple of songs, but when she started taking her clothes off to the music, a stunned Papa announced it was time to go home. We left in the middle of her performance and a visibly embarrassed Papa said no more about the incident. It was one of those occasions where we accepted his decision to leave. "Period." No questions asked.

Three months after our sister Connie's birth, the last of our United States-born cousins joined our ranks. A boy was born to Uncle Bill and Thea Chrisoula in Lansing, Michigan. He was named Nicholas, of course, after our Papou in Mercovouni.

The Forties found us living at 1516 West Madison in one of the Salvation Army Building's second floor apartments. We moved across the porch and east on Madison to become next-door neighbors of the docile but still imposing, brown grizzly bear building. The Fellas family moved to the same building and continued to be our next-door neighbors, a small step up for both our families. After the move, we bought our first electric refrigerator to keep our baby sister's milk cold. It was modern and electric, but Mama continued to refer to it as the "iceboxi." A customer who worked at the factory arranged for us to buy the Hotpoint refrigerator at a discount; Papa paid one hundred and six dollars.

At street level, the building housed the "Salvations" church and community center. The smiling, neatly uniformed men and bonneted women of the "Army" were friendly neighbors. Nick and I had previously been in the Salvation Army Building when we attended a Christmas party for deprived Depression kids. Chris Dekazos and our cousins, the Ganas boys, had come with us. Wide-eyed, we examined the inside of the simple house of worship, the only church interior any of us had seen outside of a Greek Orthodox Church. We were shocked that its only ornamentation was a single, immense, and very realistic painting of Jesus.

In 1940, neighborhood excitement peaked with the announcement that the Democratic Convention would be held at the stadium, as it had been in 1932. We wondered if F.D.R. would drive down Madison so we could cheer him from our apartment's window in the Salvation Army Building. Papa was disappointed that Roosevelt, who had already served two terms, would probably not run again. Chicago's politicians thought differently, however. Unpredictably bizarre plots have been hatched in Chicago's city hall incited by the "creativity" of her politicians. Chicago is notorious for them.

The summer of 1940 was not "an ordinary time." Eleanor Roosevelt used those words when she came to Chicago in July to address the Democratic Convention. Hitler's armies had overrun Denmark and Norway that spring. In June, Mussolini forced Italy to join Hitler's side, and by the end of June, France had surrendered to the Nazis. War had exploded in North Africa, and Germany's aerial bombardment of Great Britain was a month into the unknown future. When Democrats met at the Chicago Stadium for their National Convention in July of 1940, the United States was unnerved by a very threatened peace. Eleanor Roosevelt appeared at the Stadium in person, but unlike 1932, without her husband.

A statement from the President was read to his fellow Democrats saying that he did not expect to be nominated and that the delegates were free to vote for any candidate. At the end of the reading, a loud, unexpected, amplified exclamation burst into the huge arena. It demanded, "No! No! No! We want Roosevelt. We want Roosevelt. We want Roosevelt. The party wants Roosevelt! The world wants Roosevelt!"

The forty-five minute chant instigated a rally on the convention floor which led to Roosevelt's unprecedented third term re-nomination. The Mayor of Chicago, Edward J. Kelly, had collaborated with Chicago's Superintendent of Sewers, Thomas D. Garry, to turn the tide toward F.D.R. Mr. Garry, the unseen influence who demanded "We want Roosevelt," found fame as "the voice of the sewers." History was made, again, four blocks from the Austin Lunch.

By 1940, Steinbeck's *The Grapes of Wrath* became a movie starring Henry Fonda and Jane Darwell. Nick's new whistling and humming numbers from the Austin Lunch jukebox were *You Are My Sunshine* and *Back in the Saddle Again.* Radio gave a voice to "Superman" who had been introduced to the world in 1938. We read the thrilling comic books over at Thea Politimi's house thanks to Cousin Jimmy Ganas. Now we heard his exciting adventures on our own new floor-model Zenith radio. "Able to leap tall buildings in a single bound. It's a bird. It's a plane. It's 'Superman.'" We were breathless.

Mr. and Mrs. Jones lived only a porch away from our new quarters in the Salvation Army's building. Sympathetically, we watched their anguish over the tragic situation in England and France. Three hundred fifty thousand British troops had to evacuate Dunkirk in small boats. London and other British cities were being "blitzed," suffering devastating bombardments from Nazi aircraft.

We, too, felt anguish for our beloved families in the "old country" because once again, someone was trying to conquer Greece. This time it was Mussolini. As the Italian dictator pushed his forces toward the Greek peninsula, we kept track of the war by reading the daily Chicago newspapers. I started a scrapbook of the world's events, cutting articles out of newspapers, after Papa had finished reading them from front headline to back page. We were proud of our tough *patriotes* in Greece who, for a time, successfully fought off the Italian armies in the rugged green mountains of Epirus. The battles took place in north-western Greece, near the Albanian border. In October of 1940, the Greek Prime Minister Ioannis Metaxas answered "OXI," Greek for "NO," to Mussolini's demand that the Greeks surrender. Meanwhile, the governments of Hungary, Rumania, Bulgaria and Yugoslavia agreed to co-operate with Hitler's regime. A small force within the Yugoslav army, however, rebelled at their government's capitulation and, like the tough Greeks, struggled against the invaders. The resistance lasted until the spring of 1941 when Hitler's forces overwhelmed both the Yugoslav army and Greece. Sixty thousand British troops were sent from Egypt to help the feisty Greeks, but in the spring an airborne German invasion forced the British back to Africa. After that, Greece was occupied by both the Germans and the Italians.

December 6, 1941 fell on a Saturday. The sixth of December is the feast of St. Nicholas in the Greek Orthodox Church, and our brother's name day. Since St. Nicholas Day fell on a Saturday in 1941, always the busiest day of the week at the Austin Lunch, Mama decided to invite all our aunts, uncles, and cousins to our apartment on Sunday, December 7th, for a celebration. Sometime during dinner, we heard that the Japanese had attacked Pearl Harbor. The rest of Nick's celebration was spent somberly listening to tragic news about Hawaii on the radio.

The following morning I stopped at the store before catching the streetcar to go to school and found Papa and Mr. Jones at the counter. They were trying to figure out why the Vogels, our bakery neighbors in Mr. Prevolos's building, had disappeared overnight.

"You mean they aren't there anymore, Papa?"

"They are gone. Moved out during the night."

"What happened?"

"Nobody knows. They're German, so maybe the attack on Pearl Harbor scared them. I remember during and after the war in 1917, there were anti- German feelings in America. Hatred of Germany was taken out on innocent German immigrants who had nothing at all to do with Kaiser Bill. Maybe the Vogels were afraid it would happen again."

Mr. Jones had another theory. "Perhaps the Vogels have Nazi ties, Paul. The *Tribune* says that after Roosevelt gets his declaration of war from Congress, we'll be at war with the Japanese and then with Hitler, too. Maybe the Vogels moved out because they're bloody Nazis."

Papa didn't believe it. "I don't think so, but it's hard to figure, George. I've been next door to them all these years but didn't know anything about them. They kept pretty much to themselves. War brings strange happenings. This is only the beginning."

Arriving at school the morning after the attack on Pearl Harbor, I learned we were about to have an unscheduled assembly. Our principal gathered the entire student body of Lucy Flower High into the school auditorium to listen to President Roosevelt's national address over the radio. "Yesterday, December 7, 1941—a date which will live in infamy—the United States of America was suddenly and deliberately attacked by naval and air forces of the Empire of Japan—The attack yesterday on the Hawaiian Islands has caused severe damage to American naval and military forces. I regret to tell you that very many American lives have been lost—Hostilities exist. There is no blinking at the fact that our people, our territory and our interests are in grave danger." Continuing the speech, F.D.R. asked Congress to declare a state of war on Japan. Congress complied, and it wasn't long before Germany and Italy had declared war on the United States.

We were frightened to our very innards and most girls were in tears when we returned to our classes at the end of the President's speech. Words from F.D.R., a man I considered almost as a relative, the Patriarch of our collective American families, informing us that "many American lives" had been lost and that we were all in "grave danger" weakened my knees and left me on the verge of panic. Even the Vogels, who had been next door to Papa's restaurant for all of my life until that very morning, had mysteriously disappeared overnight. What would become of us? Would nightly air raids blitz down on us from above to terrify us out of our beds as they were doing to Mr. and Mrs. Jones's relatives and friends in England? Our own families in Greece—grandparents, aunts, uncles and cousins who I had personally hugged, kissed, cried and laughed with—were under horrific occupation by German and Italian armies. Would I watch alarming, goose-stepping Nazis march down Madison Street and Michigan Avenue as Papa, Nick and I had seen them do on Paris streets when we watched newsreels at the One Hour Show? Would they then raise that hate-filled red, white and black swastika flag over Lucy Flower High School and the Chicago Stadium? Would Japanese air force planes with suns on their wings come to bomb the Great Lakes and the Port of New York? They were petrifying questions and no one had answers.

After I arrived at English class, our teacher gave us an unexpected and unusual assignment. She told us that none of us knew what the future would bring to America, and that it was normal to be afraid. We were at war and anything could happen. An attack from Asia or Europe would change life, as we had known it, or maybe end it forever. She fretted that 1941 might be the last year for many traditions, especially a very special Chicago Christmas event. Our English teacher assigned us to go downtown to Marshall Field and Company's department store on State Street to see the beautifully decorated, giant, two-story tall Christmas tree. She told us that every year during the holidays, Field's tree was the Christmas marvel of Chicago. Put up on the day after Thanksgiving, it remained in the store for all to admire through the holidays. She said that because the world was in a precarious state, Marshall Field's extraordinary Christmas decoration might never be seen again. Our assignment was to see it before it was taken down at New Year's. We didn't have to write about it; all we had to do was see it.

The next day, I went downtown on the Madison streetcar and for the first time in my life saw the famous Christmas tree, glistening with what seemed to be thousands of exquisite ornaments. I marveled that it stood two floors high in the middle of the Walnut Room Restaurant, located way up on the seventh floor. I was overwhelmed by its color, grace and size. It momentarily took my mind off my own fears and multiple news reports bombarding us from radio and newspapers about the war. I'm extremely pleased to report that it is now more than sixty years later and Field's Great Tree continues to be a very special Chicago Christmas tradition.

A month or two after Pearl Harbor, a stranger came into the store one busy Saturday night and complained he couldn't hear the juke box. Before Papa could stop him, the man raised the volume to an almost deafening level. No one had ever complained about the jukebox before nor had anyone messed around with its controls. Papa, Nick and Mama and I were very busy with customers and tolerated the din until Papa got a chance to turn it down. Meanwhile, Mama had asked Nick to go down into the basement to tap a barrel of beer. Nick, on his feet all day working at restaurant and bar duties (even teenage bodies got exhausted at the Austin Lunch), ignored Mama's request, deciding to wait and tap a new barrel the following morning. Mama reminded him several times, but Nick never got around to it.

When Papa went down to his basement storeroom the next morning, he discovered it had been broken into through the wall of the vacant adjacent store (until December 7th it had been Vogel's Bakery). A hole large enough to allow several thieves to remove 72 cases of whiskey had been gouged out of the wall while the jukebox blared. Both our parents were relieved that Nick hadn't followed their directions that night.

In 1984, Mama made the sign of the cross over her chest as she recalled the break-in. "Your brother would have been killed if he went downstairs that night. And none of us upstairs could have heard him yell even a 'boo' for help because the damn music was playing so loud. Those guys had a lot of whiskey to steal. They wasn't going to be nice to some kid going down there to tap a barrel of beer and getting in their way. That old joint on Madison was a pain in the neck, and everyplace else. There was alloways *stenohoria* (worry), *nevrikomares* (irritations), and *sklavia* (slavery) in that *magazi*. You never knew who's coming in the door or what's going to happen. We got stress, twenty-four hours a day. Thank God, none of us got killed because the neighborhood was getting worse and worst."

Events from 1939 until the late summer of 1946 irreversibly affected the world, our immediate and extended family included. First cousins George Kuchuris (Aphroditi and Pete's son) and Jimmy Ganas (Politimi and Christ's son) were drafted into the army. Jim was in an accident during training in Utah and never went overseas. George was shipped off to Europe. Socrates Limberopulos (Jim and Koula's son) joined the Navy and was assigned to the Pacific. Mama and Papa framed and hung our cousin's pictures, handsomely dressed in the uniforms of their country, at the restaurant. Their photographs, along with those of Austin Lunch customers in the armed services flanked the slightly larger black-and-white portrait of Franklin Delano Roosevelt in Papa's restaurant. Placed over the back bar and in the vicinity of the cash register, the smiling pictures of F.D.R. and the servicemen looked down from a place that couldn't be missed by anyone who entered the restaurant. We fervently prayed for their safe returns.

HOME FRONT

We lost all contact with our families in Mercovouni, Piali and Tripolis in 1940 when war broke out in Greece. Mr. Karamitsos reported, with grave concern, that his wife and three children never made it back to America and were trapped in Nazi occupied Greece. No communication was possible, even through the Red Cross. Nick Karamitsos was completely cut off from his family. The last thing he heard was that they were living in Kalamata, a small city in southern Peloponnesos.

In the United States, blue star banners began appearing in the front windows of homes with family members fighting for their country. Each star represented a service man or service woman from that family. The background of the small patriotic standard was usually red and white, often outlined with gold fringe. The blue star was replaced with a gold one when a loved one was killed in action. The title, "Gold Star Mother," was bestowed on those unfortunate women whose children were killed in the war.

Working women, blackouts, rationing, newspaper drives, and Victory Garden plots brought the war effort into civilian lives. Thea Tasia and Thea Aphroditi grew vegetables in small Victory Gardens adjacent to their apartments so that more commercially grown produce could be available for "the boys" fighting away from home. There was no place to plant a garden in the concrete surroundings of Madison or on Lake Street at the Ganas residence. The jukebox at the Austin Lunch played the music of World War II. Hundreds of nickels were inserted into the gaudy machine to hear *I Left My Heart at the Stage Door Canteen, Praise the Lord and Pass the Ammunition, I'll Be Seeing*

You in All the Old Familiar Places, and Glenn Miller's *Don't Sit Under the Apple Tree With Anyone Else But Me.* Another popular war song, *Goodbye Mama, I'm Off to Yokohama* ("for the red, white, and blue, my country and you") was on the flip side of a 78 RPM record which urged us to "Remember Pearl Harbor as we go to meet the foe; let's remember Pearl Harbor as we did the Alamo." When Mr. and Mrs. Jones came into the store, they plugged in countless nickels to listen to *White Cliffs of Dover.*

I recall one blackout drill in Chicago. During the citywide drill, the air raid warden on our block was worried about the light that burned day and night in the dim hallway leading up to our Salvation Army apartments. All of the residents had already covered every window with blankets to seal out any glimmer of light coming from inside the apartments. The air raid warden impatiently rang all of our doorbells, but none of us tenants could turn off the hall light bulb. The socket was located far above anyone's grasp on the high ceiling. The warden was not quieted until the janitor and his extra high ladder were finally hunted down and the bulb was loosened to comply with blackout rules. That night, during the drill, we never turned on electricity but hovered around a lone candle placed far from the blacked out window in the living room. According to official rules, no glint of light was to be visible anywhere in the city in case enemy air forces attacked at night. We prayed that in a real emergency a blackout would prevent the enemy from finding and bombing two million people in their metropolis on the southwestern tip of Lake Michigan, or anywhere else.

From 1941 through 1945, American knowledge of the world was expanded beyond the Great Lakes, Atlantic States, and Pacific shores of the U.S. We learned geography the hard way, through war. Anzio, Leningrad, the Solomon and Marshall Islands, Normandy, the Philippines, Corrigidor, Saipan, Bastogne and the Ardennes Forest jumped off pages in the world atlas and became real to us because American boys we knew were risking their lives in those places. We were ignorant of the exact locations where our cousins and friends were stationed, warned by colorful, eye-catching government posters that security had to be tight because "Loose lips sink ships." History was made every minute of the day and night, not by George Washington and Patrick Henry, but regular guys like the kids we grew up with. We fervently prayed for their safety, survival and return.

By 1943 and 1944, the nation appeared to have accustomed itself to having women in the workplace, since they were needed to replace the men who were fighting overseas. "Women are fully capable as men," a proud Eleanor Roosevelt told us. "Men and women are meant to work together." Both Eleanor and Mama knew the truth, and Mama had put those words into practice more than ten years before Eleanor proclaimed them. Yet women still had to struggle to prove themselves in the workplace. And by late 1944, when the government and nation looked forward to allied victory and an economic recovery, many assumed that the women who worked outside their homes during the war would return to being housewives once the men returned. The battle for women's equality in the American workplace would drag on long after the war was over "over there."

After the war began, Uncle Charlie found employment in a downtown restaurant that paid much better than Papa ever could. Charlie Kingos's new position was more in keeping with his talents as a topnotch chef, and both my parents understood and cheered his moving up and out. Papa and Charlie's partnership ended for the second time in their lifetimes. After Charlie left, Papa decided to stop serving full meals from the kitchen, and Mama took over the job of preparing short orders on the grill. But, her additional duties proved too much for her, so Papa finally decided to stop serving food. "Period." Although many of the fine people who were good and trusted customers continued to come in, our clientele drastically changed when we stopped serving food.

Loyal customers, neighbors, relatives and friends were all flabbergasted by my parents' next decision. Without any hoopla, Papa sold the Austin Lunch in December of 1944. Compared to the suffering at the Pacific front and the Battle of the Bulge raging in Europe, the sale of a rickety old saloon in a narrow storefront at 1458 West Madison, in the inner city slums of Chicago, was insignificant. It had a tremendous impact on us, however. Skid Row had finally enveloped the fourteen- and fifteen- hundred blocks of Madison, and my parents saw the urgent need to move to a safer neighborhood. When Papa decided to sell the *magazi*, he had difficulty finding a buyer who believed the old "joint" could make any money. He finally sold it for $6,000, two thousand dollars less than he, Uncle Bill and Uncle Charlie had paid for it when they bought it from Mr. Prevolos in 1922. The new owner, Mr. Linardos, did very well and eventually acquired Mr. Prevolos's building, too.

Papa purchased property at Harlem and Higgins in the far northwest part of Chicago in January of 1945, a month after finalizing the sale of the Austin Lunch. The new location was so distant and such a drastic change from the surroundings where we had lived and worked for the previous fourteen years that I almost felt we had moved to another planet. Trees, shrubs, grasses and wildflowers became our new environment. The boundary line between the City of Chicago and the suburb of Park Ridge was a mile to the west. There were no apartment buildings nearby. Single-family homes with front yards and back gardens were the norm. There were even trees on Papa's new property.

A working farm with cornfields, tractors, and elderly bachelor farmers, named Harris, was located diagonally across the street on the southwest corner of Harlem and Higgins. In fall, the white wooden farmhouse, which lacked indoor plumbing, was framed by drying cornstalks stacked in small clumps. Every evening at dusk, a lamplighter carrying a ladder walked along Higgins Road and lit the gas lamps that lined the street. The lamplighter returned every morning to turn off each lamp. The City of Chicago replaced the colorful old lamplighter and picturesque lampposts with electricity a few years later. There were no supermarkets or grocery stores nearby. A southeasterly ride on the Higgins bus transported residents to the busy shopping corners of Lawrence and Milwaukee Avenues, an area known as Jefferson Park. The bus trip took a half hour each way.

Several of Papa's acquaintances thought that my parents had made the worst mistake of their lives by moving so insanely far, out in "the sticks." They feared they would never hear from us again. Our family continued living in the Salvation Army Building on Madison Street until late summer of 1946 because available housing was scarce following World War II. Papa opened his new liquor store and bar in a converted brick fruit stand building at Harlem and Higgins on May 12, 1945.

I finished Lucy Flower High School and graduated from Wright Junior College during the war. After completing the two-year program at Wright and before going to work in Papa's new establishment, I worked as a typist for Douglas Aircraft at O'Hare Field, the U.S. Air Base located at Mannheim and Higgins Roads. The military airfield eventually became the parent of O'Hare International Airport. Our entire family commuted from our apartment on West Madison to work and school on streetcars and buses until we were able to buy our first car, a used, light green 1940 Pontiac sedan with running boards. Nick and I became the family drivers, but we referred to it as Nick's car. Finally in the summer of 1946, we found a suitable place to live, a real single family home on Menard Avenue, several blocks north of Higgins Road, on the Northwest Side of the city.

Nick worked at the new *magazi* (store) after coming home from Austin High School, located on the West Side. My parents decided that Nick should attend Austin, which was outside our district, because it was the only public school on the West Side that offered Greek classes. The teacher, Dr. Drossos, spent most of a class period disciplining unruly Greek-American students who felt they had heard more than enough Greek in their short lifetimes. High school became a time for rebellion and Americanization for many children of immigrants, but not in our family, of course. Mama and Papa ran a tight ship and did not allow even an iota of opportunity or time for rebellion. Nick learned little additional Greek at Austin High, but as Mama said, "at least he not lose what Greek he know already." My brother graduated in February of 1946 and then attended Wright Junior College on the Northwest Side while he continued working, almost full-time, at the new bar and liquor store which Papa named Har-Hig Liquors. When Nick completed his semesters at Wright, he continued working long hours at the "Har-Hig" until Papa sold it in 1960.

The neighborhood on the Northwest Side was a refreshing change. Our jobs were easier after we stopped serving food, and most of our customers were good people with young families. We worked long hours, but not 24 hours a day. I opened the store at 10 a.m.; Papa and Nick locked up and came home at one in the morning. Our staggered work shifts still did not allow us to sit down as a family for dinner, except on Thanksgiving, Christmas, New Year's Day and Easter Sunday. Nick, Mama and I finally convinced Papa to close the store at three in the afternoon on those holidays.

In the spring of 1945 we finally neared the end of the war in Europe. Uncle Pete and Thea Aphroditi's son, George Kuchuris, was a member of the 12th armored division in General Patton's Third Army. George was one of the American soldiers who went from Normandy, through Brittany, into Northern France. They brought relief to the U.S. Army at Bastogne in December of 1944, and eventually crossed the Rhine into Germany during March of 1945. They were the first Americans to see and liberate the unspeakably horrific Nazi concentrations camps.

Franklin Roosevelt was in his unprecedented fourth term of office and it was beginning to feel as though he was the only American who could be President of the United States. We were dumbfounded by his death in April of 1945, and our family mourned as if he had been a revered grandfather. Mama and my aunts reverently repeated "*Aionia tou i mnimi*" for the well-loved F.D.R. and, after his passing, forever referred to him in Greek as *O Makaritis O Roosevelt* (Blessed Roosevelt). Disheartened and concerned for the future of our country, I wondered if anyone was capable of taking F.D.R.'s place. Until then, Harry Truman's fine character, good common sense, and superior abilities were the best-kept secrets in the country. Papa would become one of his most loyal supporters.

A month after Roosevelt's funeral, the end of war in Europe and V-E Day took the edge off the sadness we felt at F.D.R.'s passing. When V-J Day followed the Japanese surrender in August, we were sure the dread of losing more Americans was finally over. Children gathered on street corners to blow whistles and rattle noisemakers. It was better than New Year's Eve.

Our family's merriment ended abruptly, however, with numbing, grievous news. Socrates Limberopulos had been killed in Saipan a day or two before the war's end. Uncle Jim had pre-deceased him in 1944; however, Thea Koula remained and suffered the loss of another son. His sisters, too, were devastated by the tragic passing of their energetic, happy-go-lucky Sockie. Two brothers had been taken from them by early deaths, one in front of their house while he was just a child, and one in the prime of life in August, 1945 as the war in Asia was ending. At the time of Sockie's death we were unaware the end of World War II would sink our family into further mourning.

NEWS FROM GREECE

*L*etters slowly began trickling back to us in Chicago from Greece after the war was over. Little by little, we began reading about the atrocities suffered by our valiant *patriotes* and relatives during the occupation. Several years passed before we learned that Mussolini's soldiers had taken over Thea Vasiliki and Thea Stamata's house in Tripolis, and that soldiers had viciously pistol whipped Stamata about the head. She endured blackouts and severe headaches for the rest of her life. Old Thea Vasiliki lost her feistiness after foreign armies invaded and was so terrified of occupying forces that she insisted on hiding, ostrich-like, for long periods of time inside a huge empty, earthenware water container in the corner of her grapevine covered courtyard. The scrumptious grapes in Thea Vasiliki's lovely arbor, which we remembered from our 1936 travels, along with all their other food, were confiscated and devoured by malicious, occupying soldiers.

First-hand accounts of the occupation finally reached anxious Greek-American families in the United States from American citizens who had been trapped in Greece during the war and who were able to leave Greece soon after occupying forces had retreated. Nick Karamitsos's eldest son was one of the first to return. The entire family was finally reunited, after eight-and-a-half years, when Mrs. Karamitsos and the two younger children finally arrived from war ravaged Greece in February of 1946. As American civilians trapped in Nazi occupied Europe, they witnessed machine-gun killings, endured bombings, suffered severe starvation and were terrorized by German soldiers.

Early in 1941, after a Nazi bombing raid on Kalamata, Mrs. Karamitsos left that port city in the southern Peloponnesos for what she hoped would be the safety of her own birthplace in the mountains of Laconia, northeast of Sparta. She led her children on foot to her village of Vresthena, some eighty miles from Kalamata. For the remainder of the war they lived in what had been her father's house. For the survival of her children, Mrs. Karamitsos, a caring, honest and dignified lady, was reduced to begging for meager handouts from relatives and friends.

When a company of Nazis came to town to search out local guerilla resistance fighters, German soldiers took over the house where the Karamitsos family lived at the entrance of the village. It was the perfect location for military surveillance of arrivals and departures. The Germans confiscated the family's meager food supplies, forced them to live in the smallest room, then stole and defaced their sparse personal belongings. A black-and-white photograph of an adorable, dark-eyed little girl was defaced with a pencil drawn mustache by a Nazi with too much time on his hands. It surely didn't compare with the abominable and infamous atrocities that took place during that war, but is a reminder that nothing is sacred when occupying forces reign. When the Nazis left Vresthena to search and harass the next mountain hamlet, they tried to burn down the entire village by setting fire to as many homes as possible, including the one where the Greek-American family lived. Mrs. Karamitsos heroically defied them by daring to put out the house fire, even before Nazi soldiers had left the village, and singlehandedly saved her ancestral home. In February 1946, Mrs. Karamitsos was able to leave Greece and a long-awaited family reunion took place when Mr. Karamitsos transported his family from a snow-covered train station to the small house he had bought on a quiet, tree-lined street in Ann Arbor, Michigan. He was the proud owner of the Busy Bee Restaurant on Main Street in downtown Ann Arbor.

Our family was plunged into mourning when news of our grandparents, aunts and uncles in Greece finally reached us in the slow post-war mail. Our stalwart Patriarch, Papou Nicholas in Mercovouni buried his wife, two daughters and a brother during the war; Grandpa, himself, succumbed in the late Forties. His brother, Papa's Uncle George Limberopulos, who had lived in Chicago and employed our father as a shoeshine boy when Papa first came to America, died leaving a wife, two daughters and a son. Papa's older sister Panagiota perished prior to their youngest sister, Georgia, who expired in childbirth. We were further devastated to learn that our sweet, Yiayia Eleni Limberopulos had painfully wasted away from diabetic infection and gangrene under primitive, wartime conditions.

While German planes dropped bombs over Tegea in the spring of 1941, Grandpa Krilis's coffin was being carried from the church of St. Nicholas, at the edge of Alea Athena's ruins, to the cemetery at the edge of the village. Several times during the funeral procession, the pall bearers abandoned Papou's casket to dive for cover from the exploding bombs. The mourners finally realized that a large group of people making their way along the village road could appear threatening to the pilots flying high overhead. They decided that the pall bearers and village priest, alone, would carry Papou to the cemetery and bury him and that Yiayia, Papou's daughters, grandsons, and other loved ones would return home. The priest and pall bearers continued on to the cemetery, where they had to, once again, dive for cover. Papou Krilis's burial finally took place in the silence and black of night when the planes had temporarily ceased their bombing raids.

Yiayia Eleni Krilis returned to live alone in the house overlooking the ancient ruins where she had arrived fifty years before, as an eighteen-year-old bride. She had given birth to eleven children in the small home by the ruined temple of Alea Athena. She and Papou had grieved together in the house after a diphtheria epidemic killed four of their small children within forty days. They had endured loss as a result of the "living death" every time a daughter left for America. In the late Thirties they suffered the untimely deaths of both sons, including one who was to be the heir of their property and continuation of their name in Tegea.

Throughout their lives in the old house Yiayia and Papou worried about dowries. Mama reflected on the frequent conversation between her parents that she had heard as a girl.

"Dimitri, how can we afford to marry off seven daughters?"

"Eleni, God will help us find a way. '*Ti stelni o Theos pou then ta vastai i yeis?*' God never sends more than we can bear. Every married daughter will bring a new son to our family, and then we will have seven more sons."

It all came true, but immigration placed five of the hoped for new sons-in-law in an American city far from Piali and Athena's temple. When Papou died in the spring of 1941, four American granddaughters named Eleni, in Grandma's honor, lived such an unfathomable distance away that they were unable to bring comfort and childish distractions to their grandmother's grief. When war cut all communications between America and Greece, not even a black-bordered letter could arrive in Chicago from Piali. Five daughters were unaware of their father's passing and their mother's grief and loneliness. At the end, Eleni Krilis lived alone in her home with the vine that grew the sweetest grapes on earth. Only a reach away was a burlap bag with old letters postmarked "Chicago" which she saved, touched and cherished, but could not read.

For nearly a century, life in the simple little house at the center of the Greek Peloponnesos had been full of grief, tenacious commitment, hopeful endurance, and occasional happiness, all wrapped up with trust in God. The same was true of most village homes, whether in Piali, Mercovouni, Tuscany, the Ukraine, Calabria, Dobrzejewice, or County Cork. Poverty was, indeed, widespread but poverty did not wipe out faith, integrity, respect, responsibility, patience, or love for family. In fact, these qualities grew, thrived, and were exported to America from villages all over Europe on ships bringing immigrants to the new world. They were planted in modest households throughout America. The ones I remember best were modest but love-filled apartments on Chicago's 35th Street, Lake Street, Hamlin Avenue, Huron Street, and West Madison. Those imported attributes, first experienced in a plain house situated at the edge of the ruins in Tegea, insulated the Austin Lunch and made it a special business enterprise near Chicago's Skid Row.

MAMA'S AUTUMN

*I*n late summer of 1984, when we relived our pasts through the old letters from Piali, Mama was at a stage of her life in which she struggled diligently to keep herself moving. She couldn't believe she was eighty-one. As a young woman, she had feared the evils on urban streets outside her front door. In 1984 she feared becoming immobile. Sitting on a high stool in our yellow kitchen, her arthritic legs resting on a walker in front of her, Mama cooked at the stove. I was her primary "gofer" although whoever was present was expected to fetch and assist; even crippled, Mama was still in charge of the kitchen. When she couldn't raise her aching shoulders to the counter by the sink, she cleaned and chopped vegetables over a cutting board balanced on her lap. Mama never gave up. "Just because I got a tough time walking now don't mean I'm going to sit around and get rotten."

Sitting around with nothing to do had never been Mama's style. She had learned to crochet, embroider, and sew as a girl in Piali, but by the time she was eighty-one she was limited by stiffness from the miserable arthritis in her fingers. When she wasn't cooking, mending or ironing from her stool, Mama made good use of her time doing something she never had time for when she was younger. In her old age, Mama finally had a chance to sit down and read.

First, she finished the *New Testament* in Greek and pamphlets about the lives of the saints. Then we searched bookshelves in Chicago's "Greek stores" for new material and discovered abridged Greek translations of *Little Women*, *Swiss Family Robinson* and Dickens's classics. *David Copperfield* was one of her favorites; she read it twice and recommended it to her grandchildren. While she pored over *Great Ex-*

pectations in Greek, I plowed through it in English. We talked about the book everyday. She was fascinated by the eccentrics in Dickens's books because she had met so many herself. "Woman in this story make me laugh because she remind me of that Leonora who use to come in our old place on Madison." Mama spent much of her time reading books and thoroughly enjoying them.

In 1984, we lived on Odell Avenue in the Northwest part of Chicago. Mama and Papa bought the tan, brick Cape Cod in 1952. They had been married for twenty-nine years when they bought it "brand new." They chose the two-story house with a basement because it was on a quiet street within walking distance of our store at Harlem and Higgins. Neither of our parents had learned how to drive. Papa loved public transportation. He said that all he had to do when he wanted to go someplace was walk to the corner bus stop and wait a few minutes for his "limousine" to pull up. He "tipped" his chauffeur whatever the Chicago Transit Authority demanded as its fare and went anywhere he wanted in the entire city, "No fuss, no muss."

Our dear Papa died of coronary occlusion in 1964, four years after we sold the family business and he had retired. His sudden death left all of us in shock, but his loss completely overwhelmed Mama. Papa had been gone from us for twenty years in 1984. We still missed him.

Three stairs kept Mama from moving independently in the world outside her eight hundred fifty square feet. The Kennedy Expressway was a block from our door; we could be downtown in twenty minutes. The modern "El" station, that Papa never lived to see, was only three blocks away; it connected commuters to every corner of the city and suburbs. O'Hare International Airport, a thirteen minute ride from our driveway, linked Chicago to every corner of the planet. Yet Mama wasn't able to strike out on her own because of excruciating pain and three "lousy" stairs. She ached to re-conquer those three, brown linoleum, brick patterned steps. She prayed to be independently mobile, to go everywhere by herself, and to dig in her vegetable garden, but Mama's world had shrunk to four-and-a-half rooms.

My mother depended on a tubular aluminum walker which she

both loved and hated. She knew it wasn't a temporary walking aid to nurse along an ailing limb for a few months. The reality of permanent disability frustrated her. Mrs. Paul, the lady who ran circles around everyone, was crippled and stuck with using a walker for the rest of her life. With arthritis-deformed hands she painfully grasped and lifted her walker, the only way she could pick herself up from a seated position and walk. Her stride was slow but determined; Mama continued to have presence, even clutching a walker. I can't help but recall how in my childhood I struggled to keep up with her whenever we walked together.

Mama usually held her head high but she needed to bend over whenever she tried to take a step forward with her "damned" walker. Going down the three steps leading from the kitchen to the back door was especially difficult, and she couldn't do it without someone's help. Mama would steady herself by firmly gripping the top rung of the walker as I held it tightly in place on each step. When I moved it down a level, she slowly and painfully lowered each leg to the next stair, and I silently prayed she'd make it to the landing without slipping and falling down the basement steps. "Someday I'm going to lean too far the wrong way and, 'Good-bye Charlie.' I'll be in the basement so fast, there's not even going to be time to say 'ouch.' It's going to be 'Bye-bye Mama' for good."

I tried to get her out of the house at least once a week, but she refused when it was raining, snowing, or too cold because weather affected her arthritis. Mama was a human barometer and Chicago's chancy, mostly humid weather sometimes kept her home for weeks at a time. So, semi-crippled, she observed the world through windows: the large picture window in the living room, another at the front of the house in her bedroom, two in the tiny den that faced the end of the driveway and backyard, a small one above the kitchen sink, and the glass door in the small dining area. We kept a folding wheelchair in the trunk of the car for when we wanted to go to the park or shopping mall, which she couldn't manage, even with the walker. Her favorite destination was to visit Nick and his family, in their suburban home, though she complained there were "too many" steps there. But she didn't use the wheelchair at either house. Deep down, her chair with wheels was an embarrassment, visual proof she had lost her independence.

Yet, in spite of agonizing arthritis and advancing age, Mama still loved working in her garden. By 1984, she had given up putting in her yearly vegetable patch by herself, but insisted, pain or no pain, on moving herself around the backyard to plant annuals with her hand trowel. She loved planting colorful flowers in our yard, carefully placing petunias in the sun and impatiens in shade. On "feeling better'" days she asked to be helped outside to pull weeds which pestered her. Seated in a light lawn chair, she stooped and stretched over her lap and knees to cultivate her garden. On sultry days she wiped rivers of perspiration from her face with a clean white handkerchief. Mama certainly didn't give in to the heat. When one area of the yard met with her high standards, she moved, using the walker for support, and dragged her chair and garden tools to the next spot she felt was in need of attention.

Mama had planted the lofty silver maple tree in the middle of the yard as a sapling, thirty years before, when we moved into the house. Now, in late summer of 1984, it towered over the house's rectangular lot and brown roof. Its lanky branches brushed against urban telephone and electric wires that swung, like forgotten circus equipment, high above our lawn. During the fourteen years we lived on Madison Street, Mama had been deprived of a garden. The only plant she grew was still growing out of its green ceramic pot in our house on Odell: a pointy, stiff, variegated *sansevieria*, also known as "mother-in-law's tongue." She boasted it was as old as Nick. One of her dreams while we lived on Madison was to someday garden in her very own plot of black Illinois dirt; her dream had come true. Mama had been a city resident for more than sixty years, yet the farm girl was still inside her. My mother loved the countryside and enjoyed taking rides through the farmland that surrounded Chicago. These were rare in the early years when she worked at the Austin Lunch because we didn't even have a car. She said rich, black, and fertile Illinois soil was one of God's greatest gifts. She took pleasure in watching perfectly straight rows of green and healthy crops growing from it.

In later years, when Nick or I drove her to the country for refreshing outings, Mama sadly kept track of the fierce real estate development that was replacing the Illinois corn fields. The farmland she delighted in riding through appeared to recede further and further from our Northwest Side neighborhood. United Airlines had the audacity to plunk their corporate headquarters out on Algonquin Road within acreage where she had picked tender, wild dandelion greens in springtime. Other conglomerates bought farms where she had enthusiastically participated in "Pick your own tomatoes by the bushel" promotions during late summer. Mama bristled as she watched high rises springing up in rich Illinois soil. "Looks like downtown is growing here instead of vegetables," she said. When we had driven far enough to reach farm country in the early eighties, Mama looked for small produce stands. Then she delighted in getting out of the car with her walker, pocketbook conveniently dangling by its straps from the top rung. With sharp eyes and much pleasure she selected fresh green beans, tomatoes, zucchini and "picked today" Illinois sweet corn. Mama never failed to ask the farmer in charge, "You sure you pick it today? I come all the way out here for fresh stuff. I don't want any day-old corn. I'm going to bring it back if it's not extra fresh."

When our family business close to home on Odell was sold in 1960, Papa retired and my brother and I sought employment elsewhere. Nick developed his mania for cars into a successful career in the retail Pontiac business. My last job had been with the Social Security Administration. During the fifteen-and-a-half years I worked at Social Security, I traveled downtown via the Chicago and Northwestern commuter train which I boarded at the Norwood Park station, a mile from home; the same railroad had taken us to the races with Papa in our childhood. But when arthritis finally crippled Mama, I left Social Security to be her full-time companion. She never asked me to leave my job to stay home with her; it was what I wanted to do.

Leaving her in the care of a hired stranger while I was off at work seemed like betrayal and a nursing home was completely out of the question. Mama deserved better. She had absolutely earned the privilege of having a member of her own family around for help and companionship.

Much was happening in the summer of 1984; Mama and I enjoyed it all. My siblings, their spouses and children had traveled to Europe and finally congregated in Greece in late July. Mama felt good about their plans to meet up with each other on their Greek vacations. Bob, Connie and Nikos were going to stop and visit us in Chicago before returning to Los Angeles where they already had bought tickets to several events of the 1984 Olympic games. Nick and his family were scheduled to return home the first week of September. We looked forward to the mail every day. Postcards arrived from London, Canterbury, Dover, Bruges, Brussels, and finally Athens. Caught up in Olympic fever, our relatives sent us postcards from Olympia where the athletic tradition had started. Satisfied that her grandchildren were finally getting back to their roots, Mama smiled when she read that her grandson ran in the ancient stadium, dashing off from the original, millennia-old starting line.

When I left for O'Hare to pick up our first returnees from Europe, Mama waited for them, reading her book on the den sofa. As I backed our dark blue Pontiac sedan out of the driveway, I noticed she had looked up from reading to admire her tiny grape arbor. Twenty-five years earlier, she had planted the vines to sprawl over a white, ten-foot trellis she had installed alongside the concrete driveway at the back of our house. In summer she admired her grapevine's greenery and took account of the grape clusters that could be harvested in fall. The intertwining brown shoots and dry curly tendrils appealed to her in winter, too, after the leaves had fallen and white snow filled the delicate crevices of the spindly trunk. Sometimes winters were so icy cold and the snow so frequent and heavy that Mama worried about her grapevines' survival. She was never disappointed in spring when new growth appeared. Springtime was her self-appointed season for planting scarlet geraniums underneath the trellis to splash some red color around her tiny vineyard.

Arbors, grapevines and vineyards always reminded Mama and Papa of the old country. Papa had said the tradition of growing grapes goes back so far into pre-history that it runs into the god Dionysos, although the Greek god of wine and revelry never entered Mama's mind when she planted her vines. She knew she couldn't grow any of the luscious, sweet Greek grapes native to Piali and Mercovouni; only Concords survive the frigid winters of Chicago. Mama maintained her arbor so that she could pick young leaves in spring for making *dolmades* (stuffed grape leaves), enjoy its lush greenness in summer, and make jam when the grapes ripened in the fall, but most of all, so that she could be reminded of the "old country."

When our visitors and I returned an hour later, Bob, Connie and Nikos saw Mama's face in the den window. Smiling and teary, her emotions emanated right through the window screen; Mama always cried at weddings, baptisms, graduations, funerals, reunions and departures. By the time they reached the back door, she and her walker were anxiously waiting for them in the kitchen, at the top of the three steps. She hugged, kissed and squeezed them as tightly as she could. Connie noticed her hair wasn't any grayer than it had been the year before—generous streaks of gray blended beautifully with Mama's thick, short, almost black hair—however, my sister immediately noted changes in Mama's body. Our mother was smaller, slimmer and frailer than she had ever been in her life. When arthritis started bowing her legs at the knees five years before, she started losing height.

All five of us squeezed into the den to hear news of their travels and of our relatives, including news of my brother and his family who were still abroad. While Nikos's parents unpacked, Mama asked him to tell her about his trip and I took a candid snapshot. We had moved into the dining area and were sitting at our table in front of the open glass door. Through my viewfinder, I could see a bit of the lawn and fading white hydrangeas in the background, and the ever-present walker stationed in front of Mama in the foreground. Twelve-year old Nikos, tanned from the Greek sun, was smiling at his slender, bony Yiayia whose eyes were riveted on him. Her twisted arthritic forefinger was pointing at her grandson, helping make her point to him. Visible beyond the screen of the open door was the black, wrought iron chair that stayed outside on her tiny porch all summer. Beyond that, was the tall maple tree she had planted in the middle of the yard.

The little porch made it easy for Mama to get a breath of fresh air, absorb sunshine, and oversee her beloved garden herself, without needing to be helped down the three steps. Wearing a large straw hat and sunglasses in summer, Mama read newspapers and books on her little porch. At the same time she delighted in the smell of freshly cut grass and the bright rainbow of flowers. Mama enjoyed chatting with neighbors from her tiny veranda. She marveled at the squirrels that nimbly ran along the high utility cables and watched robins pull worms out of the grass. Mama loved watching orange-breasted robins because she considered them well mannered; they never attacked her grape clusters the way less civilized sparrows did. Like an admiral, Mama directed care and feeding of the backyard from her elevated position on the four-foot high cement porch. Taking careful aim with the hose nozzle, she watered flowers herself, if someone was around to turn the ground level garden faucet on and then off for her.

Sitting in the dining room with Nikos, Mama wanted to know if they ever found the grapevine that covered the courtyard and porch in Piali. She informed him that they were the "best grapes in the world." He said they searched, but didn't see grapevines anywhere on the property. Bob told us the famous Tegean cherries had been picked by the time they got there in July, but that her niece in Tripolis, Eleni, sister Stamata's daughter, had made sweet preserves from the most recent crop. Connie dug into their luggage and presented Mama with a jar of deep red, authentic Tegean cherries from Piali, along with a book and a box. The book was a Greek translation of Nicholas Gage's bestseller, *Eleni*, the story of Gage's mother's capture and execution during the Greek Civil War that followed World War II. Knowing Mama would appreciate the book but knowing she couldn't read it in the original English, they brought it to her in Greek. Mama's gnarled hands gently caressed the cover; she listened while we explained what the book was about. She struggled to open the next gift. Her crooked fingers clumsily removed shredded Greek newspaper packing. She finally uncovered a white plaster copy of a woman's head. When Bob helped her pull it out of the box, it became instantly recognizable as the ancient Greek goddess of health, Hygeia who, like Mama, had originated in Tegea. Now world famous and reproduced ad infinitum, this Hygeia was a copy of the one stolen from Piali's museum in her youth.

Before our relatives returned home to California that August, we crowded into the den to watch the opening ceremonies of the 1984 Summer Olympic Games. The television set was positioned on a large shelf of an entertainment center filled with other shelves and drawers. Mama had assigned one of the nine drawers to granddaughter Vicky when she was a toddler so she wouldn't rummage through all the other drawers in the house. Fran and Nikos were granted rights to it when they came into the family. A pair of Greek country scenes painted in watercolors hung next to the window that overlooked the backyard. One was the exterior of a rural Greek church, the other depicted a village courtyard with a wandering brown chicken. An enlarged and framed black and white photograph of Nick decorated the wall opposite Mama's sofa. Wearing well-worn coveralls and scuffed shoes, my six-year-old brother, unaware he was being captured by one of Papa's customers who was a professional photographer, leaned against a concrete lamp post and sang his heart out in front of the Austin Lunch. The scene best personifies our Depression era childhood; it's my favorite picture.

Our almost immobile Mama surrounded herself with what she considered the best of her life in the room where she spent so much time. Her den command post also contained a color television, two windows for natural light and for observing life outdoors, a clock, a telephone with an extra long cord, family snapshots, a comfortable and sturdy sofa for resting her aching bones, a "parking place" for the walker, a good lamp for reading, and memories of Papa.

The pastel bluish-green den was the one room in the house which reminded us most of Papa. He used to sit in the large, pillow-backed chair with his legs stretched out on the matching ottoman, less than a yardstick away from the sofa where Mama sat. Papa read and watched television from "his" coffee colored chair, often dozing off with bifocals on his nose and the daily newspaper on his chest. His snow white hair contrasted sharply with the dark brown chair pillow where he rested his head. When Mama tried to replace the *Chicago Daily News* on his shirtfront with her afghan, he'd open his eyes long enough to tell her a layer of newspapers was the best of all blankets. Mama was persistent in advising him that black newsprint soiled his clothing and the upholstery, too.

Titles of Papa's books inspired memories of him, twenty years later, as we brushed passed the shelves to adjust the television. *Twelve Lives of Plutarch, Thomas Jefferson, Works of Plato, History of Herodotus, Abraham Lincoln: The War Years and the Prairie Years, Aristophanes Comedies, The Life and Writings of Abraham Lincoln* were a sampling of the titles that reminded us how much he enjoyed history. One Greek title, *Theiloi Kai Skilro Stiho*, contained works of the noted Greek poet, Kostis Palamas. Papa had never enjoyed shopping, except at bookstores, especially used ones in downtown Chicago. Most of his purchases were still on shelves in the den where he had placed them.

Network television showed the sun shining brightly at Los Angeles Coliseum; in Chicago we were close to sunset. Nikos said he was pretty sure relatives in Greece were watching the Olympics "live," even though it was the middle of the night in that part of the world. Mama hung on to the remote control, wielding the power to instantly switch off programs and commercials she didn't approve of. Love scenes and Playtex foundation garments never got exposure on our R.C.A. Victor while Mama was in the room. When we heard her say "*Sachlamares!*" (unacceptable nonsense) we knew the channel would change. Mama didn't allow herself or her loved ones to waste their eyes, brains, or time on "*Sachlamares.*"

It was a wonderful visit. We took a ride into the countryside together to see corn growing and buy fresh vegetables; we spent hours together in the den and dining room. Mama wanted to know about Bob's brother, sister, and their families; she asked about friends and relatives in California. She spoke about the past as she was apt to do, talking about Papa and her sisters, telling how she missed them. Mama said events from fifty years before were easier for her to remember than what she had eaten for breakfast that morning. She discussed books she had been reading, world news she learned from television, and articles from the daily Greek newspaper she received by mail from New York everyday. Mama was threatening to end her thirty-year subscription to the paper because rates had risen drastically, and she didn't think the news they were printing was worthy enough to warrant a higher subscription price.

"You want to read *sachlamares*? This paper's full of them."

Mama looked forward to the return of her granddaughters and their parents in September. She intensely loved all three of her grandchildren and brightened up when she was with them, referring to them as her *poulakia* (little birds). Mama asked Nikos about what he was learning in school, his piano lessons, soccer, and little league. Then she encouraged him to continue doing his best in everything he attempted. She advised his parents to keep him involved in worthwhile activities. Mama was pleased Nikos liked to read, an avocation both grandmother and grandson had in common. She told him all about *David Copperfield*, again, and urged him to read it. Mama's final counsel to his parents was in Greek. "*To paidi kai ta matia sas.*" It means value, cherish and protect your child as well as you do your own eyes.

When my brother-in-law, sister, and nephew got ready to drive to O'Hare, Mama's goodbye squeezes were tighter than her welcoming ones. She cried when they left and so did my sister. Mama watched them from the sofa by the den window as they put their suitcases and themselves into the car at the end of the driveway where grapevines and red geraniums were flourishing. We saw her get up from the sofa, in tandem with her walker, and move with a determined, energetic stride out of the den. As we backed out of the driveway and pulled onto Odell, we saw Mama forcefully raising the window shade in her bedroom at the front of the house. Then she pushed aside the drapes and waved a moving, final farewell. Mama's emotions penetrated the bedroom glass and shot through the warm summer air right through the blue Pontiac's windshield. The ache in her eyes had nothing to do with arthritis.

"Is something wrong?" Bob asked.

Not realizing the finality of the moment, my explanation was incomplete. "She always has a hard time saying good-bye."

They all waved back and blew kisses. My sister was still crying as she mumbled, "I never get enough of her."

"GIVE REST, IN A PLACE OF LIGHT"

The state is feeding us.

—Christ Ganas to his father-in-law, March 1932

Nick, Angie, Vicky and Fran arrived three weeks later. Mama anticipated their return like a kid looking forward to Christmas. She exhaled with relief, hugged and squeezed them so tightly you'd never have guessed she had arthritis in her shoulders, then raised her eyes heavenward and made the sign of the cross three times. After the joyful reunion in the middle of our bright yellow kitchen, Nick returned to the car and brought in a plastic covered package the size of a loaf of bread. The letters from her ruined birth-home in Piali had arrived and as soon as she spotted the treasure in Nick's hands, she asked for disposable table coverings and rubber gloves to handle the dirty burlap bag and its contents. "It's filthy. *Tha mas piasi panoukla*" ("We're going to get the plague").

Six sets of eyes zeroed in on her yellow gloves as they slowly pulled out a handful of fragmented papers. Mama analyzed them with her bifocals, silently checking out the Greek writing. "Look here, it's my papa's name. See? Says 'Dimitrios Krilis.' That's my papa!" She smiled with pride at her granddaughters. "He write this himself." For the first time in decades she saw her father's name and recognized his large lettered handwriting. Her voice broke and tears welled as she murmured, *Aionia tou i mnimi* (May his memory be eternal) with a deep sigh. Mixed in with shards of paper she found two, small, rusty wire hoops. Enough dirty white ribbon and tattered, fabric flowers adhered to the bent wire circles to identify them. "Never expected to see anything like this—old *stephana* (wedding-crowns)." I wondered if they had united my grandparents on their wedding day, but Mama explained the old Greek custom while she gulped down more emotion. "Usually they put them in the casket and bury them with the husband or the wife when they die."

Exhausted, Nick and Angie realized how long it would take to inspect all the letters in the burlap sack—hours, maybe even days. School was to begin for the girls the next day and they decided to go home and recover. Mama didn't say too much as we began piecing together frail paper fragments and deciphering the old letters and documents. As we sifted through the papers, we found receipts and documents with official government seals. One was an inventory of farm animals, mostly sheep that Papou Krilis had prepared for the tax collector. Mama laughed at the list and then at another absurd example of bureaucracy she found inside the sack, a registration paper from 1911 for Papou's mule. I was reminded of biblical references to ancient but mercenary tax collectors. Government's long hand had stuck itself into my grandfather's pocket even as he trudged behind his plow and mule in remote Piali.

"I never know my Papa was paying taxes. Poor guy had to pay for his mule just like we pay a license for the car. God rest his good soul. Who ever expect to see this after so, so many years? Looks like this bag was my Papa's safety deposit box, just like we got in the bank for important papers."

Mingled among the bits of paper was an envelope from the Austin Lunch. Mama and I zeroed in on it together and she removed the letter folded within. She had written a letter to her parents and brother in Greek on a menu. "Country Club Beer" was printed in the company's distinctive logo at the lower edge of the page. The Greek text was in Mama's own large handwriting, positioned between the two lines of professionally printed English words. The left corner of the envelope bore Papa's familiar, neat, and legible writing in blue ink: "P.

Limberopulos; 1458 West Madison Street; Chicago, Illinois; U.S.A."
The American stamp had been carefully cut off and given, no doubt,
to a collector. Its postmark indicated the letter had been processed in
Chicago, Illinois at 10:30 p.m. on June 12. No year was indicated on
the round postmark, and the dog-eared corner of Mama's letter that
had once included the date had torn off.

"Look here, Helen. I write my letter on paper your Papa was typ-
ing new menus on every day. It cost good money to buy paper for
writing letters. So, we used free paper the brewery give us for advertising the beer." She read what she had sent to Piali fifty years earlier: "I
have written to you twice before but you have not answered, brother
Nicholas. Now I am writing again. Please take time to write and tell
us about our parents. They are elderly. We are too far away, think of
you all the time, and are very concerned." This need to know about
the well-being of her distant family was a recurring theme in all of
Mama's letters. Obviously, Nicholas did not write often enough to
suit his sisters in America.

One letter raised Mama's ire. It had been written by Christ Ganas,
Politimi's husband. "Why the devil did he complain to my folks in
the old country? What could they do for him, or for any of us? Tasia
and me try to never send complaints back about hard times, even
when they ask. We don't want to worry them. We write, *Kai mi hirotera*
(It could be worse). They had enough of their own problems. But
look at what Christ write in Politimi's name, because Politimi couldn't
write. Remember, they never send her to school when she was a little
girl.

"'America has made us poor. Christ has been sick and unemployed
for three years. The state is feeding us. So I beg you to write to us so
we can hear news of the village and forget the bitterness of America.'

"This is in Christ's handwriting. Politimi would never ask him to
write complaints to the old country. You know, Helen, I ask Politimi
many times about Christ's health. I ask, 'Politimi, what's Christ's sickness from?' Finally Politimi answer me with just one Greek word,
'*Apelpisia* (despair).'"

"What I see from these letters was that we missed them back home and wanted to get more letters. Mostly we write to ask, 'Why don't you write?' There is no important, new family history here. But these scraps of paper are precious because they belonged to my Mama and my Papa. And Helen, they helped you and me remember old times, good and bad—and lots of good people. I've been having a good time these past two days."

Clearly there were no valuables hidden in the dirty burlap. The bag contained no cash, jewelry, gold, silver, or priceless antiques; that's why it had been ignored for thirty-seven years. Papou's important papers had unbelievably outlasted life, death, World War II, and decades of the house's vacancy following Yiayia Eleni Krilis's death in 1947. They survived in a cloth bag and were retrieved from a pair of gnawing rats by Yiayia Eleni's American descendants, offspring of the letter writers.

Thanks to her unrelenting curiosity and the refreshing Lake Michigan breezes coming through the open porch door, we stayed focused on the frustrating task that opened a lifetime of memories for us. Finally, Mama gave a caressing, farewell pat to the letters Nick brought from Greece in September of 1984. For safe keeping, her arthritic fingers, encumbered by rubber gloves, gathered the pieces and slid them back into the plastic bags that had been used to transport them.

"Helen, I never, ever, think I was going to get old like this. When did it happen? I use to be the fastest worker in that old joint on Madison. I run home every afternoon to wash and iron my uniform to save twenty-five cents. I had so much energy. Even five years ago I could dig and plant a big vegetable garden all by myself. When I got old? When?

"I'm thinking about my Mama and when she got old. My poor Mama give birth to almost a dozen children. Then she end up living alone, without any one of us in the house. She got lots of grandchildren, but only see them in pictures because they was too far away in America. Thank God she still had my sisters Stamata and Garifalia close by. My Mama was such a good woman. When I was born, God blessed me with a good Mama and good Papa. We didn't have any fancy stuff, no toys, no lots of dresses, but we was alloways neat and clean. And we never was hungry. We had a Mama and Papa that watch us and care about us all the time. They was good and honest people.

"I try to be good Mama, too. But, I had to work with Papa at the store. I wish I could be home with my kids more. Your Papa and me, May God rest his good soul, we had to work hard. And when we need help to take care of you, then, your aunts, *Aionia tous i mnimi*, they help us. I try to help them, too, when I can. I hardly get any pay myself at the store all those years but I try to help my sisters with it and most of the time they refuse to take money from me. I was alloways worry we was going to lose everything when your Papa was playing the horses. I never know how much he was losing at the track. He never, ever tell. I thought to myself, 'if I can save a little money, then we won't be altogether broke if something bad happen.' You know, Helen, bad things happen real fast—in the time it take to blink your eyes. But it alloways takes such a long time for good things to happen.

"Papa was a good, good man—real honest. The only problem Papa had was the fire in him to gamble. After he retire, we use to play cards here in the kitchen. We like to play Five Hundred Rummy together. He really get mad whenever I win a game and he was real proud of hisself when he beat me. I tell him, 'Of course you going to win. You're the card player in the family.' I miss him, Helen. God take him away from us twenty years ago and I still miss him. He only had one heart attack. It was the first, and the last. It come so sudden. When Papa die, it was like when a bird fly away—unexpected and fast. It happened too quick. He didn't even make it to the hospital. Papa die in the ambulance." Tears filled her eyes. "I hate ambulances. If you don't got a heart attack when you get into one, for sure you got one by the time you come out. Papa was smart and good. But he was stubborn. He didn't go to the doctor for check-up like he should. I alloways beg him, 'Please go to the doctor, Paul.'" Mama shook her head in frustration, swallowed hard, and pulled another Kleenex from her pocket. "Papa left us too, too soon. I miss him.

"Being a close family is most important of all, Helen. We got to do good for each other and stick together. That's the way God wants it to be and God gives us the strength. *Ipomoni* (patience) is most important. We got to have *ipomoni* and we got to have hope. Me and your Papa, *Aionia tou i mnimi*, we work together to get out of the Depression, but we was alloways together like a family should be, even at the *magazi*. We know what you was doing and you know what we was doing. We know we got to keep you as safe as possible, in every way. And it wasn't easy to do in that old neighborhood on Madison. But that was our love for you. Just like I see from my own parents when I was growing up. I was proud of my Mama and Papa. I'm proud of my children. I hope my children be proud of me."

I picked Concord grapes for Mama from her arbor by the driveway before the first frost that autumn. Yellowed leaves fell off the silver maple tree in the backyard by the thousands and she watched them flutter down. Sitting on her stool, she peered out the kitchen window while she seeded grapes at the sink. "Leafs look like pieces of pure gold."

Mama insisted on cooking the luscious purple jam by herself, attentively stirring the Concords in her large stainless steel *katsarola* (saucepan) with a wooden spoon. She was perched on the tall stool in front of the white gas range, legs resting on the crosspiece of her walker. I filled small Mason jars and assisted with the canning as Mama watched and advised. I was familiar with the entire process because we repeated it together every year, but Mama advised me anyway. Then she forced her crooked fingers to tape labels that I had typed onto each purple-filled Mason jar. "Grape Jam 1984."

She started reading *Eleni*, but said that as much as it held her interest, the weight of the book was too heavy for her aching shoulders; she eventually stopped picking it up. Mama wasn't strong enough to manage the heavy plaster head of Hygeia, either. She couldn't decide whether it looked best on the coffee table in the living room or on a den shelf, close to Papa's books. I finally helped her place it in the living room.

A month after we finished making jam, Mama woke up and discovered she couldn't swallow. She hobbled into the kitchen with her walker for a glass of water in the darkness of a very early November morning and tried to drink, but water wouldn't go down. I told her I was going to call for an ambulance, but she refused to hear of it; she refused to go to a hospital. "It'll pass. Let's wait and see," she advised in a whisper.

I called the emergency department of Resurrection Hospital two blocks from home, and asked if they could send someone out to check her. They told me to bring her to them; all examining equipment was on their premises. The hospital advised me not to force anything down that she wasn't able to swallow. Nick's wife, Angie, came to convince Mama to go to the doctor, but she refused. Her condition had not improved; Nick left work early. When he arrived at our house she was more receptive to receiving medical help, even to visiting the emergency room. But her sharp eyes fired right through me when she insisted "No ambulance!" in a forceful whisper. Together Nick and I managed to get Mama down the three impossible steps, into the car at the back of the driveway, and to Resurrection in less than five minutes. After she was admitted and tested we learned she had suffered a stroke.

Mama appeared to have lost more mobility when I saw her the next morning; her speech was slightly slurred, but her mind was sharp as ever. When an I.V. was inserted, she pulled it out. "Why'd you do that Yiayia?" granddaughter Vicky asked. The answer was clear and emphatic. "'Because I don't want it!" Mama suspected it to be the first step in being hooked up to a life support system that she did not want. "Nobody need that misery."

A day later, her condition improved. She was alert, in good spirits, and her speech was clearer, although she still slumped to one side of the bed. We all sighed in relief, and I started making plans to rent a hospital bed for home. The nurses said Mama would need a special bed until she regained some mobility. Many of the nieces and nephews she loved dearly, her sisters' children, came to visit her in the hospital. She laughed and joked with Jimmy and Gus Ganas, and I felt good about it. It was a relief for Nick and me to watch her energy come back. Recovery was just around the corner.

Connie phoned continually; she wanted to come from California, but Mama repeatedly ordered my sister to stay put. "I'm much better. Don't you dare to come now. Stay home. Nikos is in school. You can't leave him alone. Bob works all day. You must not take the boy out of school. *Prosexai to paidi* (Take care of your child.) Remember," she repeated, "*To paidi kai ta matia sas* (Take care of your son as well as you care for your eyes). Come when he's out of school for Thanksgiving, if you want. But don't come before that." Mama still had presence, stroke or no stroke, even on long-distance telephone.

Bob, Connie and Nikos made an unexpected trip to Chicago from California in November of 1984. When they pulled into the driveway on Odell, the grapevines were bare. The silver maple tree had shed all its leaves except for a few deep yellow ones that stubbornly clung to gray branches in spite of sharp pre-winter winds. The red geraniums under the almost bare white trellis had shriveled with the first, second and third frosts. Mama's face was not in the den window.

Nick and I were with Mama at Resurrection Hospital, Sunday night, November 11, 1984 when she suffered a second, final stroke. Mama surrendered her very last iota of energy and God gave rest to her own exceedingly special and very good soul.

"To the souls of Thy servants who have fallen asleep do Thou, O Lord, give rest, in a place of light, in a place of green pasture, in a place of refreshment where all pain and sorrow and sighing have fled away.»

May your memories be eternal, dear loved ones, for you are worthy of blessedness and everlasting memory.

Aionia tous i mnimi.

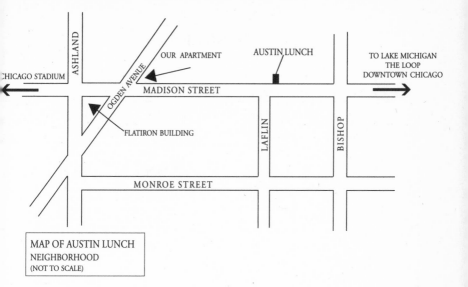

MAP OF AUSTIN LUNCH
NEIGHBORHOOD
(NOT TO SCALE)

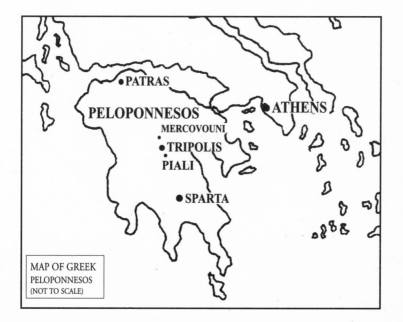

MAP OF GREEK
PELOPONNESOS
(NOT TO SCALE)

DIMITRIOS KRILIS

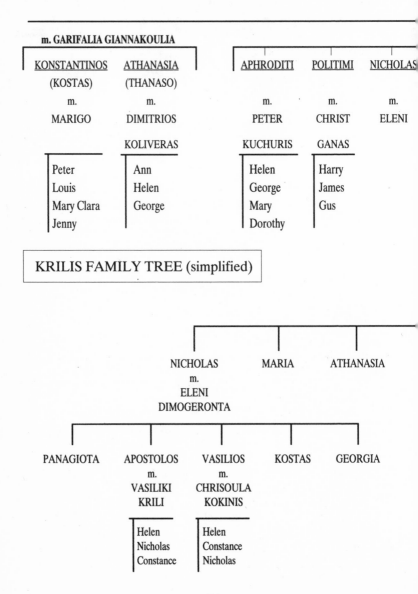

m. GARIFALIA GIANNAKOULIA

KONSTANTINOS	ATHANASIA		APHRODITI	POLITIMI	NICHOLAS
(KOSTAS)	(THANASO)				
m.	m.		m.	m.	m.
MARIGO	DIMITRIOS		PETER	CHRIST	ELENI
	KOLIVERAS		KUCHURIS	GANAS	

Peter	Ann		Helen	Harry
Louis	Helen		George	James
Mary Clara	George		Mary	Gus
Jenny			Dorothy	

KRILIS FAMILY TREE (simplified)

	NICHOLAS	MARIA	ATHANASIA
	m.		
	ELENI		
	DIMOGERONTA		

PANAGIOTA	APOSTOLOS	VASILIOS	KOSTAS	GEORGIA
	m.	m.		
	VASILIKI	CHRISOULA		
	KRILI	KOKINIS		

	Helen	Helen
	Nicholas	Constance
	Constance	Nicholas

(after Garifalia's death Dimitris re-married)

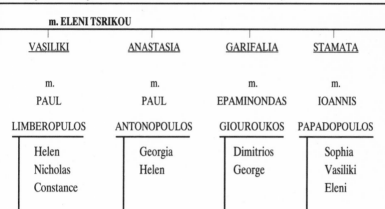

m. ELENI TSRIKOU

VASILIKI	ANASTASIA	GARIFALIA	STAMATA
m.	m.	m.	m.
PAUL	PAUL	EPAMINONDAS	IOANNIS
LIMBEROPULOS	ANTONOPOULOS	GIOUROUKOS	PAPADOPOULOS
Helen	Georgia	Dimitrios	Sophia
Nicholas	Helen	George	Vasiliki
Constance			Eleni

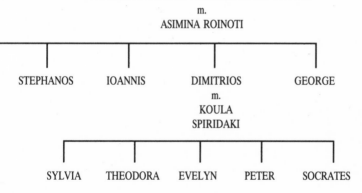

PANAGIOTIS LIMBEROPULOS

m.
ASIMINA ROINOTI

STEPHANOS	IOANNIS	DIMITRIOS	GEORGE
		m.	
		KOULA	
		SPIRIDAKI	

SYLVIA	THEODORA	EVELYN	PETER	SOCRATES

LIMBEROPULOS FAMILY TREE (simplified)